Cornell International Industrial and Labor Relations Report
Number

ORGANIZED LABOR
IN THE ASIA-PACIFIC REGION

A COMPARATIVE STUDY OF
TRADE UNIONISM IN NINE COUNTRIES

Stephen Frenkel, Editor

ILR Press
Ithaca, New York

Library of Congress Cataloging-in-Publication Data

Organized labor in the Asia-Pacific region : a comparative study of
trade unionism in nine countries / Stephen Frenkel, editor.
  p.   cm.—(Cornell international industrial and labor
relations report: no. 24)
Includes bibliographical references and index.
ISBN 0-87546-197-2 (alk. paper).—ISBN 0-87546-198-0 (pbk. :
alk paper)
1. Trade-unions—Asia—Case studies.   2. Trade-unions—Pacific
Area—Case studies.   3. Labor movement—Asia—Case studies.
4. Labor movement—Pacific Area—Case studies.   I. Frenkel,
Stephen.   II. Series: Cornell international industrial and labor
relations reports: no. 24.
          HD6796.074   1993
        331.88'095—dc20   92-42494

Copies may be ordered through bookstores or directly from

ILR Press
School of Industrial and Labor Relations
Cornell University
Ithaca, NY 14853-3901

Printed on acid-free paper in the United States of America

5   4   3   2   1

Contents

Tables and Figures

Tables

Figures

Abbreviations

ACFTU	All-China Federation of Trade Unions
ACTU	Australian Council of Trade Unions
ADB	Asian Development Bank
AP	Advanced peripheral country
ASEAN	Association of Southeast Asian Nations
AUPE	Amalgamated Union of Public Employees (Singapore)
BCA	Business Council of Australia
BRT	Business Round Table (New Zealand)
CAI	Confederation of Australian Industry
CCP	Chinese Communist Party
CFL	Chinese Federation of Labor
CIC	Christian Industrial Committee (Hong Kong)
CKTU	Confederation of Korean Trade Unions
CLA	Council of Labor Affairs (Taiwan)
CPT	Communist Party of Thailand
CSGU	Civil Servants' General Union (Hong Kong)
CTU	Council of Trade Unions (New Zealand)
CUEPACS	Congress of Unions of Employees in the Public and Civil Services (Malaysia)
DC	Developing country
DPP	Democratic Progressive Party (Taiwan)
EOI	Export-oriented industrialization
FCSU	Federation of Civil Service Unions (Hong Kong)
FKTU	Federation of Korean Trade Unions
FOL	Federation of Labour (New Zealand)
FTU	Federation of Trade Unions (Hong Kong)
FTZ	Free trade zone
GDP	Gross domestic product
GNP	Gross national product

GSP	Generalized system of preferences
ILO	International Labour Organisation
ISI	Import-substitution industrialization
ISOC	Internal Security Operation Command (Thailand)
KMT	Kuomintang Party (Taiwan/China)
LAB	Labour Advisory Board (Hong Kong)
LTRC	Long Term Reform Committee (New Zealand)
MNC	Multinational corporation
MTUC	Malaysian Trade Union Congress
NCTU	National Conference of Trade Unions (Korea)
NIC	Newly industrialized country
NKDP	New Korea Democratic Party
NTUC	National Trades Union Congress (Singapore)
OECD	Organization for Economic Cooperation and Development
PAP	People's Action Party (Singapore)
PIEU	Pioneer Industries Employees' Union (Singapore)
PRC	People's Republic of China
PTU	Professional Teachers' Union (Hong Kong)
RDP	Reunification Democratic Party (Korea)
SAR	Special administrative region
SATU	Singapore Association of Trade Unions
SCSC	Senior Civil Service Council (Hong Kong)
SDA	Shop, Distributive and Allied Employees' Association (Australia)
SILO	Singapore Industrial Labor Organization
SUP	Socialist Unity Party (New Zealand)
TUC	Hong Kong and Kowloon Trades Union Council
UMNO	United Malays National Organization

Preface

The Asia-Pacific region, variously described as "the world's power-house of industrial growth" and "the globe's hottest spot," is undoubtedly of central importance to the world political economy. Indeed, some think the twenty-first century will be the era of the Pacific Rim. Not surprisingly, interest in the region has grown immensely, especially among businesspeople and political commentators. Universities are also moving with the times. In 1991, for example, then prime minister of Australia, Bob Hawke, opened the Asia-Australia Institute at the University of New South Wales, which aims to encourage stronger academic and social ties between Australia and its Asian neighbors.

Rarely, however, have labor relations received serious attention in the success stories of Asia-Pacific countries. In fact, allegedly anachronistic labor market institutions have frequently been held responsible for retarding the economic performance of the region's few industrial laggards. Initially, this contrast intrigued me. My interest increased after resuming responsibility in 1987 for the course in comparative industrial relations at the University of New South Wales. Rather than wanting to concentrate on North America, Europe, and Japan, students increasingly were interested in the late developers within the region, particularly the "four little dragons" with which they were familiar as occasional visitors or as former or current residents. Texts and reference books, however, dealt almost exclusively with the industrialized countries. Where other countries were discussed, few distinctions were made based on their stage of economic development, historical experience, or geopolitical situation. Even now, with the exception of Frederic C. Deyo's book *Beneath the Miracle: Labor Subordination in the New Asian Industrialism* (1989)—which focuses principally on labor weakness rather than on the dynamics of trade unionism—there are no contemporary comparative studies that can be recommended to advanced students of industrial relations and human resources.

Serendipity played a role in the development of this book when in 1988 I was invited to participate in an International Labour Organization (ILO)/Japan seminar on productivity and industrial relations in Southeast Asia and Pacific countries. It was here that I made contact with senior representatives of employers' associations, unions, and government departments from whom I learned about recent developments in various countries. Following discussions with ILO officials at the seminar, the idea of a systematic comparative study of labor relations in Asia-Pacific countries began to take shape.

An introductory textbook seemed an obvious choice, but I discovered that a project on comparative labor law and systems was already under way (see S. Deery and R. Mitchell 1993). Other topics were canvassed, leading me to conclude that trade unionism was the most feasible theme based on my own expertise and the availability of data and academic talent.

Through ILO and academic contacts, I managed to assemble a group of researchers, most of whom have stayed with the project and contributed to this book. Inevitably, there have been some casualties along the way, the most notable being the research on Japan. Contemporary Japanese unionism is explored in the final chapter, however, as an essential part of a comparative analysis and discussion of trends in Asia-Pacific trade unionism.

The main aim of this volume is to describe and interpret union patterns in nine Asia-Pacific countries against the backdrop of existing theories of trade unionism. Consistent with an emphasis on comparative analysis, the project was guided by the principle of consistency: we tried to use a similar theoretical framework, to collect comparable data, and to adhere to common stylistic conventions. Briefly, the research proceeded as follows. After examining relevant literature, I formulated a theoretical framework and timetable that was circulated to the contributors. Building on their suggestions, the framework was amended and a new schedule distributed and endorsed. Work-in-progress papers were discussed at a meeting in Manila in March 1990. Here we concentrated on ways to minimize problems of comparability and focused on particular aspects of the framework requiring clarification or elaboration. Drafts of the papers were subsequently submitted to me, and I responded with detailed comments. Revisions were made by the contributors to the point where the papers became final manuscripts.

I would like to endorse the acknowledgments made by the contributors in subsequent chapters and to extend my thanks to several other people who assisted with the project. Shozu Inoue, now a professor at Hiroshima University and formerly regional adviser in industrial relations at the ILO Bangkok office, together with current incumbent, Carmelo Noriel, provided encouragement and advice. The ILO also provided some financial support, as did the Australian Research Council. Needless to say, they share no responsibility for what follows.

Professor J. C. Hong of Taiwan National University deserves mention for his hospitality in helping me get through the typhoon season in Taiwan. My visit with him was both productive and enjoyable.

Kathryn Rawson and Chris Andrews assisted in constructing the figures and tables, and Donna Wilcox brought the manuscript to what we thought was a near-zero state of completion. Erica Fox's copyediting and publication supervision by Patty Peltekos brought us much closer to this goal. I would also like to extend my thanks to Singapore University Press for permission to reproduce figure 2.1 from Lai To Lee's *Trade Unions in China: 1949 to the Present* (1986) and the *Journal of Management Studies* for permission to reproduce figure 2.2 from an article by J. S. Henley and M. K. Nyaw (1986).

Two final thanks are due: to Sheena, Lucy, and Thomas for their affection and support, and to the contributors, whose dedication, patience, and good humor testify to the immense possibilities of collaboration on Asia-Pacific themes and issues.

Introduction

1
Theoretical Frameworks and Empirical Contexts of Trade Unionism

Stephen Frenkel

T rade unionism in the core advanced societies has been of central academic concern, particularly in periods when labor presented a challenge to existing industrial and political practices. As the power of organized labor waned in response to a slowdown in economic growth, research turned to unions in crisis (Lange, Ross, and Vannicelli 1982; Edwards, Garonna, and Todtling 1986) and to management. In an era of global restructuring and high unemployment, corporations have come to be regarded as the main agents of change and the state is no longer viewed as a corporatist ally but as an economizing agent promoting market-based adjustments. Thus, in spite of national variations (Turner 1991), the future of unionism in the core advanced societies is more problematic today than it has been in any period since the Great Depression. But what of unionism in rapidly industrializing countries? Have unions gained in strength in line with increasing demands for skilled labor, or have corporations and governments moved quickly to limit union organization while simultaneously providing a safety valve in the form of steadily rising wages? And how are unions in the advanced countries on the periphery of the world economy faring? Has cooperation replaced militancy in an endeavor to compete in the new global

I would like to thank Christian Berggren, Sarosh Kuruvilla, David Levin, and Stephen Chiu for comments on a draft of this chapter and Yuen Kay for providing useful information on Singapore.

marketplace, or have unions continued to oppose change on management's terms?

Answering these questions requires a cross-national analysis of unionism in countries at different levels of industrialization. One option is to select countries in the same geographical region. This approach has four distinct advantages over a more global approach. First, situating unionism in a wider context, outside the confines of the nation-state, is compatible with the increasing significance of multinational corporations (MNCs) in world trade *and* the emergence of regional trade blocs. Second, it encourages detailed consideration of varying national contexts that appear similar from a broad perspective. Thus, Hong Kong and Singapore are both essentially ethnic Chinese city-states yet their geopolitical positions and forms of government have had lasting effects on the political economies and labor relations of the two societies. Third, a regional focus enables background considerations common to two or more countries—for example, cultural norms and practices—to be explored in relation to other causal considerations. And fourth, this approach stimulates the emergence of a body of scholarship and policy-relevant information that promotes learning and cooperation between people in neighboring societies, thereby dispelling misconceptions and reducing dependence on ideas and solutions formulated by analysts in the advanced core societies.

The Asia-Pacific region is an obvious candidate for cross-national analysis in that it includes four distinct country categories: the developing countries of Southeast Asia and China, the so-called Asian Tigers; the newly industrialized countries (NICs), or little Asian Dragons as they have come to be known; the small ex-British industrialized Pacific countries of Australia and New Zealand; and the core advanced late developer, Japan.

The subject matter of this book is unionism in nine of these societies during the 1980s. These include the developing countries (DCs) of China, Thailand, and Malaysia; the NICs of South Korea (hereafter Korea), Taiwan, Hong Kong (a British colony), and Singapore; and the advanced peripheral countries (APs) of Australia and New Zealand. Unionism in Japan is considered in the final chapter.

Our concern with the contemporary characteristics and future of trade unionism in these countries is informed by both academic and policy-related interests. There is a need for a volume that extends research and theorizing beyond jointly regulated systems (cf. Clegg 1976), complementing approaches adopted by political scientists (Martin 1989) and sociologists (Deyo 1989). Our hope is that this volume will encourage critical examination and testing of theories developed in other comparable regions (see Collier and Collier 1991), thereby contributing to a wider corpus of knowledge. From a policy standpoint, unions are important not only for labor market functioning but as vehicles of democracy, providing a base for political organization and party influence and acting as a countervailing power at the level of the enterprise. Unionism is thus not merely a technical matter of creating appropriate labor market structures and processes but a practical issue of establishing and maintaining human rights.

This chapter provides background data and analysis that should help in assessing the similarities and differences in the union patterns in the various countries examined in this book. I begin by considering relevant theories and associated hypotheses. This discussion is followed by an introduction to the Asia-Pacific region as an increasingly interdependent entity in the world economy. Key economic and political features of the nine societies are then summarized. The hope is that by the end of the chapter sufficient theoretical and empirical material will have been conveyed to justify examining unionism in each country.

Theoretical Approaches to Trade Unionism

In addition to the well-known literature on union theory based mainly on the experiences of advanced core countries (see Clegg 1976; Visser 1989; Turner 1991), it is possible to distinguish four different approaches to explaining contemporary union characteristics and trends. These are modernization theory, pursued mainly by industrial relations scholars and some sociologists; international labor market theory, preferred by some political economists and politically radical sociologists; the political science approach, pursued by specialists in comparative politics; and the political sociology perspective, which views the state as a central explanatory variable. Each of these perspectives and accompanying hypotheses will be discussed briefly.

Modernization Theory: Convergence on the United States, Japan, or Neither?

Modernization theory assumes that societies progress along a path of economic development in which economic forces play the major formative role in shaping social institutions. C. Kerr and his colleagues (1975) argued that the nature of union goals, structure, and leadership initially depended on the type of elite that presided over the industrialization process. Five ideal types were distinguished—middle class, dynastic, revolutionary-intellectuals, colonial administrators, and nationalist leaders.[1] According to this theory, as industrialization proceeded, the original forms of organization would be superseded by modern variants congruent with the demands of economic efficiency. Pluralistic industrialism in capitalist countries would involve relatively strong unions that would engage in shaping workplace rules chiefly through collective bargaining (Kerr 1983).

Some of the main problems with this schema are its assumption that the strategies put forth by elites have distinctive consequences for trade unions, that actual elites approximate the ideal types noted above, and that the strategies of any given elite do not vary substantially in different political contexts. The theory also tends to downplay the importance of product markets and industrial structure (Scoville 1973; Ramos 1990) and assumes that organized capitalism, typified by the United States, represents an end point in the evolution of economic systems (cf. Lash and Urry 1987). The theory does, however, generate the following hypotheses relevant to this work:

- At similar levels of industrialization, unionism in societies presided over by similar types of elites should be more alike than unionism in societies where the elites differ.
- Unions at later stages of industrialization should be stronger and more involved in workplace regulation than their counterparts at earlier stages.

The absence of any marked tendency in developing countries for economic unionism based mainly on collective bargaining to replace political unionism—involving support for wider social goals, close relations with political parties, and strikes in support of social objectives—led W. Galenson (1962) to argue that a limited labor supply was a necessary condition for the emergence of collective bargaining. A. Sturmthal and J. G. Scoville (1973) built on this insight, arguing that there would be a shift to economic unionism and bargaining when industrialization reached a level where the supply of labor was no longer unlimited and shortages of skilled labor emerged. At this stage unions would begin to favor collective bargaining, although there might be a lag and no simple substitution of economic for political unionism.

The idea of an economic-political continuum of union types became widely accepted (Essenberg 1981), but the typology failed to take account of the rise of enterprise unionism (Kassalow 1978) and the probability that both types of unionism could co-exist at different organizational levels (Ramos 1990). Nevertheless, the typology provides a mechanism for explaining Kerr and his colleagues' hypothesis that unions in advanced countries—where it was assumed that skilled labor tends to be in short supply—will be characterized by economic unionism. In addition, it leads to the reverse hypothesis appropriate to contemporary advanced societies experiencing deindustrialization in response to international competition:

- Where unemployment in advanced societies is persistently high by historical standards, unions will tend to adopt political rather than economic strategies in support of their goals. Thus, demands will be for national-level bargaining arrangements and laws to protect workers and their organizations.

S. Lash and J. Urry (1987) argue that such efforts will come to nothing because there are processes contributing to long-term union weakness and the incapacity of national-level bargaining arrangements to regulate employment conditions. These processes include a decline in the absolute and relative size of the manual working class; the movement of manufacturing to developing countries; the capacity of global corporations to avoid regulation by national governments as they compete increasingly in international markets; the tendency for flexible specialization in smaller workplaces, replacing mass production; and the assault on the welfare state, encouraged by fiscal crisis. These tendencies serve to "disorganize" advanced capitalism. Although the theory identifies salient changes in the advanced countries, its prognosis that decentralization and deregulation are inevitable appears myopic and overdrawn given the rise of such supranational institutions as the European Community, which is pursuing a social charter that is likely to regulate labor relations at a more centralized level. Nevertheless, in terms of industrial relations, the theory suggests the following hypothesis:

- In advanced societies, unions will decline in power and politically inspired, national-level corporatist arrangements will be replaced by decentralized bargaining and enterprise unionism.

A rather different theory, inspired by Japanese industrialization, points in a similar direction but applies most readily to the "late, late" developing societies of Asia. According to R. Dore (1974), the later industrialization occurs, the more likely the state will play a leading role and industry will start with rationalized, modern personnel systems that emphasize the rights of unions and the virtues of consultation. Consequently, the employment systems and unions will be more similar to Japanese welfare-corporatism (a late developer) than to British market individualism (the earliest developer). This theory is strengthened by the direct influence of Japanese transplants, which are likely to introduce into their host countries employment systems tailored to modern production techniques. At the same time, there may be less incentive for the host countries to adopt such systems, especially enterprise unionism, and, as Dore acknowledged, more difficulty fostering specifically Japanese practices. Nevertheless, the following hypothesis can be derived from this theory:

- Unions in the most recently industrialized countries, especially those that have been subject to high levels of Japanese direct investment, will most closely resemble Japanese enterprise unions.

The emphasis on the state's role has been taken up by B. Sharma (1985, 1991), who argues that at the earliest stage of industrialization, marked by primary commodity production, there is little pressure on the state to industrialize, and, with a virtually unlimited supply of labor, unions tend to pursue political rather than economic goals. Preindependence alliances with the ruling party continue so that cooperation is based on political support for nationalist goals. At a higher stage of industrialization, shortages of skilled labor encourage the development of economic unionism based mainly on collective bargaining. To ensure an adequate level of savings for investment purposes, however, while at the same time meeting growing consumer expectations, there is now more pressure on the state to contain union activity. This leads to conflict between the state and skilled workers' unions. Sharma cites Thailand, the Philippines, and Malaysia as examples of an apparently unstable pattern. Stability is possible, however, at a higher stage of industrialization, when there is a more favorable climate for foreign investment, thereby reducing the domestic savings constraint and permitting higher increases in wages. Under these conditions, guided collective bargaining along corporatist lines, as exemplified by Singapore, is a likely outcome (Sharma 1991:94).

Although this theory emphasizes the state's role, there is no recognition of variations in state strategies at similar levels of industrialization. State development strategies have different requirements: export-oriented industrialization (EOI) is likely to require greater unit labor cost competitiveness than an import-substitution industrialization (ISI) strategy (Bjorkman, Lauridsen, and Marcussen 1988; Deyo 1981). Consequently, the motives and pressures for changes in government policy relating to unions are complex and unlikely to correspond neatly with varying levels of industrialization. In addition, in discussing union-government relations at the highest stage of his model, Sharma does not adequately distinguish between cooperation based on the consent of autonomous unions and cooptation based on state power. Nonetheless, his position can be summarized in the following hypothesis:

- Unions will differ primarily according to the level of development of the country in which they are situated. Economic unionism will prevail in DCs with relatively high levels of industrial conflict, signaling opposition to state and employer policies. At the level of NICs, the state will tend to incorporate unions.

International Labor Market Theory

Central to the international labor market theory perspective is the notion that global capitalism has replaced monopoly capitalism (Ross and Trachte 1990). Large corporations dominating national manufacturing markets in core countries are now transnational in scope, having taken advantage of low-cost areas and modern transportation systems to shift the more labor-intensive parts of their manufacturing operations to selected peripheral and semiperipheral countries. MNCs are said to have increased in power vis-à-vis governments in the developing world, thereby reinforcing repressive public policies toward unions and workers aimed at maintaining stability, profitability, and high levels of direct foreign investment.

These changes have apparently had a profound adverse effect on workers and unions (Southall 1988:1–34; Munck 1988, chaps. 2 and 6) in both advanced and developing countries.[2] Thus, R. Southall (1988:23–24) refers to a tendency toward hegemonic despotism whereby workers' power is severely circumscribed by capital mobility and there is a tendency toward the curtailment of basic union rights. Meanwhile, union density in many developing countries remains low, and international unionism is particularly weak (Munck 1988:110–11; 195–98). New working-class movements are apparently the exception (see Webster 1988; Lambert 1990). Hence the following proposition:

- The changing division of international labor has resulted in repressive government labor policies that have contributed to marginalizing trade unions.

Comparative Politics and Political Sociology

One of the most significant contributions to union theory in recent years has been a study by R. M. Martin (1989) of the relationship between party systems and union movements. This analysis generates straightforward, testable hypotheses that stand in contrast to the work of political sociologists, whose main focus has been explicating the characteristics and consequences of the state. The wide-ranging interpretive approach adopted by scholars in this tradition makes it difficult but not impossible to derive simple hypotheses from this work. The contributors to this volume draw heavily on this tradition in conceptualizing the state and its interaction with capital (Evans 1985) and unions.

Party systems and trade union centers. Martin's (1989) theory attempts to explain variations in broad union orientations and forms at the confederation or peak council level. He argues that the basic structure and purpose of such organizations depend largely on extant party systems. Changes in party systems can therefore be expected to induce corresponding changes in union forms, although there will be "hangover" effects from the previous party system (Martin 1989:225). Systems without parties or with noncompetitive party systems—single parties and hegemonic variants—are said to produce state-ancillary unions whose goals tend to be productionist rather than consumptionist and whose structures are centralized to facilitate state control. Examples of such state corporatist (Crouch 1977) or integrative (Poole 1986) unions include those in the pre-Perestroika Soviet Union and Mexico respectively. Depending on the absence or presence of a polarizing party, competitive party systems foster unions that are either autonomous in relation to the state and employers (the United States) or ancillary to a party, that is, reflecting party goals through a structure that conforms to party demands (France and Italy). Finally, there are cases in which, despite the existence of a formally competitive party system, the major party has been able to retain power for a long time. Under such predominant party conditions, as in Japan, unions may act as surrogates for opposition political parties.

This theory does not explain a great deal about trade unions, and it raises questions about the fit of actual party systems to the typology outlined above (see Martin 1989:213–23). Nor does it say much about the causal mechanisms involved in party system–union relations. Nevertheless, it suggests the following hypotheses:

- At a general level and especially in relation to the state, unions will be more alike in countries that have similar party systems and more dissimilar in countries where party systems differ.
- The stability or otherwise of a union movement's basic form is closely related to continuity or change in the party system.

The state and trade unionism. Martin's analysis raises the question of whether parties and unions are shaped by a third factor: the interests and institutions that comprise the state. The state in Anglo-Saxon countries is frequently viewed as an output of competing group interests (pluralism or liberal collectivism) or as an institutional partnership based on cooperation between the government and large interest groups (bargained corporatism). This implies that unions as an interest group are relatively autonomous vis-à-vis the state and that the state will broadly reflect the balance of power between pressure groups. Following N. Poulantzas (1973), however, some Marxists have argued that the modern state typically operates within the confines of capitalism but nevertheless is relatively autonomous from the dominant fractions of capital.

This notion of the relatively autonomous state has been extended in accordance with the view that states can augment their power vis-à-vis dominant classes by various means but particularly through alliances with other states in the international system (see Rueschemeyer, Stephens, and Stephens 1992:64). So-called strong states have been identified in several South American and Northeast Asian countries. These states limit the autonomy of unions and other interest groups (Collier 1979; Haggard 1988; Wade 1988) and may use their discretion in a developmental or predatory manner (Evans 1989). To a greater or lesser extent, unions may be involved in making key economic decisions, either because of government preference, union demands, or both. Union power need not covary with involvement in government decision making, however. Thus, although weak unions can be involved in the decision-making process (as in Korea), it is nevertheless more common for the most powerful unions to be strong in the labor market, influential in the corridors of the ruling party, *and* involved in economic decision making (Sweden until recently).

Of relevance here is F. Deyo's (1981:15–16) conceptualization of strong states, which draws on the work of G. A. O'Donnell (1977). Two dimensions—state control of unions and union influence in the government—are used to distinguish bureaucratic from popular authoritarian states. Both involve considerable state control over unions, but in the former the union movement has little influence, while in the latter union influence is substantial. Deyo investigates factors associated with the stability of controls over the union movement in Singapore, where a bureaucratic authoritarian state prevails. These include the unity of the political elite, the elite's dependence on foreign investors and foreign governments for resources, the existence of tightly integrated institutional structures, the presence of disorganized workers, and a closely controlled mass-media communications system. Deyo argues that, in addition, the process of what he calls dependent development (based on EOI) reinforces authoritarian corporatism.[3] The desire to control the work force and to encourage worker commitment in the interest of national competitiveness and government legitimacy, however, leads authoritarian corporatism toward a more popular form of authoritarianism. According to Deyo (1981:115), Singapore is the only NIC "to systematically build the national trade union structure into an instrument not only of production but of social integration as well."

In a later work, Deyo (1989) places the state at the center of an analysis that seeks to explain the weakness of organized labor in the four NICs—Korea, Taiwan, Hong Kong, and Singapore. Weakness is assessed by reference to data on union density, strike patterns, and working conditions. Arguments based on culture and improvements in workers' welfare are examined and not completely discounted, but the emphasis is on the interplay between the state's role and structural (mainly economic) factors. Essentially, Deyo argues that the state introduced corporatist measures in various guises before industrialization so that it was in a position to defeat early left-wing unions and shape subsequent developments. With economic growth came legitimation of the authoritarian state, which served to limit the emergence of competing interest groups. The state pursued EOI strategies in the 1970s and, receiving support from foreign governments, was able to insulate itself from control by the domestic middle class. In addition, the state was in a position to establish effective labor-control systems. Though different in the four societies in terms of type (repressive or corporatist), severity (strong or weak), and level of application (centralized or local), the various systems maintained worker discipline and high productivity growth.[4]

Union weakness not only reflects the existence of state-structured labor controls but is supplemented by nonproletarian labor systems based on patrimony, kinship, and paternalism and the existence of small-scale, labor-intensive light-industry firms whose control systems make union organization difficult (Deyo 1989, chaps. 5 and 6). Looking to the future, Deyo (1989:146) notes that the continuing differentiation and complexity of industry requires more decentralized structures based on enterprise paternalism and that company unions characteristic of those in Taiwan are becoming common in Singapore. Thus, union weakness is likely to be perpetuated in a manner that recalls Dore's convergence on Japan thesis. At the same time, Deyo (1989:213) warns that class collaboration is not assured given the rise of middle-class political dissent and the possibility of a secular decline in economic growth.

Deyo's study has several weaknesses. First, he does not analyze the composition and dynamics of state elites. This is relevant, for it is unclear how the state in each of the four societies has managed to maintain its unity and strength. This is especially unclear in Korea, where there are regional antipathies, and in Taiwan, where the government has been dominated by aging mainlanders. Second, and more significant from a union perspective, he includes very little data on or analysis of unions and labor-oriented political groups beyond evidence of union weakness. Third, he does not consider public-enterprise labor relations and the role of unions. This is important in Taiwan, where such enterprises are relatively large and not confined to light industry. And, as we shall see in relation to Hong Kong (chap. 7), public-sector unions have been at the forefront of recent activity. Fourth, and finally, Deyo's analysis focuses on continuity rather than change, but in doing so he offers no explanation for the explosion of labor militancy that occurred in Taiwan and Korea in the late 1980s. These problems aside, Deyo's work has inspired hypotheses outlined later and has provided valuable insights into variations in state strategies in the four NICs.

J. J. Choi's (1989) analysis of unionism in Korean manufacturing industry between 1961 and 1980 complements Deyo's analysis. The development of the authoritarian state is explained by reference to historical and structural factors and its dynamics are explored specifically in relation to union regulation. The state's role is considered in depth in conjunction with other factors that shaped the growth, policies, internal structure, and consequences of unionism. Choi (46–47) argues that the speed of industrialization effectively prevented the development of institutionalized differences between skilled and less skilled workers and hence precluded craft unionism. The rapid spread of universal education fostered a democratic egalitarian ideology and an awareness of workers' interests that countered traditional norms and heightened the disjunction between expectations and the reality of factory despotism (71–72). Another factor of importance was the role of external groups, in particular, the churches, which raised workers' consciousness of their democratic rights and assisted workers in their efforts to organize (76).

Choi (1989:155–57) sees the state as the dominant force restraining union growth and shaping union goals in the 1970s. This restraint was achieved by the domestication of national union leaders, especially through control by the intelligence service and intervention in key union elections. Union leaders gained unique access to policy makers committed to an EOI development strategy, but they were not given positions of any influence in the corporatist system. Indeed, they apparently had little influence over the increasingly powerful executive arm of the state. The state did not simply rely on a strategy that rendered the national unions powerless, however; rather, it played an active role in fostering employee integration through the promotion of management-labor councils at the factory level coupled with an ideological program (the Factory Saemaul movement) designed to reinforce employees' work commitment (Choi 1989, chap. 7).

In the wider context of state propaganda concerning the need for industrial development against the threat of North Korea, this combined strategy of administrative control and ideological activity neutralized union power at the local level. Militant rank-and-file groups of younger, more educated workers opposed the management-oriented enterprise union leaders, however, eventually leading to a split in the union movement between official and new unions. The state reacted by introducing legislation that reduced the role of industrial unions to virtual public relations agencies of the government (Choi: 316). The new unions were thus isolated and made vulnerable to state and company attempts to force a change in leadership and thereby reintegrate these organizations into the official union system. Choi (316) emphasizes, however, that the contradiction of corporatism—combining top-down control with worker commitment to management and state goals—renders the system of control especially unstable if the political elite fragments and demands for democracy increase.

Like Deyo's study of labor in the NICs, Choi's analysis combines macro- and micro-level analysis of the state's role, but, based on detailed empirical research, he goes further in examining the mechanisms and impact of state policies. This is a significant achievement, although three main limitations should be noted. First, concentration on the state's role in relation to trade unionism tends to downplay the role of management, especially in the Chaebol, Korea's highly concentrated enterprise groups. Second, this point is particularly relevant to the 1980s, when Korea underwent political liberalization and the Chaebol achieved greater

autonomy from the state, although this did not continue without inter-
ruption in the 1990s (Song 1992). Third, Choi derives many of his
conclusions about changes in union behavior from three admittedly
large and important unions, which raises questions regarding the typical-
ity of their experiences.

Based on Deyo and Choi's studies, three hypotheses can be advanced:

- Variations in union patterns primarily reflect state power and policies that
  are influenced mainly by political and economic considerations.
- The state shapes labor relations and union behavior through a variety of
  mechanisms that tend to crystallize around a particular logic consistent
  with an overall development strategy.
- Continued emphasis by the state and employers on high-technology sectors
  encourages the growth of company paternalism and enterprise unionism as
  work force stabilization and enterprise loyalty assume increasing importance.

This brief theoretical review points to the need for a framework that
is wide-ranging in both its variables and cases, and that facilitates
systematic description and analysis. These requirements touch on issues
of strategy and methodology that are discussed below.

Research Strategy, Analytical Framework, and Methodology

In planning the research for this volume, we were guided by several
points. First, with the exception of Korea and Hong Kong, there are few
detailed published studies—in English or, as far as we could ascertain, in
indigenous languages—on contemporary trade unionism in the rapidly
industrializing and developing countries of East Asia. Second, given our
limited resources, a comparative study could be achieved only by relying
on local researchers or scholars with a special interest in the countries
concerned. Third, because of the above-mentioned constraints and the
diverse analytical backgrounds of the contributors, the most feasible
strategy seemed to be one that emphasized agreement on a few relatively
straightforward research issues and an explicit, albeit flexible, framework, that would guide the collection of data and analysis. Fourth, we
thought it important to examine unions over time because several of the
theories addressed *changes* in trade unionism and because recent political and economic developments could have significant impact. Accordingly, the project's goals were threefold: first, to describe and account
for the main characteristics of trade unionism in the nine countries over
the decade ending around 1990, a period long enough to enable changes
and trends to be identified without being so long as to stretch contributors' resources unduly;[5] second, to conceptualize and identify union

patterns and trends; and third, to assess these findings in relation to the various hypotheses outlined in this chapter.

Our study seeks a middle ground in terms of abstraction. Thus, we hope to provide an analysis of unionism in each country that is sufficiently detailed to encourage study as a single case while facilitating international comparison by using common concepts and empirical measures based on comparable data. The project draws on various perspectives, particularly those reviewed earlier, as well as many concepts derived from industrial relations. This approach, especially when combined with the use of available data—typically from official sources—emphasizes an economic rather than a political conception of trade unions. This is both a strength and a weakness, for it facilitates systematic comparisons of unions as labor market institutions but downplays union involvement in political parties and political processes, an investigation that would require intensive field-based research.

The research design we followed reflects a desire to compare patterns of unionism and, through a process of analytic induction, to gauge the importance of particular variables suggested by the theories reviewed earlier. Two methodological strategies are employed in the final chapter to do this. The first privileges particular variables as causal components in an explanation, while the second involves a search and analysis of variables after comparing the most similar and the most different outcomes.

Using the first approach, one might privilege level of economic development and nature of the party system as causal variables. Thus, societies that are similar according to the two criteria should have similar patterns of unionism. Korea and Taiwan, for example, are both NICs that operate under what might be described as transitional, single to multiparty systems. The hypothesis predicts that unionism in these societies should be broadly similar. By contrast, countries at different (albeit somewhat arbitrary) levels of economic development operating within dissimilar party systems should have different patterns of unionism. According to the hypothesis advanced above, this should be evident from a comparison between China—a developing country ruled by a single party—and Australia, an advanced peripheral country with a predominantly two-party system. Limited contrasts include comparisons of countries that differ on one or the other of the two criteria. Comparisons of this kind—for example, between Hong Kong and Singapore, which are both NICs but the former has a noncompetitive system while the latter is effectively a single-party system—should yield limited similarities. Such a comparison also permits evaluation of the relative strengths of the two variables—in this case the political factor—in comparing patterns of unionism.[6]

The second approach involves sorting the countries into two broad categories based on their patterns of unionism: those that are most similar and those that are most different according to a definition of union patterns that relies on a limited number of theoretically relevant variables. The aim is to identify and explore variables that might account for similarities and differences in unionism. Countries with the most similar patterns should share certain common causal variables and processes, while those with contrasting patterns of unionism should display major differences in some causal variables. This methodological approach conforms broadly to what D. Collier (1991) refers to as a small *N* study using most similar and most different systems designs.

The choice of countries and therefore unions was not based simply on methodological considerations. It was also determined by the willingness of knowledgeable and competent researchers to participate in the project. Originally, three additional countries were included, two developing—Indonesia and the Philippines—and Japan, the core advanced country in the region. For a variety of reasons, this research was not completed.[7] This reflects the hazards of conducting an international project on a shoestring budget within a limited time frame. Nevertheless, we would argue that the omission of these countries does not seriously impair our analysis or conclusions, especially since the important case of Japanese unionism is discussed in the final chapter.

In this volume unions are conceptualized as organizations representing members drawn from wage- and salary-earning strata. Unions typically have limited discretion over membership coverage and in enforcing compliance with leaders' requirements and union rules. As P. Lange, G. Ross, and M. Vannicelli (1982:219) have argued, unions are part of two sets of exchange relationships: between the members, on the one hand, and between employers and the state, on the other. Without membership support, their capacity to influence employers and the state is limited. Union organization and the ability to mobilize members may depend crucially, however, on the role played by the state and employers. Insofar as these differ cross-nationally, we can anticipate variations in union structure,[8] goals, strategies, and dominant methods of operation. Union structure is characterized by three features: inclusivity/exclusivity, or the extent to which unions have jurisdiction over various categories of employee (Visser 1989); unity/conflict, or the extent of cooperation or conflict between unions; and the degree of centralization, reflecting the locus of decision making (Clegg 1976; Visser 1989). Union leaders' goals and strategies vary, with redistributing social wealth and power at one end of the spectrum, and augmenting production and reproducing the existing power structure at the other.

Methods for pursuing union objectives also differ: strategies may be predicated mainly on joint regulation (through industrial or political bargaining); on unilateral imposition, by means of strikes and other forms of industrial action; or on consultation. On the basis of research in advanced societies, various combinations of these elements tend to be related empirically, so that stronger union movements are characterized by inclusive, unified, and centralized structures; redistributional goals; and extensive involvement in joint regulation at both macro and micro levels. The reverse tends to be true of the weakest union movements (Stephens 1976; Lange, Ross, and Vannicelli 1982; Gourevitch et al. 1984).

Drawing on these findings, union power in this study is assessed with reference to the amount of control exercised by the state and employers in promoting or limiting union autonomy, union structure—which facilitates or impedes organizational cohesion—and the extent of joint regulation involving participation in the determination of procedural and substantive rules affecting employees' working lives. The question of union effectiveness is considered in the chapter on individual countries, but cross-national variations in the constraints imposed on unions and variations in union objectives make it impossible to assess differences in effectiveness properly.

In keeping with the exploratory nature of this study, the determinants of union behavior were left open to interpretation. The contributors did agree to explore a set of potentially important explanatory variables, although these are not explicitly evaluated in each chapter. These variables include the history of unionism and leaders' ideologies in the context of industrialization; the structure of employment according to industry and occupation; the size, role, and strategic position of foreign-owned companies and the public sector; technology and technical change; management strategies in relation to dominant product markets; employer organization and labor-control systems; and labor market conditions and training. The characteristics of managers and workers, including their ethnic, religious, gender, and other identities, were also thought to be pertinent. The characteristics of each country's political arrangements, including the role of the government as initiator and executor of economic, social, and labor relations policies, were also regarded as important, but these characteristics proved difficult to research where noncompetitive party systems prevailed.

Economic Development and the Trend toward Regional Integration

Having explained the theoretical rationale and approach to the research, I turn now to a comparison of the levels of economic development in the nine countries. I also look at the trend toward interdependence in their economic links and labor migration patterns. Level of development indicates the size and nature of the urban wage and salary sector, which in turn influences the potential power of unions, while economic and political integration suggests the possibility of convergence in state and employer orientations to trade unionism.

Table 1.1 lists the nine countries according to five conventionally accepted indicators of economic development: average per capita income; relative size of economic sectors; extent of urbanization; literacy rate; and access to private telephones, an important medium of modern communication. The indicators tend to be positively related, the main anomaly being the city-states of Hong Kong and Singapore, which are more developed than Australia and New Zealand on two of the five indicators (economic structure and rate of urbanization). Note that the DCs continue to employ a large proportion of persons in the agricultural sector, while the NICs have the highest proportion of employees in manufacturing. The AP countries are distinguished by their relatively large service sectors.

Exports of manufactured goods from NICs to the advanced core countries have grown so rapidly that in 1988 the four little dragons lost their privileged tariff status under the Organization for Economic Cooperation and Development's (OECD) generalized system of preferences (GSP). This, together with increasing U.S. sensitivity to Taiwanese and Korean imports (Asian Development Bank [ADB] 1990:41–43), signaled the possibility of future import restrictions; hence, the diversification of NIC exports toward other Asian countries. This policy has also given the DCs an export advantage, which has been one of the factors stimulating direct foreign investment in China, Thailand, and Malaysia. How long this policy will remain is a matter of conjecture as pressure mounts on the U.S. Congress to stem imports. The American Federation of Labor–Congress of Industrial Organizations (AFL-CIO) has been active in lobbying to exclude DCs such as China, Thailand, and Malaysia from the GSP, ostensibly on the grounds of human rights abuses and exploitative labor practices.

Trade and Supply Links

Rapid growth based on foreign trade is a major characteristic of many countries in the Asia-Pacific region. In 1970, intra-Asian trade comprised 12 percent of world trade; by 1989, it had increased to 22 percent of a much larger volume (*Economist* 1991b:30). The region's share of total exports to the world (as defined in table 1.3) increased from 15.4 percent in 1980 to 19.3 percent in 1990 (Business Council of Australia [BCA] 1992:10). A summary of trade patterns and growth is provided in table 1.2.

Table 1.2 shows that by 1986 trade within the region accounted for a substantial proportion of total trade by Asia-Pacific countries—42.6 percent of total imports and 35.2 percent of total exports. More recent

Table 1.1. Development by country, 1990

Country	Per capita income (U.S. $)	Work force totals (%)			Urban population (%)	Literacy (%)	People per telephone
		Agriculture	Manufacturing	Services[a]			
DCs							
China	298[b]	60.2	17.3	22.5	21	72.6	116.0
Thailand	1,413	58.4	8.4	33.2	18	91.0	36.4
Malaysia	2,297	30.8	17.3	51.9	35	72.6	10.3
NICs							
Korea	5,569	19.5	27.6	52.9	70	92.7	3.4
Taiwan	7,332	12.3	32.4	55.3	71	91.7	2.8
Hong Kong	12,068	0.8	27.7	71.5	93	88.1	2.0
Singapore	11,245	0.5	28.9	70.6	100	90.1	2.3
APs							
Australia	13,480	5.0	14.3	80.7	86	99.5	1.8
New Zealand	11,370	10.8	17.3	71.9	84	99.8	1.4

Sources: *Far Eastern Economic Review [FEER]* 1991: 6–7; *FEER* 1992: 6–7; *Asiaweek* 1991. Services figure for Singapore is calculated from *FEER* 1990: 6–7.
[a]Includes construction, government, and public authorities.
[b]Some figures have been rounded.

Table 1.2. Foreign trade patterns of countries in the Asia-Pacific (ESCAP) region, 1977–86 (in percent)

	1977		1986		Annual average change	
	Imports from	Exports to	Imports from	Exports to	Imports	Exports
Asia-Pacific developing countries and NICs	21.2	19.8	22.7	23.9	14.4	19.7
Australia, New Zealand, and Japan	19.0	15.2	19.9	11.3	13.9	7.9
Asia-Pacific total	40.2	35.0	42.6	35.2	14.2	14.6
All countries except Asia-Pacific	59.8	65.0	57.4	64.8	11.9	14.3
Value in U.S. $ (in millions)						
Asia-Pacific total	69,439	66,039	158,431	152,727		
All other countries	172,754	188,738	371,976	433,872		

Source: United Nations 1988.
The Asia-Pacific (Economic and Social Commission for Asia and the Pacific [ESCAP]) region includes Afghanistan, Australia, Bangladesh, Bhutan, Brunei Darussalam, Burma, China, Northern Marianas, Cook Island, Kampuchea, Micronesia, Fiji, Guam, Hong Kong, India, Indonesia, Iran, Japan, Kiribati, Laos, Malaysia, Maldives, Mongolia, Nauru, Nepal, New Zealand, Niue, Pakistan, Papua New Guinea, Philippines, South Korea, Marshall Islands, Palau, Samoa, Singapore, Solomon Islands, Sri Lanka, Thailand, Tonga, Tuvalu, Vanuatu, and Viet Nam. Asia-Pacific developing countries refers to the above countries except Australia, New Zealand, and Japan. Percentages have been rounded.

Table 1.3. Foreign trade links in the Asia-Pacific region, in U.S. $ million, 1990

Importing Countries	Exporting Countries												
	China	Thailand	Malaysia	Korea	Taiwan	Hong Kong	Singapore	Australia	New Zealand	Japan	Region^a	Ex-region	Total
China	–	314	619	n.a.	n.a.	20,332	799	955	91	6,145	30,152	19,469	49,621
Thailand	825	–	1,032	817	1,420	1,076	3,490	444	82	9,150	18,681	11,643	30,324
Malaysia	372	478	–	599	1,103	579	6,873	721	165	5,529	16,801	8,510	25,311
Korea	n.a.	394	1,359	–	1,209	1,907	1,173	2,202	400	17,500	27,822	30,414	58,236
Taiwan	n.a.	449	1,004	1,343	–	1,447	1,410	1,660	191	16,011	24,680	30,048	54,728
Hong Kong	27,330	1,038	934	3,387	8,547	–	3,429	995	140	13,106	59,863	21,291	81,154
Singapore	2,017	1,696	6,751	1,534	2,199	2,615	–	1,799	120	10,739	31,616	23,996	55,612
Australia	484	373	490	1,001	1,277	1,238	1,311	–	1,727	6,926	15,542	22,037	37,579
New Zealand	51	40	67	150	195	148	204	1,954	–	1,210	4,108	3,837	7,944
Japan	9,275	3,969	4,505	12,626	8,308	4,680	4,616	10,206	1,493	–	72,619	138,959	211,578
Region^a	40,965	9,080	17,504	22,782	26,324	35,664	25,414	22,891	4,625	94,016	320,880	323,869	644,749
Ex-region	22,458	14,004	11,905	37,433	40,711	46,481	27,339	16,021	4,804	193,662	428,240	2,266,610	2,694,851
Total	63,423	23,084	29,409	60,215	67,035	82,144	52,753	38,911	9,430	287,678	749,120	2,590,480	3,339,600

Source: Business Council of Australia [BCA] 1992:8-9.
^a Refers to the ten Asia-Pacific countries in the table and Indonesia, the Philippines, and Papua New Guinea.
Ex-region refers to all other countries.
n.a. = not available.

data (not shown in table 1.2) indicate that between 1980 and 1990 intraregional trade increased as a proportion of total trade from 38.8 percent to 42.8 percent. Over the 1977–86 period, intraregional trade growth exceeded the growth in trade with advanced countries outside the region (chiefly North America and Western Europe), a point supported by export growth figures (not shown in table 1.2), which indicate that over the 1980–90 period, intraregional exports expanded at an annual average rate of 22.1 percent, compared with 17.6 percent for exports to the world (BCA 1992:10). The most rapid growth in intraregional trade involved the developing Asia-Pacific countries and the NICs, whose annual average increase in imports and exports from Asia-Pacific countries over the period was 14.4 percent and 19.7 percent respectively. This compares with corresponding figures for non–Asia-Pacific countries of 11.9 percent and 14.3 percent. For the most recent period, 1987–90, intra-Asian trade rose by an average of 21 percent per year, which was almost twice the rate of growth in trade between Asia and North America (Wu 1991:106).

Japan has played a key role in the growth of intraregional trade. Japanese exports to the region increased from 29.1 percent of that country's total exports in 1980 to 32.7 percent in 1990. This represented 29.3 percent of total regional imports. In 1990, Japan's imports from the region accounted for 22.6 percent of total intraregional exports (see table 1.3), down from 30 percent in 1980 (BCA 1992:9).

Other than China and New Zealand, the countries in the region that we are concerned with experienced growing bilateral trade deficits with Japan. Particularly large deficits were recorded by Thailand, Korea, Taiwan, and Hong Kong (see table 1.3). This is partly the result of Japanese corporate strategy, which involves outsourcing the manufacture of components to lower-cost NICs and DCs while concentrating high value-added activities—R&D, production of high-technology items, and finishing and marketing—in Japan.[9] The finished products are then exported to North America, Europe, and Asia-Pacific countries.

The importance of foreign trade and hence the need to reduce or stabilize unit labor costs varies among the nine countries in our study. Singapore, Hong Kong, and Malaysia are the strongest foreign traders (as expressed by the value of foreign trade as a proportion of gross domestic product [GDP]), while China, Australia, and New Zealand are the weakest.[10] The values of the trade flows between the nine countries including Japan are shown in table 1.3.

As evident in table 1.3, Asia-Pacific countries vary in the extent to which they export to one another. China (64.6 percent of exports), Malaysia (60 percent), and Australia (58.8 percent) export a relatively high proportion of their total exports to other Asia-Pacific countries.

This contrasts with Japan (32.7 percent) and Taiwan and Thailand (both 39.3 percent), which export mainly to North America and Europe.

Asia-Pacific countries also vary considerably in the importance of their particular trade links. China, for example, has a strong trade relationship with Hong Kong, much of it based on an exchange of low-cost, labor-intensive items and components for higher value-added products. A similar relationship exists between Malaysia and Singapore, while Thailand, which directs a relatively high proportion of its exports (of primary and labor-intensive products) to Japan, is dwarfed by higher-technology imports from that country. This resembles the Korean trade pattern and to a lesser extent that of Taiwan, which exports slightly more to Hong Kong (much of this destined for China) than to Japan. With regard to the advanced peripheral countries, Australia's exports (of mainly primary and semiprocessed products) to Japan are noteworthy, while New Zealand's relationships with Australia and Japan are significant in terms of both its exports and imports.

Foreign Direct Investment and Company Ownership

Japanese direct investment in Asia over the period 1951–88, which amounted to nearly U.S. $32.1 billion, was divided almost equally between the NICs (46.8 percent) and Southeast Asian DCs (46 percent), with the remainder going to China (6.3 percent) and South Asia (9.9 percent). The most favored countries were Indonesia, which received 30.6 percent of Japanese direct investment; Singapore, 11.9 percent; and Korea, 10.1 percent. Thailand received 6.2 percent, and Malaysia received 5.7 percent (ADB 1991:46). Japanese direct investment in East Asia continued at high levels in the 1980s, when the NICs also became major investors. The United States also remained a significant investor.[11] In 1988 and 1989, Japanese direct investment, estimated at U.S. $13.8 billion, went mainly to Hong Kong (26 percent), Singapore (19 percent), and Thailand (15 percent) (*Economist* 1990e:30). This represented only about 12 percent of Japan's total direct investment overseas, of which most funds flowed to the United States and Europe (Kidd 1992:3). In 1988 and 1989, Taiwan and Hong Kong together invested U.S. $13.5 billion in other Asian economies, an amount comparable to that invested by Japan. Taiwanese (and Korean) direct investment was stimulated by the lifting of government restrictions on capital outflows. Taiwanese money went mainly to Thailand (35 percent), Indonesia (25 percent), and China (23 percent), while Hong Kong entrepreneurs overwhelmingly favored China (72 percent) and Thailand (11 percent). H. Hill's (1990:31) observation that much of the NICs' investment in the Asia-Pacific region is underpinned by Chinese business networks,[12] together with the considerable volume of Japanese and U.S. direct investment over the last thirty years, suggests that foreign ownership may play a role in shaping trade unionism, as implied by the relevant hypothesis outlined earlier (see p. 7). This is most likely how Japanese companies, which tend to export their organizational systems (Nomura 1991a; Kumon 1991), are influential players in local economies.

The relative importance of foreign-owned companies varies among the nine countries. Among the developing countries, foreign direct investment, in the form of joint ventures, comprises a very small proportion of total investment in China, whereas Hong Kong and Taiwanese capital is playing a major role in the exceedingly rapid growth of the southern coastal region (*Economist* 1991d:18, 1992b:26; *Far Eastern Economic Review* [*FEER*] 1992:204). Japanese and Sino-Thai firms in Thailand have received large injections of capital, as indicated by the growth of Japanese and NIC investment in that country.[13] Over the period 1986–89 it is estimated that Thailand received nearly U.S. $18 billion in foreign direct investment, 45 percent from Japan and 25 percent from the NICs, with Taiwan and Hong Kong being major investors. By 1991, the accumulation of foreign investment over the decade is expected to result in foreign-controlled firms employing 20 percent of Thailand's work force and producing more than half the country's industrial output (*Economist* 1990b:28). Corresponding data for Malaysia show that the NICs—mainly Taiwan and Singapore—accounted for about 35 percent of the estimated U.S. $6.5 billion in foreign investment, with Japan contributing slightly more than 27 percent (ADB 1991:48). This suggests relatively less Japanese control and more ethnic Chinese control over industry in Malaysia than over industry in Thailand, especially since indigenous Chinese investors control an estimated 40 percent of Malaysian industry. This, together with a similar figure for foreign-controlled companies, leaves Malay nationals holding about 20 percent of company stock (*Economist* 1991c:31).

Among the NICs, Korea stands out as least affected by foreign direct investment. In the 1980s, foreign firms accounted for 2 percent of total employment and 8.5 percent of manufacturing employment (Hill 1990:26). In Hong Kong, foreign firms have become more significant; direct foreign investment accounted for 6.5 percent of gross capital formation in 1979–82 and 8.3 percent in 1983–85 (Haggard 1990:208). Foreign investment is more important in Taiwan, where investment by Chinese entrepreneurs living overseas accounts for about one-third of total investment (Hill 1990:27). Most of this appears to be in the form of portfolio rather than direct investment (Haggard 1990:208).

Singapore has the highest foreign ownership component of the NICs and indeed of all the nine countries. Over the 1980–86 period, direct foreign investment commitments in manufacturing (excluding petrochemicals) comprised nearly three-quarters of total private direct investments (local and foreign), of which the United States accounted for nearly half and Japan about 18 percent. Investors from other Asia-Pacific countries made up less than 10 percent (Economic Intelligence Unit 1991:103). Foreign investment in the NICs should not, however, be exaggerated. There appears to be more local investment in the service sector, and Singapore has a large public investment program, so that foreign investment did not exceed much more than 15 percent of gross capital formation over the 1980s (Hill 1990:26, 49).

With regard to the advanced peripheral countries, foreign ownership of Australian industry was reported to be at 35 percent in mid-1991. It has been lower in manufacturing (31 percent in 1986–87) than in mining (45 percent in 1984–85) or the ownership of registered financial corporations (38 percent in 1985–86) (Australian Bureau of Statistics [ABS] 1992, catalogue no. 5306.0:12). British and U.S. investors continue to dominate in Australia, comprising more than 50 percent of direct foreign investment. Japanese nationals increased their activity, accounting for about 20 percent of foreign direct investment in the second half of the 1980s. Investment by residents of other Asian countries was negligible (Garnaut 1989:93–94).

Foreign ownership and investment are relatively limited in New Zealand. Firms with more than 50 percent foreign ownership accounted for nearly 11 percent of the nonagricultural work force in 1990. Foreign-owned firms were most significant in manufacturing (employing 21.1 percent of employees) and business and financial services (16.2 percent of employees). Over the 1980s foreign direct investment in New Zealand accounted for an estimated average of 4.8 percent of total investment, with Australian, U.K., and U.S. firms the major investors (Callister 1991). There has been increasing cross-investment between Australian and New Zealand companies, associated with the Closer Economic Relations Agreement signed in 1988. This foreshadows a single market in goods, services, and labor in these countries.[14] Direct investment by Japanese and other Asian entrepreneurs has been minimal in New Zealand.

Labor Flows within the Region

Rapid economic growth in many of the Asia-Pacific countries has been accompanied by chronic labor shortages. One means of alleviating this problem has been through the employment of immigrant labor. Since this often involves low-skilled employees, immigrant labor may contribute to already segmented labor markets, notwithstanding the advantages of containing unemployment in the countries of origin. Estimates of labor flows are generally unreliable because of the large number of illegal immigrants working in neighboring countries. Nevertheless, based on M. I. Abella's (1991) research, the main labor flows can be summarized as follows. The first trend is toward migration from less developed to more prosperous DCs, such as Malaysia, which probably received at least thirty thousand immigrant workers (legal and illegal) between 1985 and 1988, most of them from Indonesia.

A second trend is toward a growing number of immigrant workers from DCs to NICs and Japan. According to official estimates, the flow of migrant workers increased fivefold between 1980 and 1988, so that an estimated 300,000 workers left one of the Association of Southeast Asian Nations (ASEAN) to work in a NIC. Singapore stands out as a major recipient in terms of the size of its work force. In 1991, immigrants comprised an estimated 20 percent of the country's work force (*FEER* 1992:189). This contrasts with Korea and Japan, which have relatively few immigrants—probably less than 2 percent of their respective work forces—but labor inflows have been increasing rapidly as migrant workers take advantage of labor shortages to earn high incomes compared with earnings at home (*FEER* 1992:140; Japan Institute of Labor [JIL] 1990:4).

The third form of labor flow involves immigration of labor to the APs. Over the 1981–89 period, legal immigrants to Australia from Asia increased by about 50 percent, comprising 24 percent of all immigrants in 1981 and 34.6 percent in 1990 (ABS 1982–90).[15] Only about 4.4 percent of immigrants, however, were born in Asia (ABS 1990). In New Zealand, Asian immigration is reported to have tripled as a proportion of total settlers over the 1980s partly because of the popularity of the business migrants' scheme among Taiwanese people (*FEER* 1992:169).

Summary

Broadly speaking, the economic growth, business links, and labor migration trends outlined above indicate a gradual shift toward the production of more high value-added goods and services in the NICs, with labor-intensive processes and products being concentrated in the DCs, chiefly in large cities and in economic zones that provide attractive tax incentives and low-cost labor.[16] Both the exchange of final products and cooperation based on commodity chains involving supplier-producer networks (Harris 1992) are now fostered by substantial markets and infrastructure in the region. These economic processes have been especially facilitated by the substantially lower labor costs in the DCs, the tariff advantages mentioned earlier, and appreciation of the currencies of Japan and of the NICs following the Plaza Accord of 1985.[17] Insofar as low-skilled labor is required in the NICs, immigrant labor increasingly fulfills this need. As I have noted, production in East Asia is significantly influenced by Japanese and ethnic Chinese companies in the context of growing uncertainty about U.S. and European markets. These factors, together with the growth of domestic markets, have encouraged Asia-Pacific countries to extend cooperation from security to trade matters. Progress has been slow, however, largely because of ambivalence on the part of several Asia-Pacific nations toward any trading bloc that might reduce access to the large North American and European Community markets.[18] Nevertheless, there is a strong incentive to coordinate economic policies to improve complementarities rather than intensify competition.

Finally, the AP countries experienced difficulties in the 1980s as prices for their primary exports declined relative to imports of manufactured goods. Governments have encouraged industry restructuring, including a stronger focus on exports of processed goods and services to Asia-Pacific countries, as part of the process of finding a new role for AP countries in changing world markets.

Economic Development of the Nine Countries

The following discussion focuses on trends in economic growth, foreign trade, inflation, and unemployment in the developing countries, the newly industrializing countries (which include Hong Kong, although it is a British colony), and the advanced peripheral countries.

The Developing Countries: China, Thailand, and Malaysia

Over the period 1981–90, these three countries grew rapidly. China's annual average GDP per capita increased by 7.7 percent a year, Thailand's by 5.4 percent, and Malaysia's by 3.0 percent (ADB 1991:279; World Bank 1989).[19] As figure 1.1A shows, China's very high economic growth rates began to ease off after 1984, while the economies of Thailand and Malaysia strengthened and then faltered, and then resumed their strong upward trend in the latter part of the decade.

Trends in foreign trade, shown in figure 1.1B, indicate that all three countries were in deficit for much of the 1980s. China's position was relatively strong until 1984, when it deteriorated, but was later contained by greater government control over imports and had improved significantly by 1990. The trading positions of Thailand and Malaysia fluctuated greatly over the 1980s, reflecting variations in imports of capital goods, the main effect of which was to sustain rapid industrialization. In the case of Malaysia, current account flows were more volatile in response to changes in the prices of primary commodity exports. In 1990, export earnings from palm oil, wood, rubber, and tin deteriorated significantly. Nevertheless, the growth in exports of manufactured goods—comprising 54 percent of the value of total exports in 1989—is reducing the country's vulnerability to reductions in world commodity prices (ADB 1991:103–4).

An indicator of the burden of the deficits incurred is the debt service ratio (repayments and interest on official debt as a percentage of mer-

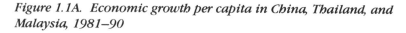

Figure 1.1A. Economic growth per capita in China, Thailand, and Malaysia, 1981–90

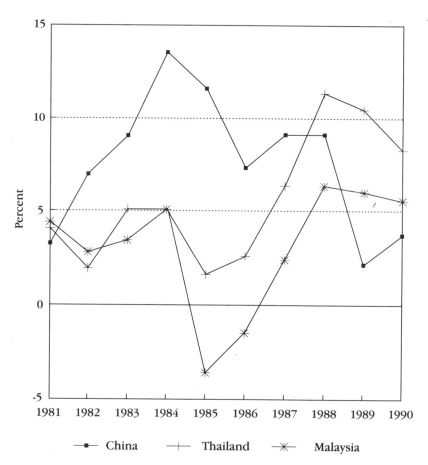

China — Thailand — Malaysia

Source: World Bank 1989; ADB 1991.

chandise exports), shown in figure 1.1C. Whereas China's debt service ratio grew slightly from a lower base, Thailand's and Malaysia's increased markedly up to the mid-1980s, mainly reflecting strongly adverse terms of trade, a contraction in the world economy, and, in the case of Malaysia, dependence on external financing to support the government's heavy-industry policy (Kuruvilla 1992). The debt position of both economies improved in the latter half of the 1980s, largely because of strong growth in exports, high levels of foreign investment, and relatively stable exchange rates. The Chinese yuan continued to devalue, and, in the absence of vigorous economic growth and a strong, sustained upward trend in exports, the country's debt service ratio remained stable.

Figure 1.1B. Balance of payments on current accounts in China,
Thailand, and Malaysia, 1981–90

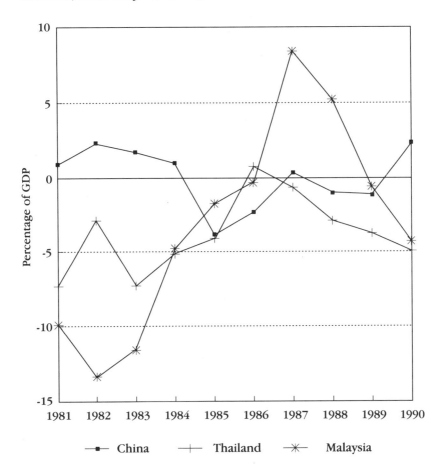

Source: ADB 1991.

By following tight monetary and fiscal policies, the Thai and Malaysian
authorities managed to reduce inflation in the early 1980s. With economic growth increasing after 1984, however, the cost of living began
to rise more rapidly. Nevertheless, as figure 1.2A shows, this increase
was much less rapid than in China's case, albeit at levels (about 5 percent
toward the end of the decade) that were beginning to threaten the
continuing success of these countries' exports of manufactured goods.

The presence of a relatively large informal sector and underemploy-
ment in agriculture mean that unemployment figures in DCs are not a
reliable indicator of the state of the labor market (Manning and Fong

*Figure 1.1C. Debt service ratios of China, Thailand, and Malaysia,
1981–90*

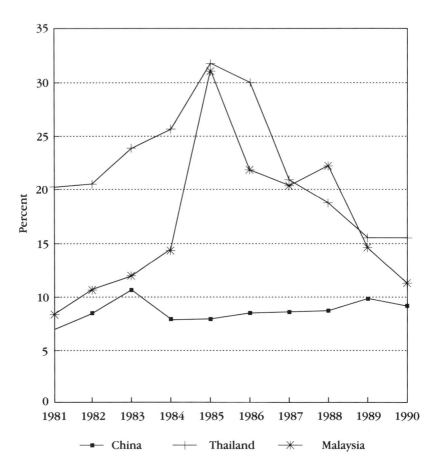

Source: ADB 1991.

1990:74). Nonetheless, the trends shown in figure 1.2B are noteworthy. They show a decline and a lower level of unemployment in China, largely because state enterprises tend to hire and retain more employees than are strictly necessary. Unemployment rose after 1985 in Thailand and Malaysia as these countries experienced downturns associated with the international recession and, as mentioned earlier, deterioration in their terms of trade. This was particularly serious in the case of Malaysia, whose economy, though changing, is more dependent on exports of primary commodities. Toward the end of the 1980s, demand picked up and growth resumed, thereby reducing unemployment, although there

Figure 1.2A. Rates of inflation in China, Thailand, and Malaysia, 1981–90

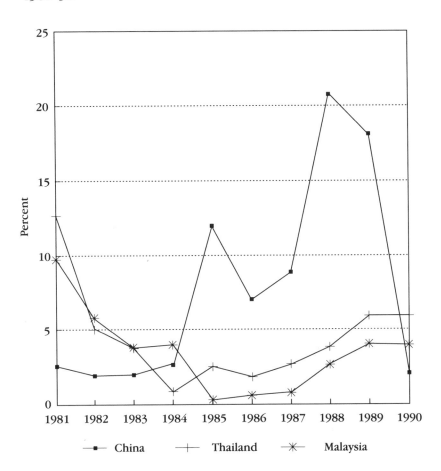

Source: International Monetary Fund 1989a, 1989b, 1991.

is substantial regional variation in both countries. In Thailand, skilled labor shortages are high, partly because the country has the lowest rate of secondary school enrollment in Southeast Asia (ADB 1991:117).

Following the period of liberalization in China in the 1980s, pressure began building for political change. The economy suffered in the short term as austerity measures were introduced. By 1990, however, economic reforms, including a reduction in the number of products allocated through central planning, more state-enterprise autonomy, and greater scope for collective enterprises (i.e., companies owned by employees, local governments, or groups of individuals) had reduced

Figure 1.2B. Unemployment rates in China, Thailand, and Malaysia,
1979–90

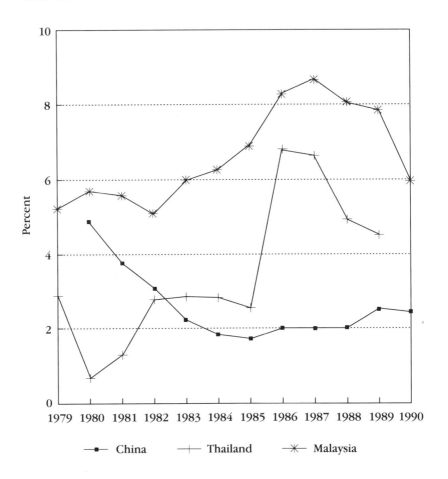

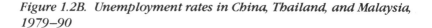

Source: ILO 1990, 1991; U.N. 1988.
Chinese data refer to urban areas only.

inflation to about 2 percent and boosted industrial production (*Econo-mist* 1991d:17–20). Despite the contradiction between economic liber-alization and single-party rule, further economic reforms along market lines continued the momentum that began in 1990.

In Thailand, the second half of the 1980s witnessed rapid economic growth based on a diverse range of exports, both in composition and destination (ADB 1990:111), although infrastructural bottlenecks in the form of inadequate harbors, roads, and telephone systems began to impede economic development and attract public criticism. Shortages of skilled personnel, especially in management and among subprofessionals and professionals, also became acute (ADB 1990:113). The government tried to ease these problems by privatizing public enterprises and, more recently, by increasing expenditures for infrastructure. These measures had not yielded much benefit by the end of the decade, however.

Economic growth in Malaysia in 1989 and 1990 was propelled more by domestic demand than by exports. This provided some protection to an economy particularly vulnerable to changes in international trade (ADB 1990:97). By 1990, manufacturing—assisted by a high savings ratio and large inflows of capital from the NICs and Japan—had overtaken agriculture as the most dynamic sector (ADB 1990:100). On the debit side, infrastructural problems in the form of inadequate electricity supply and telephone services as well as water shortages were limiting growth. In particular, skilled labor shortages represented a major problem (*FEER* 1991:164–65). More controversial was the failure of several banks and finance companies, leading to government legislation requiring much stricter control over licensed financial institutions and their managers (*FEER* 1990:174).

The Newly Industrialized Countries: Korea, Taiwan, Hong Kong, and Singapore

Annual average GDP growth on a per capita basis continued at a rapid rate in the NICs over the 1981–90 period with Korea averaging 8.0 percent a year; Taiwan, 6.3 percent; Hong Kong, 5.3 percent; and Singapore, 5.7 percent (ADB 1991:279; World Bank 1989). As figure 1.3A indicates, the growth paths of these countries showed similar fluctuations; thus, the massive decline in 1984–85 resulted mainly from a slowing of international trade. Growth resumed thereafter but at more modest levels; Hong Kong registered the slowest growth, reflecting weak export and domestic demand, a tight labor market, and rising wages (ADB 1991:61).

As figure 1.3B shows, the foreign trade position of the NICs improved steadily during most of the decade. Taiwan was exceptional in that it had a relatively large current account surplus relative to its GDP. This surplus declined sharply after 1986 following large-scale outward investment by Taiwanese entrepreneurs.

Korea's weak performance toward the end of the decade also merits comment. This resulted from a decline in export growth attributed mainly to large wage increases unmatched by high productivity growth and a substantial appreciation of the won in 1989. The weakness of the yen adversely affected Korean exports to Japan, while Korea, like Hong Kong, suffered from the slowdown in the U.S. economy (ADB 1991:69).

Consistent with Taiwan's strong foreign trade position, as figure 1.3C

Figure 1.3A. Economic growth per capita in Korea, Hong Kong, Taiwan, and Singapore, 1981–90

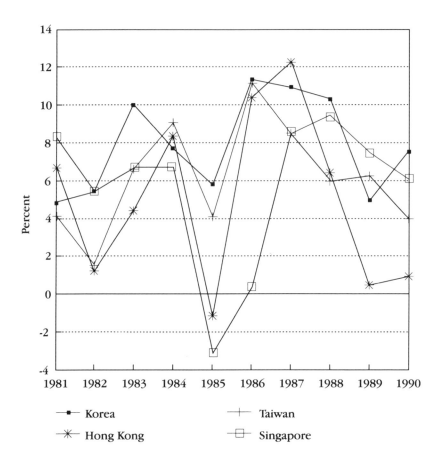

Source: World Bank 1989; ADB 1991.

indicates, Taiwan's debt service ratio was minimal in the second half of the decade (no data are available for earlier years). Korea's debt service ratio rose significantly in 1984, reflecting a high level of external borrowing, but declined dramatically in 1987 following three years of balance-of-payment surpluses, which helped pay off the debt. This contrasts with Singapore, which has tended to rely on direct foreign investment rather than loans for economic expansion; hence, the latter's debt service ratio was low and stable over the period. No information is published for Hong Kong and therefore relevant data are missing from figure 1.3C.

Inflation rates declined steeply in all four NICs until the mid-1980s,

Figure 1.3B. Balance of payments on current accounts in Korea, Hong Kong, Taiwan, and Singapore, 1981–90

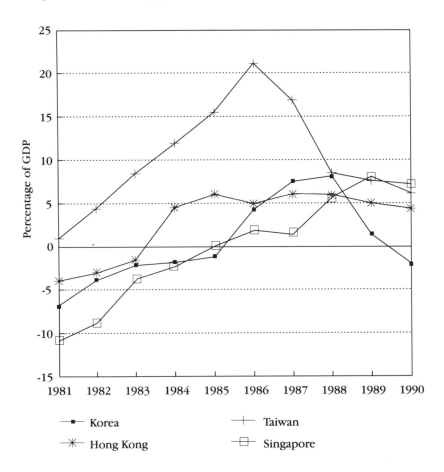

Source: ADB 1991.

when price changes began to accelerate, as shown in figure 1.4A. The lower inflation rates largely reflect the slower growth of the world economy and hence the less intense demand for exports from the NICs. In the mid-1980s, when demand increased, labor shortages and consequent wage increases contributed to higher inflation in Hong Kong. In Singapore, the government's high-wage strategy—which was intended to encourage firms to pursue high value-added production using advanced technology—had the unintended effect of exacerbating the recession (*Economist* 1988:172–78). In Korea and Taiwan, workers insisted on sharing the fruits of growth, resulting in a wave of strikes around 1986–

Figure 1.3C. Debt service ratios of Korea, Taiwan, and Singapore, 1981–90

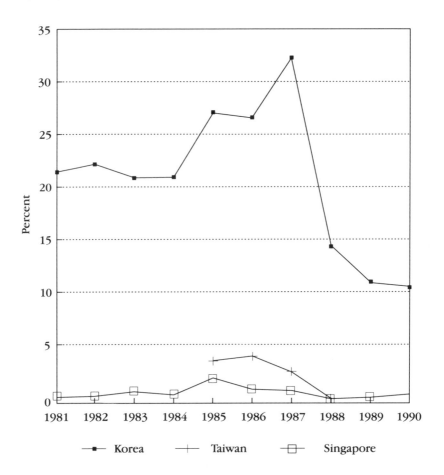

Source: ADB 1990, 1991.

87. Large wage increases thus contributed to rising inflation, which was stabilized in Taiwan by 1990 but continued in Korea, reflecting the highly adversarial labor relations that were typical of that country in 1988 and 1989.

Figure 1.4B suggests that strong growth in the second half of the 1980s reduced unemployment. This is less true of Hong Kong and Singapore. In the former case, as we have seen, economic growth declined substantially toward the end of the decade. Labor shortages were increasingly attributable to lower employment participation rates as younger people pursued education as a hedge against the uncertainty

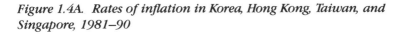

Figure 1.4A.   Rates of inflation in Korea, Hong Kong, Taiwan, and Singapore, 1981–90

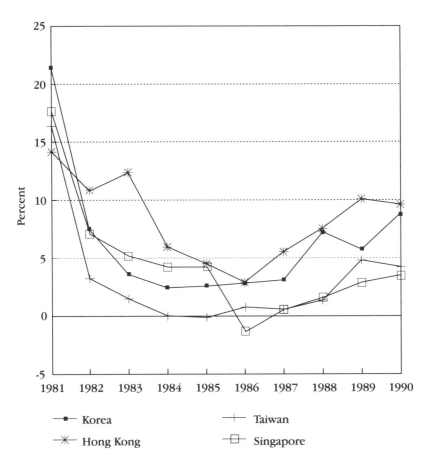

Source: International Monetary Fund 1989a, 1989b; ADB 1991.

associated with the return of Hong Kong to China in 1997. Higher rates of emigration, particularly of skilled employees, also contributed to the problem.

In the case of Singapore, unemployment more than doubled between 1984 and 1986, mainly because of the government's high-wage strategy. Following the introduction of new policies, however, including a flexible wage policy, Singapore's growth resumed. This was based on an exceptionally high rate of domestic saving—nearly 42 percent of GDP in 1989—substantial foreign investment, particularly in electronics and petrochemicals, and strong growth in services, especially tourism and

Figure 1.4B. Unemployment rates in Korea, Taiwan, Hong Kong, and Singapore, 1979–90

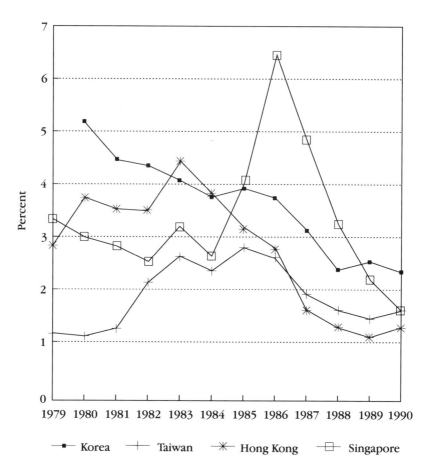

—■— Korea   —+— Taiwan   —*— Hong Kong   —⊟— Singapore

Source: ILO 1990, 1991.
Data for Singapore, Korea, and Hong Kong are for persons fifteen years and older. Data for Singapore before 1986 include family workers who worked fewer than fifteen hours per week.

shipping (ADB 1990:71). Indeed, Singapore was poised to overtake Hong Kong in container and freight handling by the end of the 1980s (*FEER* 1990:216). By 1990, the Singapore labor market was tight, giving the government cause for alarm as professionals and other skilled people continued to emigrate and controls over the employment of foreign workers were strengthened and then only partially relaxed (ADB 1991:74). The labor force is expected to grow by only 0.5 to 0.7 percent a year in the 1990s (*Economist* 1991a:27).

For most of the 1980s, Korea succeeded in maintaining rapid economic growth based on the strong export performance of the Chaebols (large enterprise groups). In 1984, two-thirds of the country's gross national product (GNP) was accounted for by sales of the ten largest Chaebols (Amsden 1989:116), and ten Chaebols accounted for more than half of Korea's exports. Toward the end of the decade, the Chaebols experienced difficulties in competing internationally because of their relatively low research and development expenditures and limited government support (*FEER* 1991:148). The highly indebted and diversified Chaebols were in fact vulnerable to failure. Despite a resumption of a high rate of growth in 1990, the stock market recorded the worst performance in nearly a decade before recovering slightly toward the end of the year (*FEER* 1991:147). Meanwhile, the movement of money into land speculation and the absence of a publicly acceptable welfare policy made for further serious political problems that the government was attempting to rectify (*FEER* 1990:158, 1991:147).

In Taiwan, export growth has been limited by the appreciation of the New Taiwanese dollar, rapidly rising wages, and other costs. Domestic demand, however, has increased sufficiently to sustain economic growth. Savings have consistently exceeded investment, resulting in a savings ratio of more than 30 percent. With Singapore and Korea, Taiwan has among the highest savings rates in the world.

Because Taiwan has not needed to borrow capital, the country's annual balance-of-payments surpluses have been very large: by 1991, Taiwan's foreign currency reserves were the largest in the world. Accordingly, there has been strong pressure on the Taiwanese government to revalue the currency further. This pressure eased toward the end of the decade when there were large-scale outflows of capital to China, Thailand, Malaysia, and the Philippines. Problems remained, however; excess liquidity led to property speculation, pushing up house prices beyond most people's reach, while sharp rises in stock exchange prices attracted many people who later suffered when the market crashed in September 1988 and again in 1990 (*FEER* 1989:236; ADB 1991:79). There was also disquiet over increasing inequalities during the 1980s and public concern about growing pollution and traffic problems, which have become important political issues.

Meanwhile, the labor market had been tight, although it eased slightly in 1990 as (mainly illegal) foreign workers entered the labor force and manufacturing firms moved to China and Southeast Asia in search of lower costs. That year, for the first time in more than a decade, the number of registered factories in Taiwan declined (*FEER* 1991:225). Like Korea, Taiwan faces the challenge in the 1990s of transition from a labor-intensive, low-skilled, export-oriented economy associated with a relatively rigid political structure to a technologically advanced, high-skilled economy based on growing domestic demand and a more democratic political system.

Hong Kong's rapid growth in the first half of the 1980s occurred in part because of China's expanding economy. By 1988, reexports from China exceeded domestic exports to China for the first time in thirty years. These reexports represented 60 percent of all of China's exports (*FEER* 1990:128). According to S. Haggard (1990:154), most of Hong Kong's labor-intensive manufacturing was being undertaken in China's Guandong province and the more capital-intensive operations completed in the colony.

After 1984, Hong Kong's economy was adversely affected by the slowdown in the Chinese economy, the weak U.S. economy, and uncertainty about Hong Kong's future, especially in the aftermath of the Tiananmen Square massacre. By the late 1980s, Hong Kong's economic activity had become part of what R. Wong (1990:xxi) refers to as "the end-game syndrome."

The Advanced Peripheral Countries: Australia and New Zealand

Troubled by low growth rates, weak international competitiveness, and rising indebtedness, the economies of Australia and New Zealand contrast with those of the NICs. Figures 1.5A, 1.5B, and 1.5C illustrate these points.

The start of the 1980s was marked by deep recession in both Australia and New Zealand. This was counteracted by government policies leading to a sharp upturn and followed by steadier growth in Australia and a more erratic experience in New Zealand. Averaged over the 1981–89 period, per capita growth rates were low: 2.2 percent and 0.9 percent for Australia and New Zealand respectively (OECD 1989a:93–94). Data for 1990 were not readily available; however, GDP growth in Australia declined from 4.4 percent in 1989 to 1.7 percent in 1990. The corresponding figures for New Zealand are −0.7 percent and 0.5 percent (OECD 1992a:175). Thus, low growth persisted. This reflected the lack of competitiveness of these two economies, which depend very heavily on exports of primary commodities and imports of manufactured goods.

Figure 1.5B shows that both countries had current account deficits throughout the 1980s, although Australia's was less severe before 1987. Both countries also suffered from the steep fall in the terms of trade that occurred in 1984. Australia devalued its currency by about 40 percent in the following two years, while the newly elected New Zealand Labour government devalued its currency by 20 percent immediately after the July 1984 election and subsequently made further reductions.

As figure 1.5C indicates, these two countries have found it difficult to stabilize their growing debt service ratio, largely because demand for

*Figure 1.5A. Economic growth per capita in Australia and New
Zealand, 1981–89*

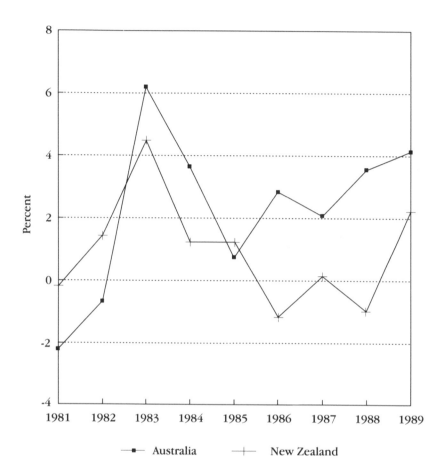

Source: OECD 1989b.

their exports is growing less rapidly than for elaborately transformed
goods. This is related to increasing protectionism, particularly of agricultural products, by the United States and the European Community. In
addition, the governments of both countries were unable to reduce
inflation and raise productivity growth to internationally competitive
levels despite relatively high levels of unemployment and tight monetary
policy toward the end of the 1980s. Details on inflation and unemployment are provided in figures 1.6A and 1.6B respectively.

Australia succeeded in moderating the rate of inflation from 1983 on,
partly as a result of a series of national-level agreements (Accords)

Figure 1.5B. Balance of payments on current accounts in Australia and New Zealand, 1981–90

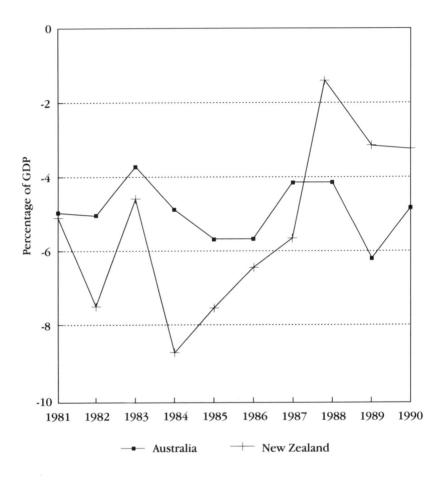

—■— Australia　　　—┼— New Zealand

Source: OECD 1989a, 1989b, 1989c, 1990, 1992a, 1992b.

between the Labor government (elected initially in 1983) and the union movement. Inflation fluctuated in New Zealand but declined when there was high unemployment. The Australian Accords covered employment and income growth, social welfare, and, more recently, microeconomic reform, including greater labor flexibility (Frenkel 1990:126–28; chap. 9). Structural adjustment has been of concern to the government, but with the exception of the deregulation of the financial system, the momentum for structural adjustment began to develop only toward the end of the 1980s. This interest culminated in a strategy document on the future of manufacturing (Pappas et al. 1990) followed by a policy for

Figure 1.5C. Debt service ratios of Australia and New Zealand, 1981–89

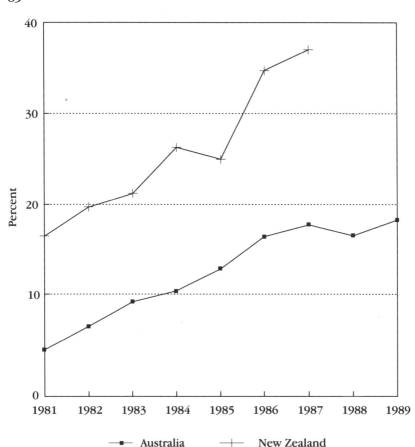

Source: New Zealand. Department of Statistics 1988; ABS, catalogue no. 5306.0.
Data for 1989 and 1990 not available.

effecting structural change (Hawke, Keating, and Button 1991). Meanwhile, companies were finding it increasingly difficult to repay loans borrowed in easier times. The collapse of several large corporations, including a state-government bank, heralded the beginning of very difficult times for Australia (*FEER* 1991:79).

The New Zealand Labour administration placed greater emphasis on structural adjustment, which had a detrimental effect on the level of employment (fig. 1.6B). Measures were taken to deregulate the economy (OECD 1989b:16) and to reduce import protection.[20] The most radical

Figure 1.6A. Rates of inflation in Australia and New Zealand, 1981–90

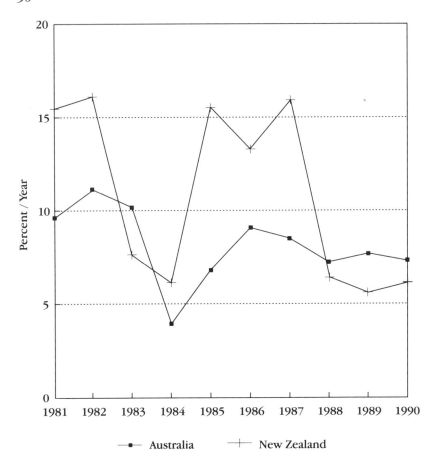

Source: OECD 1984–90; International Monetary Fund 1991.

measure was the reform of the government sector, involving a program of privatization and corporatization of government enterprises and departments respectively (Haworth 1990). New industrial relations legislation was introduced in 1987 with the aim of encouraging greater decentralization of decision making, union rationalization, and labor flexibility (chap. 10). In October 1990, the new National Party accelerated the reform program with further legislation to deregulate the labor market and reduce expenditure on social services. In the meantime, privatization was apparently improving the efficiency of certain service industries. New Zealand's ratio of exports to Australia compared with imports from Australia increased in the context of the free trade agree-

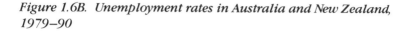

Figure 1.6B. Unemployment rates in Australia and New Zealand, 1979–90

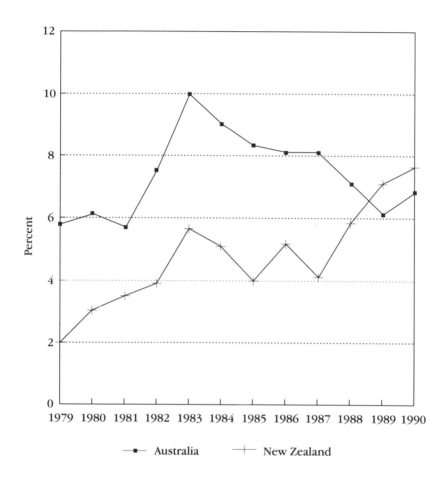

Source: OECD 1986–89; U.N. 1988; International Monetary Fund 1991.
Data for Australia refer to persons fifteen years and older.

ment, which now regulates trade between the two countries (*FEER* 1991:186). In sum, both economies were in a fragile state by the beginning of the 1990s. More changes were on the horizon. This meant a further weakening of the union movement, particularly in New Zealand.

Variations in State Structures and Development Strategies

The state has already been referred to as a major influence on trade unionism. With this in mind, a summary of the main features of the political context and the role of the state vis-à-vis unions in each of the nine countries is presented below. Figure 1.7 provides a guide.

China

China's political system is dominated by the Chinese Communist Party, which formally controls central and local administration and the military. Differences within the party leadership were evident in the 1980s, when the reformers were in a position of ascendancy. State planning and centralized controls over the economy were loosened, and freedom of individual expression and contact with the outside world were expanded (Garnaut 1989:131). Demonstrations in favor of further liberalization in 1986 and subsequently in 1989 raised fears among the party leadership of loss of control. The party's legitimacy came under threat as the economy overheated, resulting in high inflation and accusations of corruption among high-level party officials (*FEER* 1989:102). Matters came to a head in June 1989 when the military brutally reasserted the party's supremacy against pro-democracy demonstrators in Tiananmen Square. This was followed by a return to a more orthodox form of communism based on control by a conservative-dominated central committee (*FEER* 106–11). Economic reform continued at a slower pace but accelerated in the early 1990s.

Political stability in China is underpinned by coercion rather than social consensus; hence the categorization "medium" in figure 1.7 to denote its potential instability (see Redding 1990:235). State economic strategy in the early 1980s was experimental, an attempt to introduce greater autonomy and market principles into some economic sectors but within the context of public ownership of economic assets and a political system dominated by the Communist Party. The 1980s saw more emphasis placed on the production of consumer goods and services and exports to ease the shortage of foreign exchange. Toward the end of the decade, the government became preoccupied with combating inflation (see figure 1.2A) and restoring fiscal balance, eradicating corruption, and encouraging a revival of "socialist values" (*FEER* 1990:106–16).

Thailand

Thailand has traditionally been ruled by the military in conjunction with senior bureaucrats, although an elected government prevailed for most of the 1980s. The prime minister continued to be nominated by the military, however, which took power in February 1991 in a bloodless coup—the seventeenth since the inception of constitutional monarchy in 1932—so ending the six-party coalition government of former General Chatichai Choonhaven.

There appears to be an underlying stability to the political system based on the social and ideological coherence of the administrative elite (Mackie 1988), on whom a network of large-scale business leaders depend. There is nevertheless considerable competition within and between elites, which justifies our description of Thailand's power structure as being centralized yet dispersed. Since changes in government increase uncertainty in the economy, Thailand is appropriately categorized over the 1980–90 period as a country with medium political stability.

From the late 1970s through the 1980s, the state emphasized export-oriented industrialization, although this did not totally eclipse its earlier strategy of import substitution. K. J. Hewison (1989a:120–21) has noted that this reflected the World Bank's preferred strategy, which helped the Thai government become the fifth largest recipient of World Bank loans. Previous governments had created large state enterprises, but the 1987–91 development plan emphasized a shift of resources to the private sector, the elimination of fiscal imbalances, and a more equitable sharing of the fruits of economic growth (*Economist* 1988:284). The 1980s witnessed the ascendancy of large corporate groups, especially in the banking sector, where in 1983 the assets of sixteen domestic commercial banks amounted to nearly two-thirds of estimated GNP (Hewison 1989a:121). Despite rapid growth toward the end of the 1980s, deals between large companies and the government, coupled with failure to meet popular economic expectations, led to popular dissatisfaction with the Chatichai administration (*FEER* 1990:234–35) and to its eventual overthrow by the military.

Malaysia

Malaysia's political system combines traditional dynastic elements based on land ownership with parliamentary democracy. Power is shared between the central government and eleven state administrations. Nine royal state rulers elect a king every five years, and he in turn appoints a council of ministers from members of the federal Parliament.

The ruling party, the United Malays National Organization (UMNO), has been the dominant force in politics since independence in 1957. It continues as a bastion of Malay aristocratic power, which has extended into the civil service (Lubeck 1992:188). The UMNO leads a coalition of thirteen parties. In 1988, the party split, leaving one of the remaining groups as the major force within the coalition. There have also been splits within the opposition parties, leading to a complex and fluid political situation (*Economist* 1988:99).

Government development strategy switched in the late 1970s to EOI (Sharma 1985:29–30), including reduced dependence on exports of primary commodities.[21] There has been considerable enthusiasm for "looking east," which essentially means learning from Japan (Wad

Figure 1.7. Political structures and development strategies of nine Asia-Pacific countries, 1979–90

Country	Power centralization, concentration	System of representation	Political stability	Development strategy
		Developing		
China	high, concentrated	single party; Communist	medium	temporary emphasis on state control after experiment with market principles
Thailand	medium/high, dispersed	multiparty; military-dominated	medium	export-led; pro-business
Malaysia	medium, dispersed	federal; multiparty; single party predominant	high	strengthen economic position of Malays; export manufactured goods
		Newly industrialized		
Korea	medium, dispersed	transitional single- to multiparty; single party predominant	low	state-guided; mainly but not solely Chaebol-oriented; export and domestic focus
Taiwan	high, dispersed	transitional single- to multiparty; single party predominant	high, uncertain	upgrade export capacity of small firms; deregulate foreign trade
Hong Kong	high, concentrated	predominantly nonparty	high, uncertain	free trade with public commitment to provision of infrastructure
Singapore	high, concentrated	single party	high	state-led; high technology; export-oriented

Figure 1.7. (continued)

Country	Power centralization, concentration	System of representation	Political stability	Development strategy
Advanced peripheral				
Australia	becoming higher, dispersed	federal; mainly two party	high	changing from import substitution to higher value-added, export focus
New Zealand	medium, dispersed	unitary; mainly two party	high	changing from protected, regulated welfarism to a market economy

1988:218–20). The most distinctive element of Malaysia's strategy has been its emphasis on improving the economic position of the majority Malays—the Bumiputras—who comprise about 60 percent of the population (Lubeck 1992:180). There was little ethnic conflict in the 1980s, although wide disparities still existed between the mainly Chinese economic elite and the Malays and Indians. The Chinese nevertheless resent the educational and job-related advantages conferred on Malays as part of the government's Bumiputra policy.

Korea

Korea lurched toward democracy in the late 1980s. Following the assassination of President Park Chung Hee, Chun Doo-hwan seized power in 1979. Political protests followed, resulting in the Kwangju massacre in which two hundred people were killed and one thousand injured.

Chun became president in 1981 under conditions of martial law and with most of his political opponents in jail. Between 1981 and 1985, there was little opposition, but a gradual process of political relaxation culminated in the hastily constructed New Korea Democratic Party (NKDP) winning nearly one-third of the vote in the 1985 parliamentary elections. Demonstrations for direct presidential elections followed Chun's reversal of the government's political liberalization program and the nomination of Chun's military friend Roh Tae-woo as the ruling party's presidential candidate. Meanwhile, the NKDP split over the details of the demands for a democratic constitution. The majority group, led by Kim Young-sam and Kim Dae-jung, formed the Reunification Democratic Party (RDP). In June 1987, Roh gave way to public pressure, and in October he endorsed the opposition's major demand for a presidential referendum to approve a new constitution involving direct presidential elections. These were held in December 1987, the first in sixteen years. Neither of the two Kims would support the other. This led to a party split in which Roh won the election with not much more than a third of the popular vote (*Economist* 1988:212).

Roh was able to strengthen his position by permitting senior people associated with the previous regime to be fined and imprisoned on the grounds that they had been involved in crimes and corruption. Other supportive factors included publicity given to dissidents making unauthorized contact with North Korea (*FEER* 1990:156), disunity among the opposition parties, and growing concern over a flagging economy. There was, however, widespread discontent over alleged corruption, high inflation, growing inequalities, and the hard line being taken against trade unions. In 1990, in a surprise move, Roh announced a merger between the Democratic Justice Party and two major opposition parties, Kim Young-sam's RDP and the New Democratic Republican Party. Hence, the Democratic Liberal Party emerged, modeled along the lines of the ruling Japanese Liberal Democratic Party.

Development policy changed initially in the late 1970s toward heavy industry and later in the mid-1980s to small and medium-sized firms producing intermediate products. This was part of "a market-conforming policy in which the state attempted to resume reliance on market mechanisms by readjustment and deregulation" (Song 1992:7). The satisfaction of domestic demand to reduce the country's dependence on international markets was favored, but a less resilient balance of trade at the end of the decade resulted in a renewed emphasis on exports. Although the Roh government continued with its anti-union policies, it introduced several labor reforms, including a national pension scheme and an extension of public medical insurance. There have also been moves to tax capital gains on land sales to discourage escalation of house prices, which remains a major social issue (*Economist* 1990c:18).

Taiwan

Taiwan, like Korea, has been living in the shadow of a hostile neighbor. This is one factor contributing to its authoritarian, developmental state, characterized by a strong executive and high military spending. Considerable material support from the United States has helped insulate the state in both countries from local pressures (Wade 1990, chap. 10). Unlike Korea, Taiwan has been ruled continuously since 1948 by a single, all-embracing party, the Kuomintang (KMT), whose leader, Chiang Kai-shek, and key supporters fled the mainland, leaving it to the Communists.

The 1980s witnessed an easing of tension with China, which encouraged the democratization process in Taiwan. Martial law prevailed until

1987, which signaled a definite break with the past. Meanwhile, the year before, Chiang Ching-kuo—Chiang Kai-shek's son and the leader of the KMT until his death in early 1988—had begun to liberalize Taiwanese politics by restructuring the party in favor of more Taiwanese-born officials.[22] In addition, the newly formed Democratic Progressive Party (DPP) was permitted to contest the national assembly elections and won a quarter of the votes (*Economist* 1988:247). Nevertheless, the main legislative body, the Legislative Yuan, was still dominated by elderly mainlanders who had not been subject to reelection since the KMT moved its headquarters from the mainland more than forty years earlier. In 1988, 70 percent of the 360-member Legislative Yuan were more than seventy years old (*Economist* 1988:247). This had been a major bone of contention but was in the process of being resolved during the 1980s through the establishment of an early retirement scheme for parliamentarians and natural attrition (*FEER* 1990:227).[23]

The lifting of martial law in 1987 acted as a catalyst for public protest against various issues, including the destruction of the environment and the need for improved housing and better wages and working conditions. The democratization process gained momentum and has been less violent than in Korea. The political opposition has fragmented so that some former DPP supporters have formed a labor party and a socialist workers' party (*FEER* 1990:229). This has been facilitated by legislation that now permits the establishment of new political parties and greater freedom of expression.

The government has moved away from promoting energy-intensive industries such as steel and petrochemicals to encouraging light industries based on advanced technology. Since 1983, the economy has been liberalized and internationalized. There have been reductions in tariffs on many items, an easing of restrictions on capital flows, and partial deregulation of the banking industry, including plans to privatize three large banks (*FEER* 1990:232). The lifting of restrictions on personal travel has encouraged foreign trade. The government also established a Council of Labor Affairs to solve industrial relations and labor supply problems (ADB 1990:81). Efforts at improving transport and housing have been slow, however, and subject to considerable public criticism.

Hong Kong

Hong Kong's political system is a form of corporate state in which the government is run by an expatriate administrative elite in close consultation with big banks and trading companies (Wade 1990:331). The future of the system has been under intense debate as 1997—the date for handing back the colony to China—gets closer.

In the 1980s, Hong Kong was ruled by a governor in consultation with two councils, one of which was slightly democratized in 1991.[24] The

Executive Council comprised sixteen appointed members, of whom six were senior government officials and the rest leading private citizens from the professions and commerce. The Legislative Council included more than fifty members, of whom ten were heads of government departments and the rest were private citizens. Approximately half of these were appointed by the governor; the other half were elected indirectly through local governments and nine functional constituencies, of which labor was one. A system of advisory committees continues to operate, so, although political power is centralized in the British government, it is to some extent subject to the checks and balances of various influential individuals who represent powerful local interests.

The colony has enjoyed stability for many years, in large part because the government has concentrated on providing a legal and administrative framework for a growing free-enterprise economy while ensuring an adequate public infrastructure. In more recent years, when investors have tended to export capital from Hong Kong, public-sector investment has been increased to maintain confidence (*FEER* 1990:129).

Singapore

Singapore gained limited independence from Britain in 1957 and full sovereignty after its separation from Malaysia in 1965. Until his retirement in September 1990, Prime Minister Lee Kuan Yew shaped and controlled the city-state's political system. In 1989, his People's Action Party (PAP) held all but one seat in Parliament (*FEER* 1990:195).[25] Lee Kuan Yew discouraged opposition, as highlighted by the arrest of twenty-two people in 1987 for alleged involvement in a Marxist plot to overthrow the government. Failure to sustain charges subsequently led to all but two of the accused being released (*FEER* 1990:214).

Unions have been strictly controlled in Singapore through a process of incorporation: senior union leaders are members of the PAP and are chosen by the party (see chap. 6). Government policies also impinge on citizens' private lives. Examples include attempts to increase the birth rate among the higher socioeconomic classes (*Economist* 1988:189) and to harness Confucianism as a means of stemming the rising tide of professionals who have been emigrating to more liberal advanced countries (Bello and Rosenfeld 1990, chap. 20; *FEER* 1990:213–14).

In 1979, the government introduced a new development policy known as the Second Industrial Revolution aimed at propelling Singapore into a more technologically advanced niche in the world economy and thereby distinguishing it from its low-cost competitors. Indeed, the central element of the strategy was to raise wage costs to discourage low-wage, labor-intensive industries. As noted earlier, this did not work as intended, so that in 1981 the government reverted to a policy of wage moderation with selective emphasis and public investment in particular high value-added manufacturing and some service industries. This policy was designed to encourage foreign direct investment, on which the strategy depended. In addition, the creation of a more highly skilled work force through improved education and training was given priority (Rodan 1989, chap. 5).

Economic growth in subsequent years did not match official expectations, so the development policy was revised following the severe economic downturn in 1985. Now "services were earmarked as the most important growth sector of the economy, with a far greater emphasis on regional economic integration" (Rodan 1989:189). This did not mean abandoning manufacturing but rather extending Singapore's attraction to multinational capital as a regional production platform for the export of both goods and services (Rodan 1989:190–91).

Australia and New Zealand

Australia and New Zealand have common British roots, manifested in their similar political characteristics. These include a modified Westminster model of government involving a largely two-party system and a heritage of state intervention in the economy. Following the emergence of strong union movements in the late nineteenth century, after the attainment of universal suffrage, massive strikes led to the creation of statutory conciliation and arbitration systems. Both countries subsequently developed powerful labor parties that introduced state welfare provisions. Exports of primary commodities and protective tariffs for local manufacturing ensured relatively high living standards until the 1970s, but a long-term decline in the terms of trade have encouraged the governments of both countries to diversify their exports. This has meant rationalizing the manufacturing and service sectors with the aim of becoming internationally competitive.

The two countries are dissimilar in several important respects. Australia is a large and diverse country based on a federal system of government that limits the powers of the federal government, not least in the sphere of industrial relations (Deery and Plowman 1991; Dufty and Fells 1989). By contrast, New Zealand is a small country—less than 4 percent of Australia's area—and has a unitary system of government. The Labour Party's programs in New Zealand appear to have had more lasting influence than in Australia (Deeks and Boxall 1989, chap. 2; Connell and Irving 1980; Castles 1985). For most of the 1980s—since 1983 and 1984 in Australia and New Zealand respectively—the labor parties have been the dominant political force, but, as we shall see, their policies diverged markedly.

In Australia, the Labor Party attempted to reverse the divisive policies of the previous conservative administration by working with the unions to reduce unemployment and inflation while gradually reorienting the economy toward the international market, as signified by reductions in trade protection.[26] Following a substantial deterioration in the foreign trade balance in 1984–85, the government began emphasizing productivity improvement as a major goal. This was reflected in qualified tripartite support for a more decentralized approach to wage determination and microeconomic reform.

Such reforms included providing assistance to several industries, including steel, heavy engineering, and motor vehicles, to rationalize their structures in order to raise productivity and improve competitiveness. There was also progress toward improving work practices and productivity in the ports and in the shipping industry, and toward the end of the 1980s plans were implemented to deregulate telecommunications and the airlines. The government also introduced private-sector management practices into the federal public sector, but the unions and the Labor Party successfully opposed privatization. Against employer opposition, the government did succeed in introducing a training levy that began raising the level of occupational training, which was low by international standards (Australia. Economic Planning Advisory Council 1986).

New Zealand faced a growing external trade crisis: overseas debt (which arose mainly from public-sector borrowing) had risen from 20 percent of GDP in 1980 to 60 percent by 1984 (OECD 1989a:16). This called for radical reform. The incoming Labour Party government responded by embarking on a massive deregulation program, which included the following measures: the abolition of wage and price controls; the new labor relations legislation mentioned earlier; reduction of local industry protection, including a reduction of effective rates of assistance to industry from 37 percent in 1985–86 to 26 percent in 1987–88; deregulation of several major industries, including banking and telecommunications; and a variety of practices designed to model the public sector on private-sector lines (OECD 1989a:16). In sum, the program was most uncharacteristic of a labor government and more akin to the policies pursued by successive Thatcher governments in the United Kingdom.

Summary

In conclusion, most of the nine countries that comprise this study have benefited from the relative openness of the regional and world economy. As noted above, however, growth has not been smooth. In China, the economy was moving ahead fast in the early 1980s, while the reverse was true of Thailand. By the end of the decade, other countries—China, Korea, and New Zealand—were facing difficult economic problems. Thus, in attempting to assess changes in unionism, it is important to acknowledge not only differences between the countries over the 1980s but also variations within countries. Furthermore, despite similarities between some countries and a trend toward regional economic integration, variations in the structure and role of the state remain substantial. We therefore contend that economic and political differences are likely to prove useful in understanding unionism in each country and to contribute to an explanation of the broad variations in union patterns within the region.

Outline of the Volume

The chapters that follow are divided into four parts. The first comprises chapters 2 through 4, which examine trade unionism in the developing countries of China, Thailand, and Malaysia respectively. The pattern in China is shown to be markedly different from that prevailing in the other two countries. A common denominator in the three countries is union weakness.

The second part comprises chapters 5 through 8, which focus on the NICs, beginning with Korea and followed by Taiwan, Hong Kong, and Singapore. Unionism in Taiwan and Korea has similar characteristics, the most evident being that each has both official unions and unofficial militant organizations. Hong Kong's unions are quite different and have little in common with their Singaporean counterparts. Indeed, as I shall argue in the final chapter, the former are more like unions in the advanced peripheral countries while the latter more resemble unions in China.

The third part of the volume includes two chapters that examine unionism in Australia (chap. 9) and New Zealand (chap. 10). The union movements in these advanced peripheral countries are less constrained by the state than they are in Hong Kong, but unlike the latter, they have been under severe pressure to restructure and alter their priorities. As we shall see, this has taken the Australian and New Zealand unions in different directions.

The final part, comprising chapter 11, summarizes, orders, and discusses union patterns in the nine countries according to a common conceptual framework. Japanese unionism forms an integral part of this analysis, which seeks to evaluate the hypotheses touched on earlier and to anticipate the nature of trade unionism in the immediate future. The chapter ends with some thoughts about a future research agenda.

Part I.
Developing Countries

2

Chinese Trade Unions: Structure and Function in a Decade of Economic Reform, 1979–89

Malcolm Warner

his chapter focuses first on the historical dimension of Chinese trade unions. It then examines organizational changes over the last few decades and, among other themes, prospective developments. The way in which unions in the People's Republic of China (PRC) fit into existing typologies of unions, in both Western and Communist societies, is also discussed, as well as their effectiveness in representing workers' interests.

The Leninist conception of trade unions in Communist societies, which emphasized their role as "transmission-belts," has long been an intrinsic element of "democratic centralism" (see Poole 1986:92). Accordingly, the Soviet model, in ideal-typical terms, with its high levels of formal unionization, industrial unions, apex-governing structure, and dutiful implementation of party policy, greatly influenced the emergence of Chinese trade union structure after 1949 (Wilson 1987:221). Chinese trade unions soon became part and parcel of the Soviet system of planning introduced by Mao and his colleagues during the First Five-Year Plan (1953–57), but this was modified because China was a "labor-surplus" economy (Littler and Palmer 1987:268).

Trade union structure is, more often than not, a product of its history. Chinese unions are no exception; indeed, we must note their beginnings,

I am most grateful to Stephen Frenkel, Craig Littler, Martin Lockett, and Peter Nolan for their help in providing critical comments and useful supplementary data for this chapter.

especially the formative years before the "Liberation" in 1949 played a dominating role in shaping the present state of Chinese union organization. As a recent study points out:

> The current function and importance of Chinese trade unions can only be understood in the context and development of the Chinese labor movement. Trade unions evolved in the midst of the immense social upheavals which shaped modern China. The unions' present status, self-image and power reflect their role in these revolutions, regressions and reversals. Their historical development will continue to influence their future role in the changes still sweeping China (W. Leung 1988:7).

The organized labor movement came into being before the establishment of the Chinese Communist Party (CCP) in 1921, but unions had been active even before the turn of the century (see Chesneaux 1968; Chan 1981; Chen 1985). In that industrialization had been confined to the coastal areas and especially to such large cities as Canton (now Guangzhou), Hong Kong, Shanghai, and Tientsin (now Tianjin), it is not surprising that labor disputes flared up in these locations. Indeed, the workers' organizations originated there.

The formal national union structure in China has a long history, going back to the early 1920s (see Littler and Lockett 1983). The All-China Federation of Trade Unions (ACFTU) was set up in 1925 in Canton. The dominance of the Communist Party was established from the onset, with rule from above, although the union collaborated with the "yellow" unions of the Kuomintang (KMT) and with the "gray" unions of the politically unaligned workers (W. Leung 1988:10).

The right within the KMT came to power in 1927, when Chiang Kai-shek organized a coup against the Communists. As many as thirteen thousand activists were executed in the struggle for political ascendancy, and more than twenty-five thousand died in combat (Guillermaz 1972:226); labor unions were savagely treated, particularly where they could not be taken over by the KMT (Wilson 1987:221). The struggle for power resulted in the disappearance of leftist unions. As a result of this conflict, the KMT prevented the ACFTU from establishing trade unions throughout China, since the CCP could not organize all industries on a national level (Lee 1986:14). Some occupational groups could be recruited, however, and seamen, mechanics, railway workers, print workers, and miscellaneous unskilled operatives began to take over the leadership of the unions (Chesneaux 1968:400–402). By and large, the ACFTU worked mostly in agrarian areas between 1927 and 1949. Unions were set up hurriedly and often existed only on paper. The "industrial" logic was never fully pursued, and the number of experienced union cadres was very thinly distributed across the country (Wilson 1987:219).

Before 1949, therefore, the unions had a skimpy industrial spread and a limited proletarian base. This "weakened their ability to make demands on the party" (Lee 1986:30). After the Liberation, the party did not have to construct a union wing out of thin air; there was already a legacy of subordination. A new organizational basis was established by the constitution of the Sixth Labor Congress in 1948 and the Trade Union Law of 1950. From these documents, the principle of democratic centralism was consolidated. The industrial-sector basis of unionism became preeminent and, in association with geographically established trade union councils, formed a "dual system" of authority (Littler and Lockett 1983).

The historical legacy of the pre-1949 period and the difficulties of organizing nationally thus led the CCP to use the ACFTU, above all other considerations, as essentially a transmission-belt between party and "masses." The problems faced by the ACFTU in building grass-roots support in the cities probably prevented it from gaining a strong autonomous role vis-à-vis the party.

The ACFTU undertook a national role from 1949 until 1966, when it went into abeyance during the Cultural Revolution. By 1979, a speedy restoration of its structure and function had taken place (Littler and Lockett 1983). Its evolution over the subsequent decade must now be examined against the background of industrial, managerial, and socioeconomic changes, especially those accompanying the reforms initiated under Deng Xiaoping (see Warner 1987b). The organizational history of these developments will be summarized in a later section on union structure.

Socioeconomic Background

In 1980, four out of five people in China were country folk (800 million in all), but by 1986, more than one in three (37.1 percent) had become more or less urbanized, according to the State Statistical Bureau (cited in Gittings 1989:4). Out of a total population of more than 1 billion, nearly 400 million lived in or near townships and cities, with food consumers growing at the expense of food producers. If the party ideology had once greatly reflected the peasant character of the revolution, it now had to balance this with increasing concern for the urban worker, of which the "vanguard" was concentrated in state-owned industrial enterprises (Zhang 1988:11).

The total population for year-end 1988 was 1,096,140,000 (15,410,000 over 1987); birth rates fell slightly that year, from 21.04 per thousand to 20.78. By comparison, the number of Chinese in 1978 had been 958,090,000 and the birth rate 18.2 per thousand, and in 1949 the population had been 541,670,000 and the birth rate 36 per thousand.

The first World Bank report on the PRC concluded that GNP per capita expanded at 2.0 to 2.5 percent a year between 1957 and 1977 (faster than the 2 percent growth of the population). This compares with the average economic growth rate of 1.6 percent in other developing countries (cited in Gittings 1989:105–6). Chinese official statistics need to be interpreted cautiously, however. This was achieved under a command economy, but one that exercised much less detailed control than its Soviet counterpart (*Economist* 1987:11).

Between 1953 and 1978, industrial output is said to have grown at an annual rate of 11.8 percent by value and to have risen to 12.8 percent per year from 1978 until recently. Between 1978 and 1988, industrial output officially leapt from 432 million yuan per year to 1,378 million yuan per year in value. Between 1979 and 1988, GNP also rose rapidly, at an official annual growth rate of 9.6 percent per year. Agriculture also greatly expanded but less rapidly than the industrial sector. By late 1989, however, the economy was entering a period of successive difficulties, partly due to. the "overheating" and partly due to the "uncertainty" generated by the Tiananmen Square massacre, both of which adversely affected prospects for foreign credit and trade (*Financial Times*, 8 Nov. 1989:6).

Inflation greatly increased during the period in which a socialist market economy was introduced, as seen in table 2.1. Whereas prices were more or less stable in 1978, by 1988 officials admitted that urban inflation was more than 18.5 percent and by 1989 more than 25.8 percent. In reality, it was probably much higher. By March 1989, eleven thousand worker price-supervision stations had been set up by the ACFTU in forty provinces in an attempt to hold down the cost of living (BBC 1989).

Urban unemployment rose over the decade from a couple of percent to much higher levels. By 1989, there were more than 10 million people officially unemployed and another 7.5 million entering the work force each year. Estimates were that 100 million workers would be displaced from the land, with some accounts envisaging a labor surplus of as many as 250 million. Official sources estimated that there were "at least 15

Table 2.1. Inflation in the People's Republic of China, 1978–87

	1978	1980	1985	1987
Staff and workers' cost-of-living index	188.5	172.2	140.5	120.7
Consumption goods	191.7	174.2	141.6	121.3
Services	156.9	155.7	129.2	113.8

Source: Statistical Outline of China 1989:89.
1978, 1980, 1985, and 1987 are base years when inflation index = 100.

million unneeded workers in China's state-owned enterprises" (BBC 1989). In the 1980s, for example, several directors stated during my empirical investigations in Chinese factories that no new apprentices were being hired (Warner 1986). Temporary laborers were being released, and older workers retired early as the drive for higher productivity put pressure on factory directors. Wage increases averaged 18.8 percent in 1989, but this represented a fall in real wages (*China Now,* Autumn 1989:4), although (if official Chinese statistics are to be believed) there was a rising trend in the 1980s, as shown in tables 2.2 and 2.3. Some caution should be exercised in employing these figures, however.

Reliable statistics concerning labor disputes in China are not available. Even so, miscellaneous sources suggest that in the late 1980s a wave of strikes affected the Chinese economy. Accounts of disputes in the Shenzen special economic zone are described by the Hong Kong–based Asia Labor Monitor Group (see W. Leung 1988). Out of four thousand foreign-funded enterprises, only one thousand were unionized (BBC 1989). Altogether, it was officially claimed that more than eight thousand joint venture businesses in China had been set up over the decade, constituting 2.7 percent of total industrial output by 1988 (*Beijing Review,* 2–8 Oct., 20). Managers in such enterprises were said to have stronger powers to hire and fire than in state-owned firms vis-à-vis the local unions (see W. Leung 1988). The pace of change was stretching the economic system to its limits (see tables 2.4–2.6). J. K. Fairbank summed up the situation:

Table 2.2. Output per worker in industrial enterprises in China, 1978–88

Year	Labor productivity index
1978	100.0
1979	106.4
1980	108.5
1981	106.6
1982	109.0
1983	117.2
1984	126.4
1985	135.5
1986	142.0
1987	151.7
1988	n.a.

Source: Statistical Outline of China 1989:48.
The data refer to publicly owned units with independent accounting and are based on 1980 prices.
n.a. = not available.

Table 2.3. Average real wages of staff and workers in publicly owned units in China, 1978–88

Year	Real-wage index
1978	100.0
1979	107.5
1980	113.8
1981	112.4
1982	113.5
1983	115.1
1984	133.9
1985	140.4
1986	153.0
1987	153.7
1988	152.6

Source: Statistical Outline of China 1989:95.

By the Spring of 1989 the reform program of the Four Modernizations under the aegis of Deng Xiaoping had been ten years underway. Problems were accumulating. Current trends if continued would risk disaster. Population growth was not being held in check. Enterprise in agriculture was bringing material prosperity in some areas but not in others. The reform of industry was stymied and getting mixed results . . . . Corruption spread like a cancer . . . . Finally, inflation was running at 30 percent or more a year with no reduction in sight (1989:32).

External Union Structure

The current structure of Chinese trade unions is much as it has been since 1949 (see Lee 1984; 1986). The types of unions, as we shall see, have remained roughly the same, although there has been an expansion of union membership as urbanization has drawn more workers into industry. Reform of the economy has led to rationalization of labor-management relations, as one account has described:

Deng has introduced his own concept of "democratic management" and abolished revolutionary committees at the enterprise level, on the grounds that they have fulfilled their "historic duties." . . . Certainly Deng has sought to rationalize the state planning system and the productive enterprise in order to achieve greater efficiency, while management is being evaluated according to economic as well as political criteria. The labor movement has also been restructured to harmonize with government ministries on industry lines, while regional federations of unions are linked with

Table 2.4. Population of the People's Republic of China, 1978–88

Year	Population (in millions)
1978	963
1979	975
1980	987
1981	1,001
1982	1,016
1983	1,028
1984	1,039
1985	1,050
1986	1,065
1987	1,081
1988	1,096

Source: Statistical Outline of China 1989:14.

the Party structure on a geographical basis (Lansbury, Ng, and McKern 1984:57).

The composition of union membership has resulted from a somewhat elastic definition of the term *worker* and perforce *workers' organizations.* Those who were involved in "mental" as well as "physical" labor were eligible, although the number of "permanent" workers was less than the total labor force. In addition, apprentices and trainees were not enrolled. As Article 1 of the ACFTU constitution (1988) states, "membership in trade unions is open to all manual and nonmanual workers in enterprises, undertakings and offices whose wages constitute their principal means of livelihood." Thus, the scope of the Chinese labor movement has been rather wide in its definition of workers. This characteristic has resulted from the fact that previously 80, or more, percent of the labor force worked on the land as peasants, only a minority in industrial employment and an even smaller group in large enterprises, so that the unions had to be "generous" in their categorization of who was eligible and who was excluded.

Trade unions in China have long been organized on vertical lines, in keeping with both Leninist notions and Soviet "industrial" principles of organization (see Brown 1966; Pravda and Ruble 1987). Craft and occupational structures provided a lesser counterpoint, stemming in part from the older guild tradition, which characterized master-apprentice relations up to well into this century (see Ma 1955; Chesneaux 1968). As Article 11 of the ACFTU constitution (1988) states:

> The trade unions of China apply the principle of combining leadership along industrial lines with that of a locality basis. Trade union members in the same enterprise are organized in a single primary trade union organization. National and local industrial trade unions

Table 2.5. Index values of industrial output in China, by broad sector,
1978–88

	Industrial output	Light industry	Heavy industry
1978	100.0	100.0	100.0
1979	108.8	109.9	108.0
1980	118.9	130.8	110.1
1981	124.3	149.4	105.0
1982	134.0	158.1	115.5
1983	149.0	172.9	130.6
1984	173.3	200.7	152.0
1985	210.3	246.2	182.7
1986	234.8	276.3	203.0
1987	276.4	327.8	236.9
1988	332.6	401.9	281.4

Source: Statistical Outline of China 1989:10.
Values are in real terms with price increases abstracted out.

shall be formed, as circumstances require, for a single branch of the
national economy or for two or more similar branches of the
national economy.

There were, for example, more than 100,000 primary trade unions in
1951–52. After several fluctuations, there was a fivefold increase by
1988, to more than 540,000. There had been only 2.4 million union
members in 1949, but this had grown to more than 100 million by 1988,
with 470,000 full-time worker representatives. This change represents a
union density (based on members as a percentage of the number of
workers and employees) of just over one in four in the early days to
about nine out of ten today (*Beijing Review*, 13–26 Feb. 1989, 27–31).
The discrepancy between the total number of ACFTU members and the
size of the work force, probably as much as 30 million persons, is the
result of government, research, and cultural personnel not being
counted, since there is no separate public employees' union (Zhang
1988:15). There are more than 320,000 full-time officials and 100,000
staff members in national trade unions.

There were a total of sixteen industrial unions in 1950–51; the
number rose to twenty-five in the late 1950s. The number soon fell to
sixteen and fell drastically after 1966. When unions were reestablished
again after 1978, the number rose to seventeen, and there were fifteen
in 1989. In addition, there are twenty-nine provincial trade union
councils. The ACFTU is an "apex" organization, which integrates the
constituent parts. The federation held its congress in 1988, the eleventh
since 1925.

The federation has eight departments: economy, technology and labor
protection, labor and wages, women workers, propaganda and education,

Table 2.6. Gross material product (GMP) and national income (NI) of China, 1978–88

Year	GMP[a]	NI
1978	100.0	100.0
1979	108.5	107.0
1980	117.6	113.9
1981	123.1	119.4
1982	134.8	129.2
1983	148.6	142.0
1984	170.3	161.4
1985	199.7	182.3
1986	222.0	197.3
1987	251.1	217.4
1988	289.6	242.3

Source: Statistical Outline of China 1989:8.
[a]In communist economies, GMP excludes nonmaterial production as normally defined in accounting procedures.

international liaison, organization, finance and accounts, and auditing. The fifteen national unions are organized respectively by trade in the following industries: railways, civil aviation, seafaring, road transport, post and telecommunications, engineering and metallurgy, petrochemicals, coal mining and geology, water and electricity, textiles, light industry, urban development and building materials, agriculture and forestry, finance and trade, and education.

The organizational rationale for the postrevolutionary Chinese unions was to set them up along industrial lines, but a geographical principle was introduced later when local union councils were given the power to run all local industrial unions except those already definitively under strong national industrial councils. Figure 2.1 provides a schematic summary. This move was spurred largely by the relatively small percentage of industrial workers in the PRC's labor force, political considerations, and a desire to emulate the Soviet model, rather than by any logic of union organization based on "trades" (see Lee 1984, 1986).

The organizational structure of the ACFTU leadership in 1988 consisted of 1 chairperson; 7 vice-chairpersons; 27 presidium members; 10 secretariat members (including 1 first secretary); 229 members of the Executive Committee; and 7 members of the Auditing Commission, 1 chairperson, 2 vice-chairpersons, and 4 standing members (ACFTU 1988:63–64).

The main factors shaping the external union structure have been largely political, as indeed they were vis-à-vis the internal structure. The reader is referred to the standard sources on the role of the party in the PRC to learn about these ebbs and flows in detail. J. Gittings's book

Figure 2.1. Reconstruction of the ACFTU in China after 1949

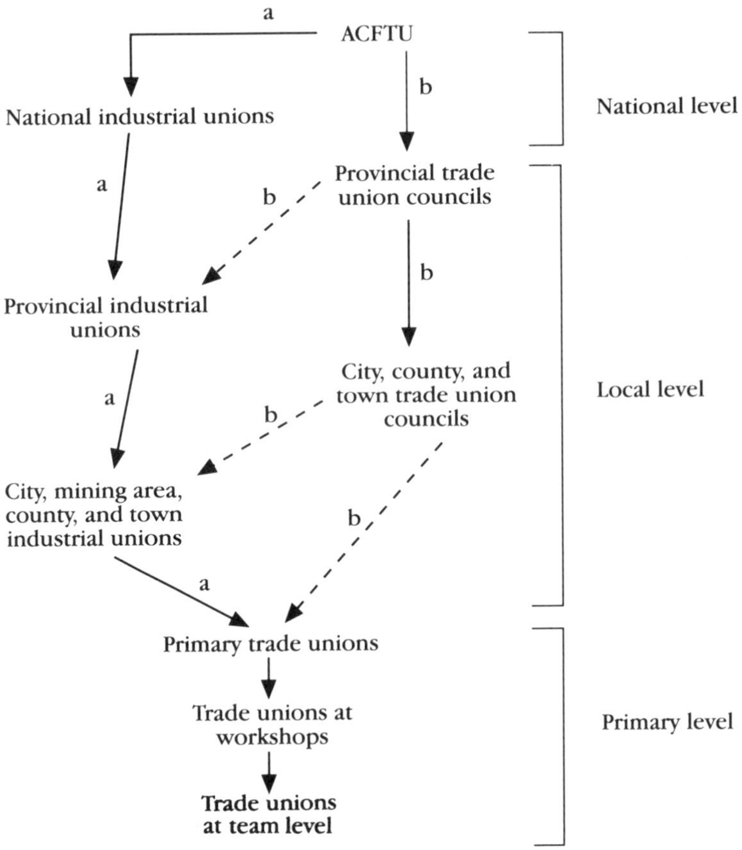

Source: Lee 1986:47.
Development proceeded along (a) industrial lines and (b) geographical principles.

(1989) summarizes the changing political currents in postrevolutionary China for the nonspecialist.

Officially, the role of the ACFTU is to "fight for workers' rights and interests" in society in general (Lee 1986:174). It plays, for example, a part in drafting new laws and regulations, at least on a consultative basis (see Wilson 1987:243). It also helps the government and the party draft legislation, as it did, for example, with the Enterprise Law of 1988, and interpret the application of such laws in the workplace. A new law to replace the older one of 1950 was promulgated in April 1992; it covers formal powers, structure, rights, and duties of trade unions. The ACFTU helped the Ministry of Labor revise this legislation. Similarly, it "advises" on social security provisions, compensation for accidents, and so on. In effect, however, its role vis-à-vis the government and party is mostly ancillary.

Internal Union Structure

The way the union leadership is chosen is broadly similar to the process in other unions modeled on Leninist lines (see Brown 1966; Pravda and Ruble 1987). The selection of union cadres and representatives takes place from the primary union level on up. From time to time, "mass participation" has been encouraged. A combination of "persuasion with coercion" (Lee 1986:44) characterizes the system. The party plays a primary role in this process.

The trade union–guided workers' congresses, of which there are said to be more than 360,000 (Zhang 1988:35; Gong 1989:3), now supplement the formal "representative function" of the unions. As T. Liu (1989) points out, enumerating its formal responsibilities in an officially sanctioned description, more is promised than may ultimately be fulfilled:

According to the provisions of the Law of the People's Republic of China on Industrial Enterprises Owned by the Whole People, the Workers' Congress is the basic form of democratic management in enterprises and the organ for workers to exert such powers. It has the right to deliberate such major issues as the policy of operations, annual and long-term plans and programs, contract and leasing responsibility systems of management; it may approve or reject plans on wage reforms and bonus distribution as well as on important rules and regulations; it may decide on major issues concerning workers' conditions and welfare; it may appraise and supervise the leading administrative cadres at various levels and put forward suggestions for awards and punishments and their appointment and approval; and it democratically elects the director (1989:5–6).

In terms of the union democracy debate, the term *oligarchic* might arguably be used to characterize the ACFTU, as opposed to *democratic* (see Edelstein and Warner 1979). The degree of electoral competition is, to say the least, limited, and alienation is now said to be widespread among many union members. A demand for direct elections of union officials has surfaced again (it had been a demand of the Democracy movement of 1979), and in one hundred enterprises sampled on-site, a third of the incumbent officials were said to have been voted out of office (Zhang 1988:23).

Factionalism has long been endemic in union politics in China. For the most part, this tendency has not resulted in membership opinion being more effectively represented, but largely reflects political forces external to labor-management relations. The main lines of cleavage are usually as they are in the party—namely, the rivalry between old-style political conservatives and reformers. The former currently hold the upper hand, but there is a balance of forces in large cities such as Shanghai and especially Guangzhou.

Union representation in the workplace—to make the workers "masters in their own house"—is formally built into the system and has been since the early 1950s (see Warner 1987a). The institutional arrangements to encourage this have evolved over four decades, although changes in form may have overshadowed shifts in function. The role of the party secretary in the enterprise, according to some observers (for example, Walder 1989), has always been, and remains, central regardless of changes in institutional arrangements, whether managerial or representative. The party committee remains responsible for "guaranteeing and supervising" policy implementation (Child and Xinzhong 1989:10). In this context, full-time union cadres may be seen as still relatively influential compared with policy-making bodies in the enterprise in that they reflect the party line. As indicated in figure 2.2, this is true regardless of whether the factory director officially has more or less power.

On sensitive work force issues, such as dismissals, management in several enterprises talks to the union officials representing the workers' congress rather than to the party committee. In other areas of decision making, discussion with members of such bodies is no more than procedural (Child and Xinzhong 1989:29).

It is doubtful that the unions play much of an independent role in the factories. Union officials support increasing production if the party wishes it, and workers' congresses are functionally not very distinct from the unions. Some sessions may be seen as just formalities. The workers elected to workers' congresses are usually drawn from the union faithful. In many of the special economic zones and joint ventures, there are no workers' congresses, although there may be local unions in the plant (see Warner 1989). In foreign-owned firms, there may be neither. The Joint Venture Implementation Regulations are said implicitly to recognize an adversarial role for unions. Union officials may deal directly with overseas partners over disputes and attend top board meetings when labor-related policy issues are discussed, but they do not vote (Henley and Nyaw 1989:284).

Union Goals, Strategies, and Tactics

The formal goals of the ACFTU were from the start to unite and improve workers' welfare. Its tasks included the development of workers' unions in China, unifying the labor movement, setting up an organizational system, directing union activities, adjudicating interunion disputes, propagating the aims of class struggle, representing Chinese

Figure 2.2. Decision-making structure of a Chinese state enterprise (national, provincial, and local levels)

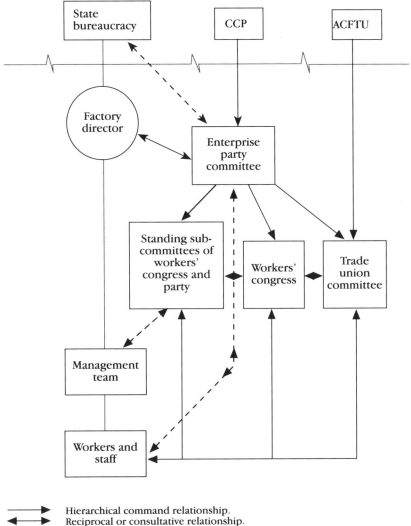

Hierarchical command relationship.
Reciprocal or consultative relationship.
Links of a weak or unclear nature.

Source: Henley and Nyaw 1986:642.

workers vis-à-vis outside countries, raising workers' educational levels, and protecting workers' benefits. As the opening paragraph of the constitution of the ACFTU (1988) states:

> The trade unions of China are Chinese working-class mass organizations led by the Chinese Communist Party and formed voluntarily

by workers and staff members, and are important social and political organizations. Trade unions should conscientiously take economic construction as their central task and should faithfully
reflect and safeguard the particular interests of workers and staff
members while upholding the interests of the people as a whole,
speak on behalf of workers and staff members, work for them, build
up a dedicated, high-minded, well-educated and disciplined contingent of workers and staff members and bring into full play the role
of the Chinese working class as the main force in developing
socialist material and cultural civilization.

The guiding principles are described as "rallying around the four
modernizations; to speak, to work and to defend the legitimate rights of
workers; to strengthen political, cultural and technical education of
workers; aiming to build a workforce with ideals, with high morals,
culture and good discipline" (W. Leung 1988:39).

Union responsibilities, Leung claims, have changed over the years. In
the past, unions concentrated mostly on problems faced by workers,
such as their dissatisfaction with wages or living conditions. Yet, more
often than not, they would do no more than report a case to the factory
director. Unions claim that they now have broader functions since "as
the union participates in the allocation of the company's profits to be
retained for its own disposal, it actively campaigns for more general
interests: asking for extra money for housing, education, a cinema, dance
hall, swimming pool, or whatever is deemed desirable" (*Beijing Review,*
13–26 Feb. 1989, 28). Over the years, the trade unions have also been
involved in educational and training activities in the enterprise, but
many of these activities duplicate those of other departments (see
Warner 1989).

Plant-level industrial relations functions, in the broadest sense of the
term, are carried out by both the trade unions and the elected workers'
congresses, as described above, which represent the work force and staff
in enterprises on the basis of one representative for ten or twelve
persons. In big plants, the basic unit is the union team, centered on the
work group, which meets once a fortnight, or monthly, as need be. The
workers' congress in an enterprise meets between one and four times a
year depending on "custom and practice" (see Warner 1987a).

The union committee in the workplace, through its full-time cadres,
provides continuity of contact when the congress is in abeyance. It is
thus unavoidable in the *danwei,* the all-important official place of work
and the building block of Chinese society (see Walder 1986). The
danwei controls much of both the managers' and workers' lives, both
inside and outside work. These work establishments not only provide
cradle-to-grave welfare services but also help shape the workers' sense
of identity. To buy a bicycle, change their job, or get married, personnel

have to get permission from their *danwei*. Given the part trade unions play in the modernization process, they tend, first, to emphasize production over consumption, according to L. T. Lee (1986) but, second, to look after the everyday welfare interests of their members (see *Gongren Ribao* [*Workers' Daily*], 19 July 1988, 2). The unions also play a role in enforcing and monitoring birth-control policies by their surveillance of women workers in the factories and offices.

The trade unions operate a "check-off" system to finance their activities. Members pay 0.5 percent of their wages each month to the union, and the enterprise contributes another 2 percent. About 5 percent of all union dues goes to the ACFTU.

Union effectiveness, as far as official policy is concerned, takes the form of the unions helping the government achieve economic growth and modernization, as well as protecting workers' welfare, providing educational facilities, and so on. Unions are expected to cooperate with management. Their role centers on "labor productivity, worker morale and welfare rather than the interpretation of national policy" (Henley and Nyaw 1986:648). They do not bargain freely or fix wage levels, but in contracted or leased enterprises they help determine the allocation of funds and the arrangement of working schedules. Normally, they are supposed to help implement resolutions passed by the workers' congresses in these areas.

In the everyday work of an enterprise, unions are also expected to defuse conflicts between the work force and management, if the latter acts out of order, for example, by reducing bonuses or canceling labor insurance and there is a stoppage by the workers involved. The union tries to intervene informally to resolve the grievance and get production restored. Chinese workers still "retain a de facto shop floor bargaining power" insofar as they can raise the productivity level by working harder if they choose to do so (Littler and Palmer 1987:268–69).

In the last few years, Chinese trade unions, on the central government's initiative, have promoted a system of collective agreements (Gong 1989). These accords are for individual enterprises to anchor labor-management relations. They are said to have been implemented in ninety-seven thousand enterprises. An officially sponsored trade union publication describes their characteristics, perhaps rather overoptimistically, as follows:

> Clearly defined in the collective agreements are the director's objectives during his term of office, annual targets in production and management, plans to improve workers' conditions and welfare and specific measures to achieve the above-mentioned objectives and targets, as well as responsibilities on the part of the director, the trade union and the Workers' Congress. Then the director and the trade union chairman sign the agreement respec-

tively on behalf of the administration and the workers and employees. This practice is well received by the workers, for it links up
the workers and the management in a community of interest in
which obligations, risks and benefits are shared by both sides
(Gong 1989:7–8).

Y. Gong argues that such agreements boost production significantly vis-
à-vis enterprises that are without them, but their overall effects are
unproved.

Nonetheless, "the Party has the final say as it leads the union organization, appoints its officials and organizes and even manipulates Congresses
of workers and staff" (Walder 1989:247). It also screens the nominations
list for all officers in the workplace, union and otherwise. Workers
therefore often turn to the party when they have grievances about
bonuses or discipline, although the union is formally supposed to be the
voice on their behalf.

Discussion

A sociological theory of trade union organization has highlighted the
twin rationales of administrative and representative functioning (see
Child, Loveridge, and Warner 1973). Using such analytical tools, we can
see that trade unions in the PRC are disproportionately geared to
administration, although it would be foolish to disregard their representative function entirely, especially at the shop-floor level. The critical
observer is forced, however, to view the macropolitical (and even more
so the macroeconomic) role of Chinese unions as relatively removed
from the life of the ordinary worker they claim to represent. An ACFTU
survey conducted in 1986 found that fewer than 30 percent of workers
had a positive view of workers' congresses, less than 40 percent viewed
the unions with enthusiasm, and 21 percent had no idea what unions do
(Li 1989:78). The ACFTU national conferences have echoed party thinking for so long that it is hard to imagine them reflecting, let alone
initiating, independent ideas or policies.

Workers' concerns about their jobs, wages, and standard of living
generally, their working conditions, and even more urgently price stability had to have been articulated more explicitly (see Rosen 1989) if the
trade unions were to live up to their prescribed roles. This was particularly evident when important changes were introduced during 1986 to
undermine the "iron-rice bowl" system, with its guarantee of job security
for life. The new policy was based on the introduction of labor contracts:

> The system involves open recruitment through examinations. No
> longer are the children of retired workers allowed to fill their
> parents' positions automatically, nor are employees' children guar-
> anteed a job, as was previously the case. At the same time, factory

directors have been given the right to dismiss workers for breach of discipline (*Beijing Review,* 24–30 Oct., 25).

Clearly, trade unions in Communist societies present conceptual difficulties for industrial relations analysts (see Littler and Palmer 1987). If trade unions are defined as organizations of workers that bargain freely and collectively, then they cannot be considered unions at all (see Banks 1974:37ff; Poole 1986:90ff).

In the mid-1950s, trade union committees in factories were subordinated to the party committee, even merged with it in some cases (see Zhang 1988:41). In this context, union officials were appointed by the party committee in the enterprise. This development probably represented the high point of integration of party and union. Lee (1986:159), for example, concludes that

> Chinese trade unions are fundamentally different from the unions in Western democracies. To use the analytical concept of structural-functional analysis, Chinese unions have little or no "sub-system autonomy." Chinese union leaders also make no pretence about this . . . . The reconstructed trade unions after the Cultural Revolution were similarly controlled by the Party. Chinese unions are essentially an arm of the executive to mobilise the resources of the society.

Any representative function of trade unions for the labor force was mitigated, however, by their "exclusive" membership requirement; "only permanent workers could join unions and were eligible to the medical care, unemployment, housing and other welfare benefits administered by trade unions" (Lee 1986:115). Temporary and contract workers were excluded from union protection, and indeed this was one reason among others for the "fall" of the ACFTU during the Cultural Revolution. Curiously, the idea of temporary contract labor was imported from the Soviet Union during the 1950s, when top officials were sent there to study their contract system in an effort to reduce overhead costs and gain greater labor flexibility (Lee 1986:115).

The failure of Chinese unions to cater to all workers was a weakness that represented a grievance that surfaced periodically during the Great Leap Forward in the late 1950s and again in the early 1960s (Lee 1986:115) when the labor contract system was used. In the early 1980s, the unions asked local committees to help recruit contract workers (Wilson 1987:229). Clearly, the growing use of such workers during the later period of economic reforms fueled the dissatisfaction with official unions as the contract system was extended nationally (see W. Leung 1988:61). By April 1987, about 8 percent of the industrial labor force was classified as employed on a contractual basis.

The chairman of the ACFTU (Ni Zhifu) outlined the official position on 22 October 1988 to the Eleventh National Congress of Chinese Trade Unions as follows:

It is necessary to introduce the mechanism of competition in reforming the labor system, to grant the enterprises autonomy in selecting workers and vice versa, and to set up an employment system which allows a reasonable flow together with relative stability of the labor force. Rational labor reorganization should be carried out in accordance with the principles of openness, equality, competition and optimal selection, while trade unions should organize democratic supervision by the workers and staff. At the same time, they should urge and assist enterprises to diversify their operations, open up new avenues of employment, make proper arrangements for the placement of redundant personnel and reduce the rate of unemployment in society (ACFTU 1988:17).

The latter part of this statement appears to be an effort to "sweeten the pill" for the workers potentially threatened by the changes.

Contracts may be for varying periods, even ten years, although some are for less than one year. They have legal validity and state the obligations of the enterprise vis-à-vis safety, training, remuneration, insurance, welfare, and so on. In that the contracts are for fixed periods, they may help in recruitment as well as training.

A mediation committee may be set up to resolve disputes that occur when contracts are introduced. There are nine members of such a body: the full-time leaders of the union committee, the part-time worker-representatives, and the personnel director. When a dispute arises, the union is supposed to look after its members' interests. If mediation does not work, the case may go to the municipal labor arbitration committee (Dong 1989:28–29).

It may be hypothesized that the greater the extent and speed of the modernization policies, the deeper the level of dissatisfaction with the official trade unions in their current form (see *Gongren Ribao,* 28 Dec. 1988, 3). Yet, according to a leading Western authority on Chinese industry (Walder 1989), for the permanent labor force, the collusive nature of the enterprise sociopolitical coalition ensured an increasing standard of living and improved working conditions over much of the last decade. If "the Party leads the union organization, appoints its officials, and organizes even manipulates congresses of workers and staff" (Walder 1989:247), then it can make sure it looks after the faithful. The ACFTU survey carried out in 1986 and noted earlier reported that more than 80 percent of those interviewed (nearly 650,000 members) believed their standard of living had improved since 1979 (see He, Hao, and Guo 1989).

Yet, although it would be reasonable to ask why one should study trade unions in Communist societies given their often subordinate importance in the decision-making process, it is possible to envisage their long-term future role as becoming more important (see O'Leary 1989). The example of Solidarity in Poland could presage both an expanded political and economic role. If the economic reforms are to be extended further in the PRC in the future, the role of unions will have to change significantly.

An alliance of workers and students, à la Polonaise, is precisely what the Chinese authorities have been concerned about since the early 1980s (see Littler and Lockett 1983). Until the spring of 1989, these streams of potential dissent had been kept as segregated as possible. Student marches, where they occurred, were keenly screened by the police for any workers who dared join the protesters. In 1987, a peak year for disputes, industrial strikes began to spread and were even reported on in the Eastern European press. There were at least two hundred major strikes in 1988, and the longest, involving eleven hundred workers, was said to have lasted three months, closing the factory (BBC 1988).

There were many, many more protests, however, some reported, others unreported. A feature of the Tiananmen Square protests in late spring 1989 was the presence of the Workers' Autonomous Federation, even if it was on the fringes of student-led dissent. Its appearance has been well documented (Fathers and Higgins 1989:66, 75, 136), as has its presence elsewhere, and indeed its leaders featured prominently in the subsequent official crackdown in that they were sentenced severely for their apparent audacity. The guiding principles of the Workers' Autonomous Federation, clearly showing its wish to be outside party control, are set out in Table 2.7.

Dissident staff of the ACFTU were said to have given out leaflets in the square in May 1989 calling for greater union autonomy and promoting the idea that "trade unions should work and speak for the workers and masses" (Fathers and Higgins 1989:66). In addition, on May 18, the headquarters of the ACFTU donated 100,000 yuan (U.S. $27,000) to the Red Cross for the student hunger strikers, a remarkable step (BBC 1989). There were even rumors of an unofficial one-day general strike in Beijing.

The activities of the "free" trade union organizations were also reported in Chengdu, Guangzhou, Hangzhou, Hefei, and Shanghai, among other places (*Echoes from Tiananmen,* 15 June 1989, 3; 15 Aug. 1989, 6). As late as 9 June, at least a thousand workers were reported marching behind the Workers' Autonomous Federation banner in demonstrations in Shanghai. The autonomous trade unions were accused of usurping the name of the working class, fabricating rumors, and, through the official press, attempting to overthrow the people's government. Such illegal organizations, it was said, "will certainly become the rubbish abandoned by history" (*Gongren Ribao,* 18 June 1989, 2–3).

Table 2.7. Beijing Workers' Autonomous Federation Provisional Memorandum

Based on the initial guiding principles, prepared by the preparatory committee of the Beijing Workers' Autonomous Federation, issued on 25 May 1989.

Preamble:

In the entire People's Patriotic Democracy movement, led by the students in mid-April, the majority of the Chinese workers have demonstrated a strong wish to take part in politics. At the same time, they also realize that there is not yet an organization that can truly represent the wishes expressed by the working masses. Therefore, we recognize there is a need to set up an autonomous organization that will speak for the workers and that will organize the realization of workers' participation and consultation in political affairs. For this purpose, we put forward the following preparatory guiding principles.

1. The organization should be an entirely independent, autonomous organization, built up by the workers on a voluntary basis, through democratic processes, and should not be controlled by other organizations.
2. The fundamental principle of the organization should be to address political and economic demands, based on the wishes of the majority of the workers, and should not just remain a welfare organization.
3. The organization should possess the function of monitoring the party of the proletariat—the Chinese Communist Party.
4. The organization should have the power, through every legal and effective means, to monitor the legal representatives of all state and collective enterprises, guaranteeing that the workers become the real masters of the enterprise. In other enterprises, through negotiation with the owners and other legal means, the organization should be able to safeguard the rights of the workers.
5. Within the bounds of the constitution and the law, the organization should be able to safeguard all legal rights of its members.
6. Membership of the organization should come from individuals on a voluntary basis, and also group or collective membership in branches of various enterprises.

Tiananmen Square, 28 May 1989

Source: *Echoes from Tiananmen,* 15 June 1989, 1.

By 25 July, the official Chinese news agency reported that "China's trade unions must work under the leadership of the CCP (Chinese Communist Party) and no trade unions opposed to the CCP are allowed to be established, (according to) Ni Zhifu, president of the All-China Federation of Trade Unions (ACFTU)" (BBC 1989). Addressing the third meeting of the eleventh ACFTU presidium, which opened in Shanghai on that day, Ni emphasized that any attempt to work outside the CCP leadership and put the trade unions into an opposition role had to be resisted: "Otherwise, we will miss the correct political orientation of trade union reform and construction, leading to great errors."

Ni then emphasized the unions' role in representing and safeguarding workers' rights and interests. He argued that "the trade unions must avoid simply acting as agents of the government and work independently so as to increase the attraction to workers and enjoy more confidence from the workers, leaving no opportunity to those who attempt to organize 'independent trade unions.' Otherwise we will also make great errors."

Worker discontent resulting from the adverse consequences of the economic reforms remains a problem (see Mirsky 1989:3). According to some accounts, only workers (rather than students, for example) associated with the Workers' Autonomous Federation were executed in the reaction to the events of June 1989 (see Goldman 1989:5), but it is hard to confirm whether students were therefore protected. In the early spring, the students had physically tried to stop the workers from marching with them, fearing they would join only for the pursuit of materialistic goals. On 17 May, the students relented, however, as a million people marched in Beijing. The fear of a Solidarity-style movement was palpable. Deng appeared to mistrust Soviet and Eastern European reforms more than he did Western ideas: "Those people who have been influenced by the free elements of Yugoslavia, Poland, Hungary and the Soviet Union have a reason to create turmoil. Their motive is to overthrow the Party" (cited in Goldman 1989:5).

Might there be a return to greater equality in pay? The question of economic rewards for work during a period of socialist transition surfaces throughout the history of the PRC (see Gittings 1989:111–14). After the Great Leap Forward, material incentives were in disrepute; during the Cultural Revolution, wage bonuses were slowly eliminated and piece-rate payments demoted. With the Dengist reforms, wage incentives were reintroduced (Warner 1986, 1987a). Bonuses rose from 2 percent of all wages in 1978 to 9.1 percent in 1980, 15.1 percent in 1985, and 16 percent in 1987.

It is questionable whether there will be a curb on performance-related bonuses and a return to more egalitarian pay structures. There was, for example, no great clamor for such a reversion in an article on "unfair income distribution" written by the incoming party general secretary, Jiang Zemin, published in early autumn 1989, in which he strongly criticized illicit and excessive incomes. He concluded that

> we must resolutely protect lawful incomes, reasonably regulate excessively high incomes and strictly ban illegal incomes. From a long-term point of view, in order to solve problems caused by unfair distribution of income, a flexible employment system should be gradually established, in which laborers will obtain relatively equal opportunities in competition. Correspondingly, a system for social security must be established and improved. Although it is impossible to solve all problems immediately, we must do the best we can (*Beijing Review,* 28 Aug.–3 Sept. 1989, 20).

Resentment has recently surfaced, however, over "forced loans" many enterprises have made their workers pay to the state in the form of compulsory bond purchases. Sometimes, these have amounted to three months' wages (*Guardian,* 7 Feb. 1990, 6). These "loans" have been imposed to raise revenue as well as to take purchasing power out of the overheated economy, rather than as a way to affect income distribution.

Conclusion

Chinese trade unions continue to play a vital role in the mobilization process. They do not, however, bargain collectively as Western unions do; instead, they try to discipline and "ensure the production commitment of the labor force" (Lee 1986:160). They are organized on both an industrial and a geographical basis. The ACFTU is for much of the time a transmission-belt of government policy and will play its part in whatever current campaign the party delegates to it, such as attempting to seek out corrupt officials or being a watchdog about excessive price increases. Its role since 1949 has been mostly consultative (see Wilson 1987:243), such as helping to shape official policy goals and targets, insofar as they affect wages and conditions of work, welfare matters, worker education, and labor protection. The effectiveness of trade unions in these tasks depends on how far they can mobilize worker support for official policies in these areas and appear to represent workers' interests credibly. In recent years they seem to have been unable to do this successfully (see Rosen 1989:4). Their future role may depend on whether or how far the Chinese leadership "turn back the clock."

While the Open Door policy has remained nominally in favor, the Four Cardinal Principles have been strongly reemphasized vis-à-vis the Four Modernizations. Even if the degree of reaction to the events of June 1989 lead to a return to "conservative" policies, these events may still prove to be a historical benchmark. It is still too early to predict their ultimate consequences in general (see Nolan 1989) and for trade unions in particular. It is doubtful that the unions will diverge from government policy in the immediate future, and if government policy involves tightening party control, in the final analysis the unions will fully support it.

The most probable scenario is that there will be "the gradual creation of an economic mechanism which combines a planned economy with market regulation" (*Beijing Review,* 12–18 Feb. 1990, xii). The ACFTU would then more than ever continue its traditional top-down role, as the Leninist model would require. This swing could probably last until the demise of China's aging leadership, when the possibilities of more extensive political and economic reform may present themselves. In this event, the Chinese trade unions may have to emphasize more strongly their representative function vis-à-vis their administrative one. Until this occurs, China's unions are likely to remain closer to the Leninist ideal type than most of their counterparts elsewhere.

3
Union Unevenness and Insecurity in Thailand

Andrew Brown and Stephen Frenkel

S trikes and other forms of protest by wage laborers in Thailand date back to the early 1880s. They continued to erupt throughout the 1890s and early years of the twentieth century, and in the 1920s Thai workers were appealing to state officials to allow them to organize. Yet, by the late 1970s, unions had been permitted to exist legally only for short periods: 1932–34, 1944–47, 1955–57, and 1972–76. Although in each of these periods workers managed to make some significant economic and political gains, progress was subsequently stalled by renewed cycles of repression. Thus, for almost seventy years, Thai workers have faced a continuing battle to secure recognition from the state for the right to organize. It is against this background that the 1980s appeared to represent greater official acceptance of trade unionism, as the government prepared to accept unions as a means of promoting worker discipline and higher productivity. As we shall see, however, history repeated itself with the 1991 coup, which threatened the future of labor organization in Thailand.

This chapter examines key aspects of union development in Thailand. In the first section, we discuss the factors that facilitated the rise in union

We would like to thank Somsong Patarapanich, Kevin Hewison, and Sukanya Daramas for supplying information. Thanks also to Fred Deyo, Kevin Hewison, and Somsong Patarapanich for their useful comments on a previous draft of this chapter. The authors are solely responsible for the contents, however.

legitimacy during the 1980s. Particular emphasis is placed on the emergence of an industrial proletariat capable of mounting challenges to employer control. The second section focuses on the institutionalized context of unions, membership growth, size distribution, and reasons for their relative weakness. In the third section, we discuss the structure of the union movement, including interunion rivalries at the peak council level. The fourth section looks at union goals and methods in relation to such issues as official recognition, employer noncompliance with the law, opposition to privatization, improved wages and conditions, and social security legislation. The fifth section assesses union achievements, while the sixth and concluding section notes the possibility of a change in government that might weaken unions even further. The postscript summarizes recent legislation introduced by the 1991 military government. Essentially, we argue that Thai unions are dualistic, relatively powerful in the state-enterprise sector and weak elsewhere. And although prospects for growth and consolidation in the 1980s were generally favorable, the environment has since become more hostile so that it is hard to be optimistic about the future of unions in this rapidly industrializing society.

Before proceeding, an important caveat must be set forth: the field of Thai labor studies is very much in its infancy; there is little primary research and therefore one must rely on secondary sources, which are often frustratingly incomplete and sometimes contradictory. In addition, there is only a limited amount of government data. Although every effort has been made to check the accuracy of the information reported in this chapter, what follows should be read as preliminary and tentative rather than as a definitive analysis of Thai trade unionism.

Industrialization and Government Attitudes toward Unions

Capitalism in Thailand dates back to the late nineteenth century, but it is only in the last three decades that development has become a principal official goal. It is in this context that unions have become acknowledged as potentially constructive agents in the process of industrialization described briefly below.

From the 1850s to the end of the 1950s, Thailand's role in the international division of labor was basically as an exporter of four primary products—rice, tin, teak, and rubber—and as an importer of Western manufactured goods. Although industrial development was limited during the pre-1932 period, a shift toward industrial production did take place. Rice and timber milling and plantation agriculture were among the first enterprises to require the services of wage laborers. In addition, infrastructural projects, such as the construction of railways, roads, ports, dockyards, and bridges, together with the growth of small-scale private industries, such as those that manufactured bricks and tiles, textiles, soaps, and matches, also led to a growth in demand for wage labor. Industrial production advanced further during the post-1932 period with the rise of a state that was determined to pursue a policy of state-led industrialization (Hewison 1989a:57). Over the following twenty-five years, the state, by taking on the functions of policy maker, financier, and model investor, actively promoted and managed a wide range of industrial activities. Though reasonably successful in furthering the expansion of capital accumulation, by the end of the 1950s the policy of state-led industrialization had become problematic. The overthrow of the Phibun Songkhram government in September 1957 not only ushered in a highly authoritarian political order but also marked a watershed in Thailand's development strategy.

After seizing power in the coups of 1957 and 1958, army commander Sarit Thanarat made clear his intention to modernize Thailand's economy and society. Turning away from the state-led industrialization policies of his predecessor, Sarit began to implement a development program in which a leading role was to be played by both foreign and domestic private capital. Under advice from the World Bank, the state was urged to assist industry by offering development assistance, improving laws related to business, expanding credit, providing necessary infrastructure, initiating development planning, and adopting a strategy of import-substitution industrialization (ISI). According to Hewison (1989a:103–21), the adoption of an ISI strategy had some negative effects, such as exacerbating the bias against rural areas, increasing income disparities, and discriminating against export industries, however it changed the structure of the economy.

During the 1960s, the contribution of manufacturing to GDP rose from 12.5 percent to 17.5 percent, and annual GDP growth averaged more than 11 percent for the period. Moreover, high protection rates encouraged domestic manufacturing, with industrial and banking capital enjoying the greatest benefits. By the early 1970s, although it had been relatively successful, ISI began to experience problems. As early as 1966, the influential Bangkok Bank had begun to argue for an expansion of manufactured exports and a revision of tariff schedules to aid local manufacturers that were producing for external markets. The shift away from ISI was hastened further by both domestic and international factors. Domestically, excess manufacturing was becoming a problem and investment began to decline. Moreover, fiscal problems began to force the government to consider the possibility of adopting export-oriented industrialization (EOI) as a way of overcoming trade deficits. Further, higher inflation in Western countries and fluctuations in the exchange rate were making Thai manufactured goods more attractive on the world market.

EOI has not completely replaced the ISI model, but it has been in the ascendancy since its formal recognition in the Third Development Plan (1971–76), and the adoption of EOI has led to some significant changes within the Thai economy. The value of manufactured exports rose rapidly from U.S. $40 million in 1970 to U.S. $270 million in 1973. By 1983, manufactured goods contributed 30 percent to total exports, compared with 15 percent in 1972 and only 5 percent in 1965 (Hewison 1989a:120).

The adoption of both ISI and EOI development strategies has fostered the growth of a fractionalized domestic capitalist class presided over by a powerful finance group (Hewison 1989a:127–206). An industrial proletariat has also grown significantly. During the period 1958–90, Thailand's population increased from about 23 million to 56.3 million and the labor force (defined as those eleven years and older) rose from 13.8 million to 30.6 million. The proportion of persons employed in agriculture fell from 82 percent of the economically active population in 1960 to 70 percent in 1979. By 1989, this figure stood at 57.3 percent. Manufacturing employment rose from 3.4 percent in 1960 to 10 percent by the end of the 1980s (Asian Business 1988:81; *FEER* 1990:7). Of the 6.5 million workers employed in the secondary and tertiary sectors, 71 percent were in the private sector and 29 percent in the public sector. Such employees were distributed over a wide variety of industries.

Managers and planners have concluded that Thailand must follow the NICs in producing higher value-added goods for export markets and to satisfy local demand. This presupposes an adequate supply of skilled and productivity-oriented urban wage labor at internationally competitive rates. It is in this context that labor relations has become an important policy problem, in that reliance on a plentiful supply of low-skilled employees who can easily be controlled through repressive measures is no longer a viable option. Economic change has thus been opening the way to a growing recognition that, rather than being "obstacles" to development—a view propagated at the beginning of the Sarit period—unions may be able to help bring stability to the labor market (Limqueco, McFarlane, and Odhnoff 1989:32). This attitude is reflected in the emergence of a progressive view of organized labor. The following comments, by the vice-president of the Employers' Confederation of Thailand, illustrate the view of some large employers since the late 1970s:

Employers must recognize that the right to organize is a universal right of the workers which is guaranteed by law. Rather than fighting against it, employers should take a more positive, enlightened approach to turn the adversaries into advocates, transforming negative energy into constructive one [sic.]. The Employers' Confederation of Thailand has contributed its part to the process of educating its members in the proper concept of labor relations. Employers have been constantly persuaded that good labor relations are conducive to better productivity and higher profit (Sopon 1991:6).

Political factors associated with discontent over wages and working conditions have contributed to a more positive view of unions among some employers, but these same factors have stiffened the anti-union resolve of others. By 1970, almost half a million factory workers were receiving a mere 7 to 10 baht (approximately U.S. $0.5) a day in wages. There was no compensation for overtime, holidays, accidents, or illness. Child labor was common, and no health and safety standards were in existence (Hewison 1989a:123).

These conditions worsened between 1971 and 1973 as the economy experienced rising inflation. Resistance to these oppressive conditions began to gather momentum, fueling wider opposition to the military, and in October 1973 led to the government's demise.

Well over a thousand strikes were officially recorded between 1973 and 1976, and by late 1976, 185 unions had been formed (Morell and Chaianan 1981:189). Moreover, two large and influential peak councils were established, the radical Labor Coordination Center of Thailand and the laborist-oriented Federation of Labor Unions of Thailand. The growth of organized labor was halted following the coup of October 1976 and the subsequent installation of an authoritarian government. But another coup, in October 1977, which brought General Kriangsak Chomanan to power, was followed by the easing of repression, leaving many believing that the experiences of the 1970s meant that the growth of the organized labor movement was irreversible (Mabry 1979:81).

While the activities and struggles of workers themselves have certainly been a major factor in forcing the elite toward a greater acceptance of organized labor, such recognition has also been facilitated by two other factors: the existence of deep divisions within the ruling class itself and the influence of external organizations. Thus, since the tumultuous events of the 1970s, the Thai political stage has been occupied by a heterogeneous group of actors: capitalist fractions, various factions within the military and civilian bureaucracies, remnants of the feudal aristocracy and nobility, peasants, and students. Also noteworthy is the existence of what A. Turton (1984:29) has termed a "secondary complex of predatory interests": localized power structures spread over the surface of Thai society that comprise networks led by gangsterlike businessmen, politicians, and hitmen who maintain complex links with the military, police, and business groups. Lack of ruling-class unity has provided opportunities for unions to secure support, if only temporarily, among influential groups, including the military and political parties.

Since the mid-1970s, the main political problem in Thailand has been establishing a suitable political forum able to respond effectively to the diverse groups that represent various interests. During the 1980s the establishment of a parliamentary democracy, albeit under military guidelines for most of the period, remained the dominant trend, culminating in the appointment of Chatichai Choonhaven, the first democratically elected prime minister since 1976. Part of the appeal of a parliamentary democratic form of rule is the characteristic institutional division between economic and political class struggle, which often operates to contain the demands of labor. As B. Jessop (1978:29) observes:

> From the viewpoint of capital the ideal position is one in which economic class struggle is confined within the limits of the market relation and political class struggle is confined within the limits of bourgeois parliamentarianism. There would be a clear division between trade union struggles concerned with wages and conditions and political struggles to promote social reforms through parliamentary majorities and the mobilization of public opinion.

The growth of a parliamentary form of politics has thus been accompanied by the reemergence of a system of industrial relations reflecting the goal of a clear institutional division between economic and political struggles. An attempt to establish a stable industrial relations framework in which unions could assist in managing conflict without it spilling over into the political arena was first made in the 1950s. The system lasted for less than a year before it was abolished by the Sarit administration. Further attempts were made in 1965 and 1972, culminating in the promulgation of the Labor Relations Act of 1975, which continues to be the foundation of contemporary (1991) private-sector Thai industrial relations.

In sum, Thai workers and their organizations have faced a continual battle for recognition and legitimacy in which opportunities have ebbed and flowed. From the late 1970s, possibilities for union expansion were more favorable, although by the end of the 1980s the future of democracy was less bright as the military showed increasing signs of dissatisfaction with the Chatichai government. Nevertheless, we shall explore the extent to which the unions were able to grasp the opportunities before the curtain once again came down on Thailand's emerging parliamentary democracy.

Union Development in the 1980s

The Thai state has a complex set of structures, including departments, committees, subcommittees, and advisory bodies, presided over by officials, that not only shape the practices of unions but also define the objectives of these organizations. The key legal document in this regard is the Labor Relations Act, which pertains to all the elements traditionally associated with "rational" systems of industrial relations. The act accords workers the right to strike, to bargain collectively, and to form trade unions *(sahaphapraenggnan),* labor federations *(sahaphanraenggnan),* and labor councils and congresses *(ongkanlukcang).* As few as ten workers may form a union on either a workplace or an industry basis. Their objective must be to secure and protect workers' interests relating to conditions of employment and the promotion of better relationships between employers and employees and among employees (Kromraenggnan 1984:306).

Two or more unions whose members are working for the same employer, or who cover employees in the same industry or in the same line of work, may apply to register as a labor federation, for the purpose of promoting better relations between unions and protecting the interests of unions and employees. No fewer than fifteen unions or federations may join together to establish a labor council, aimed at fostering education and improved labor relations (Kromraenggnan 1984:311–12). There are two important points in this regard: One, the registrar has the power to reject an application for registration and/or to dissolve an already registered union if the objectives of that union are considered likely to "disrupt public order" (Kromraenggnan 1984:307). Two, persons not employed in the relevant firm or industry cannot stand for a leadership position in union elections. Table 3.1 shows the distribution of unions in 1989.

Table 3.1 indicates that there were nearly six hundred unions in Thailand, nearly 80 percent of which covered workers in the private sector. As might be expected, state-enterprise unions are concentrated in the capital, Bangkok, whereas private-sector unions tend to be more represented in the provinces. Note that nearly two-thirds of unions are of the enterprise type, in part reflecting the tendency for state-enterprise unions to be organized along enterprise rather than industrial lines. Although not evident from table 3.1, the number of unions increased

Table 3.1. Unions in Thailand, by region, sector, and type, 1989 (in percent)

Region	Sector			Type	
	State	*Private*	*Total*	*Enterprise*	*Industrial*
Bangkok	91.9	38.3	49.4	58.7	32.0
Other	8.1	61.7	50.6	41.3	68.0
Number of unions	123	470	593	387	206

Source: Thailand. Department of Labor 1990.

substantially during the 1980s: from 255 in 1980 to 436 in 1985. Table 3.1 shows that there were 593 unions in 1989, while the most recent count, for 1990, puts the number at 713 (Thailand. Department of Labor 1990). No data on union type or sector are available for these years, but the upward trend, taking into account the slower increase in union membership over the ten-year period—153,550 in 1980, 181,851 in 1985, and an estimated 300,000 in 1990 (Damri 1990:179)—suggests relatively faster growth of enterprise than of industrial unions. A note of caution is warranted here: only about 70 percent of registered unions were reported to be active in the mid-1980s (*FEER* 1986), and most of these were of the state-enterprise type. If this was true of the second half of the 1980s, then union growth was less significant than might be supposed.

The strongest unions have as their base strategically powerful workers who are employed in large enterprises. The ten largest unions in Thailand (nine of which are state-enterprise unions) are found in the State Railways of Thailand, the Electricity and Generating Authority of Thailand, the Communication Authority, the Telephone Organization of Thailand, the Bangkok Mass Transportation Authority, the Metropolitan Electricity Authority, the Provincial Electricity Authority, the Port Authority of Thailand, the Bangkok Bank (private), and the Krung Thai Bank.

The largest number of unions are in the metal industry, followed by textiles and clothing, transportation, warehousing, communications, food, beverages, and tobacco, chemical products, and petroleum and rubber. No figures are available showing changes in the distribution of unions by industrial sector over recent years, but a survey conducted by P. Limqueco, B. McFarlane, and J. Odhnoff (1989:39) at three industrial sites in and around Bangkok indicates that union density in manufacturing was highest in modern large-scale firms, most of which were owned by multinational companies in joint venture relationships with Thai partners. Density was lowest in medium- and small-scale, labor-intensive industries, most of which were owned by Sino-Thai interests.

Thai unions range in size from fifty to twenty thousand members; the average union in the early 1980s had five hundred to six hundred members (Narong 1982:36). Since as few as ten workers may form a union, unions are fragmented. For example, Nongyao Reecharoen (1988:9) reported the presence of 74 unions in twenty state enterprises. Available data suggest that in 1990 there were 123 state-enterprise unions covering approximately sixty state enterprises.

Although unions were not prevented by law from organizing during most of the 1980s, membership remained weak. Gross union density, or total nonagricultural employment divided by total union members, an indicator that seriously underestimates real union density, increased very slightly, from 2.3 percent in 1980 to slightly under 3 percent in 1990.[1] This represents an estimated net density of about 6 percent in 1990, where net density takes into account those elements of the work force who are not available for unionization (i.e., employers, the self-employed, household labor, and child workers). In contrast to the density in the private sector (Damri 1990:179), which is very low, and among civil servants, who are prohibited from joining unions, density among state-enterprise employees is more than 50 percent (U.S. Department of Labor 1990:3).

Surveys indicate that Thai workers, particularly skilled employees, hold positive attitudes toward unions, believing that they afford protection (Limqueco, McFarlane, and Odhnoff 1989:41), so why then do comparatively few workers actually join unions? There are a number of possible explanations. First, promoters of unions are not legally protected until after a union is registered; employers have thus been able to dismiss organizers with virtual impunity (Suphachai et al. 1984:53). Second, the potential benefits of joining a union are not widely understood by the workers, who are predominantly young and inexperienced and have only recently joined the urban work force. Indeed, the industrial work force generally has limited employment experience in the nonagricultural sector, and a large proportion of the urban workers are still attached to their rural communities. Third, the effects of rapid economic change have contributed to the fragmentation of the work force. About a quarter of the work force are self-employed, and a further 14 percent are employed as household labor. Those who are employed as wage labor work in a diverse range of industries and occupations, many in small workplaces. Thus, it was estimated that in 1980, 96 percent of fifteen thousand manufacturing firms employed fewer than fifty workers and two-thirds employed fewer than ten (Mabry 1987:305). Manufacturing is based on a variety of light industries, including textiles; garments and leather products; computers and components; gems and jewelry; food, beverages, and tobacco; and plastic products. Employment in a large range of services has also grown rapidly in recent years (Sumalee 1984:6).

The composition of the work force is further complicated by the presence of seasonal immigrants, underemployed persons, and children. No data are available for persons in the first two categories, but in 1982 it was conservatively estimated that more than 1 million children between seven and eleven years—approximately 20 percent of the nonagricultural work force—were employed in the urban sector (Turton 1984:35). Underemployed workers comprised an estimated 5 percent of the nonagricultural work force in 1988, which was lower than in previous years.

In sum, the tremendous upheavals in Thai society wrought by rapid industrialization, together with the way in which workers are distributed across newly emerging industries, enterprises, and occupations, have made it difficult for unions to secure employee commitment. Without effective legal protection or union contracts, employees are liable to reprisals if they join and become active in unions. Such practices include blacklisting, sacking, and physical violence.

Union Structure and Competition

All unions that seek official registration are required to submit a copy of their regulations to the authorities. These must contain the name of the union, a statement of its objectives, the procedures through which members are admitted or expelled, the admission fee, and a copy of the union rules, which must outline the rights and duties of members as well as the organizational structure of the union. As B. D. Mabry (1979:72) observes, since most unions are enterprise-based, their internal structure is relatively simple. The rank and file elect a committee of representatives, who in turn elect an executive. An enterprise union organized at the Bangkok Weaving Mill, for example, has an elected committee of seventeen persons. These lay officials represent employees in processing grievances and in collective bargaining and pass on information from management to their constituents.

Unions provide few services for members, largely because they lack the funds. At the Bangkok Weaving Mill, the fee to join the union was 10 baht, and there was a monthly fee of 5 baht in 1984. These rates had not changed in more than ten years because the union was afraid of losing members (Hongladarom et al. 1985:22). The fee to join the sixteen thousand–member Thai Railway Workers' Union, the largest of six unions within the railways, was 10 baht, and the fee was 3 baht per month thereafter. In both these cases, as in most others, union dues represent less than half a percent of average earnings. The problem of limited resources is compounded by the large proportion of members who fail to pay their dues regularly. This is estimated at about 50 percent (Wehmhorner 1983:485).

Because of their weak finances, unions are reliant on either larger unions, federations, peak councils, or outside organizations for assistance. The number of union federations increased from six in 1980 to seventeen in 1990. There were three peak councils in 1980 and five ten years later. These are the Labor Congress of Thailand (*sapha ongkan lukcang raenggnan haeng prathetthai*) with 107 unions and 2 federations, and an affiliated membership of 78,166; the Thai Trade Union Congress (*sapha ongkan lukcang samaphan raenggnan haeng prathetthai* or TTUC), with 104 unions and a membership of 117,033; the National Labor Congress of Thailand, with 127 affiliated unions and

29,237 members; the Free Labor National Council, with 32 unions and 10,254 members; and the Thai Congress of Industrial Labor, with 11 unions and an estimated few thousand members (Thailand. Department of Labor 1990). The State Enterprise Labor Relations Group, comprising a loose coalition of state-enterprise unions, is the strongest labor organization in Thailand (U.S. Department of Labor 1990:3). These organizations are particularly important in mobilizing wider support for affiliates undertaking industrial action, assisting in organizing workers, and coordinating bargaining activity.

Various nongovernment agencies also provide training and specialized advice to unions. The most notable of these organizations are the Union for Civil Rights and Liberty, the Justice and Peace Group, the Asian Cultural Forum of Development, the Peoples' Association of Free Rights, and the Arom Phongphagnan Foundation (*Khaophiset,* 6–12 Feb. 1988). The Thailand Department of Labor also provides training seminars and workshops for union representatives.

Several international organizations also assist Thai unions in various ways. The most influential of these is the AFL-CIO's Asian-American Free Labor Institute (AAFLI), which has maintained a permanent presence in Thailand since the early 1970s. According to a recent report:

> AAFLI support was vital to pursuing Thai labor's agenda in virtually every area of concern, including labor law reform, improved attention to industrial health and safety, members' services like credit unions and child care centers, developing options to privatization, political lobbying, organization of private sector workers, promoting worker rights, et cetera (U.S. Department of Labor 1990:9).

Between 1972 and 1988, the AAFLI was reported to have conducted labor education and training programs for more than fifty-seven thousand Thai trade unionists (*Nation,* 14 Sept. 1988). Other international organizations, including the International Confederation of Free Trade Unions (ICFTU) and the ILO, have supported union demands for greater legal rights for Thai unions, a recent example being the ICFTU's request for affiliates to impose trade sanctions against Thailand "in retaliation for the government's disbanding state unions and banning strikes and other industrial action by state enterprise employees" (*Bangkok Post,* 2 July 1991, 3).

Interunion Rivalries

Although cooperation exists among unions, federations, and councils, the 1980s witnessed disunity within the ranks of organized labor. This was most apparent at the level of peak councils, in which continuing conflict seriously undermined union solidarity and organization. Such divisions were based on ideological, generational, and factional differences. In the discussion that follows, we focus on the ideological differences since these were the most visible source of problems affecting union solidarity in the 1980s.

Since the late 1940s, two broad ideological divisions have existed within the Thai union movement. On the one hand, there are those who argue that unions should restrict their objectives to the improvement of wages and conditions, that is, confine their aims to industrial issues. On the other hand, others argue that union power should also be used in the struggle for wider political and social reform. This basic division continued through the 1980s and created conditions that allowed outside elements to infiltrate the movement, thereby undermining labor solidarity. These developments can be illustrated by reference to the Labor Congress of Thailand over the past decade.

The Labor Congress was officially registered in 1979 with the support of public- and private-sector unions. The first president, Paisan Thawatchaianan, was a respected labor leader who attempted to keep the organization independent from politicians and civil and military groups. A split occurred within the Labor Congress during the early 1980s when Paisan's leadership was challenged by a rival faction led by Ahmad Kamthetthong and Sawat Lukdot. Both of these leaders had their power bases within the State Railways Union. Moreover, both were linked with the military through the Internal Security Operation Command (ISOC) through their close relationship with Prasoet Subsunthon, a former general secretary of the Communist Party of Thailand (CPT) who had been employed by ISOC as an adviser. Together with other military officers, Prasoet was influential in the formation of the government's anti-insurgency policies. These policies outlined a strategy through which politicians and the military aimed to defeat oppositional groups. Although the CPT was a central target of the strategy, organized labor represented another group against which this policy was directed.

Basically, the defeat of these groups was to be achieved through political rather than violent means. The government was to control, through cooptation, organizations that were based on mass support. Clearly, unions were a major target, and a committee comprising senior military officers was established specifically to deal with these organizations. Under plans formulated by this committee, it was decided that the military should refrain from intervening in strikes, that conflict should be resolved through a process of negotiation, and that measures should be adopted to prevent strikes and other forms of labor unrest from being used by "oppositional" political groups (Samrej 1987:158). To achieve these aims, the military decided first, to establish and support a rival congress to the Labor Congress, the Free Labor National Council *(saphaongkan lukcang raenggnanseri haengchat).* Second, a concerted attempt was made to infiltrate, coopt, and control the leadership of the

Labor Congress (Mabry and Srisermbhok 1985:625). In pursuing this latter objective, the military found two willing partners in Ahmad and Sawat, both of whom rejected Paisan's "laborism" and felt that the Labor Congress should also become involved in pressing for wider political change.

The relationship between the Ahmad/Sawat faction and various military elements became a public matter in 1983 when ISOC asked the governor of the state railways if the two unionists could work for ISOC (Wehmhorner 1983:488). This growing politicization of the Labor Congress became even more apparent during 1985. In return for a promised better deal for labor, Ahmad and Sawat began to cooperate more closely with military elements who had become dissatisfied with the Prem administration. As rumors of an impending coup proliferated, the leaders of the Labor Congress attempted to take advantage of worker dissatisfaction in both the state railways and the communication authority to further destabilize the Prem government. The politicization of these disputes was heavily criticized. Thus, during a strike by communication workers over proposed privatization plans, student groups claimed that the dispute was being used to create "political chaos" and workers were urged not to allow themselves to be used as "political tools" (*Bangkok Post*, 22 Jan. 1985).

In September 1985, there was an attempt to overthrow the Prem administration. It failed because Prem had support from key army divisions. Both Ahmad and Sawat were arrested after the failed putsch. This appeared to vindicate Paisan's warning that unions should restrict their objectives to the industrial arena and refrain from becoming entangled in politics.

After his defeat in the 1982 elections, Paisan resigned from the Labor Congress and established the rival peak council referred to earlier as the TTUC. This split divided the strongest body of organized labor throughout the first half of the 1980s.

Following the demise of Ahmad and Sawat, however, there was a growing recognition within the peak councils that greater cooperation was necessary. Thus, from 1986 on, the Trade Union Congress and the Labor Congress in particular began to discuss the possibility of merging.

Cooperation continued throughout 1986 and 1987, when it assumed a more concrete form in July 1987 in a common strategy aimed at the establishment of a national social security system and in support of other issues. Cooperation increased further during the early months of 1988 as the four major union councils joined in the labor welfare campaign and sought ways to overcome problems resulting from competition over positions in various tripartite bodies. A dispute at the Winner Textile Company over working conditions provided an additional opportunity to show solidarity.

Winner Textile Company had responded to local union demands by dismissing employees. Rallies were organized outside Government House, and scuffles with the police ensued. The dispute caught the attention of both the media and all major labor councils, and a number of arrests were reported (*Nation,* 11 April 1988). The Trade Union Congress came out in support of the workers and demanded that all workers be reinstated. Letters were sent to officials at the Department of Labor notifying the interior minister that the government had seven days to settle the dispute and ensure the workers were reemployed (*Nation,* 27 April 1988, 29 April 1988).

The protests continued over the following four months with numerous public rallies at which some workers slashed their arms and penned letters in blood to the prime minister (*Nation,* 2 May 1988, 29 June 1988, 8 July 1988). Following the election of the Chatichai government, the settlement of the dispute became a test for the new administration. A large rally was held outside Government House, which marked the beginning of a hunger strike. The government finally settled the six-month dispute after forcing management to assure the workers that they would be reinstated.

Despite the more cooperative atmosphere, divisions within the ranks of organized labor remained. And although the Trade Union Congress and the Labor Congress continued to hold discussions over the possibility of merging, disagreements remained among the four major councils over positions in tripartite bodies (*Nation,* 19 Feb. 1989, 2). Furthermore, in mid-1989, unions in Samutprakan, a relatively industrialized province, were planning to establish a fifth labor congress, which would further exacerbate union disunity (*Nation,* 2 May 1989, 8).

Union Goals and Methods

During the 1980s, unions struggled for the achievement of several goals, the most important of which were recognition of basic union rights, including employer compliance with the labor law; the defeat of government privatization plans; the improvement of members' pay and conditions, especially the abolition of inappropriate temporary work contracts; and the passage of social security legislation, in light of the high levels of unemployment and company retrenchments. Union leaders adopted various methods to achieve these goals: becoming involved in various tripartite committees; lobbying leading political figures and the press; staging street rallies, protests, and strikes; and making use of the official industrial relations machinery.

Under conditions laid down by the Labor Relations Act, a labor dispute is said to have occurred if within three days of receiving a demand either employers or employees have been unable to reach an agreement. When notification of a dispute is lodged at the Department of Labor, the conciliation officer must help resolve the dispute within five days. If the dispute remains unresolved, a strike or lockout may occur. Figure 3.1 shows the number of disputes and strikes over the years 1980–89 and strike severity (working days lost per thousand employees) over the same period.

Figure 3.1 indicates a strong surge in strikes in the early 1980s, followed by fluctuations around a declining trend. Political instability, high inflation, and a depressed manufacturing sector, which contributed to increasing unemployment, were the main factors behind the steep rise in strike activity. This rise was also facilitated by the return to workers of the right to strike in January 1981. The trend in strike severity

Figure 3.1. Industrial disputes and strikes in Thailand, 1980–89

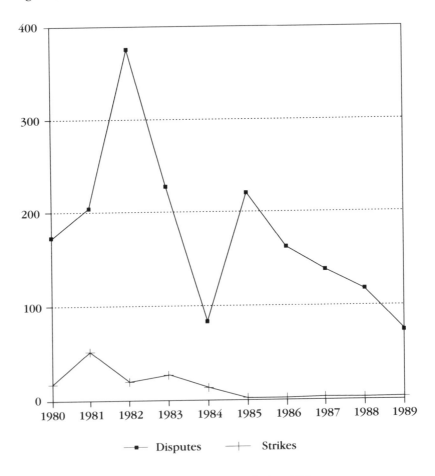

Source: Thailand. Ministry of Interior, Department of Labor. 1990.

(figure 3.2) is less clear-cut, but a decline in which the same factors are working in reverse is evident. Data for 1989 indicate that around three-quarters of the very few strikes that were officially recorded occurred in the manufacturing sector. Newspaper reports suggest that collective action tended to be concentrated in state enterprises. Dispute data for 1988 and 1989 show that the three most common grievances and demands centered on welfare issues encompassing working conditions and employee rights (34.8 percent), while nearly 20 percent concerned wages and about 18 percent focused on employment conditions (Thailand. Department of Labor 1989:126). Particular disputes will be mentioned below to illustrate issues of concern to workers and the methods used to pursue their objectives.

Figure 3.2. Working days lost (per thousand employees) in Thailand because of industrial disputes, 1980–89

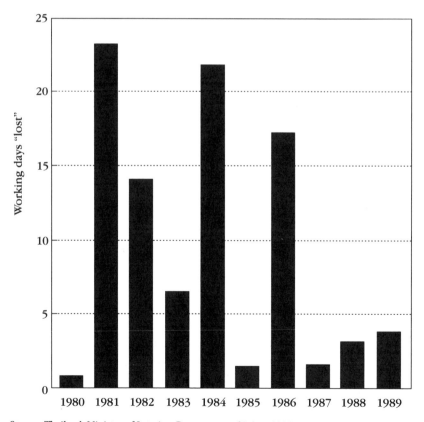

Source: Thailand. Ministry of Interior. Department of Labor 1990.

Struggles for Basic Rights and Employer Compliance with the Law

Following the military coup of October 1976, the government of Thanin issued a ministerial order that stated that all industrial disputes would be arbitrated by the minister of the interior. Strikes and lockouts were prohibited. Under the direction of the Labor Congress a decision was made in mid-1979 to conduct a campaign to force the government to rescind the order. By lobbying government officials, staging public protests, and organizing petitions and protest letters, the unions, led by the large state-enterprise organizations, were able to force the government of Prem Tinsulanonda to withdraw the order on 27 January 1981.

The lifting of the strike ban was part of what was to be a better deal for labor. Prem had reassured the unions of his government's commitment to addressing problems of unemployment, lack of education, ineffective labor law administration, and inadequate wages for state-enterprise employees. Prem also established the National Labor Development Advisory Board, a tripartite body designed to provide a "forum for discussion of labor problems and to recommend policies to deal with these problems" (Mabry and Srisermbhok 1985:622).

Linked to this campaign for basic rights, the Labor Congress also encouraged the government to ratify a number of ILO conventions. Among the most important were convention 87, which guarantees workers basic rights to associate freely and form unions; convention 98, which covers rights to collective bargaining; convention 135, which protects workers' representatives; and convention 151, which promotes union rights and reasonable employment conditions within state enterprises.

Initial letters sent to the government seeking ratification of these conventions were ignored. In 1981, a rally was organized outside the ILO office in Bangkok, and workers lodged a complaint with ILO representatives to the effect that the Thai government was violating workers' basic rights. It was not until 1983, however, that the government reached a decision on this issue. It ratified conventions 98 and 135 but not 87 and 151, the argument being that these conventions were "not appropriate to Thailand and that they contradicted . . . local administration practices" (Translation Services for Social Development 1991, appendix 3). It is noteworthy that as of 1 January 1991 Thailand had ratified only eleven of the ILO's conventions, the same number as Malaysia but fewer than China (seventeen) and Singapore (twenty-one) (ILO 1991a).

Another aspect of the struggle for basic rights related to attempts to force employers to abide by the labor law. From 1982 to 1986, the Thai economy went into recession (see chap. 1) as local capitalists faced their first "major crisis of accumulation in more than two decades" (Hewison

1989a:143). The crisis was marked by mounting foreign debt, a large increase in bankruptcies, and a significant decline in company profitability. By 1984, the problem of growing unemployment was receiving enormous press coverage and becoming the subject of widespread public debate. It was reported that 150,000 high school and university graduates were looking for work (*Matichon*, 29 Dec. 1984), while unemployment was said to have increased in 1985 from 1.5 to 1.7 million. Further, an additional 2 million persons were categorized as underemployed (*Matichon* 3 Feb. 1985). Moreover, 80,000 persons were reported to have migrated from the countryside to Bangkok, a figure expected to increase to 100,000 by 1986 (*Matichon*, 3 Jan. 1985).

With workers under pressure, employers began to pursue aggressive measures. In the first six months of 1984, 25,885 workers lost their jobs (*Matichon*, 16 Jan. 1985), and between October 1984 and May 1985, a total of 50,000 were reported to have been retrenched (Samrej 1987:173). Although some of the layoffs were the result of genuine company closings, it was becoming increasingly clear that employers were using the adverse conditions to undermine employment conditions and attack unions.

In this context the issue of temporary employment was fiercely opposed by Thai unions, which alleged that employers were making extensive use of such contracts to deny long-standing employees access to severance pay, sick leave, and other protections under the Labor Relations Act. Such contracts also tended to discourage union organization. In response to a strike threat, the government's tripartite National Labor Development Advisory Board drafted a ministerial order limiting the use of temporary contracts. This was subsequently endorsed by the government in October 1989; however, its ambiguous wording has meant that it has had only a limited impact on employment practices in the private sector (U.S. Department of Labor 1990:6).

Some employers have attempted to weaken unions directly, and unions have responded pragmatically. Thus, in 1984, management at the Thai Melon Polyester Company dismissed the entire work force. Increasingly known as the "kingdom of fear," the firm, situated in Patumthani, had been a joint venture between Sukree Bhodirattanangura, one of the most influential figures in the Thai textile industry, and French interests. In 1982, the French representative in the company was attacked by local gangsters, which led to the French withdrawing from the partnership. In 1975, two labor leaders in the factory were murdered; and in 1982 and 1983, a total of 155 workers who had been active in the union were sacked. When interviewed for positions at the company, prospective employees were informed that not joining the union was a precondition for gaining employment.

It seems that the 1984 strike was the result of a long period of pent-up frustration among the workers, as evidenced by the strike vote: 530 of the 560 employees agreed to strike. Although the dispute was passed to the Department of Labor for conciliation, no agreement was reached. A strike and lockout ensued. The company dismissed the workers and paid compensation, and the enterprise union disintegrated. The company subsequently advertised for new workers, who were to be employed under three-year contracts and paid on a daily basis (Asian Cultural Forum on Development 1984:4–5).[2]

Samrej Zeeponsekul (1987:174) highlights another example of an attempt by an employer to destroy a union. A union in a company that manufactured pet products submitted a list of demands to management. They were accepted. In 1985, when the agreement expired, the union put forward a new set of claims. These were countered by management, which sought to eliminate the pension fund, decrease wages, and change work rules to increase management control over employees. Although the union withdrew its demands, the company pursued its new policies. The factory was closed, the unionized workers were dismissed, and new workers were recruited.

A third and final example concerns the York Tyre and Rubber Company, where the owner closed his business on the day the new official minimum wage rate came into effect. Three hundred workers lost their jobs. This and other closings in the area, as well as a physical attack on the union president, were reported to have been aimed at undermining the power of the Industrial Union of Thailand (*Matichon,* 16 Jan. 1985). Formed in 1981, this union had been active and successful in raising wages and improving conditions and was said to have been the strongest local labor organization in the Omnoi region.

In some instances, unions have developed a more strategic response to employer aggression. The powerful Metropolitan Electricity Trade Union, for example, outlined a strategy for combating aggressive employers. This comprised the following seven elements. First, workers and union leaders needed to familiarize themselves better with all company regulations. Second, and related, they had to develop greater understanding of the labor law. Third, union leaders had to keep a closer watch over management to gather information. Fourth, the organizational structures and finances of unions had to be improved so that clear distinctions were made between policy formation and policy implementation, including efforts to amalgamate smaller unions into larger industrial-based unions or federations. Fifth, unions were encouraged to form alliances both with other unions and other organizations, including international labor organizations, nongovernment welfare agencies, and groups such as the Union for Civil Rights and Liberty and the Justice and Peace Group, and with political parties and student associations. Sixth, unions were urged to develop their own activities, including effective dissemination of information and the provision of better education, training, welfare, and legal services. Seventh, and finally, unions were advised to use the strike weapon more judiciously and to make greater use of company regulations and procedures that they might be able to exploit in their favor. Slowdowns, it was argued, could be an effective tactic to back up workers' demands (Samrej 1987:179–81).

With workers' rights under attack, there was an upsurge in complaints against employers for their disregard of the law. These included allegations that employers were paying below the minimum wage, refusing to recognize unions, dismissing workers unfairly, and evading compensation payments. Thus, in 1983, 3,762 cases were heard before the labor court. A year later the number had increased to 5,247. This change is also reflected in the steep rise in the number of disputes and working days lost, shown in figures 3.1 and 3.2. Most of the cases were brought by employees against employers who had not paid adequate compensation upon termination of employment. Over the two years, the court directed that employers pay a total of 120 million baht (approximately U.S. $5 million) in such compensation (*Bangkok Post,* 8 Jan. 1985).

The Labor Congress launched a campaign in late 1984 urging the government to reduce inflation and unemployment and limit widespread retrenchments and legal infringements. It also wanted the price of oil to be fixed, interest rates lowered, and more credit made available. It warned that if the government did not take the initiative, there would be a rise in labor militancy. It reiterated its position in early 1985, adding that it wanted the government to promulgate a social security law and actively to promote the further establishment of unions (*Matichon,* 24 Dec. 1984). Despite the warnings, the widespread violation of labor laws continued throughout the decade.

Opposition to Privatization

Opposition to privatization was a major objective pursued through the 1980s, particularly by state-enterprise unions, often in cooperation with the State Enterprise Labor Relations Group. In 1983, the Prem administration introduced several restructuring measures, including changes in executive boards and management systems; allowing private interests to acquire shares in state enterprises and become involved in management; and selling off existing public enterprises. This approach was continued by the Chatichai government, which, like its predecessor, did not consult the unions as part of the policy-making process.

The state-enterprise unions opposed the privatization plans on several grounds, which included the need to protect their members' wages and working conditions and because the plans constituted a potential threat to national security (Translation Services for Social Development 1991, appendix 5). It was argued that privatization could lead to essential services falling under foreign control, thereby compromising national security, especially where there was no domestic competition, as in the generation of electricity and the supply of water. The unions were supported in this position by the military.

Virtually all state-enterprise unions became involved in the campaigns against privatization. These included the port, tobacco, postal, railway, metropolitan, and water supply workers. Various strategies and tactics were used: public seminars and forums, the distribution of leaflets and other educational campaigns, public rallies, strikes, lobbying, and negotiations.

Industrial action by the port unions seemed to have a decisive impact on the Chatichai government. Disruption to port operations in 1989 and 1990, together with threats by electricity and telephone workers to undertake similar action, forced the government to postpone ongoing privatization projects pending the establishment of the tripartite State Enterprise Labor Relations Promotion Committee, responsible for achieving a consensus on policy options for state enterprises (U.S. Department of Labor 1990:5). As discussed later, following the 1991 coup, however, state-enterprise unions face legal extinction, though they may reappear in a new guise. Thus, the unions may have succeeded in halting the process of privatization but at a significant cost to their future security.[3]

Improving Pay and Conditions

Regulating wages and conditions through the establishment of collective bargaining contracts remains a key aim of the union movement. During the 1970s, negotiations were usually initiated by unions or employees' representatives; however, Samrej (1987:174) has observed that during the economic downturn of the early 1980s some employers, in an attempt to divide and destroy unions, began submitting counterdemands. The process of making claims (and counterclaims) is usually formalized. At least 15 percent of employees in any given enterprise must sign the demand. If the demand is submitted by a union, that organization must have at least one-fifth of the total number of employees in its membership. Any demand submitted by the union need not contain the names and signatures of employees. Employees' representatives in collective bargaining negotiations must be employees involved in the demands or committee members of the union or labor federation with which the employees making the demand are affiliated. The party receiving the demand must inform the opposing party of the names of its representatives, and negotiations between the parties must begin within three days from the date of receipt of the demand. If negotiations are successful, both parties typically sign an agreement, which is required to be posted for a period of thirty days at the workplace. The agreement must also be registered with the director general of the Labor Department. Agreements are not permitted to last longer than three years; most remain in force for at least a year.

Unfortunately, no data exist on the coverage of collective agreements over time, but according to the Thailand Department of Labor (1990:128), in 1989, 174 collective agreements were officially registered, 6 fewer than in the previous year. In both years slightly more than a third of these contracts were registered in Bangkok, although half the unions exist in this area. Table 3.1 shows that more than 90 percent of state-enterprise unions (which comprise close to 20 percent of all unions) are located in Bangkok, compared with 30 percent of the private-sector unions. It thus seems that private-sector unions in Bangkok are either less successful in obtaining and registering collective contracts than their counterparts in other regions—which is unlikely given the state of the labor market in the capital city and the proximity of the peak union bodies—or that state-enterprise unions conclude fewer collective bargaining contracts, assuming that they are required to register them. The explanation for this may lie in the fact that the wages and conditions of state-enterprise employees are regulated through statutory provisions rather than by collectively bargained contracts.

A strategy was devised by the Labor Congress in the early 1980s to enhance members' pay and strengthen the unions' bargaining position. According to Narong Petprasirt (1982:46), the aim was for each factory union committee to learn about collective bargaining procedures and gather information about their employer's business operations. In addition, such committees were expected to establish education programs for members to inform them of their rights and obligations under the law. Demands would then be made on the basis of increases in the cost of living, employers' capacity to pay, and awareness of pay and conditions at comparable firms. Strikes were to be used carefully; the emphasis was placed on other tactics, such as slowdowns, exposing employer secrets via the mass media, and public rallies (which included tactics such as burning effigies) aimed at highlighting workers' grievances. As figure 3.1 suggests, strike action was used sparingly, whereas newspaper reports indicate that protests and rallies were common throughout the 1980s.

Such tactics were clearly in evidence in the campaigns directed at increasing the minimum wage. Under the tripartite system, daily minimum wage levels were set by a national wages committee. Since wage levels proposed by workers' representatives have normally been rejected, attempts to increase minimum wage levels have tended to be accompanied by street protests and demonstrations. These minimum wage campaigns have met with some success: in 1978, the daily minimum wage was 35 baht (U.S. $1.40), but it was 78 baht (U.S. $3.10) in April 1989 and a further increase to 90 baht (U.S. $3.50) was scheduled for a year later (U.S. Department of Labor 1990:5). The problem of implementation remains, however.[4]

Social Security Legislation

The struggle to obtain social security protection in Thailand dates back to the 1950s, but little progress was made. A Workman's Compensation Fund provided limited benefits for on-the-job injuries and death. As mentioned above, in the late 1980s, the Labor Congress and Trade Union Congress began a renewed push for a social security law. Through public demonstrations and lobbying of politicians and political parties, the campaign eventually resulted in the promulgation of the Social Security Act of 1990. Though the act does not cover unemployment, it extends benefits for off-the-job injuries and death and maternity leave to workers in several relatively industrialized provinces, and it has provisions for extension to other areas (U.S. Department of Labor 1990:5).

Conclusion

From the foregoing it is apparent that the Thai union movement is weak and fragmented. Even though less than 5 percent of the work force is organized, there are more than seven hundred unions, most of which are organized on an enterprise basis. The existence of five major umbrella organizations complicates matters further. Our analysis suggests, however, that in assessing Thai unions we need to distinguish between private-sector unions and those organizing employees in state enterprises.

Private-sector unions, which comprise the majority, remain very weak, although their position has improved marginally over the decade. Nevertheless, without effective government support and in the face of employer opposition, the vast majority of private-sector workers remain unprotected and have undoubtedly been exploited. Over the past five years, the AFL-CIO has regularly filed petitions against Thailand alleging deficiencies in the legal provision of workers' rights. Practices cited include employer imposition of individual contracts, in effect excluding workers from sick leave and severance pay provisions, and, more generally, union protection; the dismissal of workers for union activity; inhibiting union organizing and servicing of members; making it illegal for Thai union officials to be employed as workers outside the relevant enterprise or industry; proscribing union organization among civil servants; and the employment of child labor (*Nation,* 29 April 1988). If these petitions were accepted, they would exclude Thailand from tariff advantages under provisions of the law amending the U.S. generalized system of preferences (U.S. Department of Labor 1990:6–7). The U.S.

government has not acceded to the AFL-CIO's demands; rather, it has responded by pointing to gradual progress in Thai labor law.

Amid the persistence of such problems, how is the decline in strikes to be explained? Three interpretations can be suggested. First, wages, and probably working conditions, have been improving, thereby limiting worker dissatisfaction. Thus, real earnings per employee in manufacturing increased 6.3 percent per year from 1980 to 1988 (World Bank 1991:216). This has been largely the result of economic growth and shortages in some labor markets. Second, there is some evidence that human resource management techniques are being increasingly used in the larger private-sector enterprises to increase worker commitment (Siengthai 1988). Third, an increasing number of the most resilient and enterprising workers—around 267,500 persons in January 1989 (U.S. Department of Labor 1990:9)—have been working in other countries, in effect depriving the union movement of potentially valuable resources.

The relatively strong state-enterprise unions have succeeded in advancing their members' interests. Research on comparative earnings shows that state-enterprise employees were receiving 28 percent more pay than private-sector employees in 1982, a gap that widened to 51 percent by 1987. In that year skilled state-enterprise employees were earning 91 percent more than their private-sector counterparts, while semiskilled workers in these organizations were earning 99 percent more. By contrast, state-enterprise managers were earning 11 percent less than private-sector managers (*Bangkok Post* 1988).[5]

State-enterprise unions were also at the forefront of more general struggles for basic rights in the 1980s, assisting private-sector unions in campaigns to force employers to abide by the law and protesting against unfair labor practices. Major gains were made in the political sphere, as evident in the campaign to halt the privatization of state enterprises and in the government's decision to introduce social welfare legislation. Such successes probably alarmed the military, however, which undoubtedly disapproved of the rise of labor as a countervailing political force. Hence, as described in the postscript to this chapter, following the 1991 coup, the very existence of the state-enterprise unions was directly challenged.

Although rapid economic growth and labor shortages augur well for the future, union development in Thailand depends on the outcomes of struggles in the political sphere. Should the tendency toward a parliamentary form of political representation persist, a strategically powerful, albeit small, union movement will continue to grow. If history is any guide, however, union development will be forestalled by a new authoritarian regime, especially if the military is able to overcome the internal divisions that have plagued it since the 1970s. Clearly, the Chatichai government, widely accused of corruption, is unpopular.

Postscript

On 23 February 1991, the military did, in fact, reassert control. The democratically elected Chatichai government was disbanded, the constitution abrogated, and martial law imposed. While the National Peacekeeping Council has stated that it intends to restore democracy to Thailand, the precise nature and form of this democracy are unclear at this time (July 1991), especially in light of the junta's policy toward labor. State-enterprise unions, which, as noted above, constitute the backbone of organized labor in Thailand, are to be excluded from protection of the Labor Relations Act. In April 1991, the cabinet approved two relevant bills. The first removed state-enterprise workers from the provisions of the Labor Relations Act, and the second, entitled the State Enterprises Employees Relations Act, lays down rules that will govern and regulate labor relations within public enterprises. This bill effectively undermines workers' bargaining power by removing their right to strike. State-enterprise workers will be allowed to form associations, but such bodies must restrict their objectives to welfare issues. In order not to breach international labor conventions, the government will allow these organizations to be referred to as unions. Workers found guilty of instigating work stoppages will be liable to jail terms of up to one year and fines of up to 20,000 baht. On 15 April 1991, these bills were rapidly passed by the military-appointed National Assembly and so became law.

The new legislation plunged the union movement into deep crisis. All leaders of state-enterprise unions have had to relinquish their positions on peak councils. They have also had to surrender their positions on tripartite committees. Under these conditions the immediate future of unionism in Thailand looks bleak. At the same time, state-sector unions may be able to reorganize as associations while maintaining the commitment of the rank and file. When the government reverts to civilian rule, as promised, the unions may yet assert themselves. In the meantime, private-sector unions will find it more difficult to influence both employer and government policy. Where new unions do emerge, they are likely to assume the form of company unions, reflecting the preference and power of larger employers. In the longer term, tendencies toward more advanced industrialization and democratization will encourage worker autonomy, though the extent to which unions will be an attractive option remains to be seen.

4

State Regulation and Union Fragmentation in Malaysia

Ponniah Arudsothy and Craig R. Littler

The aim of this chapter is to examine the origins and development of Malaysian trade unionism, to outline the current structure of trade unions in both the private and public sectors, and, finally, to consider the future of the Malaysian union movement. One theme should be underlined at the start: an examination of unions in Malaysia, unlike one of unions in Australia or New Zealand, does not provide a broad picture of either industrial relations or employment relations. As we shall see, union densities are low, unions are small, and the significance of the state is crucial.

A second theme of this chapter is that there has been a lack of stability in Malaysian unions. It is difficult to construct a simple narrative in connection with the Malaysian situation—the process has been one of constant flux. One argument, advanced by B. Sharma (1985), is that unionism in Malaysia has evolved from a British-patterned mode of voluntarism to one of arbitration. This argument ignores the facts, however: British-style unions were never really established in Malaysia, and as soon as a state-dominated structure of arbitration had crystallized, the state emphasized the need for in-house, or enterprise, unions.

A third theme of this chapter, and one that distinguishes Malaysia from the other ASEAN countries, is that ethnic antagonism has helped shape the Malaysian state, economic policies, and the union movement. The ethnic composition of both the union membership and leadership changed dramatically in the postwar years. For the 1984–88 period, the participation of Bumiputra (i.e., Malay) workers topped that of other ethnic groups, accounting for more than 55 percent (Malaysia. Ministry of Labour 1988:6) of the work force.[1]

One distinctive feature of Malaysian trade unionism—a constant through many changes—is the small size of most of the unions. Compared with Western unions, those in Malaysia are decidedly small: between 1946 and 1987, the average membership was never more than two thousand and was usually fewer than fifteen hundred. This characteristic has given rise to the term *peanut unions* in the context of Malaysia.

The chapter concludes by examining possible future trends in Malaysian unionism. From the perspective of 1992, it is difficult to say whether a new conception of unionism is emerging or whether there has been a "transformation of industrial relations." The palette at present is messy—traces of enterprise unions; traces of the past, marked by small occupational unions; signs of paternalism in the public sector (the Association of Female Employees in the Government Sector [PUSPANITA]); and, above all, continued constraints by the state. It seems clear that the 1990s will not bring the emergence of Western-style trade unions in an Anglo-American mold.

The material for this chapter comes from four sources. First, statistical data and discussions are derived from official reports. Although the quality of these data is high overall, they are still tainted by an optimistic interpretation of events and situations for the simple reason that the propaganda of industrial peace attracts multinational dollars. Second, the chapter is based on material from the union movement, including union journals such as *Suara Buruh*. Third, Ponniah Arudsothy has had discussions and interviews with Malaysian Trade Union Congress (MTUC) officials over many years. Fourth, and finally, we have accumulated information from a limited number of secondary sources that discuss the development of Malaysian labor relations and labor law.

Socioeconomic Background

At the time of independence, in 1957, Malaysia was essentially a primary commodities–producing country where foreign capital was heavily concentrated in the rubber plantation and tin-mining sectors. There were some associated interests in the service sector. The first government of Malaysia, made up of conservative elements from Malay civil servants, fringe members of the aristocracy, Chinese business groups, and clan leaders and middle-class Indians, tried to preserve the traditional structures of the colonial economy lest their leadership and influence be challenged by opposition groups. The new government pursued a strategy of exploiting Malaysia's considerable resource advantage in the well-developed plantation economy and the lucrative mining sector, which in combination accounted for about 80 percent of export income.

Faced with rising unemployment and the absence of further expansion in the traditional sectors of the economy, the government introduced the Pioneer Industries Act in 1958, which sought to attract foreign capital, which would be well protected by tax concessions and tariff walls. In 1957, agricultural workers, who were generally low skilled, constituted 59 percent of the total labor force, and even by 1965 they remained the dominant category of labor, at 55 percent. Corresponding ratios for industrial production workers, who were just emerging in a variety of import-substituting industries, were 6 and 9 percent respectively.

It was only after the political crisis of 1969 and the economic downturn of 1969–70 that a major move was made to liberalize foreign investment opportunities, through not only traditional tariff-based domestic market protection but free trade zones (FTZs). The impact was seen in the sectoral distribution of GDP for the period 1971–75: manufacturing showed the highest rate of growth, almost double that of trade and tourism, the second most dynamic sector (see table 4.1).

The rapid growth of manufacturing is reflected in the annual rate of increase in the Malaysian labor force (6.5 percent) during 1971–80. This was in large measure due to the promotion of FTZs in Malaysia: the approvals of export-oriented projects by the Ministry of Trade and Industry rose threefold from 1971 to 1975. Another indicator of the increasingly important role played by FTZs in Malaysian industrialization is the ratio of the value of manufactured exports to manufactured imports: this showed a phenomenal increase, from 29 percent in 1970 to 151 percent in 1982. One effect of these developments has been a rapid rise in the proportion of manufacturing workers in Malaysia: by 1990, manufacturing and trade and tourism each accounted for about 32 percent of the labor force. This dramatic growth has not had a significant impact on union strength, however, as is evident from the data in table 4.2.

Table 4.1. GDP growth in Malaysia, by industrial sector, 1971–90

	Average annual growth rates (%)			
	1971–75	*1976–80*	*1981–85*	*1986–90*
Agriculture	4.8	3.9	4.2	2.6
Mining	0.4	8.9	6.1	3.1
Manufacturing	11.6	13.5	4.9	6.4
Trade and tourism	6.3	8.2	7.1	6.3
Government services	10.1	9.1	9.8	4.1
Total	7.1	8.6	5.8	4.7

Source: Malaysia. Prime Minister's Department 1981–85, 1986–90.

Table 4.2.   Labor force structure and union strength in Malaysia,
1957–90

	1957	1965	1970	1975	1980	1985	1990
Agricultural workers (%)	59	55	48	43	39	35	32
Production workers (%)	6	9	25	28	29	30	31
No. of unions	168	286	251	267	290	296	322
Average membership of unions	888	1,146	1,475	1,992	1,868	1,920	1,778

Source: Malaysia. Ministry of Labour, various years.
The 1990 figures are estimates only. Agricultural and production workers are expressed as
a percentage of total employees.

Over the past thirty-five years, Malaysia has been transformed from a
primary commodities producer to a relatively industrialized society. The
first phase of development (1957–69) was slow and was based on import
substitution. The second phase of export-oriented industrialization
(1970 to the present, under the so-called New Economic Policy) has
witnessed rapid changes in the labor market and the broader economic
structure. During the 1980s these changes were fueled mainly by Japanese and NIC investment.

In some ways the development situation in Malaysia has been favorable. Though subject to fluctuations in the prices of commodities, a
limited skill base, and ethnic conflicts, Malaysia has a small population
(17.5 million in 1989), limited demographic pressures, and a reasonable
standard of living by Asian standards (in 1989, GNP per capita was U.S.
$1,820, compared with U.S. $650 in the Philippines).

Origins and Development of Malaysian Unions

Understanding trade unions and industrial relations practices in Malaysia today requires some knowledge of the history of the colonial period
and developments during the 1960s and 1970s. Most of the early
organizations were mutual benefit or friendly societies formed by Chinese workers to promote their interests. Such societies were registered
under the Societies Ordinance and could not legally take on the normal
functions of a trade union even though they looked after the welfare of
workers (Khoo 1972; Parmer 1964).

Authorities in the British colonial territories were not favorably disposed to legislative reforms, particularly those that sought to intervene
in the market. In the economic depression of the 1930s, however, the
Colonial Office was able to pressure the governments of the dependent
territories to adopt some model pieces of legislation (including labor
laws) with the inducement of budgetary assistance. To meet the growing
unrest in the waged labor sector caused by the rising prices of basic

necessities and declining real incomes, the colonial administration in Malaysia prepared new labor laws to regulate unions. When the colonial administration finally adopted the Trade Union Ordinance in 1940, however, giving legal status to unions, it could not be implemented because of the outbreak of World War II and the occupation of Malaysia by the Japanese. Given these events, the history of unionism in Malaysia can be said to have begun after World War II. In 1946, the British Military Administration reintroduced the Trade Union Ordinance—a set of regulations that had become common in most British colonial territories.

After independence in 1957, the government consolidated all the existing pieces of legislation on unions in a new piece of legislation called the Trade Unions Act of 1959. With subsequent amendments, this law now governs most aspects of the establishment and administration of unions, as well as their supervision and control. Thus, key Malaysian legislation embodies British colonial traditions, unlike the situation in, for example, Thailand or the Philippines.

From their inception in 1946, Malaysia's trade union laws were criticized by union leaders for their essentially undemocratic character, principally the requirement of compulsory registration. The official explanation at the time was that compulsory registration gave a union legal status, which was associated with some important rights, including the ability to take legal action in its own name (ILO 1962:62). But it soon became apparent that the colonial administration wanted to use the device of registration to supervise and control unions in the same manner as it had been used to control societies. Through the Societies Ordinance, the government had been able to control political opposition to the regime, by distinguishing between legal and illegal societies, the latter of which were subject to police prosecution (Barraclough 1984). As the subsequent history of unions in Malaysia was to show, the Registrar of Trade Unions was able to use the device of registration to favor politically acceptable unions and to discriminate against their more militant counterparts, led by the Communist Party or its front organizations.

The registrar had taken a similar approach to managing the unprecedented growth in unions after 1945, illustrated in figures 4.1 and 4.2. Between 1946 and 1947, union membership rose by about 190 percent, while the number of unions rose from 83 to 270, a staggering growth of 225 percent. Denied legal political status, the Communist Party sought to build up its support by forming unions in different industries and occupations (among both employees and self-employed tradesmen) and structuring them under centrally organized general unions. Further, Communist leaders sought to create the potential for revolution by frequently using the strike weapon and even staging armed attacks against employers in remote areas, such as plantations and mines. In

Figure 4.1.   Number of unions in West Malaysia by sector, 1946–79

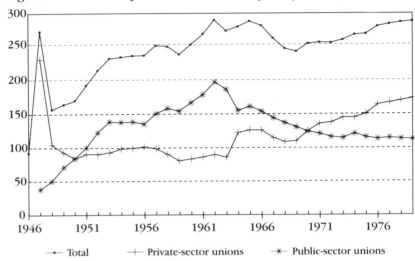

—•— Total   —+— Private-sector unions   —*— Public-sector unions

Source: Malaysia. Ministry of Labour, various.

1948, the colonial administration justified the declaration of a state of emergency throughout the country on the grounds of growing political insurgency and terrorism, and assumed extraordinary powers of arrest and detention without trial against anyone suspected of working for the Communist cause. Among those arrested were many unionists.

During 1947 and 1948—which witnessed the declaration of emergency and the registrar being given additional powers to check the growth of large "omnibus" or general unions, particularly those that were being organized by Communist groups—union membership declined by 64 percent while the number of registered unions fell by 42 percent. The clearest indication of the impact of the government's assumption of emergency powers is provided by a comparison of the period from December 1947 to December 1949, which shows a union membership decline of 78 percent (see figure 4.2; Gamba 1962:365). Thus, the early postwar period witnessed state repression of militant or Communist unions; stunted union growth, despite the legalization of unions; and the emergence of small unions as Communist-led general or omnibus unions were deregistered.

The coalition of mainly communal and elite-led parties that have formed the appropriately named Alliance government in Malaysia since independence has been even less sympathetic to the union movement than the colonial administration. Thus, despite protests by the Malaysian Trade Union Congress, the first national government of the country

Figure 4.2. Union membership in West Malaysia by sector, 1946–79

Source: Malaysia. Ministry of Labour, various.

introduced conditions that were even more restrictive to the formation and activities of unions, such as funding strikes or political parties.

Thus, in contrast to the situation in neighboring Singapore, which experienced similar sociopolitical developments and had almost identical labor laws, the Malaysian government made little effort to co-opt the trade unions into the government or party structure. While aggressive methods of forcing independent and left-wing unions into the People's Action Party mold succeeded in Singapore, in Malaysia the union movement was forced to look for support from opposition political groups, such as the Labor Party and the Parti Rakyat (Peoples' Party).

Over the decade 1965–75, the conservative parties in the Malaysian government twice invoked emergency rule, first to protect the nation against Indonesian hostility (1965) and later to preserve national unity and political stability in the wake of ethnic rivalries and riots (1969). On both occasions union laws were amended so that both freedom of association and freedom to undertake collective bargaining, as well as other rights to function independently, became severely restricted. The Trade Union Congress complied with the government imposition of a ban in 1965 on all industrial activity, in the interest of national security, but it was not prepared for the additional government measures to restrict free collective bargaining taken after the emergency. These were achieved through the introduction of an extensive body of industrial relations law that was incorporated into the new Industrial Relations Act of 1967. The setting up of an industrial court under the act was interpreted by union leaders as an attempt to shift the emphasis from free collective bargaining to compulsory arbitration and to deny union leaders an appropriate platform for worker education and mobilization, especially since unions were expected to cease all activity once a dispute was referred to the court. Moreover, the benefits of the court were denied unions in the public sector, unless prior permission was given by the *agong* (head of state). After the 1969 political crisis, which was accompanied by the suspension of Parliament for about a year, additional restraints were imposed on unions and their leaders.

In general, the early history of Malaysian unions was marked by British colonial traditions plus a series of postindependence political crises that threatened the survival of the state. Within this context, unions were regulated as political rather than economic institutions. An understanding of these processes is critical to an understanding of union formation in Malaysia.

Union Density

Between 1957 and 1989, union membership levels fluctuated with economic and political developments. Membership reached a preindependence peak of 232,174 in 1956 and declined until 1959; absolute levels rose steadily in the early 1960s to 327,673 in 1965 but declined in the latter 1960s and bottomed out in 1970. Through the 1970s and 1980s, membership levels in absolute terms increased, reaching 617,521 by the end of 1988.

The picture in terms of union density is less impressive. Overall, the data indicate that union membership has not kept pace with employment growth. Thus, whereas union membership accounted for 21 percent of total wage employment in 1947, the ratio remained at about 18 percent and declined during the latter part of the 1980s to 14 percent of nonagricultural (but including plantation) employment, even though waged labor was the fastest-growing category in the labor force.

There are some problems in estimating union density data in Malaysia, especially because of the prevalence of temporary and casual labor in construction, commerce, and services. These difficulties result in some lower estimates—as low as 9.9 percent in the latter part of the 1980s (e.g., see Hing Ai Yun 1990), compared with 18 percent in 1985 (see table 4.3). Ministry of Labour officials put private-sector union density in the range of 7 to 10 percent. Further details are given in table 4.3, which shows union density in both the private and the public sectors.

How does one explain these trends—fluctuating membership levels and a continued low, or declining, union density—in a rapidly industrializing economy? The decline in union membership during the latter part of the 1950s can be attributed to two general economic conditions—a recession and high levels of unemployment—as well as to the

Table 4.3. Number of unions and union density in Malaysia, by major industries, 1985

Industry	No. of unions	Density (%)
Plantation agriculture	28	46
Mining	4	25
Manufacturing	62	11
Construction	4	0.4
Electricity and water	7	53
Commerce	19	5
Transport and communications	69	26
Services	176	20
Sector		
Private (estimate)	161	7
Government	131	43
Statutory authority	100	49
Total	761	18

Source: Malaysia. Ministry of Labour 1988.

effects of deregistration. The deregistration of the National Union of Factory and General Workers (NUFGW) in 1957, for example, and of the Malaysian Mining Employees' Union and the National Union of Transport Workers in 1959 left a substantial number of workers unorganized. The effects of deregistration between 1957 (independence) and 1969 can be seen in table 4.4.

State opposition to unionism is not the total explanation for the slow increase in growth. Employer resistance to unionization also is a factor. Many employers have refused to recognize the rights of unions to represent the interests of workers and have victimized worker activists. Employers have used the full panoply of tactics—dismissals, intimidation, bribery, anti-union clauses in contracts, and company unionism—to discourage independent unionism. Union busting and anti-union activities increased during the 1980s compared with the 1970s, and according to an MTUC survey, indigenous companies were the worst offenders (*Suara Buruh* [journal of the MTUC], June 1988). Significantly, workers resisted threats to job security by engaging in industrial action—working days lost from strikes increased substantially in the mid-1980s—but as employment prospects picked up in the latter part of the decade, the number of strikes declined to levels below those at the start of the decade (Malaysia. Ministry of Labour 1989:43).

One area in which unionization has made little headway is in the so-

Table 4.4. Newly registered and deregistered unions in Malaysia,
1957–69

Year	New	Voluntarily dissolved	Ceased to exist	Deregistered[a]
1957	37	13	4	2
1958	35	5	17	9
1959	20	18	5	12
1960	48	17	13	6
1961	38	14	2	6
1962	38	14	2	1
1963	26	28	2	10
1964	24	12	n.a.	5
1965	23	6	4	4
1966	10	9	4	4
1967	3	18	1	4
1968	9	13	6	5
1969	7	6	3	3

Source: Todd and Jomo 1988.
[a]Action was taken by the Registrar of Trade Unions for such reasons as failing to submit annual returns, illegally constituting the union executive, participating illegally in political activities, or competing with another union already operating within the same trade, occupation, or industry.

called pioneer industries. There is a provision in the Industrial Relations Act (1967), Section 15, which protects pioneer industries during the initial years of their establishment against any unreasonable demands from a trade union. Thus, there was a three-year restriction on unionization. In 1980, the law was amended to extend the ban on unionization indefinitely (Wu 1982:78).

Many of the workers in the pioneer industries sector are females employed in electronics. There was considerable struggle over the unionization of workers in this sector during the 1980s. At the start of the decade, there were 48,500 workers in electronics; by 1985, the figure was close to 90,000 (MTUC 1985:54). The Electrical Industry Workers' Union (EIWU) was registered in 1971 and has campaigned to unionize electronics workers. Although the EIWU has criticized the MTUC for its weakness, by 1984 EIWU membership was only 8,142, and by 1989 the membership was still only a very small percentage of the potential.

A recent state policy, discussed later in this chapter, of encouraging enterprise unions along Japanese lines may have significant effects on union density since unions or work groups are now even more vulnerable to employer action. This general trend is compounded in the Malaysian case by the lack of organizational expertise among the labor force and by ethnic divisions. The Bumiputra/non-Bumiputra conscious-ness has become sharper since the early 1970s.

One barrier to the development and spread of even enterprise union-ism is the stubborn resistance of several multinational firms, especially in the FTZs, to unionization of any kind (Kuruvilla 1992). In 1989, for example, one American multinational electronics corporation was re-ported to have intimidated workers who were considering joining an in-house union. The company's security guards confiscated membership forms and pursued a union-avoidance program. The unions' pro tem president was reported as stating: " 'The management has been discour-aging workers from signing up as members and threatening them that if they did so, the plant will be closed down in three months and the operations will be moved to either Taiwan or Thailand' " (*New Straits Times,* 6 Feb. 1989).

These actions are in clear violation of the Industrial Relations Act of 1967. One reason for employers' success in avoiding unionization of their work forces is the preponderance (more than 92 percent) of females, most in their late teens or early twenties, among the production workers in this industry (Malaysia. Ministry of Labour 1988:76).

In the next section we look at the structure of Malaysian unions. Once again, it is not possible to understand union structure without consider-ing the processes of state regulation.

Structure of Malaysian Trade Unions

The Malaysian law on unions and the functioning of the office of the Registrar of Trade Unions have affected not only the external patterns of unions but also their internal structures. Government authorities have consistently had the power to investigate the internal affairs of unions, including their finances. The processes of legal recognition, or registra-tion, for example, provide an avenue for state pressure. Before a union acquires legal status, a petition signed by seven members of the union must be forwarded to the registrar, together with a list of potential officers and a statement detailing their past job and union experiences. There are no avenues of appeal against unfavorable decisions by the registrar, so that the prospective union leadership is likely to be per-suaded to adopt the registrar's suggestions and to comply with govern-ment demands rather than adhere to rank-and-file wishes.

As we have seen, the majority of Malaysian trade unions are small by Western standards. To underline this point, in 1986, slightly more than half had five hundred or fewer members, and 67.7 percent had one thousand or fewer members (Malaysia. Ministry of Labour 1988). Malay-sian unions tend to have an enterprise or local orientation and to have a simple, nonhierarchical structure; officials work for their unions part time. This is the case for unions with a membership restricted to a single enterprise or company, as in the Dunlop Industry Employees' Union. In the public sector, the registrar's rigid interpretation of the Trade Unions Act of 1959 has forced employees to form enterprise-type unions (such as the Rubber Research Institute Union or specific hospital unions) with no prospect of forming federations with other public-sector unions. Some other restricted "single" unions have been able to grow by mobilizing workers from an extended geographical area, an example being the Penang Textile Workers' Union, which now covers the island of Penang and parts of the mainland. The largest unions in Malaysia are the national unions, such as the National Union of Plantation Workers and the National Union of Transport Workers, which maintain regional branches.

Most of Malaysia's unions have the simple structure of a single union, whether they are organized at local/enterprise or state/regional levels (as most textile unions are). Only unions in the third category, those organized at the national level, maintain an elaborate structure of intermediation between the union executive and the members. Even unions organized at regional or state levels have simple organizational structures whereby members interact directly with largely untrained officials. These unions do not have branches, and supreme decision-making power is vested in the general meetings of the members. The structure of the National Union of Plantation Workers, the largest single union in Malaysia, can be used to illustrate the structural differences between unions.

The National Union of Plantation Workers (NUPW) was a product of a merger in the 1950s of several unions that were variously organized at regional, state, and workplace levels. The union has various state committees that are responsible for electing delegations to its national meetings, at which the principal officers of the union are elected. This aggregation of small and medium-sized unions into a large union with a claimed membership of about 200,000 in the early 1950s was in contrast with the forced fragmentation of other large unions into peanut unions. The process of aggregation would have occurred without the support of the colonial administration. In other words, the structural outcome had little to do with rank-and-file actions but depended on anti-Communist and ethnic politics.

At a more general level, we can distinguish between various union federations, the largest of which is the MTUC. The MTUC was formed in 1950 after suppression of the Communist unions and their leaders. It was known then as the Malayan Trade Union Council. The name was changed to the Malayan Trade Union Congress in 1956 and to the Malaysian Trade Union Congress in 1963, some six years after independence.

Whatever its name, the MTUC has not been a strong, central organization. It has had no role in wage fixing and has concentrated its efforts on labor education and political firefighting over the almost annual round of changes to labor laws and regulations. In 1980, union members in 99 affiliated unions accounted for 57.6 percent of total union membership. The most recently available data show that in 1985 126 MTUC affiliates accounted for only 46.4 percent of total union membership (Malaysia. Ministry of Labour 1988:117). Legally, the MTUC has no status as a trade union organization; instead, it is registered under the Societies Ordinance, which restricts its functions. Thus, the MTUC may not take part in any wage negotiations or assist in any industrial action. Instead, it has a Political Affairs Bureau and is involved in political lobbying.

The MTUC was further weakened in 1990 by the registration of a rival apex organization known as the Malaysian Labour Organization (MLO). The latter has been promoted by the Bank Employees' Union with "behind-the-scenes" support from the government. As of 1990, the MLO consisted of fifteen unions with a claimed membership of 142,000, compared with a claimed membership of 500,000 for the MTUC.

Figure 4.3 shows the structure of the Malaysian union movement with the apex organizations and the geographical divisions. Public-sector employees have a separate peak council, known as the Congress of Unions of Employees in the Public and Civil Services (CUEPACS).

Federations of unions are possible under Malaysian law. They can be approved by the registrar (Section 72) if they comprise unions "whose members are employed in a similar trade, occupation or industry." In other words, general federations are prohibited.

The impact of the federations on the performance of unions in

Figure 4.3. Structures of Malaysian unions and geographical divisions (MTUC, mainly private sector, and CUEPACS, the public sector)

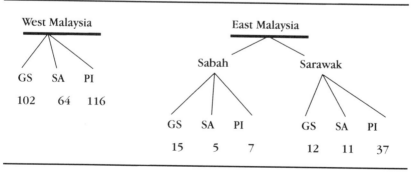

Source: Malaysia. Ministry of Labour 1989.
GS = government service; SA = statutory authority; PI = private industry.

Malaysia can be largely discounted. There have been only three such federations, all in the public sector. The largest, CUEPACS, had fifty-two affiliates and an estimated 114,475 members in 1985. The teachers' federation (Congress of Unions of Teachers in the Education Service) has eight affiliates and an estimated membership of nearly 25,000. The Sarawak Wharf Laborers' Union Federation has fifteen affiliates but only 1,324 members as of 1985 (Malaysia. Ministry of Labour 1988).

A basic split exists in the pattern of Malaysian unionism between the public sector and the private sector. In particular, the 1970s and the 1980s involved a denial of negotiation rights in the public sector. Consequently, the next two sections consider these sectors separately.

Trade Unions in the Public Sector

In the early postwar years, the colonial administration's attitude toward unionization among its own employees remained ambivalent. On the one hand, there was the view that any policy of unionization in the public service would politicize the administration and undermine the authority of the government; on the other hand, public servants formed the largest group of better educated workers and could thus set an example for the rest of the work force of how to organize and operate "moderate and responsible unions" (ILO 1962:81).

The original trade union enactment of 1940, and its replacement in 1946, prohibited "public officers" from forming or joining unions, except by special exemption "orders." After independence, the government of Malaysia retained this formula for workers directly employed by the government. This was codified in Section 27 of the Trade Unions Act of 1980, but the armed forces, the police, and the prison service were excluded, as were government employees in managerial or professional positions and those who worked in a confidential or security capacity in any government department.

Other government employees were able to join unions, provided these covered only government-sector workers. The registrar applied this rule of exclusive membership to government workers so strictly that there were practically no "mixed unions" across sectors. The only exceptions were the teachers' unions, which had members in both government and nongovernment schools. Thus, throughout the 1950s and 1960s, there were effectively three distinct groups of employees in the public sector: civil service employees; employees in local authorities, such as town councils; and employees in statutory authorities. Not only did these three segments have exclusive areas of unionization but they developed different systems of industrial relations within their work environments.

The registrar made an exception, however, of the members of the Amalgamated National Union of Local Authorities. These workers could not form enterprise unions because of the very small size of many of their establishments, especially since laws strictly limited union membership to specific trades or occupations.

Although civil service employees may have been expected to be less subject to this process of balkanization, the evidence shows that the separation between the three administrative regions was retained from the colonial past and that the registrar strictly separated employees not only according to federal and state government criteria but also based on the special "occupational" characteristics of the different ministries. Thus, in-house unions were a distinct feature of administratively structured Malaysian unions before the arrival of the Look East policy of the 1980s, discussed in more detail below (Jomo 1983:283).

From the trade unions' point of view, the problem continued to be the unchallenged powers of the registrar, which encouraged this "variety" so that the prevailing condition in the organized labor sector would be the endemic financial and organizational weakness of the multiplicity of peanut unions. This financial weakness is evident insofar as no public-service union has a paid union organizer.

The 1969 emergency regulations and the 1971 amendments to the Trade Unions Act of 1959 extended the requirement of exclusivity applied to unions of government employees, to workers in statutory authorities. Workers in statutory authorities were additionally constrained, however, by a requirement that they had to belong to a union organized within the particular authority that employed them. Within an enterprise, hierarchical occupational gradations took over, so that in each statutory authority there are unions catering to different categories of workers. In the National Electricity Board, for example, four different unions were established to represent the different grades of workers, embracing senior officers, junior officers, technical staff, and general staff respectively.

As an ILO mission observed of the nature of Malaysian unions generally: "What is characteristic of the unions in Malaysia is their variety. The only common feature among them all is that they must be registered by the Registrar of Trade Unions" (ILO 1962:38). University unions (covering academic and nonacademic staff), for example, were refused permission to form national federations even though they were from a similar trade/occupation/industry, on the grounds that they would represent workers from "different" statutory bodies. The only exceptions were financially autonomous local authorities, whose unions were permitted to organize workers from "different" local authority establishments, some of which were too small even to provide the minimal seven persons required for the pro tem committee to organize the application to the registrar. Further, the coverage of the term *statutory authority* was extended by the Trade Unions (Amendment) Act of 1980, so that it now means "any authority or body established, appointed or constituted by any written law, and includes any local authority." Recently, government policy has moved strongly in the direction of not permitting unionization of the professional, managerial, and executive grades of workers in the whole of the public sector.

A major reason for the separate development of the different categories of unions in the public sector was the differences in industrial relations practices. While workers in statutory and local authorities were able to engage their employers directly in negotiations about pay and conditions and to have collective agreements signed between the parties, government-service workers were persuaded to settle their grievances or demands through a system of joint consultation, namely, the Whitley Council system, which extended from the departmental to the national joint council level. Here again we can see the influence of British institutional traditions.

The Whitley Council system began a long decline after independence as the government began to resent the growing strength of public-sector unions and their relative autonomy, which allowed them to criticize government policies publicly. It was also felt that the decentralized system of negotiations and bargaining that Whitleyism represented took up too much of the time of senior officers and that it went against evolving general principles of remuneration (based on objective criteria) for the whole of the public sector. With the introduction of salaries commissions in the late 1960s, the government thought that ad hoc negotiations at the department level should be discouraged. Thus, since the late 1960s, much of the activity of public-sector unions has been devoted to presenting memoranda to cabinet-appointed salaries commissions for specific sectors or professions in the economy and challenging the findings of such commissions in order to effect modifications before they are implemented by the government.

A more centralized system of national joint councils—representing broad categories of workers in the public sector, such as civil servants, industrial, manual, and general workers, the police, and teachers, as well as employees in statutory and local authorities—was established in 1973 to replace the Whitley system of decentralized negotiation. But even this mild form of worker participation in influencing pay and conditions of work has been regarded as a serious threat to policy making. Thus, early in 1989, the government suspended all national joint councils, although the unions continue to exist.

There are increasing signs that the current Malaysian government dislikes the adversarial role adopted by trade unions, especially in the government sector, and would rather such organizations devoted their energies to social and cultural activities. Women workers in the government sector have already been organized along these lines by the formation of PUSPANITA, an association of female employees in the government sector. Since 1983, such organizations have been formed in most ministries, covering most of the female employees of government departments. The structure of this organization is shown in figure 4.4.

The Ministry of Labour claims that PUSPANITA is intended to "foster good-will and harmony among the female employees and wives of employees of the civil service irrespective of rank, including the families" (Malaysia. Ministry of Labour 1985:7). It may well be that organizations such as PUSPANITA are intended to be alternatives to unions, which are regarded by the government as an unacceptable "cultural import."

Trade Unions in the Private Sector

In the private sector, workers in all categories may form or join unions provided they adhere to the registrar's guidelines on membership. Under Section 9 of the Industrial Relations Act, however, any union whose majority membership is constituted by nonmanagerial ranks is prohibited from negotiating with the employer on behalf of the following categories of workers (even if they are members of the union): those working in a managerial, executive, confidential, or security capacity. This rule appears redundant given the registrar's wide powers to regulate union membership and in view of the divergent interests and responsibilities of the workers concerned. It may have been designed to discourage workers from forming unions with a broader membership, which could present an effective challenge to the employer, particularly given the expertise of senior staff. There have been frequent disputes between unions and employers on the above exclusion clause since the terms have not been defined in the relevant act, and the parties were forced to seek the help of the Industrial Court to ascertain its proper application. Since 1969, such disputes no longer go to the court but ultimately, after investigations by the director-general of industrial relations, are ruled on by the minister (whose decision cannot be challenged in any court). Union leaders have frequently protested that the minister's rulings on what constitutes managerial, executive, confidential, or security posts in an enterprise are often arbitrary or politically motivated and, since no reasons need be given, tend to be inconsistent from one decision to the next.

Unlike the public sector, where special rules govern unionization, in the private sector the registrar is the principal influence on the pattern and growth of unionization. The proliferation of small unions is due largely to the registrar's application of the concept of a union as comprising only workers "within a similar trade, occupation or industry." The growth of larger unions has been hampered by the application of the same criteria for amalgamations and federations. The attempts by the Electrical Industry Workers' Union in the early 1970s to organize

Figure 4.4. Structure of PUSPANITA

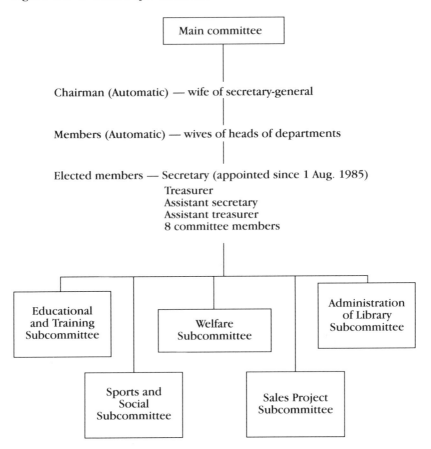

Source: Malaysia. Ministry of Labour.

workers in the newly established electronics factories were thwarted by the registrar on the grounds that they were dissimilar industries. Appeals to the High Court and subsequently to the Federal Court were fruitless since it was held that "the Court must decline to exercise its discretion in making any declaration which would fetter the Registrar." Such a challenge to the decisions of the registrar were denied unions after 1969, however, when all appeals of the registrar's decisions to the courts were disallowed. Subsequently they have been reviewed by only the minister of labor, whose decision is final and conclusive; it cannot be reviewed by any court.

These changes in the trade union laws have left those in the labor movement in Malaysia bitterly dissatisfied about the state of workers' freedom of association. The MTUC's attempts to persuade the government to ratify ILO Convention 87 (1948) on freedom of association also failed. Further, federations or amalgamations of unions have been discouraged in the private sector. Thus, the National Union of Transport Workers was prevented from organizing workers in railways, shipping, or port facilities, and particularly in the airlines industry. The largest of the private-sector unions, the National Union of Plantation Workers, is the only union that engages in industry-level bargaining with an association of employers. The terms of the agreement do not have industrywide coverage, however, since most of the smaller employers are not members of the employers' association and have tended to rely on nonunion casual labor. Most other large industrywide unions, such as the National Union of Banking Employees or the National Union of Transport Workers, continue to bargain at the enterprise level, either because there is no association of employers or, as in banking, because enterprise bargaining has become established as the preferred mode.

Figure 4.3 shows that the structure of Malaysian unionism is largely the outcome of trade union laws introduced during the colonial period and subsequently interpreted by the Registrar of Trade Unions. In the first instance, unions fell into the three broad categories of government or civil service, statutory authority, or private industry, according to the nature of their members' employment. Since the formation of Malaysia in 1963, however, incorporation of the East Malaysian states of Sabah and Sarawak has meant that this structure has been repeated in each of the three principal administrative regions of Malaysia. Industrywide unions such as the National Union of Banking Employees and the National Union of Transport Workers, could not organize on a pan-Malaysian basis because the law restricted union operations to their traditional pre-Malaysia regions. Amendments to the Trade Unions Act made in 1989 will now permit such pan-Malaysian organizations, but each case will have to be specifically approved by the Registrar of Trade Unions. As of 1990, only the National Union of Banking Employees had been approved by the registrar to organize on a pan-Malaysian basis.

The balkanization of unions in Malaysia has thus been ensured by laws that separate private- and public-sector unions and within the public sector restrict workers in all statutory bodies to forming in-house unions. This is clearly illustrated in table 4.5.

Table 4.5 shows that in 1985 there were eighty unions in the statutory authority sector, although its membership share was only 16 percent of the total. This contrasts with the private sector, which had twice as many unions and three times the membership. There are strong indications, however, that these differences between public- and private-sector unions may become less pronounced in the future. It is worth noting that although the number of unions in Malaysia as a whole increased over the period 1980–88, union membership increased very slightly.

Table 4.5. Trade union structure in Malaysia, 1985

Region/sector	Government service	Statutory authority	Private industry
Peninsular states (West Malaysia)	102	64	116
Membership share (%)	35	16	49
Sabah (East Malaysia)	15	5	7
Membership share (%)	50	11	39
Sarawak (East Malaysia)	12	11	37
Membership share (%)	67	9	24
All Malaysia	129	80	160
Membership share (%)	36	16	48

Source: Malaysia. Ministry of Labour 1988.

This aggregate picture masks a significant change, however: private-sector unions have generally contracted in size, while the well-established public-sector unions appear to have grown in size, if only moderately.

Trade Union Strategy and Tactics

The 1980s were not kind to the Malaysian union movement. After nearly four decades of independence, the vast majority of workers remain unorganized, and most of those who are organized are members of peanut unions. In addition, the legislative noose around the necks of unionists has been progressively tightened by an unsympathetic government.

What are the major problems facing the labor movement in Malaysia in the 1990s? Four key issues can be identified. These are the right to organize in both the public and private sectors; the right to negotiate over the terms and conditions of employment, which, as we have seen, is a particular problem in the public sector; static or declining union densities; and, finally, organizational and financial weakness.

The problem of unionization levels is a serious one for the Malaysian labor movement. Union density is dropping because the union membership is aging and mostly male. Efforts to recruit women have been limited and restricted by government policies that have prevented workers in the FTZs from joining unions. The general problem of membership levels has stimulated the spread of welfare schemes, and, in spite of financial constraints, some of the larger unions provide welfare services to members. Such services include retirement, sickness, death, and educational benefits. The levels of these benefits are very low, but they are intended to act as membership incentives. Particularly in the public sector, where unions are denied negotiation rights, the advantages of unionism to potential members are not obvious.

In the private sector, unions are also losing ground, as highlighted by the decline in collective bargaining. Thus, in 1983, 137 collective bargaining agreements covering 30,021 workers were vetted by the Industrial Court (as required by law). By 1986, only 105 agreements were considered by the court, and these covered 23,179 employees, nearly 23 percent fewer than three years before (Malaysia. Ministry of Labour 1988:124).

The union movement has seen some benefits in pushing for minimum wage legislation to gain members, but at present Malaysia does not have a minimum wage except for hotel employees. The MTUC has argued for a minimum monthly wage of M$400 (approximately U.S. $145) for all industries, but it has repeatedly encountered government opposition.

The membership and financial problems of Malaysian unions have led them down avenues that have compounded their difficulties and rendered them more vulnerable to government pressure. Since the early part of the 1970s, a number of unions have moved into commercial activities: the so-called New Frontiers policy. The argument has been that unions should be allowed to promote economic development by participating in business ventures either unilaterally or in partnership with domestic or foreign capital. Singapore was suggested as a model in this regard. With the ready availability of cheap land, most unions began to build substantial buildings for commercial letting as well as for their own use. Subsequently, these were used as collateral for purchasing equity in multinational joint ventures. CUEPACS, for example, set up an investment corporation registered as a limited company. This corporation invested in the housing industry and developed a number of large housing schemes.

Over the period 1975–86, the assets of unions in peninsular Malaysia increased by 336 percent, while membership rose by only 17 percent (Malaysia. Ministry of Labour n.d.; 1988). The rapid rise in union assets does not reveal the extent, however, of debt and cash-flow problems that all the major unions faced in the latter part of the 1980s. In 1989, for example, the MTUC was forced to raise affiliation fees to avoid bankruptcy proceedings, and the National Union of Plantation Workers was forced to mortgage some of its principal assets. Trade union debt to the government-funded trading banks have left the unions very vulnerable.[2]

The New Frontiers policy has not been without its critics. For example, K. George, writing in the May 1987 issue of *Suara Buruh,* raised a series of questions that have not been answered satisfactorily:

> How many unions are in a position to invest in business? Should the unions confine their enterprises to cooperatives? Or should

they go into private enterprise? If they want to go into private enterprises, should there be joint ventures with capitalists and the government? Is there a conflict of interest? Will business enterprises lead to corrupt practices? Is it desirable for a trade union leader to become a director of a private business? Will it not lead him to play a dual role at times? In a conflict between workers' rights and protection of investment, what would be his tendency? Will he or will he not be forced to compromise trade union principles and workers' rights to obtain favors from the government and the capitalists for his enterprises?

The financial independence of unions is not helped by their low dues. In the public-sector unions, for example, the average dues are still around M$2.50 per month, which is around 0.5 percent of the average member's earnings. It has been very difficult to raise dues because of a provision of the Trade Unions Act (section 40: 30) that states that dues may be raised only after a majority of the members have voted for the increase by secret ballot.

Future of Malaysian Unionism

In the early 1980s, the government policy of Malaysia was changed dramatically to emulate that of Japan, whose management strategies were publicly extolled as providing the best model for Malaysia. In the labor sector, this policy switch saw the Ministry of Labour emphasizing not only corporatist labor-management styles but also the appropriateness of Japanese-style unionism. As a preliminary step, statistics were published on Malaysia's in-house, or enterprise, unions. Until then these statistics had remained unpublicized because of the general criticism leveled against the Malaysian government that it fostered weak peanut unions.

Although the Look East policy of Prime Minister Mohamed Mahathir did not go into effect until the early 1980s, Malaysian trade unionism was already well set in that direction, in that 47 percent of all unions were already organized on an in-house basis. This relatively high ratio was due to the dominant position of in-house unions in the statutory authority sector, a circumstance that could be traced directly to colonial labor policies of the 1950s rather than to the constraints of accommodating Japanese and NIC multinational investors. Indeed, the private sector had the lowest ratio of enterprise unions, while their share in the government sector was almost double that in the earlier part of the decade. Recent trends in the growth of enterprise unions are shown in table 4.6.

In 1984, there were only forty-three in-house unions in the private sector, making up 28.2 percent of all unions in that sector, while their

Table 4.6. Growth of in-house unions in Malaysia, 1984–88

Sector	1984	1985	1986	1987	1988
Total	177	189	199	210	224
Share of all unions (%)	49.3	51.2	52.5	51.3	54.5
Private sector (%)	28.2	32.5	36.1	36.7	38.2
Statutory authority (%)	94.8	95.1	95.1	95.1	96.6
Government service (%)	45.8	47.2	47.6	47.2	46.7

Source: Malaysia. Ministry of Labour 1988; n.d.

presence was almost twice as great in the government sector. By contrast, throughout the 1980s in-house unions were almost exclusively the only type of union found in the statutory authority sector, representing about 95 percent of all unions in that sector.

It is likely that during the 1990s trade union realities will catch up with the rhetoric of the 1980s. With government support, enterprise unions will become an increasingly significant feature of private-sector unionism, as indicated by their significant rise from 28 to 38 percent over the period 1984–88.

In early 1989, the Trade Unions Act was amended specifically to accommodate enterprise unions. Workers in any single enterprise can now form a union, regardless of the earlier occupation/trade/industry criteria, which had been used to emphasize the homogeneity of union membership. The registrar (who under the 1989 amendments was renamed the director-general of trade unions) has indicated that in-house unions may be favored over traditional unions in recognition cases.[3] The relative ease with which enterprise unionism can be instituted in Malaysia clearly derives from the early policies of limiting the size and national extent of unions.

Enterprise unionism is likely to continue to be a trend through the 1990s. Another trend is the shift in the public sector toward unitarism and paternalism. The increasing pressures exerted by the government on public-sector unions in the hope that they would become "instruments" and propagandists for government policy and abandon traditional adversarial activities have made them extremely passive and docile organizations. Since the suspension of the national joint council system in early 1989, which suddenly deprived about sixty-five thousand civil servants of consultative machinery, it is quite probable that there will be a significant reduction in public-sector unionization (*New Straits Times,* 21 March 1989). Just as women employees in government service are being organized into social clubs such as PUSPANITA, the existing public-sector unions may be diverted into taking a more active interest in their business ventures, encouraged by financial assistance and the granting of exclusive licenses to run services in a specified geographical area.

Several Malaysian unions have sought alternative roles to their limited one of defending the economic interests of their members. Activities of a different nature have been offered in place of traditional union services as union leaders fear membership decline and the accompanying loss of income from dues. With the model of Singapore unionism before them, many Malaysian union leaders have sought to develop business and entrepreneurial unionism. Most of their financial ventures have failed, however, and many unions are burdened with extra debt service commitments and little prospect of recovering their initial investments. Government domination of the banking sector has meant that union leaders very often find themselves obliged to adopt a conciliatory stance with the government to secure their investments. Further, many vital union assets, such as land and buildings, have been put in jeopardy by the failure of these business ventures. Banks, which are closely supervised by government agencies, have the power to agree to the rescheduling of union debts. There is therefore a strong tendency for unions to split up into new "business groups," each trying to build an empire of joint-venture capital, and thus to neglect both union education and the traditional concerns of workers (*Asiaweek*, 30 June 1989).

Finally, the government has been actively trying to split the union movement by emphasizing differences between the CUEPACS and the MTUC and by giving informal support to the Malaysian Labour Organization.[4] It is widely expected that these efforts will continue through the 1990s, fueled by ethnic divisions.

Will the Malaysian labor movement survive through the 1990s? Will the combined effects of enterprise unionism, public-sector paternalism, the failures of business unionism, and continued government attempts at union fragmentation result in the demise of unionism? The answer is probably no. In our view, unions will survive in some form in Malaysia, but there is little evidence that a labor movement will develop that is capable of adequately protecting and advancing workers' interests.

Part II.
Newly Industrialized Countries

5

The Korean Union Movement in Transition

Hwang-Joe Kim

The labor movement in Korea takes various forms, including trade unions, labor-oriented parties, and the cooperative movement. Unions remain the major element of the labor movement, although, as in most developing countries, union growth and organizational strength have been retarded by a hostile environment. Since mid-1987, however, the nature of unionism has changed dramatically. To understand the magnitude and character of these changes, it is necessary to grasp the historical and political context in which unionism has found it so difficult to prosper. Accordingly, this chapter begins with a brief analysis of union development. The contemporary status of the union movement is then discussed, including its leading participants, organizational structures, main objectives and tactics, and effectiveness. Major issues facing Korean unions are sketched in the concluding section, as well as the prospect for the future. In essence, I shall argue that the nature and structure of Korean unions reflect their politicization. In the past, this divided the industrial working class, but more recently it has resulted in a vibrant and militant movement that grew spectacularly following the democratic reform commitments made by the government in June 1987. Although unions remain divided along ideological lines, the decline of the old geopolitical order based on cold war assumptions

I would like to thank Sang-Heon Lee, Dong-Ouk Eom, and Dae-Sik Hur for their research assistance, Moo-Ki Bai for comments on an earlier draft, and Steve Frenkel for making the manuscript more concise and readable.

and the consequent warming of relations with North Korea signal the possibility of greater union solidarity and improved bargaining relations with employers over the longer term.

Historical Development

Spontaneous and scattered unions in the form of friendly societies developed in seaport areas following the opening of trade to foreign merchants in 1876.[1] Mining by foreign companies also encouraged the emergence of unions. The first major labor disputes by dock workers occurred in the 1890s, and many disputes took place in the early 1900s. The most important sources of conflict were economic issues, but these often included a political dimension. This was especially the case after the Korea-Japan protection treaty in 1905, which resulted in criticism of the transfer of mining and lumbering rights to Japanese capitalists; protests against expropriation of rural land by the Japanese colonial regime through the national land survey project; opposition to the Japanese prohibition on investment by local entrepreneurs; and disquiet concerning Korea becoming integrated into a wider Japanese market. In addition, there remained a tendency for managers to treat workers harshly, reflecting the remnants of a precapitalist mentality associated with the rigidly stratified Korean Empire. Japanese managers were no better. They tended to ignore or suppress the demands of Korean workers, who received at least 50 percent lower wages than their Japanese counterparts doing similar work.

Union demands at this time were simple: more pay and the abolition of discrimination at foreign-operated mines and at open seaports. Continued employer suppression of workers' demands frequently led to violent strikes, however, and the breaking of machines.

Gradually, the workers' movement began to adopt new tactics, including boycotting foreign commodities. Protests crystallized into demands for national independence based on the conviction that industrial justice could be achieved only when the precapitalist, centralized, and stratified social system was abolished and foreign capital and Japanese colonial rule brought to an end. Spontaneous and scattered unions based on these notions began to emerge throughout industry (Cho 1978:74–75).

The suppressed anger against Japanese rule since Korea had opened its ports burst into nationwide popular demonstrations in the wake of the declaration of independence on 1 March 1919. The Japanese colonial regime practiced an appeasement policy until the mid-1920s, and it was during this period that various nationwide labor organizations were formed. These included the Korean Labor Mutual Aid Association in 1920, the Federation of Korean Labor in 1922, and the Confederation of Korean Labor and Farmers in 1924.[2] There were many labor disputes similar to the Pusan seaport workers' strike aimed at abolishing discrimination based on low wages and long working hours but ultimately directed at eliminating Japanese imperialism from Korea. On the whole, local unions were organized and operated by rank-and-file members, while national labor organizations were led by intellectuals, doctors, and lawyers, some of whom were socialists.

In response to emerging labor opposition, the Japanese colonial regime began to suppress the union movement severely through legislation, in particular the Public Peace Act of 1925. The formation of unions was made much more difficult, and the Japanese police adopted a variety of tactics to suppress union activity, including prohibiting workers' rallies, closely inspecting union activities, and arresting union leaders. Furthermore, since many events—for example, the organization of the Korean Communist Party in 1925, the 10 June demonstrations, and the 1927 student protests at Kwangju—were encouraged or sustained by the union movement, the Japanese colonial regime increased its suppression of worker organizations. Consequently, in 1930, the union movement went underground.

Reemergence of Unions in the Cold War Era

In the wake of the economic disorder resulting from World War II, including the partition of Korea, widespread shortages of managers, technical personnel, and raw materials resulted in large-scale factory closings. Unemployment, commodity shortages, and inflation ravaged the Korean economy, which was now suddenly separated from that of Japan. Although the plight of workers was a major problem, the most critical issue facing the nation after independence was the creation of a unified government in the context of severe conflict between left- and right-wing groups. The latter made suppression of the Communist labor movement its first priority.

Many intellectuals and labor activists who led the independence and socialist movement under the colonial regime organized the Communist-inspired National Council of Korean Trade Unions (NCKTA) in November 1945, comprising sixteen affiliated industrial federations and nearly twelve hundred local unions. This peak council constituted the mainstream of the union movement under U.S. military rule until it was challenged and attacked by right-wing anti-Communists under the so-called nationalist banner. The latter faction established the Confederation of Korean Trade Unions (CKTU) in March 1946.

Confrontation between the two peak councils occurred over a major railway dispute that escalated into a general strike and ended in victory for the CKTU. The latter was supported by the U.S. occupation regime's police and the Labor Youth Association. The NCKTA was declared illegal by the occupation regime in March 1947 and went underground until its dissolution two years later.

After the establishment of the Korean government in 1948, a legal framework permitting independent unions was introduced. The three basic rights of workers—to organize, to bargain collectively, and to strike—were allowed under the new constitution. Specific regulations were set out in the Trade Union Act of 1953, the Labor Disputes Adjustment Act, and the Labor Committee Act of 1953. At that time, however, unions were fragile, and employers opposed any union involvement in setting wages and conditions. In addition, CKTU leaders competed for control of their organization and were manipulated by the ruling Democratic Liberal Party, leaving them separated from their constituents. In 1958, the National Conference of Trade Unions (NCTU) was organized by a small group of union leaders in an attempt to unify the union movement, but it had no influence on the government-controlled confederation.

Political and economic corruption under the Liberal Party regime led to the student revolution of April 1960, catalyzed by the fraudulent presidential election in the previous month. The union movement sought to distance itself from the government, so that the NCTU demanded the resignation of CKTU board members. At that time, however, the NCTU was not organized strongly enough to pursue its demand. Thus, after many twists and turns, a combined meeting was held on 25 November 1960, resulting in the founding of the Federation of Korean Trade Unions (FKTU). Before the executive board members of the FKTU had been elected, however, the labor movement divided again.

In summary, the union movement after the student revolution can be characterized as a struggle by rank-and-file workers to assert the legitimacy of union activity independent of the government. The revolution gave workers a brief opportunity to seek an autonomous path, but this, together with the student revolution, failed in the wake of the 16 May 1961 military coup d'état. In consequence, the unions returned to their illegitimate status. The FKTU was disbanded temporarily, but after August 1961 it was allowed to be reorganized and collective action resumed. The FKTU emphasized political neutrality and financial independence as a new direction for the union movement, consistent with legislation prohibiting union involvement in politics, enacted by the new government that assumed office in 1963.

In the late 1960s, the FKTU abandoned its position on political neutrality and encouraged its officers to run in local and national assembly elections. The federation also demanded the elimination of the clause in the Trade Union Act banning union political activity. As a result, some union leaders were eligible for election to the national assembly. Most union leaders did not act to protect workers' rights and interests, however, which gave rise to direct action facilitated by the increase in the size of workplaces. This, in turn, fostered rank-and-file union organization. Some strikes—for example, at Gold Star in 1963 and at the Chosun Gongsa shipyard in 1969—were large and intense, but there was little violence.

Legal Containment of Unions and Worker Militancy

More restrictions were imposed on unions during the 1970s as the relationship between South and North Korea worsened and the economy showed signs of instability. In 1971, the Special Act for National Security was introduced, whereby collective bargaining and industrial action were severely limited and made subject to decisions by the government. In response, workers began to use violence, which the unions had little power or inclination to stop. An extreme example was Chun Tai-il, who burned himself to death in 1970 as a protest against extremely poor working conditions. In the following year, the main building of the Han Jin Company was set on fire in the midst of a workers' riot. More generally, a strong workers' movement emerged separate from the formal union organizations. This was understandable given that the government's severe restrictions on unions had suppressed union activity.

Spontaneous stoppages, such as at the Dong-il Textile Company and at the Bando Company, led to criticism of unions from outside groups. Some of these organizations—for example, the Urban Industrial Mission—stepped in to assist in educating and organizing workers. Workers also looked to political parties for support. Employees of the Y. H. Trade Company, for example, engaged in demonstrations inside the headquarters of the opposition party, demanding its support. Violent labor disputes occurred in April 1980 at the Sabuk coal mine and the Dongkuk Steel Company in the context of the political vacuum that arose following the assassination of President Park Chung Hee in October 1979.

The constitution was amended at the start of the fifth republic, and the labor laws were changed in December 1980. These laws were aimed at weakening unions and making industrial action ineffective. Although the Special Act was lifted in December 1981 so that workers' rights to bargain and act collectively were formally restored, restrictions had been imposed on union activity through the amendment of the labor laws the previous year. The cooling-off period had been extended from twenty to thirty days in ordinary enterprises, and union shops had been made illegal. Most significantly, the law had provided for the restructuring of unions from an industrial to an enterprise basis. For an enterprise union to be legally recognized, the consent of at least thirty workers or one-fifth of the total workers in a designated workplace was needed. Other controversial clauses had the effect of barring union federations from assisting enterprise unions in negotiations and dissolving unions such as the bus and taxi drivers' unions that were organized on a regional basis. Many union leaders thus lost their positions.

The weakness of unions in collective bargaining also resulted from the government's emphasis on consultation through legally prescribed labor-management councils. The Labor-Management Council Act of 1980 required that such councils be established in most sectors in workplaces employing one hundred or more regular workers (reduced to fifty by an amendment to the act in April 1988) and in all unionized workplaces, regardless of the number of employees.[3] Management is required to consult employee representatives about productivity improvements; employee welfare, education, and training; and the handling of grievances. Firms must submit the rules of their labor-management councils to the minister of labor, who has the authority to dissolve the councils or to order reelection of their members. Since representatives of the union and other persons commissioned by the union are members of the councils, unions are expected both to bargain and to consult. Collective bargaining is usually conducted at the workplace level (Kim 1984:79–88); thus, the establishment of an alternative consultative mechanism has been regarded by many union leaders as a means of limiting the scope of bargaining and hence their authority.

In sum, the 1970s were a difficult time for unions. Compulsory reorganization from industrial to enterprise organizations, together with the new legal requirements for enterprise unions, resulted in declining union power, highlighted by a substantial reduction in union membership after the labor law was amended in 1980. The FKTU (1984b:134) observed that its control was weakened by the 1980 amendment of the Trade Union Act, which encouraged the dispersion of local unions. It argued that since enterprise unions were only loosely affiliated with the federation, obligations by such unions to the FKTU were frequently ignored. Some unions apparently intentionally reported reduced numbers of members to avoid paying membership fees to the FKTU. Moreover, unions were destroyed or virtually paralyzed by the increased unfair labor practices engaged in by employers. Further, there were very few newly organized unions to counter the trends. Thus, unions were hampered by the 1980 labor legislation, employers' resistance to bargaining, and internal dissension within the union movement.

Leading Participants and Structures in the Emerging Korean Democracy

Between June and October 1987, there was a nationwide eruption of strikes immediately following massive student demonstrations and civilian protests that signaled the Korean people's accumulated disaffection with authoritarian rule and against the widening inequalities in wealth

(Bai 1990:14–15). The strikes led to the declaration of democratic reforms (referred to above), although these did not explicitly affirm the rights of independent unions. Nevertheless, a large number of new unions were established as workers engaged in widespread industrial action aimed at obtaining higher wages and improved working conditions. Workers demanded such reforms through industrial and regional consultative union organizations since there was no comprehensive union movement strategy or strong organizational base. The 1987 surge in union activity marked a turning point in Korean labor relations, however, in that it introduced marked changes in the leading participants and the organizational structures of the movement. These are discussed below.

Changing Membership Characteristics and Union Activity

The first point about recent union developments is that male workers employed in large companies, especially in the iron and steel, metal-fabrication, and chemical industries, have replaced female light-industry employees as the leading participants in union activity. Since the 1970s, the concentration of male workers in large establishments has accelerated, owing to the rapid expansion of workplaces in the above-mentioned industries. Union activity in the Masan and Changwon machine industry complex and in the Ulsan area of Kyongnam province reflects this change; there was a burst of strikes in 1987, beginning in these areas and spreading nationally. The size of these strikes, indicated by the number of strikers, was very large in spite of the relatively small number of disputes. Some more general characteristics of the recent labor disputes are outlined in table 5.1.

According to table 5.1, disputes in large establishments (employing more than three hundred employees) accounted for 23.7 percent of the total labor disputes in 1987. But the occurrence rate of such conflicts was much higher; for example, the occurrence rate in the largest establishments—those with one thousand or more regular employees—reached as high as 69.3 percent in 1987. It was less marked in the two subsequent years but nevertheless continued to exceed considerably the rates for smaller-scale establishments. These data are consistent with Deyo's (1989:35) proposition that labor protest has tended to be concentrated in large-scale, heavy, capital-intensive industries that provide a stronger base for union power and effectiveness. If anything, this argument will carry even greater weight in the 1990s.

The second important point about recent union developments is that white-collar workers, such as clericals, professionals, technical workers, and salespeople, have begun to participate in unions. This is suggested by the rapid increase in the number of new unions among employees in these occupations. Except for workers at commercial and government-

Table 5.1. *Labor disputes in Korea, by establishment size, in percent and by occurrence rate, 1987–89*

Establishment size (no. of employees)	1987 distribution	1987 occurence rate	1988 distribution	1988 occurence rate	1989 distribution[a]	1989 occurence rate
5–49	14.5	0.6	11.2	0.2	14.4	0.2
50–99	22.3	8.7	27.1	5.3	20.8	3.2
100–299	39.5	24.5	37.7	11.7	40.0	10.1
300–499	16.8[b]	39.2	8.4	16.4	8.5	13.2
500–999	–	–	7.0	20.5	7.1	16.7
1000 +	6.9	69.3	8.6	43.0	9.1	35.4
Total	100.0	3.4	100.0	1.7	99.9[c]	1.4
Number of disputes	3,749		1,873		1,585	

Source: Korea. Ministry of Labor 1990.

Note: Occurence rate is the ratio of number of establishments that have disputes to the total number of establishments.

[a]Data are for first eleven months only.

[b]Includes figures for 500–999 size category.

[c]Total does not equal 100 because of rounding.

run banks, union activity among white-collar employees remained dormant until the beginning of the 1980s. After the establishment of a union at the Hanil Investment Financing Company in June 1983, however, unionization gradually spread into other financial-sector organizations, including stock exchanges and insurance companies. Following the strikes of 1987, enterprise unions were established by almost all groups of white-collar workers, including research workers at private and government-financed institutes. Furthermore, the organizational base of the unions of clerical, professional, and technical workers was significantly strengthened in the first half of 1988, and the scope of their activities was greatly enlarged. Organizations of white-collar unions are also being developed to build solidarity across occupations.

The causes of white-collar union growth are the relative decline in the privileges and rewards accruing to routine white-collar work as the number of white-collar employees has expanded in line with the rapid growth of the Korean economy (see Kwanmo 1989:9–10). Thus, the proportion of professional and technical employees to total employment increased from 5 percent in 1963 to 20 percent in 1987.

The third, and a more general, point is that the number of legally recognized unions has grown remarkably since June 1987. This can be seen in figure 5.1. There were 2,725 local unions and 16 industrial federations in Korea at the end of June 1987. By December 1989, the number of locals (more than 90 percent of which are enterprise organi-

Figure 5.1. Local unions in Korea, 1963–89

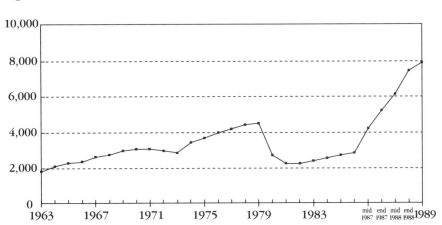

Source: Korea. Ministry of Labor.
Branches of unions and local unions were amalgamated under the category "local unions" on 31 December 1980 in conformity with the Labor Union Act amendment. Mid-year and end-of-year figures are provided for 1987, 1988, and 1989.

zations) had almost tripled to 7,883, while the number of federations had increased to 21. A substantial increase in the number of local unions occurred during the latter part of 1987; the growth in federations occurred slightly later. As figure 5.2 shows, union density has also increased substantially since 1987, particularly among male employees. In mid-1987, union density stood at 14.7 percent. It had risen to 23.7 percent by the end of 1989, most rapidly among men, for whom the rate went from a low of 15.6 percent to 26.0 percent. Although density figures according to plant size are not available, unions tend to be concentrated in large establishments. According to M. K. Bai (1990:28–29), 72.9 percent of manufacturing plants with more than three hundred employees are unionized. This he interprets as union penetration rapidly approaching saturation. These changes do not necessarily mean that unions as organizations are more powerful. T. Kim (1990:11) notes that because of the recent rapid growth of enterprise unions, the average size of such organizations has declined: from 385 members in June 1987 to 247 in June 1989.

The increase in union members and the number of unions over the recent period underline noteworthy interindustry differences, as indicated by the data in table 5.2. Larger increases in the metal and printing industries highlight the greater activism among more highly skilled blue-collar workers, while the considerable growth of the National United

Figure 5.2. Union density in Korea, by gender, 1970–89

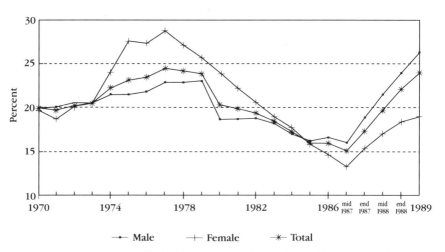

― Male   + Female   ✳ Total

Sources: Korea. Ministry of Labor for union members and *Monthly Statistics of Korea* for number of employees.
Union density is defined as the number of regular employees at nonfarm establishments divided by the number of union members expressed as a percentage. Mid-year and end-of-year figures are provided for 1987 and 1988.

Table 5.2. Union membership and rate of growth in Korea, by industry, 1987–89

	Membership				Rate of growth (%)		
	mid-1987	end 1987	end 1988	end 1989	1987	1988	1989
Korean Railway Workers	30,276	30,305	31,041	31,181	0.1	2.4	0.4
Federation of Korean Textile Workers	111,331	123,889	139,691	155,331	11.3	12.7	11.2
Federation of Korean Mine Workers	56,663	56,858	52,845	44,305	0.3	−7.1	−16.2
Korean National Electrical Workers	19,634	19,548	25,467	26,517	−0.4	30.3	4.1
Federation of Foreign Organization Employees	21,609	24,949	37,535	38,416	15.5	50.4	2.3
Korean Communication Workers	65,717	66,406	47,754	50,366	1.0	−28.1	5.5
Korean Federation of Port and Transport Workers	36,508	37,962	39,994	46,668	4.0	5.3	16.7
Korean Seamen's Union	81,995	78,444	86,099	83,455	−4.3	9.8	−3.1
Korean Federation of Bank and Financial Workers	99,384	125,521	114,349	120,571	26.3	−8.9	5.4
Korean Monopoly Workers	10,204	10,861	10,574	10,238	6.4	−2.6	−3.2
Federation of Korean Chemical Workers	152,267	180,529	179,931	206,429	18.6	−0.3	14.7
Federation of Korean Metal Workers	147,658	229,016	402,184	448,583	55.1	75.6	11.5
National United Workers' Federation	60,773	101,521	188,514	237,597	67.0	85.7	26.0
Federation of Korean Printing Workers	5,449	6,439	21,932	26,887	18.2	240.6	22.6
Korean Federation of Auto and Transport Workers	142,372	164,626	92,195	121,161	15.6	−44.0	31.4
Korean Tourist Industry Workers	8,581	10,898	18,637	24,107	27.0	71.0	29.4
Korean Federation of Postal and Telecommunication Workers	—	—	21,160	21,949	—	—	3.7
Korean Federation of Insurance Labor	—	—	13,016	21,063	—	—	61.8
Federation of Korean Taxi Transport Workers	—	—	101,333	117,284	—	—	15.7
Federation of Korean Rubber Workers	—	—	65,278	67,728	—	—	3.8
Federation of Clerical and Financial Workers	—	—	17,939	32,579	—	—	81.6
Total	1,050,201	1,267,457	1,707,456	1,932,415	20.7	34.7	3.2

Source: Korea. Ministry of Labor 1990.

Workers Federation, which represents workers in miscellaneous manual occupations, indicates the extent to which unionism has gained momentum among the urbanized working class. The growth of white-collar unionism is evident from information on organizations that cover tourist industry workers and clerks and financial service workers. Moreover, these data understate the true picture of white-collar union growth insofar as several organizations that have grown substantially in size are not legally recognized and are therefore excluded from the official statistics.[4] Despite the high capital intensity of the chemical and stevedoring industries, table 5.2 shows that union growth has also increased among workers in these strategically powerful industries.

Interunion Solidarity and Cleavage

Unionized workers are also attempting to strengthen their multiunion activities by organizing joint union councils within their region, industry, and enterprise. These have developed in response to the weaknesses of enterprise unionism. Most of the unions that belong to these consultative councils are those that are organized in small and medium-sized firms. Some of the unions are affiliated with the Federation of Korean Trade Unions but tend not to follow the federation's directives. The FKTU inherited its anti-leftist ideology from the CKTU and has been accused of being too close to management and the government. As of February 1989, FKTU affiliates comprised about 870 unions covering 236,000 members or 14 percent of Korea's total union membership (Korea Labor Institute 1989a:37).

Regional consultative councils have been the most active interunion organizations. These began to be organized during late 1987 and were activated again during the 1988 spring wage offensive. By the end of that year, formal regional councils were established in major cities and provinces, as shown in table 5.3.

Through the councils, local unions support one another by exchanging information, sharing common training and public relations activities, and coordinating strike action. By means of these joint activities, they have tried to foster workers' consciousness of labor problems beyond the factory gates. The regional councils are loosely organized, however, so that internal unity and the maintenance of external solidarity, as well as the narrowness of the scope of their activities, pose problems. Without the power and experience of union leaders from larger workplaces, the councils lack expertise.

There are several occupational/industrial councils. These include the council of hospital employees' unions; the council of researchers', professionals', and technicians' unions; the council of democratic publication and press unions; and the council of university employees' unions. The councils of the clerical and financial workers' unions and that of the journalists' unions have developed into independent entities as legally recognized federations. These occupation/industrial councils generally comprise relatively homogeneous union members of comparatively new unions (most of which were organized since mid-1987), which gives them greater organizational cohesiveness than their regional counterparts. They have minimal interest, however, in labor problems outside the boundaries of their own occupations or industries.

Since late 1987, solidarity movements of a less formal nature have emerged in other industries. There is a council of public servants' unions, for example, which includes postal workers and railway workers. And there are regional unions of clothing workers, shoemakers, and printers. The council of hospital workers' unions and that of unions in government undertakings are also active.

Enterprise joint union councils began to be organized after 1975 following the establishment of the Lucky Gold Star Group council. They did not attract much attention, however, until the Hyundai Group council was set up on 8 August 1987. The Hyundai council played an important role in 1987 in the labor-management struggle of the Hyundai Group workers over recognition of unofficial unions. This conflict involved massive action, intimidation by company agents, and violence (Ogle 1990:118–20).

Enterprise councils were also established in other major conglomerates, such as Sunkyong, Kia, Ssangyong, and Daewoo. These councils are not legally recognized organizations but function to reinforce solidarity among affiliated unions and support collective bargaining at the enterprise level. Many large Korean enterprises are conglomerates, however, with geographically dispersed workplaces characterized by different wage levels. Consequent policy differences between unions and the problem of subcontracting companies affiliated with particular enterprises, which are not usually council members, make it difficult to achieve a united front for bargaining purposes.

There are two final points to be made about organizational change among unions in Korea. First, new types of unions are on the increase following the amendment of the Trade Union Act of 1987. These are characterized by rank-and-file determination. Typical examples are regional industrial unions, unions that protect daily and temporary workers, and the council of unions, which covers employees of subcontractors affiliated with big firms (Korea Labor Institute 1989b:31–33).

Second, since October 1988, there have been vigorous attempts by the "democratic trade unions" to create a second national association to compete with the conservative, business union–oriented FKTU. The more radical National Alliance of Trade Unions (NATU) was established on 22 January 1990 with the participation of fourteen regional union

Table 5.3. Councils of trade unions in Korea, by region and industry,
1988

	Date of establishment	Affiliated unions	Membership
Consultative councils by region			
Federation of Masan Changwon Unions	12 Dec. 1987	30	26,000
Council of Seoul Unions	29 May 1988	108	34,081
Council of Incheon Unions	18 June 1988	46	7,000
Council of Seongnam Unions	25 June 1988	28	4,500
Council of South Kyunggi Unions	28 Dec. 1988	52	13,933
Council of Daegu, Kyungbuk Unions	7 Dec. 1988	35	4,500
Council of Pusan Unions	6 Aug. 1988	21	3,100
Council of Cheonbuk Unions	21 Aug. 1988	30	6,262
Council of Jinju Unions	17 April 1988	12	1,200
Council of Kwangju Unions	16 March 1989	30	5,000
Total		392	105,576
Consultative councils by industry or occupation			
Council of Researchers', Professionals', and Technicians' Unions	16 July 1988	38	12,000
National Federation of Clerical and Financial Workers' Union	27 Nov. 1987	85	25,000
National Federation of Journalists' Unions	26 Nov. 1988	43	13,600
National Federation of Hospital Unions	17 Dec. 1988	98	35,000

Table 5.3. (continued)

	Date of establishment	Affiliated unions	Membership
National Council of Construction Unions	10 Dec. 1988	22	14,142
National Council of Foreign-Invested Firms Unions	11 Dec. 1988	70	15,000
Council of Democratic Publication and Press Unions	16 Jan. 1988	18	1,752
National Council of University Employees' Unions	1 Feb. 1988	54	9,200
National Council of Unions of Facility Maintenance Employees[a]	28 Jan. 1989	50	4,500
Total		478	130,194
GRAND TOTAL		870	235,770

Source: Council of Seoul Trade Unions 1989.
[a]As of 23 Feb. 1989.

consultative councils as well as two occupational/industrial consultative councils; several other councils attended in an observer capacity.[5] Representatives of 574 NATU-affiliated unions (8 percent of all unions), covering some 190,000 employees (16 percent of all of Korea's union members), were in attendance.

Subsequent government suppression of the NATU leadership and affiliated unions led to a reduction in the association's organizational base. Thus, by the end of June 1990, 116 unions were reported to have disaffiliated from NATU (*Chosun Daily,* 16 July 1990, 11). This is likely to be only a temporary setback, however, for NATU is regarded as the most authentic voice of labor at the national level. With a loosening of political control over the union movement, NATU is likely to grow rapidly.

Union Activity

Union activity in Korea tends to be oriented toward economic and political ends, which are usually related. Collective bargaining is a traditional form of economic activity, while the struggle for institutional reforms, including the amendment of the labor laws, is supported as a means of facilitating workers' self-determination in both economic and political spheres.

Enterprise Unions and Collective Bargaining

At least until the summer of 1987, unions were inactive as far as collective bargaining was concerned. This was largely because of government restrictions on union activity as well as strong employer resistance. This is evident from an FKTU study (FKTU 1984a:5–7) of collective agreement clauses based on 184 contracts in 1984. Only 70.2 percent of the agreements had clauses regulating wages, and 21.9 percent of the contracts stated that wage decisions were determined unilaterally by management. Clauses concerning union security were far more common: exclusive bargaining rights for particular unions were guaranteed in 94.3 percent of the contracts, check-off of union dues in 88.6 percent, and recognition of full-time union officers in 60.5 percent. These data indicate that Korean unions have been more successful in obtaining union security than in negotiating improvements in pay and conditions for their members.

The weakness of collective bargaining in Korea is partly due to the organizational structure of Korean unions and the limited skills and experience of union leaders, who have a high rate of job turnover (Kim and Sung 1990:16). Enterprise unionism makes for small-scale unions that lack resources and bargaining strength. By law, unions cannot levy members more than 2 percent of their monthly earnings in union dues. The typical proportion levied is 1.4 percent. Union members can entrust negotiations to the industrial federation with which the union is affiliated, but this practice is rare. In any case, federations have limited resources and rely mainly on levies of affiliated unions. For example, the membership fee for a national federation affiliated with the FKTU in 1987 was less than .07 percent of the average worker's wage (Kim and Sung 1990:17).

Enterprise unions also have difficulty retaining their independence from management, which has been able to commit legally defined unfair labor practices, such as discrimination against union activists and refusal to bargain over particular issues, with virtual impunity. In addition, the existence of labor-management councils encourages management to consult rather than bargain. Union leaders prefer to bargain over a wider range of issues. The councils have thus given rise to confusion by designating issues subject only to consultation when there is little agreement on the legitimacy of this distinction (Kim 1988:6).

Collective Action as the Major Means of Achieving Gains

Successive Korean governments have pursued export-led, low-wage policies that have fostered rapid economic growth at the expense of workers' welfare. Before the 1987 declaration of democratic reforms, the suppression of unions and the outlawing of industrial action went hand in hand. Without much encouragement to bargain, unions tended to use industrial action as an initial tactic rather than as a last resort. Employers relied on the government to resolve such disputes, but this strategy was largely unsuccessful insofar as the relevant state institutions lacked legitimacy in the eyes of employees and were inadequately equipped to resolve such issues expeditiously. Disputes in Korea therefore assumed a political character and hence became more difficult to settle.

Strike waves occurred whenever there was a political vacuum, for example, after the assassination of President Park on 26 October 1979 and following the 29 June 1987 declaration of democratic reforms. As shown in table 5.4, the number of disputes suddenly jumped in 1980 and in 1987.

Table 5.4 indicates that with the exception of 1980, the period 1975–86 was relatively dispute-free, largely because of government and employer suppression of open conflict. Wage increases and protests against underpayment of wages were usually the most frequent sources of the disputes. The proportion of disputes over wage increases ranged from 20 to 44 percent during the 1975–86 period except during 1980, 1982, and 1983, which were years of economic recession. In 1987, wage disputes exploded, highlighting workers' accumulated dissatisfaction with low wages and inferior working conditions.[6] This dissatisfaction continued through 1989, though to a lesser extent. One authority interpreted these developments as follows:

> Facing absolute poverty Korea's workers were eager to improve their standard of living. To do so they were willing to invest long hours of work at relatively low wage rates. . . . However, at some point during the past five to ten years workers and the public seemed to shift from a concern over absolute poverty (or well-being) to a concern over relative poverty (or well-being). Expectations began to increase in step with rising GNP and labor productivity growth rates. Social activists and students demanded political democracy and workers were encouraged by them to begin claiming a greater return on their two and a half decades of perceived sacrifices which enabled the nation to achieve its present level of economic prosperity (Bognanno 1988a:435).

Disputes over employers' alleged failure to pay adequate wages decreased substantially after 1986, against a background of an overheated economy and tight labor markets. Disputes over unacceptable working conditions were a common source of disputes, however, particularly between 1982 and 1987.

A final point worth noting in regard to the issues occasioning disputes

Table 5.4. Labor disputes in Korea, by issues, 1975–89 (in percent)

Year	Wage increase	Underpayment or non-payment of wages	Working conditions	Unfair labor practices	Dismissals	Shutdown or working hours reduction	Collective agreement	Other	No. of disputes
1975	31.6	24.1	3.0	14.3	7.5	5.3	–	14.3	133
1976	28.2	33.6	3.6	7.3	2.7	7.3	–	17.3	110
1977	37.5	31.3	2.0	6.3	4.2	4.2	–	14.6	96
1978	44.1	28.4	–	2.0	1.0	2.9	–	21.6	102
1979	29.5	34.3	–	2.9	5.7	4.8	–	22.8	105
1980	9.3	70.5	3.4	–	1.2	2.7	–	12.8	407
1981	20.4	37.1	17.2	2.2	4.8	5.9	0.5	11.8	186
1982	8.0	29.5	23.9	–ᵃ	2.3	4.5	5.7	26.1	88
1983	8.1	35.7	19.4	–ᵃ	6.1	9.2	6.1	15.3	98
1984	25.7	34.5	12.4	6.2	4.4	1.8	–	15.0	113
1985	31.7	23.0	15.5	4.5	8.3	4.5	–	12.5	265
1986	27.2	17.4	17.4	5.8	12.3	4.0	–	15.9	276
1987	70.1	1.2	15.1	1.7	1.4	0.3	4.5	5.7	3,749
1988	50.5	3.2	7.3	3.2	5.9	1.1	17.5	11.5	1,873
1989	45.9	3.7	1.3	0.6	5.0	1.9	26.4	15.3	1,616

Source: Korea. Ministry of Labor 1990.
ᵃThe unfair labor practices for 1982 and 1983 are included in the "other" category.

is the significant increase in 1988 and 1989 in conflicts over collective agreements. This increase represented a determined thrust by unions to secure collective contracts against entrenched opposition by employers who favored unilateral determination of employment conditions.

Although not shown in table 5.4, disputes over management-controlled company unions have also taken place, sometimes leading to extreme violence, as at the Sabuk coal mine in 1980, when workers rioted after discovering that their union leader had been receiving large payments from the company to ensure industrial peace. Company union disputes were prevalent in the summer of 1987 when this issue was raised in 21 out of 114 unionized establishments. Incumbent union leaders were ousted in ten of the twenty-one establishments (Korean Productivity Center 1987:21–23).

Disputes in Korea have tended to focus on more than one issue. According to a Korean Productivity Center survey based on 1987 data (1987:30–34), unions averaged 4.2 major demands (they were classified into fourteen categories) per establishment; improvements in wages and bonuses, payment of vacation leave, welfare facilities and lunch subsidies, and union organization were the most common demands. The increase in union activity, together with the recent rapid rise in wages, have probably widened the scope of bargaining. Issues now on the unions' bargaining agenda include the introduction of a service-related severance pay, bonus increases, and workers' participation in decision making (Bai 1990:33).

The incidence of industrial disputes by industry is not shown in a table, but manufacturing accounted for 52 percent of strikes in 1987 and 42 percent in 1988. Transportation, the other strike-prone sector, accounted for 37 percent of strikes in 1987 and 46 percent in 1988 (Bognanno 1988b:17). Mention has already been made of the rising militancy of male heavy-industry employees, while disputes in transportation reflect the strengthened joint activities of the taxi drivers' unions through their regional union councils. Organizational drives among taxi drivers have accelerated since 1988 when the independent Federation of Taxi Transport Workers' Union was established following its departure from the Federation of Auto and Transport Workers.

In manufacturing, unions also engage in joint preparations for wage struggles, including synchronization of strike action. This coordination is achieved through regional or industrial consultative councils. Their joint actions are, however, not so systematic and strong as might be expected of full-fledged industrial unions.

Finally, industrial disputes tend to be positively associated with establishment size, as is evident from table 5.1. Larger workplaces are more difficult for employers to direct unilaterally and afford greater opportunities for workplace union organization. The types of collective action used in labor disputes are shown in figure 5.3.

Strikes and sit-in protests have been the major forms of industrial action, and the latter have assumed greater significance since 1985. Although not shown in figure 5.3, three further points are worth noting. First, until 1988 the vast majority of disputes were illegal. Second, and partly stemming from government intervention, a large minority—perhaps up to 40 percent of industrial disputes—have involved violence. Third, in a large minority of disputes, industrial action has occurred in nonunionized workplaces (Bognanno 1988a:435). This may decline in the future insofar as unions have organized most large-scale establishments.

Although the number of industrial disputes has decreased drastically since 1988, some conflicts have been much longer in duration, as illustrated by the Yonhap Steel Company Ltd. dispute, which lasted from 1 October 1988 to 2 February 1989. By the end of February 1989, the number of companies that had experienced disputes lasting more than a month had reached a high of twenty-two. In aggregate terms, the severity of industrial disputes (as measured by working days lost per thousand nonagricultural workers), declined from 1,240 in 1988 to 1,040 for the first six months of 1989. This was higher than the severity rate for the second half of 1987, which was estimated at 790 working days lost per thousand employees. There has, however, been a much lower incidence of violence.

Figure 5.3. Industrial disputes in Korea, by types of action, 1975–89

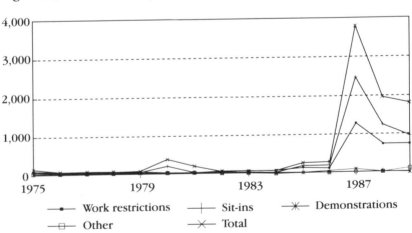

Source: Korea. Ministry of Labor.
The 1987 total of 3,749 disputes includes 126 that occurred before the declaration of democratic reforms on 29 June 1987.

In addition to industrial action focusing on workers' immediate demands, unions have begun to mobilize at regional, industrial, and national levels to exert pressure on the government to amend the labor laws. At the end of October 1988, this action assumed the form of a national-level struggle by the so-called democratic unions, which were organized mainly during and after the 1987 summer strikes, and the regional and industrial councils, whose organizational cohesiveness was strengthened during the spring wage offensive of 1988.

In June 1988, some labor leaders in regional and industrial union councils organized the National Trade Union Special Committee for the Reform of Labor Laws. This committee was reinforced by the participation of additional councils, each of which set up its own special committee for labor law reform and encouraged action appropriate to the circumstances of the region and industry in which the particular council was located. Other informal organizations composed of enlightened workers and activists transformed the existing Joint Committee against the Suppression of the Labor Movement into the National Council of Labor Movements Organization. Its aim was to help the special committee explore ways to engage in joint struggle and to try to unite the unofficial union movement with the official trade unions. In August 1988, the National Council and the special committee established objectives and principles for labor law reform at a joint national meeting in Daejun.[7] A further joint meeting, which included union delegates, was held on 6 October 1988. Several important strategies were decided, including that regional rallies would be held, the three opposition parties pressed to amend the labor laws, all democratic groups supporting labor law reform would be unified, and a national headquarters established for the struggle for labor law reform and wage increases.

The first meeting of delegates to the national struggle headquarters took place on 28 October 1988, where it was decided that a group of metropolitan union leaders would join sit-in protests organized by the Seoul Council of Trade Unions at the headquarters of the Party for Peace and Democracy. Tactics were also explored to change the passive attitudes of political parties and members of the National Assembly toward amendment of the labor laws.

At another meeting of delegates in Daejun toward the end of 1988, it was decided that sit-in protests would be staged at the headquarters of the three opposition parties, especially the Party for Unification and Democracy. The intention was to encourage amendment of the labor laws during the 1988 session of the National Assembly. It was also decided that rallies and general meetings of union members would be held simultaneously in as many regions as practicable.

Sit-in protests at the headquarters of the Party for Unification and Democracy from 29 November to 1 December 1988 completed the year's political activities.[8] Similar political actions were conducted during 1989, and the school teachers extended the struggle by demanding legalization of the National Teachers' Union. The bitter confrontation between the union and the government led to the loss of 1,527 teachers' positions by the end of June 1990.

The most important historical event for the Korean union movement in 1990 was the establishment of the National Alliance of Trade Unions on 22 January 1990. NATU called a nationwide strike by its members on 1 May to protest police action against strikers at the Hyundai shipyard. Other demands included immediate withdrawal of police troops deployed inside and outside the company, the release of detained workers, and the resignation of the cabinet ministers who had ordered the police raid. The May Day strike call did not, however, receive much support from affiliated unions. Most of NATU's senior leaders were subsequently arrested or pursued by the police.[9]

Effectiveness of the Union Movement

Unions in Korea influence wage levels, relative wages, labor productivity, and other aspects of employment relations. One caveat is that union influence in Korea is not confined to unionized establishments. Thus, in comparing the wages and conditions of unionized and nonunionized employees, one should not assume the latter are independent of the former. Differentials may be smaller than anticipated if union influence matters in the workplace. Reinforcing this view is the fact that labor shortages were most severe in the period 1987–90, contributing to higher levels of inflation and hence limited economic growth.[10] In this environment employers were eager to retain and recruit skilled workers and hence were bidding up wages. Union influence is also likely to be less evident because, as noted earlier in relation to industrial disputes, a large minority of disputes are prosecuted by workers in the absence of unions. And it is mainly through industrial action followed by negotiations rather than collective bargaining that Korean workers have achieved gains in the workplace. With these qualifications in mind, I shall draw on recent research I conducted with B.-N. Sung (1990), based on a random sample of more than sixty thousand employees covered by the official 1987 and 1988 occupational wage surveys.

Relative Wages

The union wage effect was estimated by fitting average earnings functions to micro cross-section data on wages, union existence, and other variables, controlling for differences among workers in working conditions and worker quality. From the estimated results, it is clear that most of the observed union/nonunion average wage gap can be explained by differences in worker quality and working conditions. These estimates are summarized in table 5.5, which distinguishes between gross (uncontrolled-for) wage differentials and net differentials, which take into account variables other than union presence.

Table 5.5 shows that in 1988 the average wage for male production workers was 30 percent higher in the unionized sector than in the nonunionized sector but that the gap closed considerably (2.2 percent) after controlling for human capital attributes and other structural variables. Since 29 June 1987, however, the relative wage gap has increased and unions have won much larger gains for blue-collar than for white-collar workers. In the case of male unionized workers, the relative wage effect was negative for both production and nonproduction workers in 1987, as shown in table 5.5. In 1988, the wage effect continued to be negative for male nonproduction workers, but it was 2.2 percent for male production workers. For female production workers, there is no significant difference in the union wage effect between 1987 and 1988. The analysis of the 1988 data yields an estimate of the union relative wage effect of 0.4 percent for nonproduction workers and 2.8 percent for production workers as a whole.

A noteworthy point—not evident in table 5.5—is that for male workers, the union relative wage effect declines as establishment size increases. The union relative wage effect in 1988 was 4.1 percent among workplaces with 100 to 499 employees, compared with − 4.1 percent among firms with 500 or more employees. For female workers, however, the union wage effect increases as establishment size increases. There are several possible reasons for this. First, the labor market may be tighter for males than for females, thereby limiting the independent effect of unionization on males. Second, females tend to be employed in

Table 5.5. Gross and net wage differentials in Korea, by union versus nonunion status, 1987 and 1988 (in percent)

	1987		1988	
	Gross wage differential[a]	*Net wage differential*	*Gross wage differential*	*Net wage differential*
	Male		*Male*	
Nonproduction workers	5.6	− 1.6	19.9	− 2.2
Production workers	12.0	− 2.9	30.1	2.2
	Female		*Female*	
Nonproduction workers	3.7	1.8	11.9	0.4
Production workers	3.9	2.9	7.8	2.8

[a]Percentage gap between union and nonunion average monthly earnings in sample data.

smaller establishments, so that the impact of unionization is likely to be greater when they work among militant male employees in larger establishments. Third, a higher proportion of males are white-collar employees who work in larger establishments. Their wage differential with blue-collar workers has been compressed in recent years. This reduced bargaining power is reflected in the lack of a positive association between establishment size and wage differentials for male employees. Finally, there are considerable variations in the union wage effect by industry, region, educational level, and length of service (Kim and Sung 1990:79–82).

Effect of Unions on Wage Inequality

To examine the effect of unions on wage inequality, Sung and I calculated and then compared wage differentials by sex, occupation, establishment size, and educational level for the unionized and nonunionized sectors separately. We found that the male-female net wage differential with respect to production workers in 1988 was lower in the unionized sector (1.189) than in the nonunionized sector (1.255). Table 5.6 provides additional data.

Table 5.6 shows that unionism reduces male production workers' wage differentials by establishment size and by level of schooling, controlling for other factors, while the opposite is the case for females. One possible interpretation is that unions work to equalize earnings for the dominant gender (males), but this has the effect of encouraging employers of unionized labor in larger establishments to employ a greater proportion of lower-paid, less educated females in less-skilled occupations.

Since Korean unions are organized mainly among blue-collar workers and union wage gains have been much larger for blue-collar than for white-collar workers, occupational wage differentials are much lower in the unionized sector, as shown in table 5.6. In 1988, for instance, in the nonunionized sector, male nonproduction workers who were high school graduates received 17.6 percent higher wages than comparably educated male production workers, even controlling for other variables including marital status, establishment size, industry, region, and average monthly working hours. In the unionized sector, however, nonproduction workers received 1.5 percent lower wages than production workers. While female nonproduction workers with the same qualifications received 26.0 percent higher wages than their production worker counterparts in the nonunionized sector, those in the unionized sector earned only 8.2 percent higher wages. Thus, it would seem that unions exert a substantial equalizing effect on wage differentials.

Table 5.6. Net wage differentials in unionized and nonunionized sectors of Korea, by occupation, establishment size, and workers' level of education, 1988

	Male		Female	
	Unionized sector	Nonunionized sector	Unionized sector	Nonunionized sector
Occupation[a]				
Nonproduction workers Production workers (middle school graduates)	0.969	1.216	1.002	1.204
Nonproduction workers Production workers (high school graduates)	0.985	1.176	1.082	1.260
Establishment size				
≥500 employees 10–99 employees	1.118	1.197	1.147	1.126
≥500 employees 100–499 employees	1.092	1.184	1.213	1.131
Level of Education				
High school Elementary school	1.177	1.244	1.199	1.171
High school Middle school	1.119	1.146	1.187	1.153

[a]Calculated for production workers only.

Effect of Unions on Labor Productivity

Union activity represents an alternative to quitting, thereby saving employers hiring and training costs. Workers also contribute to improving productivity by encouraging more effective plant administration and higher employee commitment. Lower turnover facilitates the accumulation of specific human skills through on-the-job training, further enhancing labor productivity. Data limitations prevented analysis of all these possible effects, but indirect evidence that unions stimulate the long-term attachment of workers to their employers was investigated. By fitting equations to cross-section data on wages, union status, schooling, age, and other labor market structure variables, it was found that even controlling for human capital attributes, wages, and structural variables such as establishment size, region, and industry, the data indicate that workers in the unionized sector stay with an employer longer than in the nonunionized sector. For example, length of service in the current job is about one year longer for male workers in the unionized sector. This result represents indirect evidence that Korean unions play a positive role regarding labor productivity.

In addition to the aforementioned economic impacts, unions have had a significant influence on workers' consciousness and attitudes, on employers' views concerning the treatment of employees, and on industrial relations more generally. The revitalized union movement that has developed since mid-1987 has made workers aware of their rights, as reflected in their strong demands for higher wages, reduced working hours, and better treatment by management. Workers have also been made aware of the need for unity in their struggle for institutional reforms (Christian Institute of Industrial Development 1990:274–76).

Surveys have confirmed that workers' attitudes are changing. Specifically, manual employees are voicing more radical opinions than their white-collar counterparts. A recent survey concluded that "blue collar employees feel stronger class consciousness and relative deprivation. They also have a stronger desire to participate in decision making as well as a more negative view of the labor laws of Korea" (Korean Productivity Center 1989:238). This awareness has contributed to the strengthening of worker solidarity within unions and has facilitated a more national approach to labor issues.

The solidarity of the "democratic unions," illustrated by the establishment of the National Alliance of Trade Unions, caused anxiety and a reassessment of employer and government policies while at the same time encouraging the FKTU to become more responsive to workers' demands. Before electing its new executive members in 1989, the FKTU asserted that it intended to take a firm stand against the government's unfair interventions in labor disputes and would support political parties that emphasized protection and advancement of workers' interests. The FKTU also formally established a political activities committee. As a sign of change, and in contravention of government policy, the FKTU held a May Day ceremony in 1990. Although the response by workers to this major event was not very enthusiastic (partly because it meant losing a day's pay), it was the first time the FKTU had asserted itself in this way since the banning of May Day activities thirty-four years before.

Union activity has also led to the adoption of more capital-intensive production techniques and two opposing trends in the management of human resources. One is toward a more enlightened approach, including acceptance of the legitimacy of unions as representatives of labor's interests and as means of developing common sets of interests based on labor-management cooperation. The other is toward a hard-line approach, highlighted in many newspaper reports on the use of such unfair labor practices as refusal to bargain, intervention in union activities, employment of "save-the-company squads" to intimidate employees, and discrimination against union activists (see *Korea Labor News, Han-Kyoreh Shinmun,* and *Mahl*).

The National Council of Economic Organizations (NCEO) was created on 24 December 1989, one month before the National Alliance of Trade Unions was established. Through the NCEO, employers began to orchestrate a response to workers' demands and to apply sanctions against companies that did not abide by their policy directives. Moreover, following the emergence in early 1990 of the new ruling Democratic Liberal Party after the merger of three conservative parties (two in opposition and one in power), the government tightened control over the labor movement. This was partly in response to lobbying by the NCEO, which had insisted on the principle of "no work, no pay" in strike situations. The NCEO had attempted to enforce this principle jointly with the government. This campaign has been interpreted by union leaders as an attempt to weaken unions on the grounds that it is impossible for unions to accumulate strike funds when monthly union payments cannot legally exceed 2 percent of monthly wages.

Union activity after 1987 initially led to a more compromising position by the government, but since mid-1989 its position has been reversed. The government has attempted to blame the unions for fueling inflation and causing recession through excessive wage demands. The police raid on Hyundai Heavy Industries Company (which employs about twenty thousand employees) in April 1990 highlighted the government's resolve to support employers against what had been regarded as excessive union claims backed by illegal industrial action.

Conclusion

Korean unions have always been concerned with both economic and political issues. They were at the forefront of resistance to Japanese colonial rule and thereafter continued pressuring for democratic reform. As noted earlier, however, for most of the subsequent four decades, until 1987, this was an uphill struggle characterized by splits in the movement and the failure of union leaders to patch up their differences, especially around 1960–61, when there was a unique chance to unite opposing union factions. Consequently, the official union movement, represented by the Confederation of Korean Trade Unions and later by the FKTU, was neutralized, leaving only a militant minority of unions to oppose the lack of organizational freedom typical of union activity for most of the next twenty-five years. Union strategies were thus characterized by either their subservience to capital and the state, or their resistance, mainly through industrial action. Repressive legislation and harsh penalties ensured, however, that independent union activity was effectively suppressed.

The government's promise of democratic reforms and the measures that followed, aimed at fostering union-management cooperation, stimulated union activity and resulted in the creation of many new autonomous ("democratic") unions (see Deyo 1989:74). As noted, the official conservative unions tended to adopt policies independent of those of the government. Union density increased substantially between 1987 and 1990 in response to the successes registered by unions. Hence, we may speak of the late 1980s as a period of transition.

Some characteristics of the future union movement are already evident from the changes that have occurred so far. Male production workers in large companies, especially in the heavy-metal and chemical industries, have become leading participants, and white-collar workers have become more prominent actors on the union stage. There has been a strengthening of multiunion activities through regional, industrial, and company-based consultative councils. Last but not least, a new national association, the National Alliance of Trade Unions, has been established by the democratic unions in competition with the conservative but somewhat revitalized FKTU.

Whereas unions have lacked the capacity to bargain for the reasons discussed earlier, the changed economic and political context, including more enlightened attitudes by some employers, has assisted unions in strengthening their position in this regard. Moreover, since 1988, political action at regional, industrial, and national levels has foreshadowed the possibility of changes in labor legislation that may extend unionism and collective bargaining in the future. As I noted, however, reactionary employers, whose power is largely based on patrimonial rule (Biggart 1990), still retain significant influence in Korea. With government support, the spread of unionism and collective bargaining has been temporarily stemmed. There is even talk of anti-union legislation being introduced by the ruling party, whose dominance in Parliament is currently overwhelming. Thus, in the short term, the prospects for a transition toward a more united union movement based on strong bargaining relationships with employers and close consultation with the government look remote. In the longer term, however, with the decline of the cold war and the process of unification on the government's agenda, the issue of national security will be a far less convincing argument for maintaining authoritarian control over independent pressure groups. In addition, the government is mindful of demands by the more educated and younger generation, whose propensity to violent agitation has been amply demonstrated. Last but not least, it is unclear how stable the current merger between the three main political parties will prove to be.

The major challenges facing the union movement are threefold: first, how to establish ideologies and goals that encourage worker support and are realizable without substantially alienating large employers and the government; second, how to devise strategies and tactics that extend internal union democracy and strengthen union organization as a safeguard against state or party domination, which transforms unions into dependent substructures; and third, and most important, how to encourage leaders and activists of different unions to work more closely, especially at the national level, to ensure the creation of a framework for the joint regulation of wages and working conditions and extensive tripartite consultation on national economic policy.

6

The Resurgence and Fragility of Trade Unions in Taiwan

Stephen Frenkel, Jon-Chao Hong, and Bih-Ling Lee

The mid-1980s marked the beginning of major political change in Taiwan as numerous interest groups began to demand freedom of expression and improvements in the quality of life both inside and outside the workplace. Trade unions under younger, more militant leaders were among the most important of the forces that encouraged the lifting of martial law in 1987, thereby permitting legitimate pressure group activity for the first time in thirty-eight years. By the end of the year, many disputes over annual bonuses brought the development of Taiwan's union movement to a new stage. The number of unions grew at an unprecedented rate, and the nature of industrial relations changed significantly. A study of the Taiwanese union movement therefore needs to explore the seeds of this new development if one hopes to understand the changing characteristics of unions and their significance.

Accordingly, this chapter begins with a brief history of trade unionism in Taiwan, drawing attention to the context in which unions have blossomed in recent years and the factors responsible for this development. In the second section, we discuss changes in Taiwanese unions by referring to data on union growth and intra- and interunion organizational characteristics. The third section examines changes in union goals and strategies with special attention to union activity, particularly the

We would like to thank Peter Chen and Chung-Chen Lin for their observations. Responsibility lies solely with the authors, however.

rise in industrial conflict and the political and managerial responses to it. In the fourth and final section, we discuss the achievements and limitations of trade unionism and probable future shape of trade unionism in Taiwan.

Political Control, Old-Style Unionism, and the Democratic Challenge

Immediately following World War II, Japan—which had colonized Taiwan for fifty years and had prohibited trade unionism—was forced to hand back Taiwan to China. Unions were encouraged, resulting in the growth of more than one hundred mainly craft unions. After several strikes by the miners' unions in 1947, labor organizations were banned by the Kuomintang Party, which was recognized as the rightful heir of China by Western governments. Chiang Kai-shek had failed to defeat the Communists and had fled with his army and supporters to Taiwan, where they had taken over the government of the island and established it as a base from which to reclaim the mainland. Considering themselves as formally at war with the People's Republic of China, the KMT imposed martial law on Taiwan, leading to severe restrictions on civil rights. Opposition political groups were strongly discouraged. There thus developed something of a siege mentality among the population. At this time, the government was dominated by KMT stalwarts, most of whom differed ethnically from the Taiwanese and who comprised less than 3 percent of the total population (Ying 1990). Under these circumstances it was very difficult for workers to develop autonomous unions.

The KMT's perception of unions as sources of political opposition and as potential social welfare agents led to the formulation of labor laws that effectively outlawed strikes but fostered trade unionism under KMT control. By 1950, there were 175 unions representing 7.9 percent of nonagricultural employees (Lee 1988:186). Thereafter, union growth was relatively slow, but it grew more rapidly between 1970 and 1984 so that by 1984 the number of unions had reached 1,924 and they represented 22.8 percent of the nonagricultural work force.

According to J. S. Lee (1988:188–91), four of the five most important reasons for this growth had to do with the major role played by the state. First, the Trade Union Law was amended. Until 1975, it had required unions to be established in workplaces in most sectors with more than fifty employees. This threshold was reduced to thirty employees in 1975. Second, having been forced to relinquish its seat in the United Nations in 1971 in favor of the Communist government on the mainland, the Taiwan government was feeling increasingly isolated. Unions were encouraged by the government as a means of fostering relations with other countries. Third, the government wanted to give the impression that it was democratic. Fourth, self-employed persons were showing increasing interest in joining unions in order to become eligible for social insurance.[1] Fifth, and finally, with economic growth, the secondary sector expanded from 28 percent of employees in 1970 to 42.3 percent in 1984, making unionization more likely.

Unions remained subservient to the government, however, and helped it promote international relations and mobilize workers to support the KMT in local and national elections. The unions provided limited welfare and educational services for their members and lobbied for favorable labor legislation (Lee 1988:191). It was not until 1985 that unions independent of the KMT began to emerge. Before discussing this, it is worth noting that the KMT appears to have been able to control unions through the legal arrangements surrounding union elections, which continue to this day.

Various aspects of union government in Taiwan are legally prescribed (see Ying 1990:43–44). Unions must have a certain structure of members, representatives, and executives. Representatives are elected by groups of five to thirty members. Representatives in turn elect union executives, who then elect standing executives, who ultimately elect the union president.

Registration of a new union can be delayed by the government, which may encourage management and worker support for a rival organization if the union making the application does not support the KMT.

Until 1987, the KMT guided most unions through local government control over the nomination and election of union officials, through the fostering of KMT cells and branches at workplaces, and through "supervision" by larger affiliates of the sole national union peak council, the Chinese Federation of Labor (CFL). The CFL did not conduct a single election for its congress or its executive officers between 1950 and 1975 (Lin 1988:384), ostensibly because it was a national organization and, it was argued, because the mainland was occupied by hostile forces, a national congress could not be held. Officials of the CFL monitored union affairs, persuading union representatives and other union functionaries to act in line with KMT policy.[2]

The CFL had been established on the mainland by the KMT to replace the Communist-dominated peak union organization, the ACFTU. After its transfer to Taiwan, the ACFTU came to exercise substantial control over trade unionism as a result of receiving financial support from the government, thereby enabling it to develop an extensive hierarchy that spread down to provincial and county levels. According to H. S. Ying (1990:14), the CFL has about twenty-two hundred union affiliates, representing 20 percent of the work force. As we shall see, however, the CFL has attracted criticism from union activists and is now under challenge from several new labor federations.

Legal Context of Union Development

We have already touched on the centerpiece of old-style unionism: incorporation by the government, coupled with severe restrictions on industrial action, leading to union quiescence. The government also promoted cooperation at the workplace level by legislating (and amending or adding to the original legislation from time to time) worker protection and limited involvement in decision making. The key law is the Labor Standards Law of 1984, which was introduced in response to the rise in worker militancy. This law requires employers (except in government, education, and the defense industry, which together comprise 17 percent of the work force) to observe certain minimum standards with respect to such matters as termination of the employment contract, overtime pay, payment of wages in arrears (to prevent bankrupt employers from reneging on their employment obligations), work hours and holidays, sick leave, workers' injury compensation, and wages.[3]

Another important law is the Labor Insurance Act of 1958, which requires employers with more than five employees to deduct wages and contribute to a central fund for the provision of social security covering such matters as nonwork- and work-related medical and disability benefits, unemployment benefits, and pensions. Under this law, employers must also establish a retirement benefits fund and deduct between 2 and 15 percent of their total monthly wage bills for transfer to the fund.

The Employee Welfare Fund Law of 1943 requires all employers to establish an employee welfare fund for such welfare activities as supporting employee housing and children's schooling, arranging sporting events, organizing singing, dancing, and other forms of entertainment, and supervising the workplace canteen. The law prescribes the proportion of funds to be allocated to this fund (Taiwan. Council of Labor Affairs [CLA] 1989a:315).

Finally, the Labor Safety and Health Law of 1974 proscribes certain dangerous activities and prescribes precautions to be taken.

With regard to employee and union participation, the Labor Standards Law requires relevant firms employing more than thirty employees to establish a consultative committee with an equal number of workers and employer representatives. Members of this committee are elected by union members if a union exists in the workplace or, in the absence of a union, by the workers directly. The role of this committee is broadly to foster cooperation between management and labor by management's provision of information on business conditions and production plans and by addressing matters of mutual concern (CLA 1989a:115–19). The Factory Law of 1929 required a similar body to be set up in which workers' representatives are elected by all the nonmanagerial employees in the workplace (CLA 1989a:423).

Unions are expected to play a role in the supervision and administration of various employee benefit programs. For example, according to the Labor Standards Law, the supervisory committee of each enterprise's retirement fund must be composed of a majority of worker representatives, who are elected by the union or directly by the employees where no union exists (Taiwan. CLA 1989a:133–35). Under the Employee Welfare Fund Law of 1943, not less than two-thirds of an employee welfare committee must be union representatives. Where there is no union, it is customary for the employer to organize a welfare committee with employee involvement.

The Trade Union Law of 1929, which regulates unions, envisages these organizations to be employee protectors, promoters of workers' welfare, and contributors to the development of productive enterprises (CLA 1989a:203). Provision is made for unions to bargain with employers under the Collective Agreement Law of 1930, which also requires that agreements be submitted to the government for approval (CLA 1989a:267).

The Settlement of Labor Disputes Law of 1928 prohibits industrial action before a dispute has failed to be conciliated or arbitrated (CLA 1989a:289), but this provision did not apply before 1987. The same law states that a union cannot legally strike in favor of a wage claim that exceeds the standard wage (CLA 1989a:223). As we shall see, this has not prevented unions in recent years from striking over bonuses, which traditionally had been a discretionary item paid by the employer at the end of the year according to the profitability of the business. The custom of giving bonuses has been institutionalized by the Labor Standards Law (see CLA 1989a:25).

In summary, although the union's role has been cast by the law as a bargaining agent, the emphasis has been on unions as organizations that carry out welfare functions on behalf of employees. Until 1987, the prohibition on industrial action under martial law (which overruled the Labor Disputes Law of 1928) made it impossible to bargain, while government control over unions through the supervision of elections prevented the rise of a workers' movement until the mid-1980s, when labor rights were part of the people's wider democratic agenda. Union development was also restricted, paradoxically, by a tight labor market, resulting from rapid economic growth and reduced population growth. This situation encouraged employers to increase wages without union pressure. Thus, it seems that the environment permitted union activity aimed at protecting and advancing workers' interests but only within narrowly prescribed limits. This is how one authority described Taiwanese unions before the period of democratic reform:

Trade unions were instruments advocating government decrees; all the organizations and activities were operated in accordance with the government's predetermined policies. Their forms resembled those of western official labor unions but they were company unions controlled by representatives of the employers. Within a trade union numerous factions contradicted each other and the quality of the union's cadre was rather uneven. Instead of actively promoting labor's interests, the union's function dwindled into passively handling such matters as labor insurance. Furthermore, the financial self-sufficiency of the trade union also suffered from the workers' lukewarm willingness to join the union. As a result, the general state of the union movement in the past can only be portrayed as "lethargic" (P. T. Huang 1988:77).

With the abolition of martial law, which included the lifting of bans on industrial action, workers could collectively and publicly express their discontent. They quickly challenged the ways of old-style union leaders. Before examining the changes that ensued, it is worth noting the broader forces that generated the democratic movement.

Factors Encouraging Political Reform and New-Style Unionism

Among the main factors that have contributed to the liberalizing tendency in Taiwan, several are particularly noteworthy. The first factor is the contradiction between the slow development of labor rights and Taiwan's rapid economic growth. Arguably, labor's rights have been constrained by the government's undue concentration on the economy, which experienced the highest postwar (1953–85) growth rate (8.6 percent per year) in the world (Ying 1990:10). The implementation of new legislation—the Labor Standards Law—designed to protect workers more effectively had been eagerly anticipated, but deficiencies in the law, difficulties of interpretation, and lack of enforcement resulted in the persistence of health and safety problems, discrimination against women workers, and employer evasion of limitations on weekly working hours (Ying 1990:24–30).[4]

The second factor is the changing occupational structure and employees' expectations; these have changed considerably with new job roles and rising educational levels. The proportion of workers with secondary and tertiary qualifications has increased in line with the growth in trades and white-collar occupations. In 1979, for example, 18 percent and 8.9 percent of employed persons had graduated from secondary high school (or the equivalent) and tertiary institutions respectively. Ten years later, these proportions had increased to 28.9 percent and 15.4 percent (China. DGBAS, n.d.:13) in a nonagricultural civilian work force some 42.6 percent larger and a white-collar work force whose size relative to the total work force had expanded by 28 percent (China. DGBAS, n.d.:2– 10). More highly educated workers are looking to unions to advance their interests, and it is these workers who are providing much of the activism in the new union movement.

The third factor affecting workers' consciousness has been the tendency for workers to turn away from the countryside and focus on cities. Whereas in earlier years employees had looked to the countryside to supplement their income and find work if they experienced unemployment, by the 1980s Taiwan was substantially urbanized and the great majority of workers were dependent solely on wages from labor.[5] This has stimulated workers to fight for employment rights. Moreover although large establishments are comparatively rare in Taiwan (Deyo 1989:40), increasing numbers of Taiwanese work in factories and large cities (Chiu 1989:59).

The fourth factor affecting industrialization is the disintegration of the traditional work ethic. According to Chinese custom, labor-management relations were modeled on that of benefactor and beneficiary, and the latter obeyed the former unquestioningly. This convention is being substituted by a modern notion of work relationships based on integration of, and respect for, persons occupying specialized and increasingly skilled work roles. In addition, a minority of workers have left their jobs in buoyant times to gamble on the stock market. This occurred in 1987 and 1988, but since then share prices have declined considerably, encouraging these workers to return to the job market.

The fifth factor is the tendency for income inequality to have increased in recent years. In 1988, the total income of families in the highest 20 percent income category received 38.3 percent of gross national income, while those families in the lowest 20 percent of income earners received only 7.9 percent of national income. Thus, recipients in the highest income category received nearly 4.9 times more than those in the lowest category; 1988 was the eighth year in which income inequality increased.[6] Workers' feelings of relative deprivation have therefore provided a strong motivation for seeking improvements in earnings and working conditions.

More specifically, political issues have played a major role in focusing discontent. The notion that Taiwan was at war with the PRC and would eventually assume power on the mainland had after three decades become a fiction. This made it increasingly difficult for the government to maintain the legitimacy of martial law and a gerontocracy of unrepresentative legislators. In addition, by the 1980s, Taiwan was becoming politically isolated as many countries recognized Beijing and switched their diplomatic representation accordingly.

Taiwan's economic success also served to undermine the island's one-party government. The United States was becoming increasingly sensitive to its massive foreign trade deficit with Taiwan, leading to demands for improved labor rights (which would increase the cost of Taiwan's goods and make them less competitive) and fewer import restrictions. There was also the possibility that the United States would withdraw Taiwan's most-favored-nation status. This would have been a significant blow to a country that exports more than 40 percent of its goods to the United States (Ying 1990:93). In addition, the Taiwan government was beginning to realize that if the country's growth record was to continue into the 1990s it was necessary to restructure the economy. Success in the United States and other overseas markets had pushed up the Taiwanese dollar. A strategy based on cheap labor with limited democratic rights and a narrow range of markets was coming to be seen as untenable. Moreover, labor militancy in countries such as South Korea and the Philippines, where democratic movements were consolidating, encouraged labor relations reform. Hence, there was a tendency for government officials to think more in terms of the production of higher value-added goods based on new technology and a highly skilled and committed work force. To accomplish this, a new labor relations strategy was deemed to be necessary.

Demands for greater participation in political decision making were manifested in demonstrations by various groups, beginning around 1984, against pollution and nuclear power and in favor of consumer protection. As part of this social movement, workers sought improved working conditions and the right to form new unions (Ying 1990:35). In September 1986, the Democratic Progressive Party (DPP) was established as the first expression of open opposition to the KMT in many years. Although it was illegal, the party was allowed to survive. The following month, martial law was lifted (including the ban on strikes), although this was not formalized until July 1987.

The lifting of martial law, together with reduced restrictions on travel to the PRC, signaled a major shift in government policy. This, together with the emergence of a free press and competition between political parties—the Labor Party was registered in 1987—gave the social movement further impetus. In late 1986, the opposition parties won two of the five seats reserved for union representatives in the legislative branch of the government.[7] These developments caused the government to reevaluate its labor policy and to expand and raise the status of the labor administration department, which was a branch of the Interior Ministry, by establishing an autonomous cabinet-level Council of Labor Affairs (as part of the executive branch). This council began operating in August 1987.

The council did little to stem the rising tide of industrial militancy, so the government established six labor courts and amended the Labor Disputes Settlement Act in the summer of 1988. This did not prevent the Maioli bus drivers from striking, however, and the dispute from widening into a challenge to the government's labor relations policies (Lee 1988:178).

A national labor administration conference was held the following year at which the government's support for the protection and improvement of workers' interests was emphasized. In addition, major legislative changes were foreshadowed.

The next section begins by examining trends in union growth in terms of the number of unions and their membership. The changing internal dynamics of unions are then discussed, followed by some observations on relations between unions.

Number of Unions, Union Membership, and Union Size

The number of unions and union members increased sharply over the period 1979–89. Table 6.1 summarizes the data at selected points during these years.

Table 6.1 distinguishes between enterprise and occupational unions from 1986, when such data became available. The Trade Union Law of 1929 requires that there be only one union per workplace, so that employees of different manufacturing occupations belong to the same enterprise union. Although the law encourages employers to establish a union where more than thirty workers are employed and requires all employees to join the union (CLA 1989a:207, 211), employers have been reluctant to obey the law. Unions are most common in larger establishments, where they receive as much support among higher-educated employees as from their less formally well-qualified counterparts.[8] Employees in smaller establishments have tended to join occupational unions based outside the workplace, which bring together members of the same occupation in the same locality.

The fragmented nature of the Taiwanese union movement and the

Table 6.1. Number of unions and union members in Taiwan, by union type and density

| Year end | Unions | | National Federations | Membership (in 1,000s) | | Density[a] |
	Enter-prise	Occupa-tional		Enter-prise	Occupa-tional	
1979	1,637	–	n.a.	1,028.7	–	20.4
1984	1,924	–	n.a.	1,370.6	–	22.8
1986	1,201	989	5	478.4	1,067.7	26.9
1989	1,453	2,009	5	577.3	1,766.8	32.6

Sources: China. DGBAS, n.d.:3, 11, 29; Taiwan. Council of Labor Affairs 1990a.
[a]Denominator in the union density calculation is the number of persons in the nonagricultural labor force.
n.a. = not available.

growth of unions, particularly since the end of 1986, are evident from table 6.1. Thus, the number of unions increased by 58.1 percent between the end of 1986 and the end of 1989, compared with an increase of 33.8 percent in the seven-year period ending in 1986. The increase is most noticeable among occupational unions: their number more than doubled between the end of 1986 and the end of 1989.

A similar picture emerges when membership growth is examined. The most rapid period of growth was between the end of 1986 and 1989, when the number of union members increased by 51.6 percent. The number of members of occupational unions rose during this period by 65.5 percent, versus 20.7 percent for enterprise unions. These changes are reflected in the union density estimates, which show an accelerating trend most evident from the end of 1986.

Before attempting to explain these changes, it is worth noting that the number of national union federations and provincial and municipal federations (not shown in table 6.1) remained relatively stable, although one major new-style federation—the National Federation of Independent Unions, comprising some twelve unions—remained outside the formal system and was therefore excluded from the official statistics from which the data are drawn.

Three reasons can be advanced for the accelerated growth of union membership, particularly in occupational unions, during the late 1980s. The first reason is that the lifting of martial law in 1987 acted as a catalyst for many people to participate in public affairs. Thus, many employees joined occupational unions because their workplaces lacked statutory support (they had thirty or fewer employees) or because their employers opposed unions despite the law. Both factors applied to the growing white-collar private-service sector, which, by the end of 1986, accounted for 41.5 percent of the work force (China. DGBAS, n.d.:9). Thus, workers in the finance and banking sector formed unions with the aim of establishing a national organization, while teachers protested against the union law that prevented them from establishing a union (CLA 1989a:205). The police and public servants, together with employees in defense industries, continue to be prohibited from organizing (Kleingartner and Peng 1991:434).

The second reason for the accelerated growth was that the Labor Standards Law of 1984 gave workers the opportunity to join an occupational union as a means of contributing to, and receiving, various social insurance benefits. By 1986, information about this opportunity was widespread, and consequently many employees not previously covered by insurance, especially those in uncertain jobs in small firms or working as self-employed contractors, as well as persons not in the paid work force, such as women working at home, joined occupational unions for insurance purposes.

The third reason for the rapid growth in occupational union member-ship has to do with changes in the official definition of occupation. Following enactment of the Labor Standards Law in 1984, the govern-ment began to define occupations more narrowly, thereby considerably increasing in number. This process has been a continuous one and has resulted in new unions registering to cover the new occupational groups.

An important implication of the above analysis is that union member-ship data and estimates of union density are a poor guide to the strength of the Taiwanese union movement. The inclusion of both workers and nonwage earners (subcontractors and unpaid persons) in occupational unions for reasons having to do with the labor insurance warn against an interpretation that emphasizes a significant increase in union power.

No data are available except for 1988 on the changing size distribution of Taiwanese unions. These are summarized in figures 6.1 and 6.2.

Figure 6.1 shows that most enterprise unions have one hundred or more members but that less than 10 percent report having a membership of one thousand or more. There are proportionately more larger occu-pational unions (fig. 6.2), which is not surprising given that members of such organizations are not confined to a single employer. Nevertheless, the small size of these unions indicates that they are limited in geograph-ical coverage and by the narrow definition of occupation referred to earlier. The data on enterprise unions are consistent with the small size of establishments in Taiwan: in mid-1989, only 15.5 percent and 6.3 percent of employees worked in establishments with one hundred to fewer than five hundred or five hundred or more employees respectively (China. DGBAS, n.d.:31).[9]

Changes in the Nature of Trade Unionism: Individual Unions

The statistics presented above and the ensuing discussion do not convey the change in union character that has occurred since 1986. So-called new-style unions, characterized by greater militancy and auton-omy from the KMT, some of which are affiliated with other political parties, emerged in the latter part of the 1980s. In some cases these organizations began as workers' associations established as alternatives to existing unions and served as bases from which elections for union positions could be organized. Successful examples include the Taiwan Petroleum Workers' Union, the Nan-Ya Plastics Corporation Union (Ying 1990:45), and two state enterprises, the Taiwan Power Company Union and the Taiwan Sugar Company Union (J. Huang 1988:283). Old-style unions have also changed as the leadership has responded to a more demanding rank and file, who are less likely to acquiesce to KMT "supervision." Ying (1990:40) puts the number of new-style unions at more than one hundred, or nearly 6 percent of the total number of

Figure 6.1. Size distribution of enterprise unions in Taiwan, 1988

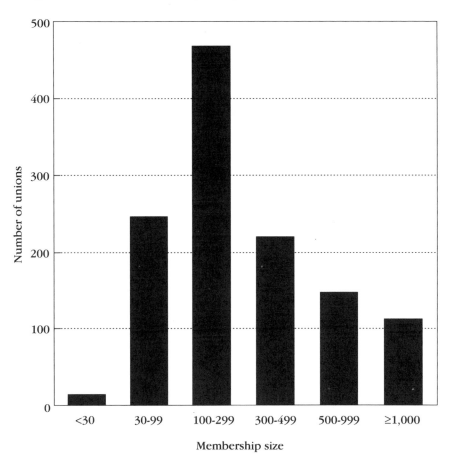

Source: Taiwan. Council of Labor Affairs 1989b.
No data were available for sixty-three unions.

unions. In terms of membership and influence within the union movement, however, their impact has been far greater. At the same time, the
consensus among labor specialists is that by mid-1990 these unions were
losing their momentum as the rate of economic growth declined and
employers showed their determination not to give in to union demands.
This new attitude was illustrated by management at the Hsin-Ya Electric
Company, which closed the factory rather than accede to employees'
demands. Publicity given to a rapid increase in outward investment by
Taiwanese manufacturing firms also contributed to a less determined
rank and file.[10]

Reflecting the emergence of a more vocal rank and file, the internal

Figure 6.2. Size distribution of occupational unions in Taiwan, 1988

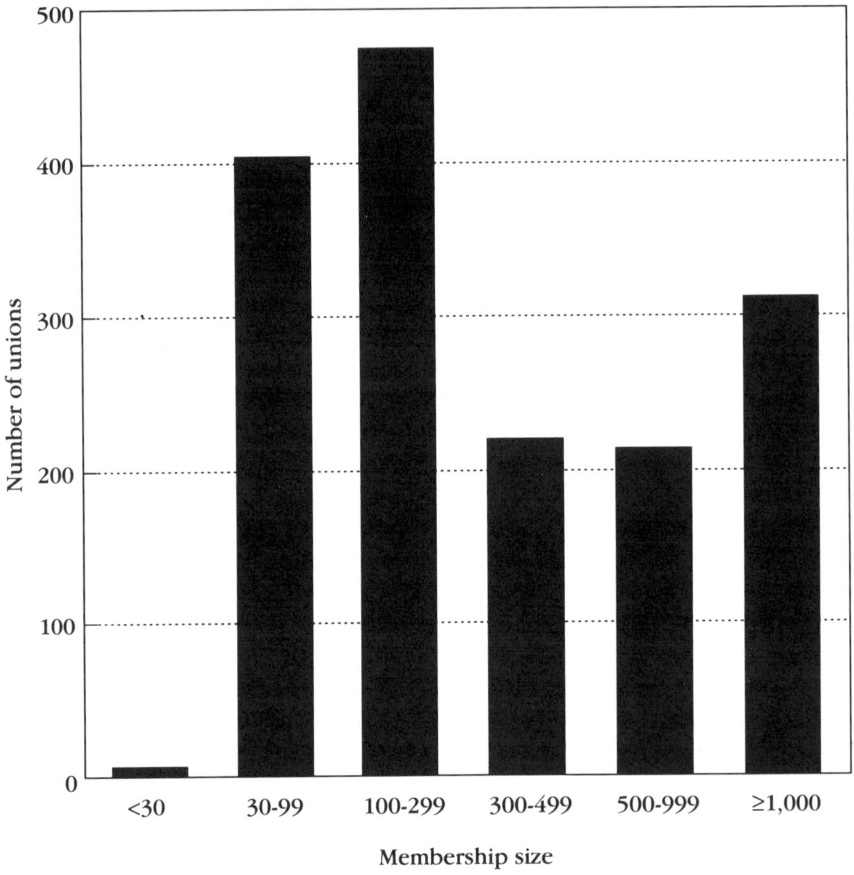

Source: Taiwan. Council of Labor Affairs 1989b.
No data were available for forty-six unions.

operations of unions have also undergone change. In the past the representatives' conference was the most authoritative meeting of a union, yet conferences were held only once a year (triennially for a national federation). Most members were either unfamiliar with, or indifferent to, the activities of their union, so union policy was effectively set by the union officials. Members are now playing a more substantial role in conference proceedings, however, to ensure that officials are more responsive to their demands. This is reflected in the increased number of proposals discussed at union conferences. In 1988, for example, as many as three hundred proposals were discussed in the union representatives' conference of the Oil Industry Union. Increasing rank-and-file participation is also evident in the longer time taken to conduct such conferences. This also reflects the diversity of members' opinions that have had to be accommodated, their inadequate knowledge, and the occasional abuse of conference regulations.

Finally, some unions have felt it necessary to explain their policies to members. An example of this is the Taiwan Railway Union, which, in an effort to increase organizational unity, took the unprecedented step of conducting several campaigns in 1988 to explain its views to members of eighteen branches.

Union Elections and Factionalism

As mentioned earlier, the abolition of martial law in 1987 provided an opportunity for emergent oppositional political groups to challenge KMT hegemony in the union movement. Consequently, the number of candidates for union positions increased substantially. Competition has grown keen, and there are rumors of bribery in union elections. Both the KMT and employers have found it difficult to retain their influence over union elections. An example of the opposition to traditional unionism is the Chun Sin Paper Company Union, in which the incumbents, supported by the provincial government, lost the elections in 1988. In other cases, as mentioned earlier, dissident elements have established rival organizations from which to launch elections.

At the same time, the independence of workers in enterprise unions should not be overstated, for the law prohibits rival unionism and requires that leaders of enterprise unions be employees of the relevant companies. This encourages union officials to adopt moderate policies and limits the extent to which outside organizing expertise can be recruited (Lin 1988:300). In a survey of manufacturing workers conducted in 1986, 27.1 percent of the respondents expressed the view that union leaders were nominated or assigned by management, 18 percent said this was not the case, and most of the remainder (53 percent) expressed no opinion on the matter (Social Department of Taiwan Provincial Government 1986:196).

Despite opposition, the KMT retains substantial influence on unions. C. Lin (1988:386) estimates that at least 30 percent of union leaders are KMT members, and most of the subsidies to federated municipal- provincial-, and national-level unions come from the government. Opposition political parties have nevertheless been active in support of new-style union leaders, a matter that has received widespread attention in the media. This was particularly true of elections in seven national unions during early 1988: the Electric Power Union, the National Federation of Railway Unions, the Seamen's Trade Union, the Taiwan Petroleum Workers' Union, the National Posts Alliance, the National Mining Federation, and the Chinese Federation of Labor. A member of the Labor Party was elected to the executive branch of the Taiwan Petroleum Workers' Union, an unexpected result given the KMT's vastly superior resources. A further change was prompted by a declaration by the CFL that thirty-one union officials elected many years earlier would be retired to make way for new blood. This led to the election of union officers from the municipal and provincial levels who were more responsive to members' demands. This change was limited, however, in that seventeen out of the fifty-one directors of the CFL continued since they were elected for life at a congress held before the establishment of the KMT's control over Taiwan (Lin 1988:384).

Fostered by competing political groups, factionalism within the union movement has been inevitable as union officials have been encouraged to identify with one or another political faction to protect their positions (Chen 1986:184). The factionalism tended to increase with the split in the Labor Party in 1988 when the more radical socialists broke away and formed the Lao Kong Tang (Workers' Party) in 1989. Since then, union leaders have tended to emphasize industrial rather than broader political issues in order to avoid criticism from members who have become impatient with politically inspired rhetoric and competition. Such criticism in turn has made the task of developing a viable political opposition more difficult.

In addition to intraunion rivalry occasioned by union law, which requires that elections for union positions be held every three years (CLA 1989a:215), limited resources continue to constrain union development. Membership dues are the main source of revenue. The average annual membership fee of an enterprise union in 1988 was estimated to be about 0.8 percent of an average manufacturing employee's earnings and that of an occupational union slightly more than 2 percent of the estimated average income of a service-sector employee. There are four main reasons for this disparity. First, many enterprise unions are subsidized by management and therefore can keep their dues to a minimum. Second, because these unions have been inactive in the past, members are unwilling to pay high dues. Third, the government subsidizes the union dues of workers joining occupational unions (to encourage labor insurance coverage), so there is an incentive for them to charge higher dues than enterprise unions. Fourth, and finally, occupational unions are in a monopoly position vis-à-vis labor insurance coverage for employees working in small establishments; this may also encourage them to charge higher dues than otherwise would be the case.

Despite an increase in membership, an official survey showed that in 1987 only half the unions reported being in better financial shape than five years earlier (mainly through increasing the number of members and to a lesser extent raising their dues), 11 percent claimed to be worse off (mainly because of membership loss and a reluctance to raise their dues), while 39 percent maintained that their financial position had remained unchanged (CLA 1988:304–5).

Changes in the Nature of Trade Unionism: Interunion Relations

According to official statistics (CLA 1988:272), there were twenty-five general federations of unions, twenty-three federations encompassing enterprise unions, and sixteen federations of occupational unions in 1987. The general federations include enterprise and occupational unions, and the three types of federations operate at the municipal, provincial, or national level. No data are available showing trends for these organizations over time; however, data are available from December 1986 to December 1989 for municipal and provincial federations grouped together. These show an increase from nine to twelve federations associated with a small (5.2 percent) increase in membership (CLA 1990a). Thus, union growth in recent years seems to have been concentrated at the local level, though to a greater extent outside than inside the workplace.

The main functions of these higher-level union organizations, which rely mainly on the local unions for their income, are to assist local unions in organizing workers and to coordinate support for unions in disputes. They also provide conciliation services and training for union officials, for which they may receive assistance from the government. Some new federations have served as organizing bases for persons competing for union positions in enterprise and occupational union elections. An example is the T'ao-Chu-Miao Brotherhood Union (TBU), which was formed in late 1987 and comprises sixteen new-style unions in northern Taiwan. It was closely associated with the Labor Party, but following the split in 1988, this relationship was apparently dissolved.

Another example is the National Federation of Independent Unions (NFIU), which was established in 1988 by the leaders of twelve unions. Attempting to remain independent of political parties, it doubled the number of its affiliates and eighteen months later it represented about thirteen thousand workers (Ying 1990:74).[11] Since 1989 it has lost ground, however, as economic conditions have become less certain.

Finally, two other labor organizations are associated with the growth of new-style unionism. These are the Federation of Union Cadres and the Labor Rights Association. The former was formed in early 1988 and consists of a network of individual unionists drawn from nearly seventy unions, mainly in southern Taiwan. The federation conducts education programs and assists unionists in industrial disputes. The Labor Rights Association is engaged in similar activities but is quite different in form. Some observers consider it to be the labor department of the Workers'

Party that may form the basis for a new socialist-oriented, pro-PRC union federation (Ying 1990:77).

Union Goals and Strategies

In the past the absence of a vigorous independent union movement in Taiwan and the ineffectiveness of the government in administering labor law meant that workers' rights could be easily overridden in practice. An official investigation based on 1987 data showed that in enterprises with more than seven hundred employees, 65.1 percent of the 232 enterprises examined prolonged working hours beyond the standards stipulated in the relevant regulation (no. 32) of the Labor Standards Law (CLA 1989a:27–28), 58.8 percent violated the regulations concerning workers' rest hours and holidays, and 56.9 percent defied the law by not insuring their employees for workers' compensation purposes or by reporting false payroll numbers for setting insurance premiums (Chen 1988:107). Moderation and indirectness were the guiding union principles, often manifested in attempts to influence labor legislation, to report workers' opinions to government organizations, and, to a lesser extent, to conclude collective bargaining agreements with the help of KMT coordination. Annual bonuses and ownership of company shares were supported, but these efforts did not satisfy employees' growing expectations and hence a more militant trade unionism emerged.

The goals and strategies pursued by unions since the abolition of martial law can be summarized as follows. The first goal has been to protect workers against unfair competition with a view to improving their working conditions. For example, the Seamen's Union protested to the Ministry of Communications against permitting the employment of foreign seamen; the Construction Association opposed the recruitment of immigrant workers; the Kaohsiung Longshoremen's Union denied the right of nonunion workers to work in the industry, and workers of the Hsin-Ya Electric Company took over the factory after management declared that the workplace would be closed and that operations would be transferred to another country.

The second goal has been to ensure that employee rights enshrined in legislation are translated into practice. For example, bonuses are paid for working on public holidays and overtime rates are applicable for work undertaken at times other than normal working hours.

The third goal has been to achieve reasonable wage and welfare standards. Under this heading are better wages, salaries and annual bonuses, and opposition to the current health insurance system. Some unions have demanded equality of wages between lower-paying locally owned firms and their multinational counterparts. The health insurance system has also been criticized for restricting the choice of hospitals open to employees requiring medical treatment.

The fourth goal involves information disclosure and participation in decision making. There have been growing demands for regular information on company operations and market conditions and some support for employee ownership schemes. Many unions have protested management arbitrariness in transferring employees to jobs and in attempting to close down operations. For example, in 1988, the Shin Kong Spinning Company decided to shut down its Shih Lin plant and move operations to a rural area. This was strongly opposed by the work force despite a company offer to pay higher severance pay than that stipulated in the Labor Standards Law (J. Huang 1988:285).

The fifth and final goal has been to improve unions' finances by seeking to establish union banks. This objective has not yet been realized.

In sum, unions, particularly those independent of the KMT and management, have put pressure on employers and the government to uphold the law and take workers' interests more seriously.

Union Activity: Collectivism without Collective Bargaining

In the 1986 manufacturing survey, employees were asked how helpful unions are to workers. More than four in ten (43.7 percent) respondents stated they were very or quite helpful, while a similar proportion (43.3 percent) said they were only a little helpful. These figures suggest that unions are seen as furthering manufacturing employees' interests at least somewhat. There are three main ways in which this is attempted: first, by advancing members' welfare (e.g., organizing recreational, cultural, and educational activities) through welfare committees, which, as noted earlier, employers are legally obliged to support[12]; second, by supporting higher bonus claims on behalf of employees; and third, by advising workers of their legal rights in relation to work and employment (Social Department of Taiwan Provincial Government 1986:208–9).

Despite an increase in collective bargaining, the formalization of this adversarial relationship remains limited. According to official statistics, in 1986 there were 285 collective agreements; by 1989, the number of agreements had increased to 346 (CLA 1990a). This represents coverage of less than 5 percent of enterprises. While collective bargaining may be more common in manufacturing, Lin (1988:388) has estimated that only about 9 percent of manufacturing employees are covered by collective bargaining agreements, and employees in larger workplaces are more likely to be under the protection of such contracts. Thus, Lin found that 21.3 percent of employees working in the largest size plants (employing five hundred or more employees) were covered by a collective bargaining agreement. Finally, to underline the point about the weakness of collective bargaining in Taiwan, Lee (1988:192) and Lin (1988:388) maintain that many collective bargaining agreements do little more than restate employees' rights under existing legislation.

Industrial action of various kinds, including strikes, work to rule, collective absenteeism, and sit-ins, have been commonly used to exert pressure on management in recent years. Estimates of the average number of workers involved in disputes (only some of which entailed industrial action, as explained below) indicate that the average number of workers involved nearly doubled over the period 1985–89 (16.3 workers involved) compared with 1980–84 (9.8 workers involved). Lin's (1988:391) analysis suggests that in nearly half the disputes reported in the newspapers over the 1983–87 period, when industrial action did occur it took the form of presenting a petition to the authorities and/or engaging in street demonstrations. The latter activity has the potential to attract additional workers and unions, thereby broadening the conflict into a classic class confrontation. A prime example is the 1988 Maioli bus drivers' strike.

This dispute began over a wage claim and escalated into a conflict over "two laws and one case" between a large number of new-style unions, political parties, and civil rights groups on the one hand and employers and the government on the other. The "two laws and one case" referred to the application of the union law and the Labor Standards Law; the one case was a lawsuit taken out by the employer against five of the strike leaders. The dispute ended in a compromise but highlighted the difficulty of conducting a legal strike under existing legislation (see Ying 1990:66–70).

Trends in the incidence and major attributed causes of industrial disputes during the 1980s are shown in figure 6.3. Before interpreting trends, it is important to note that in Taiwan an industrial dispute represents notification to the government (at the local level) of an industrial disagreement, which may be collective or individual. Thus, figure 6.3 should not be read as necessarily referring to strikes or other forms of industrial action or indeed to union involvement, but it does signify the potential for such expressions of conflict to occur and to be resolved by union representation in negotiations, conciliation, or arbitration.

Figure 6.3 indicates that the number of industrial disputes began to rise intermittently in the early 1980s and, despite fluctuations, continued with a strong upward trend. Between 1983 and 1988, disputes over bonuses, particularly the customary end-of-year bonus, comprised the highest proportion of the disputes, although these declined substantially as the decade ended under less prosperous business conditions.[13] Bonus disputes symbolize the reinterpretation of the traditional norm of noblesse oblige in favor of a notion of equitable gainsharing on the part of

Figure 6.3. Industrial disputes in Taiwan, by major causes, 1980–89

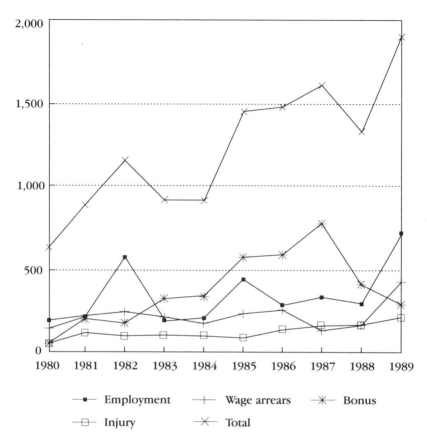

Sources: Taiwan. Council of Labor Affairs 1989b, 1990a.

the work force. As T. C. Chao, C. S. Wu, and H. L. Wu (1988:579) have argued, these conflicts have tended to focus on two related concerns: demands for participation in decision making over bonuses and the fairness of the bonus relative to the return appropriated by the business owners.

An underlying theme of most of the remaining disputes has been an increasing determination to ensure that workers' legal rights are upheld in the workplace. Disputes over wage arrears have focused on workers' claims that employers have failed to pay employees' wages. Employers have sometimes argued that business failure prevented them from doing so. This is contrary to the law (see earlier regarding the wages contingency fund), although it is likely to be a common phenomenon in economies characterized by rapid structural change and small enterprises that rely on numerical flexibility. Wages owed in cases of layoff also come under this category. Again, the employer is legally obliged to compensate the employee, but evasion is apparently not uncommon.

Alleged lack of proper pay for work undertaken outside standard working hours as defined in the Labor Standards Law is another common problem.[14] Such disputes are more likely in times of strong demand, especially given Taiwan's tight labor market in the 1980s.

Employment disputes fall into two main categories: those in which employers are accused of wrongful dismissal and those in which the reason(s) given for discontinuing an employee's employment or the conditions of termination are challenged (see CLA 1989a:11–17). Figure 6.1 shows that employment disputes have tended to rise in less prosperous periods (1982 and after 1988). This is consistent with data indicating that the most widely adopted management practice for dealing with declining product demand is employment reduction (CLA 1989a:118).

Yet another major issue giving rise to industrial disputes occurs when the employer allegedly fails to pay compensation in accordance with the Labor Standards Law (CLA 1989a:51) relating to injury, sickness, incapacitation, or death as a result of an incident at work. Although these disputes account for a relatively small proportion of total disputes and show no evidence of increasing, they highlight what some observers see as inadequate health and safety standards.[15]

Given the weakness of collective bargaining and the close connection between state politics and union dynamics, it is not surprising that workers seek government intervention to resolve disputes after being rebuffed by management. In three-quarters of the cases analyzed by Lin (1988:392), however, government authorities did not respond to allegations of legal infringement of workers' rights under the Labor Standards Law.[16] Nevertheless, political and party leaders seem to have been active in most settlements of large labor disputes in recent years. Examples of such political involvement include a case at the Kaohsiung steel mill of the Tang Eng Iron Works Company in which workers invited members of the legislative opposition to negotiate a new payment system on their behalf. And at the Hohsinghsing Company, the leader of the local KMT branch was asked to lead the workers' representatives in discussions with management on a claim involving wages in arrears (J. Huang 1988:287).

Although the new-style unions have been more inclined to encourage industrial action to achieve their objectives, they and, more particularly, their conservative counterparts have used other strategies to attain their goals. These include urging employees to vote for representatives to the legislative branch who are committed to improving labor legislation; influencing political parties to support union goals; articulating their views on government policies through the public media; concluding collective bargaining agreements; resolving industrial disputes; and supporting cooperative projects, such as bonus and share-holding schemes. At the same time, management has devised ways to prevent or limit industrial conflict. The most common practices include making higher contributions to employees' welfare funds, increasing bonuses, and, more generally, introducing quality circles and employee-participation mechanisms (Chao 1988:266–70). Evidence from official sources indicates that some 38.8 percent of firms in 1987 had some form of employee participation. The incidence rose with firm size.[17] The most common forms of participation were consultative committees and profit sharing with consultation, focused mainly on working conditions, fringe benefits, and production and marketing issues (CLA 1989a:367–69).

Management has also adopted aggressive tactics, including threatening to close and actually closing factories (an example being the Ta-Ming Battery Company in Kaohsiung), constructing "black lists" of active union members, transferring more militant employees to other workplaces, and dismissing workers. In addition, as in the Maioli strike, employers have cooperated in attempts to defeat striking unions. According to A. Kleingartner and H.-S. Peng (1991:432), "Employers seem less open to unionism in their organization today than in the past because of the greater militancy of unions."

In concluding our discussion of industrial conflict, it is worth inquiring into the extent to which industrial disputes (assuming most are collective in character) have substituted for labor turnover, the traditional way of expressing discontent. Estimates of the voluntary separation rate (resignations divided by work force size) for manufacturing (all-industry data are unavailable) indicate that labor turnover varied from year to year, averaging 37.9 percent per year over the 1980–84 period and 36.1 percent for 1985–89. This contrasts with the all-industry industrial dispute rate, which, as we saw earlier, tended to rise and then accelerate from 1985 to the end of 1989. So, although there was a slight decline in the labor turnover rate between the two periods, it was too small to support the argument that workers substituted industrial disputes for quitting.[18] Rather, it seems that in recent years workers have by and large kept to their customary form of conflictual behavior but have added "voice" to their repertoire.

To summarize, the second half of the 1980s witnessed the emergence of a democratic movement in Taiwan that began to assert people's rights in the workplace. That unions had been controlled by the government for many years and that statutory regulation of employment relations were not strictly enforced led to worker opposition, which heightened after the abolition of martial law. Further research is needed, however, on the extent to which unions are involved in industrial disputes (as defined in Taiwan) and on trends in industrial action. A dominant view is that industrial action increased from 1985 through 1988 but began to decline in 1989 as workers became more aware of the expanded government conciliation services and slower economic growth. So, although industrial disputes increased in 1989, the number of disputes involving industrial action declined and was thought to be declining further in 1990.

Conclusion

Trade unions in Taiwan have grown considerably since the abolition of martial law in 1987; their character has also changed. The new-style unions have been in the vanguard, demonstrating their independence from the ruling political party and a willingness to engage in industrial action to assert their members' legal rights. Although very much in a minority, they have influenced the broader union movement, whose leaders have become receptive to a more assertive rank and file. The close connection between democratization and the emergence of opposition political parties with an interest in securing working-class support has inevitably led to increasing competition in union elections and to the growth of new union federations less favorably inclined to the government. This politicization has complicated union affairs and led unions to favor disassociating from political parties, particularly in light of conflicts within and between the fledgling organizations. The main effect of these conflicts has been to limit any meaningful challenge to the KMT, a predicament made more difficult by the growth of under-resourced enterprise and occupational unions. Together with the less than effective implementation of labor law by the government, the politicization has meant that workers are often obliged to threaten industrial action to realize employees' rights.

The brief period since the lifting of martial law in 1987 when unions have been permitted more freedom of expression makes it difficult to evaluate the Taiwanese union movement. Some tentative observations can be made, however, in relation to members' assessments of their union, the trend in real wages, changes in productivity and unit labor costs, and the political consequences of trade union development.

Earlier we noted survey evidence that suggested support for unions by manufacturing-sector workers. Judging from the rapid growth of occupational unions, many of which cover white-collar workers, such support is probably more widely shared among employees. Although workers have suffered in the course of rapid industrialization—witness the persistently high injury rates in manufacturing and evidence of employer neglect of workers' rights—living standards have increased considerably. Between 1979 and 1984, average real wages in manufacturing rose by nearly 4 percent a year and more than doubled in the subsequent five-year period. Although it is difficult to establish the contribution of unions to this growth, it is noteworthy that in the years from 1987 to 1989, when unions were most assertive (assisted by a tighter labor market), real earnings increased even faster, at an annual average of 11 percent (China. DGBAS, n.d.:18–19).

Although unions may have contributed to the higher living standards, is there any evidence that they have fostered productivity growth and helped keep unit labor costs down? By helping to ensure that employers meet their obligations regarding employees' job rights, welfare, and payment of reasonable bonuses, management has been encouraged to introduce new technology to raise productivity. In manufacturing, labor productivity growth averaged more than 2.7 percent a year between 1979 and 1984, and it accelerated to more than 7 percent a year in the period 1985–89 (China. DGBAS, n.d.:22). Between 1987 and 1989, the period of relative union militancy, labor productivity growth averaged more than 10 percent a year. Of course, unions are only one among several factors contributing to this enviable record, but at the very least they cannot be said to have jeopardized productivity growth. Further, unions may have assisted in limiting the growth of unit labor costs in manufacturing, which averaged slightly more than 7 percent in the years 1979–84 and declined to about 3.5 percent a year over the subsequent five years, albeit with an annual average increase of more than 5 percent between 1987 and 1989.

In discussing the political consequences of unionism, it is necessary to distinguish between politics at the workplace and the national level. Regarding the former, management is now more aware of the adverse consequences of unsystematic human resource practices. This stems from both the persistently tight labor market, supporting high rates of labor turnover, and growing industrial assertiveness by employees claiming their legal rights and a greater share of income from economic growth. As noted earlier, employers are building on a paternalistic tradition: improving welfare benefits and introducing employee participation as ways of containing industrial conflict. Given continuing high economic growth, the larger private-sector firms will probably be able to incorporate or at least contain union activity. The unions may, however, develop stronger organization in such strategic sectors as transportation and communication. In smaller firms, the challenge will lie outside the workplace, with the occupational, municipal, and regional unions, which thus far have not been very successful in fostering union activity in small firms. In short, the balance of power at the workplace will vary, but, in general, unions will not pose a threat to management hegemony.

This brings us to state politics. Although the reform of labor law reflected the growing power of unions in the 1980s, the changes foreshadowed in the Trade Union Law currently being debated in the legislative assembly are, on balance, unlikely to assist the union movement. Although union organization may improve by permitting unions to provide services to members through cooperatives and allowing them to appoint full-time union officials who need not be union members, the disadvantages are more substantial. These include a proposal to make membership in enterprise unions voluntary while extending the coverage of collective bargaining agreements to include all workers in an establishment where at least two-thirds of the employees are union members. These changes are likely to make it more difficult to unionize employees in larger establishments by, in effect, eliminating the postentry closed shop and encouraging free riders. Moreover, it is proposed that workers be allowed to organize new occupational unions with minimum legal requirements in order to promote union competition and hence the provision of better services. This measure will probably further fragment and hence limit the capacity of the union movement to influence the government. Severe limitations on industrial action and more effective penal provisions are also being considered.

Just as government failure to enforce legislation in the recent past reflected union weakness at the national level, so too these changes symbolize the inability of new-style unionism to influence the government significantly. This is in spite of the fact that militant trade unionism was one of the forces that encouraged the government to abolish martial law. This militant trade unionism was part of a general people's movement, however, that went beyond workers' interests. Without wider support, particularly by a united political opposition, unions will be forced to rely on public protests to guarantee themselves a floor of rights on which stronger union organizations can be built.

In sum, although Taiwanese unions have increased in number and membership and have become more assertive, they will remain fragile as long as they act mainly as administrators of social welfare programs and agencies of protest. While they increasingly play a role in resolving industrial disputes, their capacity to negotiate with employers and the government is limited. Without legislative support, they are unlikely to achieve much success with workplace collective bargaining, given management's preference for either a nonunion environment or co-opted unions. Unions might do better, however, in prosecuting areawide or regional collective bargaining agreements that are the responsibility of groups of occupational unions based in a municipality or region. Whatever the future holds, the fate of Taiwan's unions, as in the past, is inextricably bound up with national and international politics, particularly the democratization process that began in 1987, and Taiwan's relationship with the People's Republic of China.

7
Dependent Capitalism, a Colonial State, and Marginal Unions: The Case of Hong Kong

David A. Levin and Stephen Chiu

A decade ago, the Hong Kong union movement appeared to observers to be ineffective. It was numerically weak relative to employment, fragmented, and largely powerless at the enterprise, industry, and societal levels. Instead of concentrating resources on promoting the employment interests of members, the two main trade union federations focused more on organizational maintenance through the provision of social, cultural, and welfare benefits to members (Turner et al. 1980:30–31; England and Rear 1981:163–66).

The marginal role of the union movement is surprising given a set of conditions that might be expected to produce high levels of worker discontent and a more powerful union movement. These conditions include an elitist political system excluding participation by most of the Chinese population, the postwar industrial revolution with its accompanying work deprivations, the lack of channels within most privately owned enterprises for the expression of grievances, and a generally permissive government policy toward the formation of trade unions. Moreover, in the past, the Hong Kong working class has shown considerable solidarity and capacity for collective action.

In the first section, we trace briefly the historical development of the union movement in Hong Kong. The subsequent sections explore aspects of continuity and change in the union movement in the 1980s. Thus, the second section focuses on union density, external union structure, and internal union governance. The third section is devoted to union activities—union finances, workplace activities, and political participation.

One of our main themes is that despite the more visible political role of the union movement in the 1980s, economic and political forces still constrain its effectiveness. We illustrate this point in the fourth section with reference to the role of trade unions in two public issues. The fifth section assesses the influence of cultural, economic, and political environments in Hong Kong in reinforcing the marginal status of the union movement. The final section summarizes our main points about continuity and change in the union movement in the 1980s and concludes with an assessment of its future effectiveness.

This chapter uses a variety of sources. A basic source of information on the numbers, membership, and finances of Hong Kong's unions over the past decade is the annual reports of the Hong Kong Registrar of Trade Unions.[1] We also used documents produced by trade unions and union officials where available, newspaper accounts, and other secondary sources. Three limitations to our data and analysis should be noted. First, our account of the historical development of the union movement up to the late 1970s is necessarily selective. Second, there are aspects of the contemporary trade union movement for which only sketchy information is available. This is particularly true for the internal governance of trade unions. Third, we did not interview key leaders of the union movement specifically for this paper. Our account is informed, however, by interviews conducted with selected union leaders in the mid-1980s.

Historical Development of Trade Unions

Hong Kong Island came under British colonial rule in 1841, Kowloon was added in 1860, and the New Territories were leased from China in 1898 for ninety-nine years. As Hong Kong's entrepôt economy developed during the nineteenth century, it attracted a growing number of immigrants from South China. By the turn of the century, several guilds had been formed. The first wave of trade union organization dates from the early 1920s, stimulated by the successes of two powerful unions, one composed of Chinese machinists and the other the Seamen's Trade Union. The union movement was rapidly politicized, however, as both the Kuomintang and the Chinese Communist Party sought to expand their influence in Hong Kong. This first wave peaked with the massive 1925–26 Canton–Hong Kong strike-boycott in protest against British actions in Shanghai and Canton (Chesneaux 1968:290–318). To prevent future general strikes, the colonial government enacted the Illegal Strikes and Lock-outs Ordinance of 1927, which imposed stricter controls on the union movement.

The Japanese occupation of Hong Kong ended in August 1945, and in May 1946, a civilian government replaced the British military administration. The main institutions of British colonial governance were reestablished in their prewar form, with power concentrated in the hands of the governor, who was advised by a nominated Executive Council. A nominated Legislative Council passed the laws. Appointees to both councils were drawn mainly from the business and professional classes (Rear 1971; Davies 1977).

Unions quickly reemerged after the war. The Trade Unions and Trade Disputes Ordinance of 1948 made union registration compulsory, and by 1951 there were 199 unions of employees, most in the private sector.[2] Membership boundaries were diverse: there were occupational, industrial, and enterprise unions. The political division within the union movement was formalized in 1949 with the registration under the Societies Ordinance of the pro-China Hong Kong Federation of Trade Unions (FTU) and the pro-Taiwan Hong Kong and Kowloon Trades Union Council (TUC).

The early postwar years were characterized by high levels of industrial conflict, mainly over wage levels and cost-of-living allowances in the context of an unstable economy recovering from wartime devastation. Between 1946 and March 1951, some 664,381 working days were "lost" in fifty-one industrial disputes, roughly equivalent to the number of working days "lost" in work stoppages over the next sixteen years. Strike indexes—number of strikes per 100,000 workers (19.8 in 1948) and days "lost" per 1,000 workers (5,428.57 in 1947)—reached their highest levels for the entire postwar period (W.K.S. Chiu 1987:113, 116).

Some of these disputes were resolved through a form of centralized bargaining with major (often British) employers (England and Rear 1975:189–90). This experience did not lead to institutionalized collective bargaining, however, partly because the involvement of FTU-affiliated unions in these conflicts was primarily designed "to generate and sustain militancy amongst the workers and to promote in them a consciousness of class solidarity" (Turner et al. 1980:90–91). The costs of militancy became evident in 1950 when the Hong Kong Tramways Company, following a bitter dispute, withdrew recognition from the FTU-affiliated union and dismissed union activists.

In retrospect, it appears that the major features of the postwar industrial relations system were taking shape by the early 1950s. The government had set two basic rules of the game. The first was that unions (and employer associations) were required to register, which enabled the government to regulate their objects and internal administration. The second was that the government left employers and unions to decide how to regulate their relationships. This meant that employers were not legally required either to recognize unions or to negotiate with them.

The goals and methods of the FTU and the TUC also crystallized about this time. The first goal was political, not in the sense of pursuing power and influence in the Hong Kong polity but rather in terms of expressing and mobilizing support for the policies of the People's Republic of China and Taiwan respectively. The second goal was to expand their influence among workers, which meant they had to demonstrate a concern for workers' welfare. This did not take the form of seeking systematic bargaining with employers, however.

After the early 1950s, the FTU became less overtly involved in industrial actions against major employers and began to concentrate more on building up worker support by expanding educational, cultural, and welfare services to members. The TUC adopted a similar strategy.

The structural features of the union movement solidified and changed little between the early 1950s and the mid-1960s, even though Hong Kong was undergoing a major economic transformation from a predominantly commercial to an export-oriented industrial colony. The number of unions remained at about 240 for most of this period and declared union membership in 1966—171,623—was more or less comparable with that of the early 1950s. Most unions were small.[3] The FTU became the dominant federation, accounting for some 60 percent of declared union membership in 1966, compared with 23 percent for the TUC and 17 percent for neutral unions.[4] Neither the FTU nor the TUC managed to make substantial inroads among the growing industrial working class. Of the 512,000 persons in manufacturing in 1961 (about 43 percent of the total working population), only about 10 percent were union members, compared with 40.6 percent in utilities and 78 percent in transport, storage, and communication (Chiu 1987:205).

Following mass social disturbances in 1966 and 1967,[5] a third wave of unionization began. One dimension of this wave was membership growth among private-sector unions. Those in manufacturing added 52,000 members, and those in transport, storage, and communication added 38,000 (England and Rear 1981:148). The FTU-affiliated unions recorded very large gains, so that their combined membership more than doubled, from 96,062 in 1968 to 214,858 in 1978. A qualitatively new dimension to this wave was the proliferation of unions and growing union membership among nonmanual occupational groups in community and social services. This included the civil service, where the number of registered unions more than doubled, from thirty-four to ninety-three, over the period from 1967–68 to 1977–78 (Arn 1984:238–39).

New unions were also formed by non–civil service employees in health, education, and welfare, where terms and conditions of employment were affected by civil service standards. Of the 95,345 union members in community, social, and personal services in 1978, about half were in public administration and one-third were in social services. These new unions were distinctive in another way: nearly all of them remained independent of both the FTU and the TUC.[6]

Structural Continuity and Change in the 1980s

Despite the growth of unions and union membership in the decade from 1968 to 1978, observers believed it added little to the overall effectiveness of the union movement for two reasons. First, union proliferation simply reinforced organizational fragmentation. Second, membership growth in the case of the FTU affiliates did not entail expansion into new areas or major policy changes in the direction, for example, of seeking formalized bargaining arrangements with employers. The civil service and white-collar unions, though politically independent and more job-oriented, were considered to be a special case (Levin and Jao 1988:1–5). Observers thus portrayed the union movement as stagnant if not moribund. Its goals, methods, and organizational boundaries were considered unlikely to change and likely to continue to be fragmented and to have marginal influence in the wider society. To what extent has the experience of the 1980s validated these predictions?

Union Density

As figure 7.1 shows, overall, the union movement is weaker than it was a decade ago. After peaking in 1977 at just over 400,000 members, union membership fell sharply over the next four years. It then began to climb upward, exceeding the 1977 figure in 1988.[7] Since the labor force also expanded over this period, the overall density rate of about 17

Figure 7.1. Union membership and density in Hong Kong, 1976–89

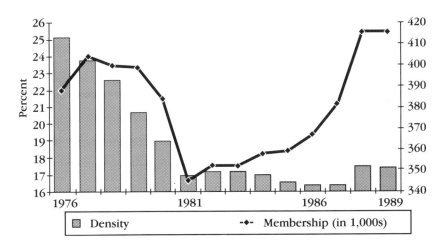

Source: Union membership from Hong Kong. Registrar of Trade Unions, various. Employment figures from Hong Kong. Census and Statistics Department various.
Density calculations are based on number of employees, excluding all other activity status categories.

percent in 1988 remains considerably below the 1976 peak of about one-quarter of all salaried and wage earners.

Paralleling the overall decline in union density were substantial declines in union density by major industrial sector over the decade 1976–86, especially between 1976 and 1981, as shown in table 7.1. The only exception is in the community, social, and personal services sector, where union density rose between 1976 and 1981 and then stabilized. Within this sector, the major growth has been in the community and social services. These trends are mirrored in the fortunes of the thirteen largest unions (comprising 51.1 percent of total union membership), shown in table 7.2.

Unions of civil servants, teachers, and nurses have experienced substantial growth in membership over the decade, while those in manufacturing and transport have experienced either membership declines or at best marginal increases. The growth of public-sector union membership has altered the social demography of union membership in two ways. First, until the early 1970s, the union movement was confined mainly to manual workers. The spread of union membership among the white-collar occupations means that the movement has become as much a middle-class as a working-class phenomenon. Public-sector unionism has also contributed to the rising proportion of women in the trade union movement, from 12.1 percent of union members in 1968 to 22.7 percent in 1978 and 25.5 percent in 1988. As shown in table 7.3, over the 1976–

Table 7.1. Union density in Hong Kong, by major industrial sector, 1976, 1981, and 1986

	Percentage of unionized employees		
Industrial sector	*1976*	*1981*	*1986*
Manufacturing	14.7	7.2	7.1
Electricity, gas, and water	49.2	25.2	22.5
Construction	20.0	8.6	8.4
Wholesale and retail trade, import and export, and restaurants and hotels	25.6	15.2	10.0
Transport, storage, and communication	82.0	50.7	46.5
Finance, insurance, real estate, and business services	38.9	16.0	11.5
Community, social, and personal services	27.9	33.1	33.0

Sources: Hong Kong Registrar of Trade Unions various; Hong Kong. Census and Statistics Department 1979, vol. 2, table VI3; 1982, vol. 2, table C4; 1986 employee data from unpublished records of Hong Kong. Census and Statistics Department.
Calculations are based on number of employees, excluding all other activity status categories. Census years are used because they provide the most comprehensive and accurate information on distribution of employees by industry.

Table 7.2. Membership trends in the thirteen largest Hong Kong unions, 1978–88

Union	Affiliation	Membership (1988)	Membership growth (%)
Hong Kong Chinese Civil Servants' Association	none	49,425	+526
Hong Kong Professional Teachers' Union	none	40,912	+120
Motor Transport Workers' General Union	FTU	26,853	−6
Hong Kong Union of Chinese Workers in Western Style Employment	FTU	16,388	−14
Hong Kong Seamen's Union	FTU	14,393	−48
Hong Kong and Kowloon Restaurant and Cafe Workers' General Union	none	12,587	+45
Hong Kong Civil Servants' General Union	none	11,113	+688
Hong Kong and Kowloon Spinning, Weaving, and Dyeing Trade Workers' General Union	FTU	10,023	−49
Government Employees' Association	FTU	7,174	n.a.
Hong Kong Printing Industry Workers' Union	FTU	6,623	+17
Government, Armed Forces, and Hospitals Chinese Workers' Union	FTU	5,875	−63
Association of Government Nursing Staff	CSGU	5,807	+98
Eating Establishment Employees' General Union	FTU	5,313	−37

Source: Hong Kong. Registrar of Trade Unions, various.
n.a. = not applicable since union was not registered until 1986.

86 decade, about one-quarter of female employees in the community, social, and personal services sector belonged to unions, whereas union density among female employees in most other sectors fell. In general, however, women remain disproportionately unorganized compared with men.

Membership declines in manufacturing are due in part to the shifting employment structure resulting from Hong Kong's changing role in the international economy. The share of the working population in manufacturing fell from 44.8 percent in 1976 to 31.9 percent by the third quarter

Table 7.3. *Union density (in percent) in Hong Kong by sex and industry, 1976, 1981, and 1986*[a]

Industry	1976		1981		1986	
	Male	*Female*	*Male*	*Female*	*Male*	*Female*
Manufacturing	17.0	10.6	9.2	4.9	8.8	5.0
Electricity, gas, and water	53.0	7.0	27.5	3.4	24.7	4.6
Construction	20.8	7.9	8.9	3.5	8.9	1.3
Wholesale and retail trade, import and export, and restaurants and hotels	29.8	13.4	19.4	6.1	13.7	3.7
Transport, storage, and communication	88.8	11.2	55.9	12.7	52.5	12.8
Finance, insurance, real estate, and business services	38.2	40.4	16.7	15.0	11.5	11.6
Community, social, and personal services	28.4	27.0	36.0	28.8	39.3	25.7
All industries	32.7	17.5	20.4	10.6	20.1	10.4

Source: Same as table 7.1.
[a]Calculations are based on number of persons who are employed.

of 1988 (Ismail 1989:95). In some industries, such as spinning and weaving, employment has declined because of a combination of factors, including technological change, the relocation of manufacturing operations to the special economic zones of China or to other countries, and competition from other developing countries. K. Y. Ting (1988:120–23) has attributed the declining membership in the Seamen's Union, for example, to containerization and rationalization in the shipping industry.

Nonmanual occupational groups in the public sector have shown a propensity to join unions, but this is not the case in the private sector. Union density in the financial sector, for example, has declined over the past decade. The different employment context of the two sectors is probably one contributory factor. In the public sector, where labor turnover is relatively low,[8] the problems of employees are not job insecurity but rather status advancement in a relatively sheltered and highly structured internal labor market. Given the government's obligation to set an example of good labor relations practices by recognizing and consulting (if not actually negotiating) with its employees, there is little risk in using trade unions as a means to advance occupational status. In the private sector, employment is less secure and labor turnover is higher as workers pursue advancement through the external labor market. Additional obstacles to unionization among white-collar employees in the private sector include employers' unwillingness to recognize unions and the growing share of women in these occupations (Lui 1989:50).

Other explanatory variables may also be influential. One factor is material improvements in the standard of living. Real income from main employment grew at an estimated average annual rate of 7 percent for 1976–81 and at 2.2 percent in the period 1981–86 (Hong Kong. Census and Statistics Department 1988:33). H. A. Turner (1988:180) found substantial increases between 1976 and 1985 in the proportion of employees receiving payment for holidays, a Chinese New Year bonus, and sick pay or other medical provisions. Growing affluence, improved working conditions, and a tight labor market (the unemployment rate rose from 2.8 percent in 1978 to 4.5 percent in 1983 but then fell to 1.4 percent in 1988) may have reinforced individualistic market strategies. The government's role in extending employee rights under the Employment Ordinance (enacted in 1968 and continuously amended), in improving employee compensation for occupational accidents, and in establishing channels for workers to seek redress for their grievances[9] may also have undercut the perceived need for trade union protection against employer exploitation.

Whether attitudes toward trade unions have changed is uncertain. Comparing surveys conducted in 1976 and again in 1985, Turner (1988:184) found that the percentage of respondents "knowing what unions do" fell from 78 to 55 percent.[10] Yet when respondents were asked in the 1985 survey their reasons for not belonging to unions, only 22 percent indicated they were opposed to unions; by comparison, the figure in the 1976 survey was 35 percent. Ignorance seems to play a role: 30 percent of respondents in the 1985 survey gave "lack of knowledge" as their reason for not belonging and another 23 percent "don't know how to join."

External Union Structure

Two main developments in the 1980s were the continuing prolifera-tion of unions and the formation of new federations. There were 104 more registered trade unions in 1988 than in 1978. Continuing a 1970s trend, the majority of new unions were formed in the service sector, mainly in the civil service. The only other sector to record a substantial increase was transport, storage, and communication, where the number of unions increased from forty-four to sixty-one over the 1978–88 period. This proliferation has not substantially altered the size distribu-tion of unions, however, as shown in table 7.4.

About 66.6 percent of the trade unions in 1978 had between fifty and one thousand members; in 1988, the proportion of unions in this size category had fallen to about 64 percent. Unions with more than one thousand members continue to represent the bulk of all union members, however, more than 80 percent in both 1978 and 1988.

In the 1970s, there was little formal integration among the indepen-dent unions, but in the 1980s they formed three new federations, listed in table 7.5. Two of these federations are composed of unions in the public sector. The Joint Organization of Unions was originally known as the Liaison Office of Public Service Unions, a research, education, and service organization with membership open to all labor organizations. In

Table 7.4. Union membership concentration in Hong Kong, 1978 and 1988

Membership	Percentage of total unions		Percentage of total members	
	1978	*1988*	*1978*	*1988*
<50–51	12.3	17.9	0.4	0.6
50–51 to 250	39.9	38.6	3.8	4.6
251 to 1,000	27.3	25.1	11.6	12.4
1,001 to 5,000	15.0	15.3	25.1	31.3
>5,001	5.5	3.0	59.1	51.1
Total	326	430	399,995	416,136

Source: Hong Kong. Registrar of Trade Unions 1979, 1989.

Table 7.5. Trade union federations in Hong Kong, 1988

Federation	Affiliated unions	Other affiliates
Hong Kong Federation of Trade Unions	78	–
Hong Kong and Kowloon Trades Union Council	69	–
Federation of Hong Kong and Kowloon Labor Unions	18	4
Joint Organizations of Unions—Hong Kong	17	2
Federation of Civil Service Unions	30	1

Sources: Hong Kong. Registrar of Trade Unions 1989; Y. H. Leung 1989:204–6.

1984, its name was changed to the Joint Organization of Unions—Hong Kong (JOU) to attract a broader membership from outside the civil service. The Federation of Civil Service Unions (FCSU) was initially affiliated with the JOU but withdrew in 1986. In addition, the Hong Kong Civil Servants' General Union (CSGU), though formally registered as a trade union in 1978, functions in practice as a federation.[11] The Hong Kong Chinese Civil Servants' Association (CCSA), the largest trade union in the civil service, has since 1975 allowed other trade unions in the civil service to have an affiliated status.[12] In the private sector, a group of independent unions inaugurated the Federation of Hong Kong and Kowloon Labor Unions. Its core members had been brought together by joint campaigns in the late 1970s to seek legislative reforms to benefit manual workers. The motivation for the formation of new federations seems to be twofold: to pool resources and coordinate efforts in trade union education and to enhance the effectiveness of the independent unions as social and political pressure groups.

Though not a trade union, the Hong Kong Christian Industrial Committee (CIC) has also been a highly visible actor in the labor scene since the 1970s. The CIC considers itself to be a specifically Christian labor organization and a pressure group committed to fighting for workers' rights and promoting unity among labor groups through education, organizing, and action (P. L. Leung 1988:117). Although it is not a trade union, it advises workers with employment problems, encourages workers to join unions, and has assisted in the formation of a number of trade unions, including in 1987 a new industry federation among independent unions in the transport sector, the Federation of Hong Kong Transport Workers' Organizations. The CIC has also functioned as a "linking pin" over the past decade in bringing together reform-oriented organizations to lobby the government on issues of broader public concern.

One major consequence of the above changes is a continuing shift, shown in figure 7.2, in the relative distribution of unions and union members among the FTU, the TUC, and other federations. The new

Figure 7.2. Distribution of unions and union membership of the FTU, TUC, and other Hong Kong federations, 1978, 1983, and 1988

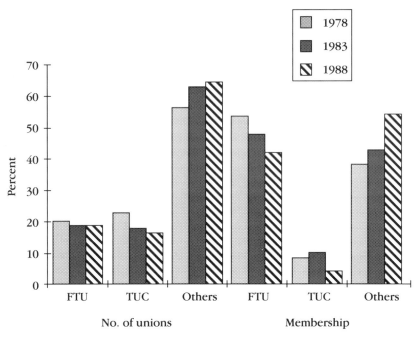

Source: Hong Kong. Registrar of Trade Unions, various.
Total number of trade unions was 327 for 1978, 383 for 1983, and 415 for 1988. Total union membership was 399,995 for 1978, 352,306 for 1983, and 416,136 for 1988.

independent unions have thus altered the balance of power within the trade union movement. In the past, the major division within the movement was between the pro-China FTU and the pro-Taiwan TUC. With the waning of the influence of the TUC, the principal groups are now the FTU and the independent sector of the trade union movement. As the independent unions have grown, conflicts have occasionally erupted with established unions where both have organized in the same workplace.[13]

Orientations of the Federations

How different are the orientations of the established and newer federations? In some respects, the orientation of the FTU has changed considerably since the mid-1970s. In 1976, during the Cultural Revolution in China, the FTU's policy statements reflected the world view of the Chinese leadership at that time: supportive of liberating Taiwan and of participating in the anti–United States and anti–Soviet Union movement, critical of Confucius, opposed to rightist elements in the CCP, and supportive of socialist revolution and strengthening nationalism and anti-imperialism among the working class. In practice, the FTU drew sharp boundaries between itself and other organizations. The FTU and its affiliates at that time refused to cooperate with other unions or to participate in elections to the Labour Advisory Board, the institutional channel created by the Hong Kong government for trade unions to advise on labor policy.

With the downfall of the Gang of Four and the new policy of the Four Modernizations in China, the FTU's rhetoric and policies began to change. The 1984 Sino-British agreement on the future of Hong Kong as well as local political reforms further stimulated a rethinking of the FTU's role. In 1985, the FTU's chairman stated that "while fighting for, and protecting, workers' rights, [the FTU] also participates actively in social affairs and democratic political activities, and works together with all social strata for the progress and stability of Hong Kong" (Cheng 1988:114). This statement is indicative of the new orientation of the FTU toward politics, labor-management relations, and other sectors of the union movement. Regarding politics, the FTU's role has been to encourage active participation in the drafting of the Basic Law (the post-1997 mini-constitution for Hong Kong) and in local elections. Building up good labor-management relations has been seen as important for maintaining Hong Kong's prosperity and stability. Thus, although contradictions between labor and management are still seen as having "an objective existence in a capitalist society," the view is that they can be "easily resolved" through mutual concession, negotiation, and consultation. While recognizing that unions hold "divergent political beliefs and viewpoints," they nevertheless also acknowledge that they have a "common aim in fighting for workers' rights and benefits." The basis for interunion cooperation is seen as "seeking common points while tolerating differences" (Cheng 1988:114–15).

In contrast with the FTU and the independent unions, the TUC appears to be a dying organization. Both its membership and number of affiliates are shrinking. Also in contrast with the FTU, where a second generation of younger members has moved into leadership positions, the leadership of the TUC and its affiliates is aging. The TUC's political allegiance to the nationalists in Taiwan is increasingly seen as a liability in recruiting new members (Li 1990). Moreover, the TUC affiliates are the traditional craft unions, which have suffered from diminishing employment in their industries. Even their leaders have doubts whether the TUC will be allowed to exist after China resumes sovereignty over Hong Kong (*Sing Tao Evening News* 1989; Li 1990).

While the newer federations are concerned with members' economic interests, they tend to define their mission in broader social terms. The

Joint Organization of Unions, for example, has taken the view that trade unions should not fight solely for their own economic interests but should play an active part in promoting social development. Though the FCSU is a federation of civil service unions, its leadership has actively supported proposals for improvements in labor laws that would benefit the working class as a whole. The leadership of the Hong Kong Professional Teachers' Union, a major independent union, defines its primary function as safeguarding members' legitimate professional rights, but its goals have evolved to include a keen interest in the quality of education and in social and political issues affecting the quality of life in general in Hong Kong (Law 1988:166).

Internal Union Organization

Regarding the internal structure of trade unions, Turner et al. (1980:30) commented that "the internal organization of Hong Kong unions appears flimsy: union staffs, branch and workplace organization appear skeletal and—outside the civil service, at least—direct member participation in union management seems low." Given that most unions are small and cannot afford full-time officials, their internal weakness is perhaps not surprising. The largest trade unions, however, are able to devote some resources to strengthening internal administration. In the 1980s, the FTU consciously sought to strengthen its internal organization and administration by sponsoring training courses for union personnel and shop stewards and using a more modernized management style in the handling of union affairs. It has also encouraged its affiliates to economize by sharing offices (Hong Kong Federation of Trade Unions 1988).

Solid data on changes in rank-and-file membership participation in union activities are lacking. Turner (1988:183–84) found from his 1985 survey that indicators of participation in union activities among those who did report belonging to trade unions were "high by comparison with the record of trade unions in other capitalist economies." For example, 35 percent of union members reported attending meetings occasionally and 11 percent regularly; 43 percent reported participating in union social activities; and 10 percent reported attending union courses or study groups.

The extent to which members are able to voice their preferences and influence union leadership is not known. In the case of older unions, however, especially those affiliated with the FTU and the TUC, outsiders have criticized their oligarchic tendencies.[14] In 1989, signs surfaced of rank-and-file discontent with the accommodative stance of the FTU leadership in negotiations with two bus companies. In one case, rank-and-file members compelled the more moderate leadership of a bus company branch of the FTU-affiliated Motor Transport Workers' General

Union to launch a strike that paralyzed public transport for two days. At another bus company, more than two hundred members of the same union took out a newspaper advertisement to announce their withdrawal from the union, citing as their reason the union leadership's acquiescence to the company (*Sing Tao Jih Pao,* 16 Dec. 1989).

The FTU is not alone in facing internal dissension. In 1988, the largest affiliate of the TUC pulled out, reportedly because leaders of much smaller (and largely moribund) affiliates had been appointed to top positions in the TUC, while leaders of the larger unions were excluded (*Hong Kong Economic Journal* 1988).

The independent unions seem to be run more democratically, as indicated by the ability of the membership to replace leaders. In 1989, for example, the chairman of the FCSU was voted out on the grounds that he had made several decisions without adequately consulting and discussing them with affiliates.

What Do Unions Do?

In reviewing the activities of trade unions in the 1980s, we first consider the unions' financial resources. We then turn to workplace activities of unions and their consequences and finally to their political activities.

Income and Expenditures

In 1980, total income reported for all employees' unions amounted to about H.K. $39.5 million, of which about 39 percent came from members and the remainder from other sources. Of the latter, the most important source was business and undertakings, as shown in table 7.6.

In 1988, union income rose to H.K. $93.5 million, and the proportion coming from members fell to about 35 percent. If total income from members is divided by the number of estimated paid-up members in 1988, the per capita figure is about H.K. $91.40 (compared with H.K. $35.59 in 1978). To put this in perspective, the figure for 1988 is about 0.4 percent of the estimated average annual income of an assembler in electronics, one of the lower-paying industries, and only 0.2 percent of the average annual income of a lockstitch sewing machine operator.[15] The low membership fees are one reason for the slender financial resource base of trade unions in Hong Kong.

Union expenditures more than doubled between 1980 and 1988, from H.K. $39 million to H.K. $90.5 million, matching the increase in income. Figure 7.3 shows how expenditures were distributed. Three points are worth emphasizing. First, the proportion of total expenditures spent on salaries and allowances has been relatively minor, a reflection of the lack of full-time trade union leaders and the minimal administrative staff one

Table 7.6. Sources and growth of trade union income in Hong Kong, 1988

Source	Percentage of total income	Percentage change in income (1980–88)
Members	35.1	+111
Schools	2.4	+87
Clinics	4.1	+40
Donations and commissions	1.1	+122
Loans	3.1	+1177
Bank interest	1.3	+2
Rent	3.5	+427
Business and undertakings	34.2	+152
Miscellaneous	15.2	+191
Total	H. K. $93,515,600[a]	+136

Source: Hong Kong. Registrar of Trade Unions, various.
[a]H. K. $1 = U.S. $0.128 at prevailing exchange rates as of December 29, 1991.

finds in anything but the very large unions. Second, the single largest item of expenditure in 1980, accounting for nearly one-third of the total, was business and undertakings, though by 1988 this had fallen to 21.8 percent. The general category of other expenditures, which includes taxation, repayment of bank loans, and depreciation, has risen proportionately because of rising property prices. Other unspecified outgoings rose from 17.7 percent in 1980 to 25 percent of all expenditures in 1988. Third, relatively minor amounts were paid out as benefits to members. The death benefit accounted for just over half of the cash benefits paid by unions in 1980 and one-third in 1988. Very small sums were distributed for unemployment relief, disputes, and sickness and accidents.

The importance of business and undertakings in union accounts merits further discussion. In 1988, unions operated 3 schools, 32 clinics, and 201 business undertakings (Hong Kong. Registrar of Trade Unions 1989:3). Business undertakings included canteens, restaurants, cooperatives, travel agencies, book shops, housing schemes, and recreation centers (England 1989:138). The motivation for these undertakings varies, but most fall into one of two categories—they provide services to members or they are sources of income.

In earlier periods when unions functioned more as mutual aid societies, union benefits such as dormitories, clinics, and schools were a principal reason for workers to join. As the government delivery of public goods has increased over the past two decades, however, the second motivation has become more important. One of the main sources

Figure 7.3. Distribution of trade union expenditures in Hong Kong, 1980 and 1988

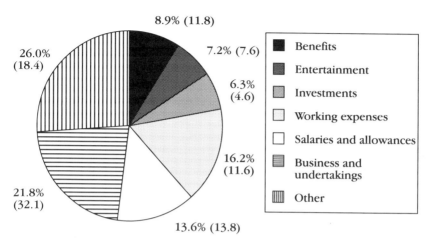

Source: Hong Kong. Registrar of Trade Unions 1980 and 1988 annual reports. Benefits include unemployment, disputes, sickness and accidents, marriage and maternity, death, education, and other relief. 1980 percentages in parentheses. 1980 total = H.K. $39,026,100. 1988 total = H.K. $90,597,200.

of income for the FTU has been a five-story restaurant it operates, while for many years the TUC has depended on rent collected from the restaurant operating on its premises. These union activities may reflect in part the entrepreneurial orientation of the work force or they may simply be evidence that the economic environment is conducive to small businesses and that unions have been able to capitalize on this situation as a way of generating income. The weakness of the union movement as a whole and hence the difficulty in raising sufficient funds from dues also compel unions to make use of business undertakings.

Workplace Activities and Their Consequences

The commonly accepted assessment of Hong Kong trade unions a decade ago—that they were weak at the workplace level—still applied on the whole to the private sector in the 1980s. Collective bargaining resulting in written agreements at the enterprise or industry level was rare. Wage levels were normally fixed by individual agreement between employers and workers (Hong Kong. Labour Department 1989:20). It has been estimated that only about 4 percent of the labor force is covered by collective bargaining agreements, and even these agreements are often not in detailed form.

In some trades with long guild traditions, general wage agreements are negotiated between craft unions and employers' associations on an annual or a periodic basis. These agreements are often ritualistic, focusing mainly on minimum pay rates and overtime payments, but lack detail on procedural matters or other substantive terms of employment and have little effect on the actual practices of individual employers. An exception is the printing industry, in which there is an established union tradition and open-ended agreements exist between the FTU-affiliated union and an employers' association covering holidays and workers' compensation. The closest approximation to the Western idea of collective bargaining in the private sector exists at Cable and Wireless Ltd., where in the early 1970s, following a bitter industrial dispute, management extended voluntary recognition to a staff union as the legitimate bargaining agent for employees (Leung 1983:123–33).

In major manufacturing sectors, such as clothing and electronics, union membership is low and collective bargaining apparently nonexistent. "Quasi-bargaining" has taken place, however, in cotton textiles, where unions have existed since the 1950s. A similar situation exists in the restaurant trade, where unions and an employers' association have reached agreements on standards defining the provision and arrangement of annual leave and other holidays. Bargaining over employment conditions occurs occasionally in some of the larger companies, such as the bus companies, where trade unions have an established position. Negotiations also take place between unions and management in some of the Hong Kong British companies, such as Cathay Pacific, but the frequency and content of these negotiations are not known.

Although many employers are undoubtedly opposed to collective bargaining, there are other reasons for its underdevelopment. The more powerful FTU affiliates, such as the Seamen's Union, prefer not to negotiate over wages and conditions of employment but to handle grievances that arise over the interpretation of crew agreements drawn up unilaterally by management (England and Rear 1981:168). What little direct evidence there is suggests a persistent weakness in the role of trade unions at the workplace level. In Turner's 1985 survey, of those respondents who reported being involved in disagreements with their employers over the previous five years, "in no single case reported was a trade union involved in the workers' representation" (1988:183–84).

There seems to be little pressure from employees for labor-management relations to take the form of collective bargaining. In both his 1976 and 1985 surveys, Turner asked respondents to indicate their preferences for various methods of job improvement. Trade union negotiation was preferred by only 12 percent in 1976 and 9 percent in 1985. Government legislation was preferred by 32 percent in 1976 and by 25 percent in 1985 but formal joint consultation by 31 percent in 1976 and 36 percent in 1985. Further evidence that trade union negotiation is not considered a route to job improvements comes from a 1986 survey of

481 female factory workers in Tsuen Wan (an industrial district in the New Territories). Respondents were asked the following open-ended question: "In your opinion, what is the best way to increase your income?" No respondent mentioned explicitly the possibility of trade union negotiation (Tsuen Wan District Board 1987:180).[16]

Another indicator of workplace-level activity by trade unions is participation in strikes.[17] Contrary to the expectations of observers in the early 1980s, the level of manifest industrial conflict, as measured by the number of strikes or working days "lost" because of strikes, did not rise. If anything, as shown in figure 7.4, strikes seemed to be less frequent. W.K.S. Chiu (1987:220) found a drop, after the 1967 disturbances, in participation by labor organizations in strikes. During 1968–70, only 36 percent of strikes involved labor organizations and during 1971–75 only 21 percent. Over the decade 1978–88, however, more than 40 percent of all strikes involved at least one labor organization, though not always trade unions. The character of union involvement in industrial action, when it occurs, can best be described as "defensive economism," in that most actions do not touch on issues relating to job control but focus on matters relating to wages or fringe benefits. The defensiveness of unions is also suggested by the fact that their involvement tends to ebb and flow in a countercyclical manner. Chiu found a strong inverse relationship between the business cycle and the proportion of strikes in which labor organizations were involved.

What difference does workplace-level union weakness in the private sector make? We suggest that adverse consequences do tend to follow

Figure 7.4. Strikes in Hong Kong, 1970–89

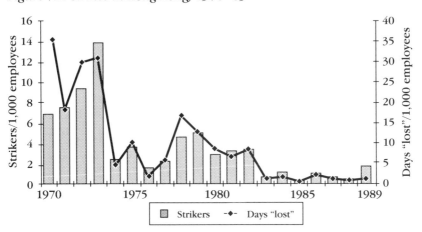

Source: Pre-1986 data from Chiu 1987:116. 1986–89 data extracted from unpublished records of the Hong Kong Labour Department.

vis-à-vis the welfare of workers, judging from two indicators of their well-being: income distribution and industrial accident rates. Although real wages have risen, albeit at lower rates over the decade 1978–88 than in the first three postwar decades, as shown in figure 7.5, increases in annual real wages have lagged far behind increases in labor productivity. The absence of collective bargaining tends therefore to reinforce the general situation of the labor market, and the increase in workers' real income has fallen behind the additional wealth they have created. Moreover, while the number of employees increased by 11 percent between 1980 and 1986, compensation of employees as a percentage of value added increased by only 7.7 percent (Hong Kong. Census and Statistics Department 1989a:38).

With regard to industrial accidents, the situation seems to be worsening. The number of industrial accidents in 1988 stood at a record level—55 percent higher than the comparable figure for 1979. As figure 7.6 shows, the industrial accident indexes have been rising even after controlling for increases in employment. Unions are naturally concerned about the situation (as is the Labour Department), but their ineffective role at the workplace, or their absence in most cases, means that unions are practically powerless to do anything about safety problems at the place of work. Consequently, their efforts are devoted more to helping workers claim compensation, pressing for more legislation designed to

Figure 7.5. Growth in productivity and real wages in Hong Kong, 1979–88

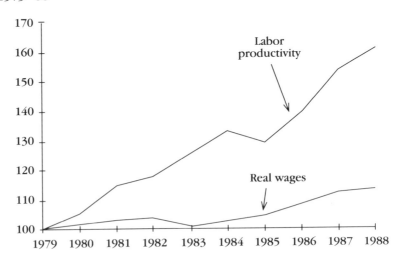

Source: Hong Kong. Census and Statistics Department, various.
Both productivity and real wages are transformed into indexes for which 1979 = 100.

Figure 7.6. Industrial accidents in Hong Kong, 1979–88

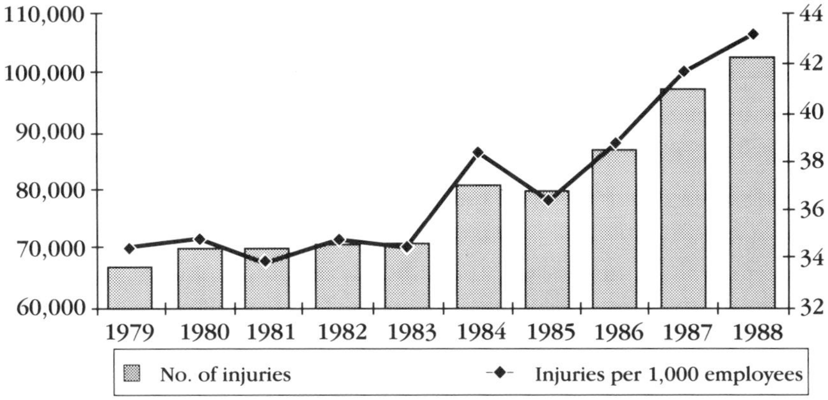

Source: Hong Kong. Labour Department 1989.
Only nonfatal accidents are included in the figure.

enhance workplace safety, and participating in tripartite industrywide committees set up to improve safety consciousness.

Unions in the civil service are in a more advantageous position to affect their members' terms and conditions of employment. Joint consultation has become the primary institutional channel for trade unions to exert influence. At the central level of government, the oldest consultative forum is the Senior Civil Service Council (SCSC), on which three servicewide staff trade unions are represented.[18] Only issues with servicewide implications are discussed in the SCSC, such as the annual pay revision for civil servants. Matters affecting individual grades are normally discussed within departmental consultative committees. In 1982, a separate staff consultative committee was set up to provide manual employees in the civil service (about one-third of all civil servants) with their own consultative forum (Tso 1988:62).[19]

The past chairman of the FCSU, which is not represented on the SCSC, has been critical of the restricted representation from the staff side on the SCSC, on the grounds that the three staff associations that sit on the SCSC represent only a minority of civil servants following the growth in the number of civil service trade unions and in union membership since 1968 (Wong 1988a:150–56). Another issue is whether the SCSC can be an effective channel for trade union participation given that the staff side has only consultative and not negotiating status. The president of the Hong Kong Chinese Civil Servants' Association, which is represented on the SCSC, has argued that the distinction between consultation and negotiation is, in practice, blurred on decisions such as the size of the annual pay adjustment for civil servants (Kwok 1988:147–49). The effectiveness of the existing consultative framework in reducing conflicts is hampered, however, by the problem of representativeness mentioned above. For example, during a conflict in 1986 between civil service unions and the government on the size of the annual pay increase, the three unions represented on the SCSC agreed to the government's proposed pay raise while a number of civil service unions excluded from the SCSC opposed the agreement.

Trade Unions, Political Participation, and Social Protest

Given the weakness of unions at the shop-floor level, one would expect unions in Hong Kong, as in other developing countries, to pursue their objectives through political channels. This became increasingly the case in the 1980s, in the context of two major political developments—the Sino-British agreement on the future of Hong Kong and the opening up of the local political system to wider participation. We first review the forms and extent of union political participation over the decade in two institutional contexts—the Labour Advisory Board (LAB) and the Legislative Council—and then trade union involvement in issue-oriented movements.[20]

For many years, the sole official channel for trade union participation in a public policy advisory capacity was through the Labour Advisory Board, which advises the commissioner of labor on matters affecting labor, including legislation and international labor conventions. The origins of the LAB predate World War II, but its composition has changed over the years (Miners 1988). In 1977, the LAB's membership was increased to twelve: six employer and six employee representatives. Of the latter, three were elected by trade unions and three were appointed by the governor. In 1985, the number of elected employee representatives was increased from three to four (offset by the reduction of appointed employee members from three to two) and as of January 1989 from four to five (leaving only one appointed employee member). The commissioner of labor or his deputy is the ex-officio chairman of the LAB.

Because of the Federation of Trade Unions' boycott of the LAB, the turnout rate in LAB elections during the 1970s was low. In 1977, for example, of 316 registered trade unions eligible to cast a vote, only 61 did so. In 1980, the turnout rate rose to one-quarter, but in the 1981 election (for 1982), it suddenly shot up to 52 percent (188 unions out of 363). It was just below 50 percent for the next two years, but in 1984 it rose again, to about two-thirds of all registered trade unions (K.Y.P. Chiu 1986:37).

The rising participation rates reflect the decision of the FTU to become more involved in the labor policy consultative framework of the Hong Kong government and the growing interest of the new public sector white-collar unions in LAB elections. With the involvement of the FTU and the independent trade unions in LAB elections, the distribution of elected seats changed. Thus, between 1978 and 1981, all three elected seats from labor's side were from affiliates of the Trades Union Council. In 1982, following the participation of the FTU in the LAB election, one elected representative came from the FTU, one from a civil service union, and one from a non–civil service independent union. This remained the pattern between 1982 and the 1987 election, except that for the election for the 1985–86 term of office, there was a fourth elected worker representative, who came from the TUC. By the end of the 1980s, the distribution of seats reflected the different groups within the trade union movement; there was one each from the FTU and the TUC, two from the civil service, and one from an independent union other than the civil service.[21]

Critics have viewed the LAB as an ineffective body, used by the government mainly for politically symbolic purposes (England and Rear 1981:9; Miners 1988:44). Though the contested elections among trade unionists for seats on the board might seem to indicate that unions now take it more seriously, union leaders are aware of the LAB's limitations. According to the chairman of the FTU: "The government still dances to the tunes of the employers. If a proposed legislation is opposed by the employers' representatives, it has to be referred back to the executive departments for amendment. This delays the legislative process for labor protection" (quoted in Li 1990:10).

A case in point is the issue of foreign labor, favored by employers in view of the labor shortage in the late 1980s. In LAB discussions on the issue, labor representatives unanimously opposed the employers' proposals to import labor. Nevertheless, the government still approved a scheme to allow for the import of three thousand foreign skilled workers, although this was a far lower figure than the employers had sought. In May 1989, the labor representatives walked out of a LAB meeting to protest the government's decision and the ineffectiveness of the LAB's consultative procedure (*Ming Pao* 1989b).

The Hong Kong government's moves during the 1980s in the direction of forming a more representative political system began with the opening to election in 1982 of some positions previously filled by nomination of the governor on the Urban Council and district boards. Following the 1984 white paper on "The Further Development of Representative Government in Hong Kong," a system of indirect elections to the Legislative Council was implemented. In place of a council composed solely of official members (civil servants) and appointed unofficial (non–civil service) members, the composition of the council from late 1985 was restructured to include twelve members elected by an electoral college (composed of all members of district boards, the Urban Council, and a new Regional Council), twelve members elected by nine functional constituencies, twenty-two members appointed by the governor, and ten official members. Of the nine functional constituencies, three—the commercial, industrial, and labor—returned two members each.

This corporatist form of political representation thus opened a new institutional channel for organized labor to participate in the making of public policy. The electorate for the labor functional constituency is the same as for the LAB—all registered employee trade unions—and each union that registers as an elector is entitled to one vote. Only individuals substantially connected with the labor functional constituency can stand for election (the exception is civil servants, who are not permitted to run), and they must be nominated by at least ten unions to become a candidate. A preferential voting system applies to the election of the two candidates.

With the exclusion of civil servants as candidates, the potential field for election from the labor constituency was only non–civil servants. In the first election in 1985, only two candidates were nominated, one from the FTU and the other from the TUC.[22] The influence of elected labor representatives on the Legislative Council is structurally limited, however, since they are outnumbered by those from the government, business, and professional classes.

The FTU encouraged members to register as voters in the 1985 district board elections and the 1986 Regional Council elections. In the district board elections, the FTU claimed 10 out of a total of 525 candidates were from member unions, of whom 5 were elected. The TUC reportedly put up seven, of whom two were elected. By comparison, members of the Professional Teachers' Union (PTU) reportedly won twenty-four seats on the district boards. Both the FTU and the TUC are also reported to have drawn up lists of candidates whom members were asked to support (Miners 1988:45).

During the 1970s, trade union participation in social protest was fairly muted. M.T.T. Tso (1983:24) suggests that the lack of involvement by the FTU and the TUC in social issues was not the result of indifference but rather a matter of "whether involvement can gain any political privilege by, say, discrediting the Government or, conversely, supporting the Government, in the light of the action of the rival camp." From the late 1970s, however, certain labor organization and trade union leaders began to participate more visibly in community protest movements. These protests were organized by temporary alliances of labor and community groups as a means of putting more effective pressure on the government (Aldrich and Whetton 1981:385–408).

In the late 1970s, a campaign was launched to promote industrial safety and improvements in employees' compensation. This resulted in a statement signed by forty-one unions, including thirteen belonging to the FTU and two to the TUC, together with other labor groups. In 1981, a Coalition against Bus Fare Increase was formed that included leaders of the PTU and initially the FTU, as well as church and student groups. During the latter stages of this campaign, some civil service unions also became involved.

In 1982, a Coalition for the Monitoring of Public Utility Companies was formed after utility companies raised charges. Trade unionists from the PTU, the FTU, the Hong Kong Social Workers' General Union, and several civil service unions joined with church and student activists in this coalition. This campaign was effective in that for the first time the government agreed to publish the scheme of profit control for seven utility companies. The coalition subsequently mobilized other pressure groups to petition the governor in late 1982 regarding the setting up of a central provident fund scheme. A signature campaign and lobbying among unofficial members of the Executive Council and the Legislative Council followed (Tso 1983:24–36; K.Y.P. Chiu 1986:56–69).

On May Day 1983, in the context of a deteriorating economy, rising indirect taxes, a fall in real wages, and a relatively low pay increase granted to civil servants, a mass rally was organized that involved some three hundred representatives from eighty labor organizations. A petition was submitted to the governor for a comprehensive social security plan, laws to protect workers from unfair dismissals, for a wage compensation fund, and for a law to make Labor Day a paid legal holiday.

Proposals by the Hong Kong government for political reforms stimulated another joint trade union venture in September 1984, when unions formed a Joint Conference on Representative Government. Some eighty-eight organizations participated, including seventeen independent unions (K.Y.P. Chiu 1986:62–66). Trade unionists who had played a leading role in earlier protest movements were among the principal leaders.

These events seemed to herald a new degree of interorganizational cooperation and enhanced political clout for the trade union movement. Tensions between the FTU and independent unions over the pace of local political reform and over the post-1977 political system for Hong Kong have made it difficult, however, to sustain united trade union action.

Can Labor Shape Its Own Future?

During the latter half of the 1980s, the union movement confronted two issues with long-term repercussions: the drafting of the Basic Law and the struggle for a central provident fund. A brief look at these two issues reveals both continuing tensions within the union movement and its lack of effectiveness in shaping a better future for working people in Hong Kong.

Drafting of the Basic Law

The dominant political development of the 1980s was the agreement reached in 1984 between the governments of the United Kingdom and the PRC on the future of Hong Kong, under which China will resume sovereignty over Hong Kong on 1 July 1997. Under the terms of the agreement, Hong Kong as a special administrative region (SAR) of China is supposed to enjoy a high degree of autonomy after 1997 except on matters concerning foreign affairs and defense.[23]

In 1985, China created the Basic Law Drafting Committee to draft Hong Kong's post-1997 mini-constitution. It appointed sixty-nine members to the committee, including twenty-three Hong Kong members, of whom two were trade unionists.

In 1986, another body, the Basic Law Consultative Committee, was appointed with 180 members, including 13 representing labor organizations, of whom 6 were from civil service unions and 7 were from other labor organizations. The nomination of these 7 members was to become a source of controversy within the labor movement.

Before the formation of the Basic Law Consultative Committee, a Joint Conference of Labor Groups on the Basic Law was formed in September 1985, open to all trade unions, to collect and express the views of labor on the Basic Law, and by October, some 167 organizations had joined. The Joint Conference was allowed to nominate seven members to the Basic Law Consultative Committee, while the civil service unions were asked to nominate six. It was agreed that these nominees would be decided by election. Because the TUC unions had refused to participate in the Joint Conference,[24] the FTU affiliates had a majority of votes in the election on a one-union, one-vote basis. Concerned that the FTU group would command a majority in the election, the Christian Industrial Committee and some other labor organizations bargained for the allocation of one of the seven seats on the consultative committee to be a representative from the CIC, two to be from the FTU group, and two each to represent independent labor federations and independent unions.

Just before the election, the CIC's director was informed that some of the FTU member unions would not support him in the election. Two unions close to the CIC then withdrew from the Joint Conference, and they were followed by another twenty civil service unions in protest against what was perceived as manipulation and discrimination against the independent unionists. In the October election for labor nominees to the consultative committee, three of the seven members who were elected were from the FTU group, three were from independent unions, and one was from an independent labor federation (Liang 1986).

This split over labor representation on this committee highlights the cleavages that have long beset Hong Kong's union movement. Another example involves attitudes toward political change. The independent unions have generally lobbied for a more democratic political framework for the future SAR as well as for more substantive rights for labor. They have demanded that future legislation enable a higher proportion of representatives to be elected by universal suffrage and have called for inclusion of such labor rights as organization, bargaining, and social security in the Basic Law. The FTU and its affiliates, although largely concurring with demands for labor's substantive rights, part ways with the independent unions on the future political system. Echoing the line of China's leaders that the primary task is to maintain Hong Kong's stability and prosperity, they have rallied for moderation in the pace and degree of democratization in Hong Kong's political development. In 1988, the FTU proposed a blueprint for the future SAR legislature whereby 45 percent of the seats would be allocated to representatives from functional groups, 40 percent would be filled by direct elections, 15 percent would be filled by an electoral college, and all representatives would sit in a single chamber (FTU Press 1988).

Following the June 1989 events in China, China's leaders became strongly suspicious of Hong Kong because of the support many in Hong Kong gave to the students and democratic movement in China. The Chinese government considered it necessary to install checks and balances in the future political system for Hong Kong to prevent it from becoming a "base of subversion." A so-called one-council, two-chamber or bicameral model was then proposed by local political groups said to have close connections to the Chinese government. Chinese officials quickly expressed their support for the scheme.

China's changing position on the political system created a dilemma for the FTU. On the one hand, shocked by the Tiananmen Square episode, the FTU publicly condemned the suppression of the democratic movement (FTU Press 1989a). Toward the end of 1989, however, the FTU backtracked on its earlier proposal for the future SAR legislature and proposed a model that bore a strong similarity to the one-council, two-chamber model supported by China.[25] It is not known whether the FTU's new proposal was influenced by the preferences of the Chinese government. FTU leaders have maintained that the model was derived from consulting with their members and eliciting opinions from the wider society. Some members of FTU affiliates issued public statements, however, criticizing the FTU's support for the bicameral model and pointed out that rank-and-file members were not consulted before the FTU announced the proposal (*Ming Pao* 1989b).

The final draft of the Basic Law was ratified by China's National People's Congress in early 1990. Trade union assessments of the law varied. The FTU and its affiliates considered it to have done "justice to the interests of all circles." Independents were disappointed with the outcome, while the TUC remained silent.

While it is difficult to assess how much influence the union movement as a whole had in the drafting of the Basic Law, its limited influence does surface in those areas that most unions agree upon. The right to strike and the right to participate in trade unions are included in the law, as is reference to legal protection of "welfare benefits and retirement security of the labor force" (Basic Law, chap. 2, art. 27, 36). Both the FTU and independent unions also demanded recognition from employers and the right of collective bargaining. On this score, however, even FTU leaders have expressed reservations about the provisions in the law.

Some political commentators have considered the union movement largely irrelevant to the drafting process. As they see it, the major players were the CCP, the British government, and the capitalist class in Hong Kong (Lo 1989). On the one hand, unionists were a minority on the Basic Law Consultative Committee and had only token representation on the Basic Law Drafting Committee. On the other hand, members of Hong Kong's capitalist class visited Beijing frequently and CCP leaders were well versed in their needs and worries. Under these circumstances, it is not surprising that unions had only a marginal influence in shaping their political future.

Struggle for a Central Provident Fund

The second issue that preoccupied Hong Kong's unions in the 1980s was the debate over a central provident fund. Demands for a scheme that would provide retirement benefits to workers were first raised in the 1980s and the FTU was one of the earliest proponents, but the Hong Kong government's position was to encourage voluntary retirement schemes. As a result, only a small proportion of workers, notably civil servants and employees of major public utilities, enjoyed a pension or other retirement benefit scheme.

During the 1980s, the three major union blocs supported the establishment of a central provident fund. It was a feasible objective for the FTU to pursue because it did not touch on the thorny question of democratization and enabled the FTU to demonstrate its efforts on behalf of the working class. The independent unions, led by the CIC, were a spearhead in putting pressure on the government. The TUC also supported the fund, content to deal with an issue not connected to the Basic Law. Nevertheless, the independent unions and the FTU differed on the pace for establishing the fund. The FTU, with its concern about maintaining stability and prosperity, was ready to accept a watered-down government proposal in 1985 for a payment scheme to compensate dismissed workers with long tenure as a first step toward the eventual establishment of a fund. The independents were less compromising and staged a protest in front of the Legislative Council when the bill to establish this scheme was passed (*Ming Pao* 1985). The FTU was more inclined to work within the institutional framework and largely abstained from the protests of the independent unions and other labor organizations. For the latter group, mobilization of the public, arousing public consciousness, and direct protest actions were the key methods of struggling for their objectives.

Despite the trade unions' united front on the provident fund, the interests of the capitalist class prevailed. In 1987, consistent with the position of employers, the governor announced that the proposal for such a fund had been rejected on the grounds that the local economy would be adversely affected. The government was also concerned about its own financial solvency and the additional fiscal burdens of a central provident fund (*Hong Kong Hansard* 1987–88:34). Thus, the fundamental nature of Hong Kong's political economy and the imbalance of class power frustrated the unions' effort to seek some safeguards for the working class.

Explaining the Marginalization of the Union Movement

The preceding discussion has revealed how limited the influence of unions in Hong Kong has been on the important issues affecting their future. This section seeks to account for this marginalization by synthesizing three strands of analysis: cultural, economic-structural, and political.

Role of Culture

One stock answer to the question of why unions remain weak in the private sector of Hong Kong emphasizes cultural values. The general argument is that the conception of the employment relationship as adversarial does not fit the dominant value orientations of employers or workers in Hong Kong (Tsui 1979:20–28). This view echoes the recent literature on the "Confucian model of East Asian development." H. C. Tai's (1989:19–20) recent contribution to this thesis, for example, contends that the impact of a Confucianist tradition manifests itself in the employment relationship in a strong sense of identification with the interests of the employing firm and a corresponding industriousness and willingness to comply with managerial authority. If this characterization applies to Hong Kong's working class, then the marginality of the union movement is hardly surprising. This thesis is difficult to sustain empirically, however. A comparison of Hong Kong and South Korea, another neo-Confucian society, reveals sharp differences in the strength and behavior of their union movements. Furthermore, the union movement in Hong Kong has been considerably more influential historically than it is at present. An undifferentiated Confucian explanation does not account for these comparative and historical variations.

Another cultural explanation, one tailored more specifically to Hong Kong, emphasizes the impact of the "refugee mentality" on workers' industrial attitudes and behavior. A substantial portion of the rapid growth of the Hong Kong population after World War II was composed of refugees fleeing from the political turmoil and changes in China (Podmore 1971:25–26). These refugees encountered in Hong Kong a laissez-faire economy and had to depend to a large extent on the familial group for economic survival. As a result, an ethos of "utilitarianistic familism" developed in which familial interests tended to take precedence over societal or other group interests (Lau 1982:72). This familism, combined with a strong motivation to seek individual economic advancement and a desire for a stable political environment, is said to have generated psychological resistance to trade unions, which were seen to be extensions of Chinese politics. The impact of the refugee mentality in preventing union growth should not be exaggerated. It cannot explain the widely divergent fortunes of unions across different economic sectors. Moreover, if the refugee mentality were operative, it would be difficult to explain why so many workers have joined the politically oriented FTU and TUC.

In the case of employers, a culturalist explanation would predict that employers' attitudes toward unions should vary depending on their cultural predisposition. Yet J. England and J. Rear (1981:94) claim that the dominant managerial style in Hong Kong is a mixture of paternalism and authoritarianism, and most employers, regardless of ethnicity, are opposed to trade unions. An employers' spokesman has characterized the typical attitude of larger employers toward trade union recognition as follows: "The law does not require it; the union does not seem to be pressing too hard to be recognized; indeed, what is there in it for me if I did?"[26] (Cheetham 1988:79). American-owned electronics factories in Hong Kong are reported to impose tight controls over labor and to oppose trade unions as a matter of corporate policy (Djao 1975:284; England and Rear 1981:93). Thus, an employer need not be a Confucian or a refugee to be predisposed to a union-free environment.[27]

This does not mean culture is irrelevant in explaining the weakness of unions in Hong Kong, only that the affective or normative effects of culture should not be overstated. Cultural values do not dictate uniform patterns of action. Rather, culture "is more like a 'tool kit' or repertoire from which actors select differing pieces for constructing lines of action"

(Swidler 1986:277). This imagery alerts us to how rational social actors respond to different circumstances by drawing on their cultural repertoire of strategies. Confucian traditions, especially the familial ethos, and the refugee mentality, did affect workers' orientations, but the prevalence of individualist modes of action at the expense of collective ones has to be accounted for by how different contexts activated different responses from among a broader set of cultural repertoires. This point suggests the importance of the economic and political contexts of action.

Structural Context of Dependent Industrialization

The particular pattern of Hong Kong's postwar industrialization is a crucial determinant of the nature and strength of its labor movement. For a century up to World War II, entrepôt trade was the mainstay of Hong Kong's economy. As shown in our historical survey, this pattern of capital accumulation was more conducive to the development of a militant and strong union movement, associated with the peaks of union activities in the 1920s and the late 1940s. While craft unions burgeoned in the traditional trades, the structural characteristics of the major industries, which mainly served the local community and the trading sector—large firm size, stable employment relationships, and a skilled and predominantly male labor force—also proved to be congenial to the growth of industrial unions. That most major firms were owned and managed by the British also contributed to tensions at the workplace and hence to the growth of union organization.

After World War II, the emergence of a new international division of labor in the capitalist world and the incorporation of Hong Kong into this network of exchange and production transformed Hong Kong from a trading port to an industrial city (So 1986). This process led to a rapid change in the contours of the union movement. First, previous union strongholds such as shipbuilding and repairing declined. Second, the emergence of export-oriented light industries set in motion a process of "structural demobilization" of labor: "It is clear that the preponderance of industrial jobs in the light-industry export sectors characterized by low-skill, minimal advancement opportunities, and job insecurity, along with a workforce dominated by young women who do not anticipate long-term industrial employment, militate against effective class politics or organization" (Deyo, Haggard, and Koo 1987:51; see also Deyo 1984, 1989).

Consequently, the proletariat created by Hong Kong's postwar industrialization differed qualitatively from its prewar counterpart. The composition of the capitalist class also changed. The bourgeoisie, which was dominant in the prewar entrepôt period, was still visible in the postwar economy, but a new generation of industrial entrepreneurs also emerged. Some, like the Shanghainese textile manufacturers, were established industrialists in China who transferred their investment to Hong Kong in response to the Communist takeover in the late 1940s. But the majority of Chinese entrepreneurs were men of fairly humble origins who started small factories with little capital (Sit and Wong 1989). Foreign investment in manufacturing grew (mainly in electronics) from the 1960s, but Chinese-owned factories still predominated. Thus, the ethnic factor that had contributed to industrial relations tensions before the war largely evaporated in industry; a more personal and paternal strategy of labor control could be exercised at the enterprise level, especially in smaller firms. These Chinese employers could invoke the cultural imagery of a benevolent patriarch in managing their firms and disciplining their work force (Djao 1981).

As demand for labor soared in the labor-intensive manufacturing sector from the late 1950s, and competition for labor intensified, workers discovered that they could get higher pay through individual action via exit (or the threat of exit). The feasibility of the exit option was enhanced by the spatial density of firms as they rapidly proliferated (especially in clothing, toys and plastics, and electronics), by the low level of skill required in these industries, and by the widespread use of piece-rate systems of pay. Because market forces led to continuous increases in real wages, "labor mobility [became] an acceptable alternative to collective wage bargaining and grievance resolution" (England and Rear 1975:44). Furthermore, the combination of a tight labor market and the familial ethos among workers enabled the working-class family to pursue a strategy of survival and mobility by pooling family resources. In particular, the patriarchal arrangements in the Chinese family enabled working-class families to appropriate the income of their unmarried working daughters (Salaff 1981).

In brief, Hong Kong's particular pattern of industrialization has engendered structural forces that in turn triggered a vicious cycle of individual (or familial) strategies of market behavior and weak class formation among the industrial working class. This process has inhibited union growth in the manufacturing sector, and the union movement as a whole has stagnated as manufacturing has become the largest employment sector in the economy.

The surge in white-collar and civil service unionism in the 1970s has created pockets of union strength outside the manufacturing sector. Nevertheless, the growth in white-collar unions has failed to compensate for the decline of manufacturing unions, as evidenced by the drop in overall union density in the late 1970s. Moreover, white-collar unions are primarily job-oriented in that they seek to defend and advance their status within bureaucratic organizations. In this respect, white-collar unionism has emerged disarticulated from the struggling blue-collar unions. Although white-collar unions have played a leadership role in the labor movement's intervention in wider societal issues, they are incapable of alleviating the structural weakness of unions at the shop-floor level in the manufacturing sector.

The Colonial State and the "China Connection"

If the structure of the economy has been a major impediment to a more viable union movement, the role of the state, or political factors broadly conceived, has exacerbated the difficulties of union organization. The colonial state has occupied a rather peripheral position in the postwar structure of accumulation. It supplies the infrastructural supports, maintains law and order, and provides some basic social services, but it has not become involved directly in production. Contrary to the experiences of many late industrializers in the Third World, private entrepreneurs rather than the state have played the pivotal role in economic development. Corresponding to this arm's-length approach to the economy, the colonial government has claimed to follow the British voluntarist tradition in industrial relations (Ng 1982). Given the power imbalance in the workplace, this approach has served to buttress managerial prerogatives rather than facilitate labor organization.

Though the government has not intervened in labor relations directly, it has not always been a neutral referee. When union actions took on political and anti-colonial overtones in a number of industrial conflicts in the early 1950s, militant workers were arrested and union leaders deported. During the 1967 disturbances involving left-wing unions and workers, the government once again did not hesitate to crack down on these unions. Nevertheless, unlike the situation in many other developing countries, direct political repression has not been the principal strategy for controlling labor in Hong Kong.

After the disturbances of 1966 and 1967, the government took a more active role in labor relations and began to compete with the unions in rendering assistance to workers in settling individual and collective disputes with employers (Turner et al. 1980:114). The rising expenditures by the government since the late 1960s for public goods—housing, education, and welfare—are seen by some as undermining unions by providing an alternative source of tangible benefits to those offered by some unions (Lau 1982:141; Scott 1989:152–70). The government's housing policy has also had an unintended adverse effect on the union movement by disrupting working-class communities in squatter areas formed in the immediate postwar period. As workers in these areas were dispersed among different housing estates, the spatial basis for reinforcement of group cohesion and collective consciousness was undermined, and the pace and extent of this change seriously outstripped the unions' ability to organize among them.[28]

Ultimately, however, the key political influence crippling the union movement has not been the colonial state but the China factor. Nationalist sentiments were a stimulus to working-class organization before World War II. The civil war between the Communists and the nationalists created a permanent division within Hong Kong's union movement, however. Competition and infighting among right-wing and left-wing unions not only caused the proliferation of unions but also facilitated the divide-and-rule strategy used by employers and the state.[29] The failure of a single union to speak for the entire work force in a particular firm or sector has often been used as a pretext for employers to refuse to negotiate with unions.

Conclusion

In some respects, the broad features of the Hong Kong union movement have not changed over the past decade. On the one hand, it continues to represent only a minority of employees, to remain structurally and politically fragmented, and, outside the civil service, to be ineffective at the workplace level. On the other hand, the independent union wing of the movement has become a more prominent actor, and the union movement as a whole has become more outspoken and involved politically than it was a decade ago, responding to the political transformations of the 1980s. Nevertheless, as this chapter has also shown, the union movement has not normally been able to translate this political voice into political outcomes favorable to the interests of the working class, in large measure because of the environment in which the movement operates.

Although there have been signs of a renewed workplace militancy since late 1989, it is by no means clear that the union movement is entering a new stage.[30] Most trade unions in Hong Kong remain relatively small, their leadership serves on a voluntary basis, and their financial resources are minimal, limiting what they can achieve. Recently, however, union leaders have raised the issue of collective bargaining rights. For example, on May Day 1991, union officials petitioned the government and organized demonstrations demanding collective bargaining rights. If eventually guaranteed by law, this would be a breakthrough for the union movement. Yet, judging from the past experience of labor legislation in the colony and the opposition of capital to any fundamental change in the power structure of the workplace, it is unlikely that union recognition or collective bargaining will be required by law in the near future. Moreover, the economic context is likely to continue to work to the unions' disadvantage. Given the continued vulnerability of the economy to international competition, employers (except for those in some sheltered sectors) will remain extremely cost-conscious, making it difficult for unions to extract concessions from them. With the probable continuing decline of manufacturing, unions in this sector are expected to be preoccupied with problems of retrenchment and bankruptcy. The aging of the labor force is likely to keep the issue of retirement benefits on the unions' agenda, but relatively few companies are in a position to spare resources to provide retirement plans. If this issue is pursued, it will most probably have to be through political channels.

A major question is the extent to which the political clout of the union movement is likely to increase in the future. In 1991, the composition of the Legislative Council was altered to include eighteen seats filled by direct elections.[31] Both the FTU and the independent trade union groups will be important players in future direct elections because of their numbers, organizational skills, and, to a lesser extent, financial resources.[32] Whoever runs for direct elections will undoubtedly wish to court the trade unions, especially the larger unions and the federations, for their support in mobilizing voters. The chairman of the FTU has announced that the federation itself may even field candidates for direct elections (*South China Morning Post* 1990a).

To pool their resources, to push for more political influence within Hong Kong, and to enhance their own prospects for survival in the face of future political uncertainties, independent unions had to form a confederation of labor. This is precisely what happened. Preparations, under way since early 1989 for the formation of an alliance of independent trade unions, resulted in the registration in early 1990 of the Confederation of Trade Unions of Hong Kong, with twenty-one unions and a membership of 80,000 (*South China Morning Post* 1990b).[33] It is thus the largest trade union group after the FTU, replacing the TUC in the polarized union movement. It will be interesting to see how well the confederation can mobilize both manual and nonmanual independent trade unions to work together, whether it will compete head-on with the FTU in politics (and at the workplace) or work out a modus vivendi, and whether it will be able to articulate a vision of unionism that proves attractive to the mass of unorganized employees.

That an alliance of independent unions that encompasses the majority of both white-collar and blue-collar unionists could become a major political force is not likely, however, for several reasons. First, white-collar unionists are themselves divided in a number of ways—between those in and outside the civil service, between those in higher and lower ranks within public bureaucracies, and between those who define the primary role of a trade union to be representation of the sectional interests of members versus those who wish to see the union movement develop into a major political actor. Second, the growing involvement of white-collar unionists in political issues of the 1980s was, according to one commentator, motivated by a desire for "guarantees that their recent economic gains, personal liberties and lifestyle would not be threatened" by China's resumption of sovereignty over Hong Kong (Scott 1989:238). Once China made it clear that it would not support greater democratization after 1997, it left the salaried middle class with difficult choices, which can be summarized as exit, apathy, and voice options. Those who distrust China's intentions toward Hong Kong can adopt individualist strategies of emigrating, which many have done and will continue to do until 1997.

Among those who intend to remain in Hong Kong, many are undoubtedly pessimistic and feel it is no longer worthwhile to devote their energies to political action. The voice option is probably attractive to a minority who want to pursue their political struggle to advance the interests of labor, although options for influencing future political changes have now been effectively closed off. But even this vocal minority is likely to be distracted from broader social and political issues by immediate economic interests, such as the security of pensions after 1997 or the magnitude of annual wage hikes. It remains to be seen which set of issues will be given a higher priority in the transitional period.

What the union movement will be like after 1997 when Hong Kong becomes a special administrative region within China is unclear and hinges on the role the leadership of China has in mind for Hong Kong. Certainly the status of the FTU will be enhanced after China regains sovereignty. If the rights to form and join unions are upheld in practice, however, then one can expect the continued survival of an independent trade union movement, although Chinese authorities view some outspoken independent trade unionists with suspicion. Nevertheless, the political influence of the union movement as a whole in the initial post-1997 legislature will be diluted by the system of functional representation. China, like the colonial government, seems to prefer this arrangement since it leads to more predictable outcomes than the uncertainties associated with direct elections. Given the above set of economic and political circumstances, it seems unlikely that there will be any dramatic advances in the effectiveness of unions in Hong Kong in the foreseeable future.

8
Corporatist Trade Unionism in Singapore

Chris Leggett

In 1982, an amendment to section 2 of the Singapore Trade Unions Act of 1941[1] substituted the trade union objects of consensus and productivity improvement for the confrontational objects of the original ordinance. That the trade unions were able to revise their rules and constitutions accordingly is an indication of the extent of the transformation of industrial relations in Singapore since the emergence of unionism following the end of World War II. This transformation has mostly defied categorization except that it has been observed to be "an amalgam of elements familiar to those in Western Europe, the USA, Australia and Japan, but . . . distinctive in that the overwhelmingly predominant role is played by the state rather than unions or management" (Levine 1980:78). At the same time, it has been acknowledged that Singapore unions offer a sense of inclusiveness for what otherwise might be an atomized work force, and it is argued here that they serve to legitimize the economic and social imperatives set for Singapore by its ruling elite.

The corporatist labor relations thesis has been outlined as follows. (1) Politicized Third World trade unions destabilize political regimes or make economically damaging wage demands. (2) To develop productionist and socialization roles for unions, governments have suppressed their opposition and incorporated them into a dependent relationship with the state. (3) The long-term stability of corporatism depends on the disorganization of nonincorporated bodies and a unified political elite. (4) Corporate state labor relations are accompanied by labor force atomism and a lack of worker commitment to elite-imposed norms. (5) As a result of worker demoralization, governments may attempt to reinvigorate trade unions with more "popular" modes of authoritarianism so that they can be more effective in their socialization and productionist roles. (6) Where development is dependent on foreign investment, industrialization is associated with the state's consolidation of "authoritarian corporatism" (Deyo 1981:109–15).

The effectiveness of authoritarian corporatist labor relations in Singapore was clearly evident during the 1985 recession when the National Trades Union Congress (NTUC) carried the work force with it through a labor cost-cutting program that reversed, for the time being, a government-sanctioned high-wage policy, although the NTUC did permit a concessionary strike against a victimizing foreign employer.[2]

Before analyzing the roles and functions of incorporated trade unions in Singapore since it achieved NIC status, it is useful to trace the development of trade unionism leading up to the government's 1979 decision to restructure the economy. The trade union history of Singapore has been well documented (Pang 1981; Pang and Cheng 1978), and a review will help to place the post-1979 changes in perspective.

Emergence and Development of Trade Unionism

Eng Fong Pang (1981) divides the history of Singapore's industrial relations to 1976 into four phases, but for this chapter they are conflated into the pre-1965 struggle for control of workers and the attainment of work force compliance between 1965 and 1979. The 1980s, it has been argued elsewhere, was a period marked by the management of work force compliance (Wilkinson and Leggett 1985).

Struggle for Control, 1945–65

Because of the Japanese occupation of Singapore during World War II, union ordinances passed in 1940 and 1941 by the British administration were not effective until 1946. By then, the Malayan Communist Party (MCP) was promoting disruptive unionism as part of its anti-colonial strategy. Militancy was somewhat curtailed by the state of emergency, declared in 1948, under which suspected left-wing subversives, such as C. V. Devan Nair, who was destined to play a major role in the reshaping of unionism for the People's Action Party (PAP) government, were detained. To counter the "leftist" unions, the colonial administration in 1951 backed the Singapore Trades Union Congress (STUC), which went on to support David Marshal's Labor Front government in 1955. Militant and politicized trade unionism increased in the first half of the 1950s, however, so that working days lost because of strikes peaked at close to a million in 1955.[3]

Although the Labor Front government was short-lived, important labor legislation was passed during its tenure. This included employment ordinances (consolidated in 1968 as the Employment Act), the Central Provident Fund Ordinance of 1955, and the Criminal Law (Temporary Provisions) Ordinance of 1955, which restricted industrial action in "essential services." More legislation followed the election to full self-government of the PAP in 1959, with Lee Kuan Yew as prime minister. The Trade Unions (Amendment) Ordinance of 1959 prevented the development of splinter unions and multiunionism, but it was the Industrial Relations Ordinance of 1960 that regulated industrial relations comprehensively by providing Ministry of Labor and Industrial Arbitration Court regulation of collective bargaining and dispute settlement. These controls were consonant with the recommendations of the Winsemius report, by a visiting United Nations technical commission, to industrialize Singapore rapidly to relieve its unemployment (United Nations 1961).

Meanwhile, a political struggle between "leftists" and the Lee Kuan Yew faction in the PAP was extended to the labor movement and came to a head over the prospect of Singapore's inclusion, favored by Lee, in a proposed Malaysian Federation.

When the leftists broke with the PAP to form the *Barisan Socialis* (Socialist Party), they sponsored the Singapore Association of Trade Unions (SATU), while the PAP, through C. V. Devan Nair, supported the newly formed NTUC. The SATU was refused registration in 1963, and the NTUC was formally registered in 1964. In the event, Singapore left Malaysia in 1965 to become an independent sovereign state but not before the leftists had been rendered politically impotent by the detention of many of their leaders.

From 1946 to 1964, union membership grew from 18,673 to 157,050, peaking at 189,032 in 1962. In 1964, the NTUC organized nearly 65 percent of all unionists in fifty-five affiliates. By 1965, this figure had risen to 73 percent in fifty-seven affiliates. Of these, the Amalgamated Union of Public Employees (AUPE) recorded 21,000 members in 1963 (Lee 1979:13) and the Singapore Mercantile and Manual Workers' Union 16,000, but most had fewer than 1,000 members and a number of "house" unions organized fewer than 100 employees (NTUC 1970:225–28). Density averaged 34 percent between 1957 and 1965, and in the exceptional year of 1962 reached more than 40 percent, levels not approached in the more orderly industrial relations of the postindependence years.[4] Details of union structure are not available for the pre-1965 period, but, using the Ministry of Labor's current classification, from their names, the forty-one NTUC affiliates in 1967 are discernible as fifteen "house," twelve "craft/occupational," eleven "industrywide," and three "omnibus" unions (NTUC 1970:225–28).

Attainment of Work Force Compliance, 1965–79

To assure the ascendency of the NTUC among Singapore unions, the Ministry of Labor had, in 1962, established a Labor Research Unit to assist unions in negotiating, and the Industrial Relations (Amendment) Ordinance of 1965 made union recognition by an employer compulsory where a ballot confirmed the union had the majority support of the workers in the proposed bargaining unit. The more militant leftist unions were constrained by the Trade Unions (Amendment) Act of 1966, which tightened the qualifications for union office holding and introduced compulsory strike ballots, and the Trade Unions (Amendment) Act of 1967, which made sympathy strikes illegal and fragmented public-sector manual unions. As intended, the number of work stoppages fell—from 928 between 1960 and 1964, with more than a million working days "lost," to 58, with 151,843 working days "lost," between 1965 and 1969 (Singapore. Ministry of Labor, annual)—but so also did union membership after 1966.

Although the earlier legislation had aimed at containing unions within an economic frame of reference, the 1968 legislation curtailed both the procedural and substantive content of collective bargaining and fundamentally changed the character of industrial relations in Singapore. While the Employment Act of 1968 set minimum employment conditions for manual workers, the Industrial Relations (Amendment) Act of 1968 made those conditions the maximum in collective agreements covering workers in industries essential to Singapore's industrialization. Further, the Industrial Relations (Amendment) Act of 1968 made it illegal for unions to bargain over management prerogatives. Since collective agreements were required to be certified by the Industrial Arbitration Court, were legally binding on the parties, and were of legally fixed duration, the unions had no choice but to comply and work out a new role for the movement if they were to have any appeal to the workers.

The NTUC organized a seminar in 1969 entitled "Modernization of the Labor Movement" (NTUC 1970) at which both PAP and NTUC leaders charted a course for labor that involved the setting up of commercial cooperatives, the provision of welfare services, and, generally, a role in worker socialization to raise productivity. C. V. Devan Nair was briefed to bring the NTUC into a more national scheme of things.

Union incorporation was furthered in 1971, when the government legislated a tripartite National Wages Council to recommend annual wage increases from 1972 on, in line with economic development. The authoritativeness of the council restored NTUC credibility with the workers but further limited the scope of collective bargaining in that the Industrial Arbitration Court was empowered to change collective agreements to include the National Wages Council's recommendations. With these measures, the institutional framework was in place for fine-tuning labor's compliance with the imperatives to be set and revised by the PAP government. The network of established institutional controls ensured the decline of overt industrial conflict. In addition to the legal provisions inhibiting industrial action, the NTUC's Industrial Affairs Council vetted its affiliates' disputes, advising or cautioning them on what courses to follow. In 1969, no work stoppages were recorded, and between 1970 and 1979, forty-four stoppages resulted in only 11,456 working days "lost," compared with 1,400,000 in the previous decade (Singapore. Ministry of Labor, annual).[5]

Union structure did not change much in the 1960s, although membership fell. Even in the 1970s most unions belonged either to the house or craft/occupation categories, but membership was largest in a small number of industrywide and omnibus unions. In this last category, with the AUPE and the Singapore Mercantile and Manual Workers' Union, were the Singapore Industrial Labour Organization (SILO) and the Pioneer Industries Employees' Union (PIEU), which, until their dismemberment after 1979, were the largest unions in the private sector, organizing workers in the manufacturing industries that had been attracted to Singapore. Of the eighty-three unions on the register in 1989 (see table 8.1), thirty were registered before 1960, thirteen before 1969, and fourteen before 1979; of these pre-1979 survivors, twenty-one were house, twenty-two craft/occupational, twenty-one industrywide, and two omnibus unions.

The pattern of unionization by industry reflected but did not keep pace with Singapore's changing industrial structure. In 1979, for example, 15 percent of unionized workers were employed in manufacturing compared with 29 percent of the work force, whereas in transport, storage, and communication, the distributions were the same but the union density was twice that in manufacturing. In the public sector,

Table 8.1. Structure of unions in Singapore in 1989 and years registered

Years registered	House	Craft	Industry	Omnibus	Total
1946–59	6	17	5	2	30
1960–69	8	2	3	1	14
1970–79	7	3	4	1	15
1980–89	16	1	8	0	25
Total	37	23	20	4	83

Sources: Singapore Ministry of Labor, various, and Leggett, n.d.

community, social, and personal services accounted for 28.5 percent of union members but 21 percent of employees, and the union density was 28 percent. Although the AUPE dominated membership in community, social, and personal services, the number of unions, many quite small occupation or house unions, was higher in 1979 than in any other industrial sector.[6]

Following the successful industrialization of Singapore and aided by the "modernization" of the labor movement, in 1979 the PAP government announced a change of development strategy and set new imperatives for labor. What followed was a restructuring of the unions and a phasing out of "old-guard" leaders as the NTUC and its affiliates were infused with younger technocrats more committed to realizing the high-technology future projected for Singapore.

Economic and Trade Union Restructuring

By the mid-1970s, Singapore had been transformed from dependence on entrepôt trade to an NIC dependent on multinational corporation investments in export-oriented manufacturing. The prospects for further economic growth were limited by the likelihood that Singapore would lose its qualification for the American generalized system of preferences; increasing competition from the other NICs in American, European, and Japanese markets; and Singapore's tightening labor market. Deciding that the time was appropriate, in 1979 the PAP government adopted a new development strategy of economic restructuring to free the economy from the impasse and avoid falling into the low-wage trap. Economic restructuring meant, first, upgrading current economic activities by increasing the value added of each worker through higher productivity and increased automation and, second, by attracting investment in higher-technology manufacturing and services (Singapore. Economic Committee 1986). For restructuring to be successful, the compliance of labor was required, and it was to this end that the NTUC leaders directed their affiliates in the 1980s.

The NTUC and the Management of Compliance, 1980

The new role of the NTUC was symbolized in 1979 by the succession of a public-sector bureaucrat, Lim Chee Onn, as secretary-general in place of the "old guard" C. V. Devan Nair, and its importance demonstrated when Lim, already a member of Parliament, was given a position in the Cabinet. Lim's zealousness led to the prime minister announcing Lim's replacement in 1983 with the current (as of 1992) incumbent, Ong Teng Cheong, who is also second deputy prime minister (*Straits Times*, 13 April 1983).

By an amendment to the NTUC's constitution in 1978, cadre members were able to participate in policy making and there continued a steady infusion of young, career-oriented technocrats—some, PAP members of Parliament—into the offices of the NTUC. Their contributions were particularly important as the NTUC began a two-stage restructuring of its affiliates.

The first stage of restructuring, begun during Lim's secretary-general-ship, involved breaking up the omnibus SILO and PIEU into industrywide unions, partly to prevent a recurrence of the concentration of individual power within the NTUC that Phey Yew Kok had wielded. Phey, a PAP member of Parliament who had been a successful organizer for the NTUC, at one and the same time had held the offices of general secretary of both SILO and PIEU, president of the Singapore Air Transport Union, president of the NTUC, and executive secretary of its Industrial Affairs Council (Deyo 1981:44). Indicted for financial improprieties concerning SILO, Phey had fled Singapore, leaving the NTUC somewhat discredited.

Another reason for restructuring was to align workers more closely with the industries in which they were employed. By 1982, an NTUC "task force" had created nine industrywide unions with a combined membership of 73,500, or about 34 percent of unionized workers, from SILO and PIEU.[7] In keeping with Lim's requirement of administratively efficient unionism, each of the new unions was supplied with an executive secretary from among NTUC-PAP cadres and an NTUC-appointed negotiating officer. Before the efficiency of the new structure could be demonstrated, however, a government committee on productivity had reported on the feasibility of Japanese employment practices for Singapore, among them house unionism, it having being surmised that house unions contributed more to labor productivity than did other types of unions (Singapore. National Productivity Board 1981). Task forces were set up by the NTUC to form house unions—some from the newly created industrywide unions—but this time the secretary-general was faced with opposition from affected officials.

Most resistant was the old-guard R. Doraisamy, general secretary of the Singapore Air Transport Union, representing employees of Singapore Airlines and its subsidiaries. His resistance was overcome early in 1984 by a combination of events, including the Ministry of Labor's withdrawal of the Air Transport Union's check-off facility, Singapore Airlines ending Doraisamy's privilege of working full-time on union matters, and the "overnight" registration of each of three house unions by the requisite minimum of seven employees (Blum and Patarapanich 1987:394–96; Leggett 1988:248–49). Resistance from the United Workers of Petroleum Industry collapsed the same year when, under pressure from the NTUC, it rescinded a resolution authorizing its executive council to discipline officials seeking to form house unions from any of its branches (*Straits Times,* 18 Aug. 1982). Nevertheless, some delegates to the 1984 NTUC

Ordinary Delegates' Conference braved Secretary-General Ong's wrath when they sat on their hands rather than vote for the NTUC's house union policy.

All told, only thirteen house unions were created in this second stage of restructuring. All but one, the Metal Box Employees' Union, were in the public sector, and only the Resources Development Corporation Employees' Union had not been a branch of an NTUC affiliate. In 1984, the seventy NTUC unions consisted of twenty-eight house, eighteen industrywide, twenty craft/occupational, and four omnibus unions, organizing 20, 52, 10 and 18 percent of NTUC membership respectively.[8] Since 1984, however, all new unions that have been registered have been of the house type.

Union membership, which had peaked at 249,710 in 1979, fell during the union restructuring and after—by 23 percent between 1979 and 1985, as shown in table 8.2. Although the new house unions had higher membership densities than the branches they replaced, these increases did not offset the overall decline in membership, which was attributed by NTUC spokesmen to a combination of structural change and worker complacency (*Sunday Times*, 31 March 1985). Work force complacency was associated with the tight labor market and the high wage policy, which the National Wages Council had pursued from 1979 to 1983 as part of the government's economic restructuring strategy. Singaporean workers had been publicly upbraided for their tardiness and "job hopping" by both government and NTUC leaders, and it is likely that the NTUC's moral tone did not endear it to the discerning young, whom the NTUC aimed to recruit. Neither did the NTUC's endorsement in 1980 of the National Wages Council's recommended second-tier bonus payment, to be paid by employers to selected "above-average" workers and deducted from the total wage bill. Finally, the ignominious treatment of

Table 8.2. Number of unions, membership by affiliation, and union density in Singapore, 1979–88

Year	Number of unions	Membership	Percentage in NTUC	Density (%)
1979	86	249,710	94.7	24.5
1980	83	243,841	94.9	22.8
1981	86	224,362	95.7	20.2
1982	89	214,337	95.7	18.8
1983	90	205,155	96.4	17.6
1984	86	192,394	96.8	16.4
1985	84	201,133	97.4	17.4
1986	83	200,613	97.0	17.5
1987	83	205,717	97.7	17.2
1988	83	210,918	97.8	17.0

Source: Singapore. Ministry of Labor, various.

Singapore Airlines pilots by the NTUC president after their illegal work to rule in 1980 probably did not improve the NTUC's standing among these employees (Leggett 1984).

Restructuring had some effect on the size distribution of unions, as shown in table 8.3. In 1980, the nine unions with five thousand or more members constituted 70 percent of total membership; by 1989, these unions had increased to eleven, but they had 63 percent of total membership. Most of the newly created unions had fewer than five thousand members, but there was a decline in those with fewer than one thousand. Thus, the new unionism, as intended, was more stream-lined and had a less top-heavy structure and fewer small unions.

In 1989, Singapore's ten largest unions, all NTUC affiliates, listed in table 8.4, organized 124,733 employees, or approximately 60 percent of the country's organized workers, the NTUC as a whole having made up nearly 98 percent of all union membership in 1988 (table 8.2). Reflecting the thrust of the 1979 new economic strategy, the largest union in 1989, the United Workers of Electronics and Electrical Industries, was registered in 1981 as one of the industrywide unions restructured from the omnibus SILO and PIEU. Six of the top ten unions were products of restructuring—either house or industrywide—while the other four were established unions representing the public sector, teachers, manual workers, and bank employees.

Complementing both union and economic restructuring was the Trade

Table 8.3. Union membership in Singapore unions, by size, 1980 and 1989

	1980		1989[a]	
Membership	Percentage of total unions	Percentage of total membership	Percentage of total unions	Percentage of total membership
< 50 members	6.0	0.1	1.4	0.0
50–249	22.9	1.0	12.7	0.7
250–999	39.8	7.0	32.4	6.2
1,000–4,999	20.5	21.6	38.0	29.9
5,000–9,999	4.8	10.1	8.5	21.4
10,000 and more	6.0	60.3	7.0	41.8
Total[b]	100	100	100	100
N	83	243,841	71	206,000

Source: Singapore. Ministry of Labor 1984:84; figures supplied by the NTUC, Singapore.
[a]Percentages are for NTUC affiliates only, as of September 1989. At the end of 1988, there were thirteen non-NTUC unions, which organized 4,695 workers, or 2.2 percent of trade union members (Singapore. Ministry of Labor, various).
[b]Percentages in each column may not add up to exactly 100 because of rounding.

Table 8.4. Ten largest unions in Singapore, by membership, September 1989

Union	Membership
United Workers of Electronics and Electrical Industries	28,693
Amalgamated Union of Public Employees	22,979
Food, Drinks and Allied Workers' Union	12,510
Singapore Mercantile and Manual Workers' Union	11,167
Singapore Teachers' Union	10,770
Union of Telecom Employees of Singapore	9,371
National Transport Workers' Union	8,074
Singapore Airlines-Staff Union	7,840
Metal Industries Workers' Union	6,815
Singapore Bank Employees' Union	6,514
Total	124,733

Source: Figures supplied by the NTUC, Singapore, September 1989.
All ten unions are affiliated with the NTUC and comprise approximately 60 percent of organized workers in Singapore.

Unions (Amendment) Act of 1982, which, as mentioned at the outset of the chapter, fundamentally altered formal union goals. To enforce union compliance with the new legislation, unions were given a grace period of one year to amend their rules and constitutions. The Ministry of Labor's Registrar of Trade Unions was authorized to deregister a trade union if any of its rules were "oppressive or unreasonable," a broad authorization that might have applied in the case of the disciplinary resolution of the United Workers of Petroleum Industry mentioned above, had the union not rescinded it. In the event, only a few non-NTUC employer-dependent organizations were unable to meet the new criteria.

Symbolically, the Trade Unions (Amendment) Act of 1982 amounted to a redefinition of trade unionism. There was little debate over its implications, perhaps reflecting the fact that it simply put into legal form what was already the practice. More overtly contentious was subsequent legislation, which bore more directly on terms and conditions of employment. The Employment (Amendment) Act of 1984, which increased the discretion management could exercise in scheduling work and overtime to the employer's advantage, was contested only by a church group (Church and Society Study Group 1985). Meanwhile, the NTUC had endorsed the rationale that management flexibility led to higher productivity, increased wages, and, consequently, worker identity with the employer, as demonstrated by Japanese companies.[9]

The management of work force compliance in Singapore was not severely tested until 1985. Official statistics (Singapore. Ministry of Trade and Industry, annual) show the new economic strategy continuing the relatively high annual growth in GDP as electronics forged ahead and investment commitments remained high—at S. $1.8 billion in 1984. Productivity growth averaged 4.5 percent between 1980 and 1984, recording 6.7 percent in 1984. Although the tight labor market had elicited complaints from employers in 1980 that workers were job hopping, and this, according to the NTUC's secretary-general (NTUC 1985a:10), helped contribute to the decline in union membership, some flexibility in the labor market was called for to facilitate economic restructuring. Both NTUC and PAP leaders inveighed for a time against job hoppers, and the government legislated in the Employment (Amendment) Act of 1984 a link between holiday entitlements and length of service with a single employer, but the longer-term policy was to move the locus of control away from the government and toward the employers as workers' wages and benefits became more associated with the productivity growth rates of individual companies.

Dependence on foreign workers, despite an intention to phase them out, remained high. In 1984, it was estimated that as much as 12.5 percent of the Singapore work force comprised foreigners on short-term permits, of whom 40 percent, most of them Thai nationals, were employed in the construction industry (*Straits Times,* 9 July 1984). There was no attempt to unionize these workers, and they were largely excluded from the mainstream of Singapore industrial life. The euphemism "guest workers" indicates the intended temporary nature of their sojourn (see Patarapanich, Wilkinson, and Leggett 1987). Their conditions of employment were in any case diluted by the large number of illegal immigrants in their midst.[10] While the Ministry of Labor has attempted to ensure minimum standards for foreign workers and has handled individual and communal grievances, the NTUC has taken little interest in this substantial (the government does not publish detailed figures) proportion of the Singapore work force and it has been left to church groups and the relevant foreign embassies to draw attention to occasional abuses.

The continued dependence on foreign workers did not depress wages for indigenous workers insofar as the National Wages Council's corrective wage policy led to an annually averaged almost 12 percent increase between 1980 and 1984 (Singapore. Ministry of Labor, annual) and the higher employer and employee contributions to the Central Provident Fund served to keep inflation low.[11]

Structurally, between 1980 and 1989, the Singapore work force changed only marginally to reflect the restructuring of the economy, but the industrial distribution of union membership underwent some changes. There was a small increase in the ratio of white-collar to blue-collar workers, mostly due to a more than doubling of the number of workers in the professional, technical, administrative, managerial, and executive category and an increase in the number of service workers, as shown in table 8.5.

Percentage changes in employment by industry are summarized in table 8.6. The employment distribution in 1989 was similar to the distribution in 1980, although in numbers the service industries, especially in the private sector, saw substantial increases. Nevertheless, manufacturing remained the largest employment sector and saw the largest increase in numbers employed. Union membership figures by industry are available only for 1986.

It is clear from table 8.7 that the rate of membership growth in manufacturing and transport was faster than the growth in employment. Membership growth was even more striking in private-sector services, while the losses, which contributed to the overall decline in union membership, occurred in public-sector services. The low unionization rate in the construction industry was due to the exclusion of the large numbers of foreign construction workers living on site.

Although economic restructuring led to some retrenchment, redundant workers were quickly reabsorbed into the work force and a Basic Education for Skills program, organized by the NTUC and the government, was among a number of institutional measures introduced to facilitate the reabsorption. The real test of work force compliance came with the economic recession of 1985, however.

Table 8.5. Percentages of employed persons fifteen years and older in Singapore, by occupation, 1980 and 1989

Occupation	1980	1989	Percentage change (1980–89)
Professional, technical, administrative, managerial, and executive workers	13.7	19.6	69.9
Clerical and related workers	15.6	15.1	15.5
Sales workers	12.3	12.0	16.4
Service workers	10.4	13.3	51.7
Agriculture and animal husbandry workers and fishermen	1.9	0.7	−56.5
Production and related workers, transport equipment operators, and laborers[a]	40.4	35.1	2.9
Workers not classifiable by occupation	5.8	4.1	−14.8
Total[b]	100	100	18.6
N (in 1,000s)	1,077.1	1,277.3	200.2

Source: Singapore. Ministry of Labor, various.
[a]Excludes construction workers living on sites.
[b]May not add up to 100 because of rounding.

Table 8.6. Percentages of employed persons fifteen years and older in
Singapore, by industry, 1980 and 1989

Industry	1980	1989	Percentage change (1979–89)
Manufacturing	30.1	29.0	15.1
Construction[a]	6.7	6.6	16.9
Commerce	21.3	22.8	26.8
Transport, storage, and communications	11.1	9.9	5.3
Finance, insurance, real estate, and business services	7.4	9.2	47.5
Community, social, and personal services	20.8	21.4	21.8
Other[b]	2.5	0.2	−45.5
Total[c]	100	100	18.6
N (in 1,000s)	1,077.1	1,277.3	200.2

Source: Singapore. Ministry of Labor, various.
[a]Excludes construction workers living on sites.
[b]Agriculture and fishing, mining and quarrying, utilities, and activities not adequately defined.
[c]Percentages may not add up to 100 because of rounding.

Trade Unionism in the Recession and Beyond

That the 1985 recession did not lead to a revision of the corporate controls of Singapore's trade unions is evidence of how well-established these controls had become. The NTUC leaders made some token gestures to "grass-roots" representation and, as has been noted, permitted an affiliate to strike, but otherwise the NTUC remained a central institution of the government's development policy. Structurally, decentralization had occurred with the creation of industrywide and house unions, but these had been carefully nurtured by the technocrats in the central body to conform to the government's strategic imperatives (Deyo 1989:140).

One effect of the 1985 recession, measured by a 1.8 percent shrinkage in the economy, was a halt in the post-1979 decline in union membership. By 1984, membership density had fallen to 16.4 percent and membership to less than 200,000. There was not, however, a subsequent significant increase in membership density since the rate of work force expansion exceeded the rate of membership growth (see table 8.2). Trade unionism became more attractive to employees vulnerable to retrenchment in manufacturing because, although the Industrial Relations (Amendment) Act of 1968 prohibits the negotiation of redundancies, it does allow negotiation of retrenchment benefits, and the NTUC encouraged "positive discrimination" in the payment of such benefits in

Table 8.7. Union membership in Singapore, by industry, 1979 and 1986

Industry	1979		1986		Percentage change (1979–86)
	Percentage of total unions	Percentage of total membership	Percentage of total unions	Percentage of total membership	
Manufacturing	18.8	15.0	26.5	25.3	35.8
Construction[a]	2.4	0.6	2.4	0.5	–29.8
Commerce	11.8	6.9	9.6	8.5	0.0
Transport, storage, and communications	20.0	12.8	19.3	22.1	38.5
Finance, insurance, real estate, and business services	5.9	3.2	8.4	10.5	160.8
Community, social, and personal services	34.1	24.5	27.7	21.7	–28.7
Other[b]	7.1	37.0	6.0	11.4	–75.4
Total[c]	100	100	100	100	–19.7
N	85	249,710	83	200,613	–49,097

Source: Singapore. Ministry of Labor, various.
[a]Excludes construction workers living on sites.
[b]Refers to agriculture and fishing, mining and quarrying, utilities, and activities not adequately defined.
[c]Percentages in columns 1 to 4 may not add up to exactly 100 because of rounding.

favor of union members. Whether the NTUC affiliate's strike over victimization by an American-owned company was intended to restore the credibility of unionism in the eyes of workers or to warn employers against exploiting Singapore's temporarily difficult circumstances is difficult to assess. Perhaps it was a bit of both, but it signaled to workers where, for the time being, the protection of their interests lay.

Another measure to restore worker confidence in the NTUC was an attempt to reestablish "grass-roots" representation in the NTUC's central committee and secretariat (*Straits Times,* 30 April 1985). It is unlikely, however, that this attempt was seen as more than a token by the rank and file in that policy was clearly determined by the key PAP cadres in the NTUC.[12]

A more immediate task for the NTUC than assuring its credibility was the maintenance of work force morale while the government dealt with the recession by, among other things, labor cost cutting. Employer monthly contributions to the Central Provident Fund were cut by 15 percentage points (from 25 to 10 percent of wages), and NTUC affiliates were persuaded to forgo the National Wages Council's recommended wage increases for 1985. This action anticipated the beginning of a revision of the wages policy, and in 1986 the National Wages Council began a "wage reform," which has involved relating annual wage increases to the performances of individual companies (Singapore. National Wages Council Secretariat 1986). That the economy was turned around (GDP growth increased from 1.8 percent in 1986 to 11 and 9.2 percent respectively in 1988 and 1989) is testimony to the strength of the institutional controls, including the agency of the NTUC, over labor in Singapore, especially as average earnings since the recession have lagged behind GDP growth and, except for 1988, productivity growth. This is shown in figure 8.1.

The prospects for unionism in Singapore are found in the visions of the city-state's ruling elite in the late 1970s and early 1980s. In his 1981 National Day speech, Prime Minister Lee said: "If you ask me I say I move towards the Japanese. It's a safer method. It binds the link between the worker and the company" (cited in Chua 1982:327).

For the NTUC, this direction is apparent in the establishment of house unions and the linking of pay with productivity at the workplace. Company welfarism and joint consultation (in its various manifestations) have been slow to catch on in Singapore (Wilkinson and Leggett 1985:13), but that was anticipated by the government. As Prime Minister Lee foresaw: "It may take 15 to 20 years to get Singaporeans as productivity conscious as the average Japanese or Korean. A change in outlook cannot be achieved in a productivity month. It is only the beginning" (*Productivity Digest* 1984:35).

In spite of some Japanization, however, Singapore's industrial relations

Figure 8.1. Changes in GDP, productivity, and average monthly
earnings in Singapore, 1980–89

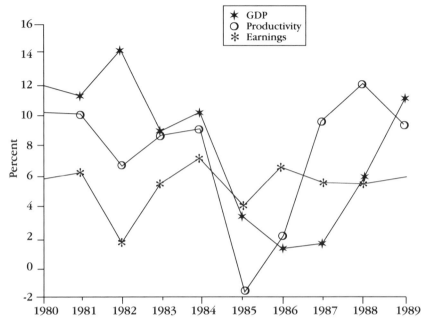

Source: Singapore. Ministry of Trade and Industry, various.
GDP statistics for 1980 to 1987 are at 1968 factor cost and for 1987 to 1989 at 1985
market prices.

still reflect institutional structures inherited from the West. Although the
NTUC's secretary-general regards resorting to conciliation and arbitration as "unhealthy" (NTUC 1984:1), the Ministry of Labor and the
Industrial Arbitration Court remain integral to Singapore's industrial
relations tripartism, as does the National Wages Council. However constrained it is by legislation and exhortations to abandon sectional interest, the collective agreement is central to most union officials' work and
the rank and file hold these officials accountable for its terms and
conditions. Even social welfare is more associated with the NTUC than
with its affiliates, especially since the establishment of the Singapore
Labour Foundation in 1977, to which all NTUC affiliates subscribe and
which provides facilities similar to pre-Perestroika Soviet unions.

Assessing Singapore's Trade Unionism

An evaluation of Singapore's trade unionism, because of its incorporation in government, inevitably involves an assessment of the govern-

ment's performance. The role of unions has been a distinguishing feature of Singapore's economic development (Harris 1987:61) and one that the PAP government has assiduously cultivated. The quality of labor-management relations and worker commitment, in addition to economic development and the standard of living, may be evaluated, as well as the functions and dysfunctions of the self-styled "symbiotic" relationship between the PAP and the NTUC.

Economic Development and the Standard of Living

Leaders of the NTUC constantly argue that the PAP's transformation of Singapore's union movement made possible the relatively high standard of living Singaporeans now enjoy. Addressing NTUC delegates in 1979, Secretary-General Lim Chee Onn echoed C. V. Devan Nair's rhetoric when he affirmed:

> History and current precedents in other countries show us that our success in raising our workers from the quagmire they were in would certainly have not been possible had there not been an enlightened trade union movement which puts the survival of the nation before everything else. . . . This is the fundamental thinking of the NTUC and its affiliates (NTUC 1979:4).

Workers benefited from the government's employment-creation strategy of the 1960s, but it was after 1972, with full employment and the creation of the National Wages Council, that wages began to increase substantially. Between 1972 and 1979, earnings averaged a 9.5 percent increase and between 1979 and 1981 more than 14 percent, but they fell back thereafter, as indicated in figure 8.1.

Employer and employee contributions to the Central Provident Fund were stepped up toward the end of the 1970s and into the 1980s so that in 1985 each was contributing the equivalent of 25 percent of an employee's wages, but in 1985 the employer's contribution was reduced to 10 percent. It has since been increased by a few percentage points, but in 1990, for the first time, the National Wages Council included this "built-in wages" component in its recommendations for overall productivity-related wage increases (*Straits Times Weekly,* overseas edition, 5 May 1990). Partly because of the high employee contributions to the Central Provident Fund, increased wages were not eaten away by inflation in spite of the booming economy after 1978. The consumer price index did record more than 8 percent increases in 1980 and 1981, but it fell to 3.9 percent in 1982 and averaged only 1.5 percent annually between 1982 and 1989 (Singapore. Ministry of Labor, annual). It should be noted that such benefits as publicly provided but privately owned housing, price-regulated public transport, and community-based amenities served to maintain a standard of living and a quality of life in the 1980s in Singapore unequaled in other Asian countries. The NTUC's claim to the credit for these achievements is based on its commitment to the government's interpretation of the national interest. Commitment is exercised through representation on key statutory boards and other public bodies. In addition to representation on the National Wages Council and the National Productivity Board, NTUC officials sit on, among others, the Economic Development, the Housing and Development, the Vocational and Industrial Training, and the Public Utilities boards. Worker participation in policy making by these boards, it has been claimed, contributes significantly to industrial democracy in Singapore (NTUC 1979). Benefits to the community and to union members are also provided by the NTUC's consumer cooperatives, covering transport, retailing, insurance, and dental services. Managed as commercial enterprises, NTUC cooperatives both provide revenue for the trade union movement and check profiteering by private enterprises.

It has not been the practice of the NTUC to address the issue of income inequalities. The emphasis has been on income generation rather than distribution. The single-minded pursuit of economic growth has not, however, widened existing disparities, and Singapore, along with other East Asian NICs, has a relatively equitable income distribution (Deyo 1989:96). It may have been that the centralization of wage control through the National Wages Council made lower-income workers more aware of the disparities. The National Wages Council has linked pay increases to performance, and after 1974 it made concessions to equity by including a flat-rate component in its annual recommendations (Pang 1982:68). These concessions may have lessened the inequalities a little, for production workers' earnings increased by 183 percent between 1972 and 1982 compared with 152 percent for other workers (calculated from Singapore. Department of Statistics 1983:39). Since 1982, the increases for production workers, who were most affected by the 1985 recession, have, on average, been the same as for all workers—about 5 percent per year—thus maintaining the differentials (Singapore. Ministry of Labor, annual).

Labor-Management Relations

On the one hand, the absence of industrial action is one measure of the quality of labor-management relations in Singapore. On the other hand, the extent to which management and labor use the dispute settlement machinery provided by the Ministry of Labor's Labor Relations Division is another, bearing in mind that if voluntary conciliation fails, the minister of labor may call a compulsory conference of the parties. From 1978 to 1988, the Labor Relations Division's annual caseload averaged 380, having declined from 548 in 1979 to 340 in 1988.

Most disputes were settled by the Ministry of Labor and concerned wage increases; a few disputes were over retrenchment benefits and bonus payments. Likewise, the number of cases referred to the Industrial Arbitration Court declined—from 156 in 1979 to 50 in 1988—and most of these cases concerned variations or continuations of awards and therefore did not constitute proper disputes. The seven real disputes referred to the court in 1988 were settled through informal mediation by its registrar. Recognition disputes, still substantial in numbers but declining, were usually resolved by the Ministry of Labor during the 1980s; only two up to 1988 were referred to the Industrial Arbitration Court.[13] By these criteria, it would seem that the NTUC's norm of nonconfrontational labor-management relations with minimum resort to official machinery has been on the whole achieved. The extent to which this achievement can be attributed to the Ministry of Labor's "preventive mediation," whereby specialist labor officers exercise vigilance to head off disputes, rather than to the proselytization of cooperative employment relations, is more difficult to assess.[14]

While the NTUC endorses the Ministry of Labor's policies, its capacity to mobilize the work force for productivity is somewhat constrained by its exclusionary policies toward foreign workers, among others, and the elitism of its cadres. As an instrument of public policy, the NTUC needs both an active and a substantial membership, but the work force's response, in accordance with its immediate economic interests, tends to be calculative, as in the 1985 recession. The leaders of the NTUC have made it clear that they regard Singapore as fortunate to have been spared confrontational trade unionism, especially the stereotypical British version (Nair 1976; Leggett 1984:35). Poland's Solidarity was represented by the NTUC's secretary-general as the product of an overbearing government—in contrast to that of Singapore—rather than as an inspiration to the labor movement (*Straits Times,* 13 Oct. 1980).

Advantages and Disadvantages of Incorporation

The PAP government's rationale for incorporation is "pragmatism." According to Chua Beng Huat (1985:31), the PAP sees economic growth as "the best guarantee of social and political stability [to the extent that] all aspects of social life are to be instrumentally harnessed to this relentless pursuit." Thus, following the suppression of militant unionism in the 1950s and early 1960s, collective bargaining was constrained by legislation, wages were kept in bounds by the National Wages Council in the 1970s, and, in the 1980s, unions were restructured and work force compliance was reoriented by amendments to the Trade Unions Act and the Employment Act. The legitimacy of the government's intervention in the labor movement and of the NTUC in the work force's orientation to work derives from their justification as pragmatic—*Socialism That*

Works (Nair 1976). For Prime Minister Lee, "Political leaders must triumph [over unions], if necessary, by changing the ground rules to thwart the challenge [by unions], using legislative and administrative powers, and, when necessary, backed by the mandate of the electorate" (Wong 1983:266; Chua 1985:32). Illustrative of the NTUC's subordination to the government-set imperatives is the NTUC secretary-general's endorsement of the recommendation by the National Wages Council in 1980 of discriminatory two-tier bonuses. He explained:

> The NTUC and our affiliates accepted this two tier approach to wage increases because we are convinced that it would lead to the creation of a more disciplined, productive and better rewarded workforce. We would have pressed for the usual one tier system. It would have made our task easier. But we chose to support the new approach largely because national interests take precedence in our scheme of things. We have no doubt that this will in the final analysis result in greater good for the workers of Singapore (NTUC 1980).

As it happened, the two-tier system proved unworkable and had to be abandoned after only one year. The NTUC leaders' unequivocal acceptance of it indicated how out of touch they were with the realities of the workplace insofar as their single-minded pursuit of a new ideology of workplace relations prevented a dispassionate evaluation of a proposal presented as consistent with their ideology.

The contradictions between the corporate imposition of policies and strategies in Singapore have been identified by Linda Lim and Eng Fong Pang (1984:30–31), who anticipated that the government would relax some of its policy commitments. As has been noted, the incorporated institutions—the National Wages Council and the NTUC in particular, but also the National Productivity Board and others—were so committed to the directions they had already taken at the onset of economic restructuring that they were unable to make compromises until the severity of the 1985 recession induced an awareness of a need for speedy reform. Such bureaucratic inertia is a weakness of incorporation in that it prevents questioning of policies and directives that might have averted crises. At the same time, it could be argued that the effectiveness of crisis measures, once they were taken, justified authoritarian control.

Based on the PAP's own criterion, that is, its contribution to economic growth, the PAP's incorporation of trade unions through NTUC hegemony has been beneficial, but the effect on the union rank and file has been demoralizing, as manifested in the membership declines following "modernization" in 1969 and restructuring in 1979, and the failure of the NTUC to continue to attract workers to unions as it did following the 1985 recession.[15] With little direction other than the paths of compliance assigned to them by the PAP government, the younger generation of discerning and affluent workers may choose to opt out by privatizing their lives or emigrating. Singapore's concern with attracting immigrants from the culturally Confucianist countries of South Korea, Taiwan, and Hong Kong, who are willing to accept the values of respect for authority and workplace discipline, rather than from the source countries of the current "guest workers" (Thailand, the Philippines, and the Indian subcontinent), with their allegedly weaker work ethic, is partly occasioned by the reluctance of educated Singaporeans to maintain population growth and by the growing number of younger Singaporeans who are seeking more liberal lifestyles overseas. The implication for the NTUC is that it could become moribund unless it is able to make membership in its affiliates more attractive to the younger generation of workers in the new occupations that economic restructuring has created. It seems that the sense of inclusion that the NTUC may have provided to blue-collar workers who joined SILO and PIEU in the 1970s has not been as persuasive in relation to white-collar workers and the house unions of the 1980s.

Conclusion

Applying Deyo's framework for corporatist labor relations as an elite response to the imperatives of dependent development, this chapter has traced how Singapore's PAP government suppressed politicized unions in the early 1960s and established control over labor with its own protégé, the NTUC. Through the PAP-NTUC special "symbiotic" relationship and labor legislation, the PAP government determined not just the regulation of unions but the purpose of trade unionism itself. Thus, the NTUC became a conduit for downward communication from the ruling elite, which set the imperatives for dependent development, to the work force. Until the late 1970s, the mode of this communication was "inculcation," but this changed in the 1980s to persuasive communication, to suit the more sophisticated sensibilities of the better educated work force and to be more consistent with the human relations ideology proselytized at the time throughout Singapore's incorporated institutions. With the goal since 1979 of restructuring the dependent economy to one based on capital-intensive high technology, the PAP government has attempted to shift the locus, if not the source, of work force control away from itself toward management. This has proved difficult because of the heavy reliance on such centralized institutions as the National Wages Council, but the recession of 1985 had the effect of speeding up the process a little, at least with regard to wage reform.

That the PAP government has been able to impose its pattern of labor relations and mold the unions into agencies of public policy may be attributed to a number of political and structural factors. The first such factor is that when it came into office in 1959, the PAP inherited structures from the British administration that it chose to build on rather than abandon. The NTUC was a PAP creation, but it had its progenitors in British attempts to support economistic, apolitical unionism, and although the legislation has been subsequently amended, it has continued to recognize the centrality of freedom of association and collective bargaining. However contrived the NTUC affiliate's strike in 1985, its legitimacy derived both from its legality and the right of workers not to be victimized by employers for engaging in union activities. Paradoxically, this contrasts with the rights of workers in ostensibly pluralistic Hong Kong, where, in the only case ever brought by the Labor Department against an employer for victimization, the court ruled in favor of the employer (*South China Morning Post,* 28 June 1990).

The second factor is that the opposition to the PAP that has emerged since the mid-1960s has not found much support in workers' organizations. It has either been discredited as subversive and its activists detained under the internal security legislation inherited from the British, or made to look absurd in contrast to the polished performances of PAP cadres. By monopolizing and incorporating administrative talent, both the PAP and the NTUC have had little difficulty outwitting dissenters in the political system or in the union movement as, for example, in the case of their opposition to house unionism. In addition, the legitimacy of the PAP's hegemony has been strengthened by electoral mandates, and the authority of NTUC officials by strict observance of constitutional proprieties. The PAP-NTUC elite is intolerant, however, of analyses of industrial relations that do not conform to its official representation,[16] and foreign newspapers and journals that publish critical articles are liable to have their circulation reduced to uneconomic levels. Consequently, employees are not exposed to alternative views that might enable them to make informed judgments of the policy choices their government and officials make on their behalf.

The third factor that has contributed to the elite's control of the union movement is that the PAP government has been unquestionably successful with its economic development policies, so that NTUC leaders have earned credibility by association. Unemployment ceased to become a problem after the mid-1970s, falling as low as 3 percent in 1980, and it increased only temporarily, to more than 6 percent, in 1986 (Singapore. Ministry of Trade and Industry, annual). Favorable employment prospects for male and, increasingly, female workers in the industries the government successfully attracts to Singapore, coupled with the government's housing and welfare provisions, have helped ensure that Singaporean workers do not "rock the boat." Singaporean workers are quite able to see—they are constantly reminded by NTUC leaders if they are not—the link between their attractiveness to foreign investors and the standard of living they enjoy. They are also conscious of the fragility of this small nation the PAP has created since it came to office in 1959 and that its survival and prosperity depend on the quality of its human resources.

The fourth factor that may help explain the acceptance by the work force of government-controlled unionism is the extent of preentry work force socialization. All males are required to complete two and a half years of national service in the armed forces at an age when they are most likely to be developing lifetime attitudes to work. In addition to the defense purpose of this national service, which reinforces sensitivity to national goals, there is a public policy element, in that it prepares the young men for disciplined employment. Similarly, moral education syllabi in schools are intended, among other things, to contribute to the maintenance of a work ethic and an identification of work excellence with the patriotic sentiment of nation building.[17] The Singapore government has a particular problem here because of its dependence on foreign employers. Thus, it continually has to demonstrate to Singaporean employees how working diligently for, say, a Japanese electronics firm is good for Singapore. To an extent, the restructuring of the NTUC unions into industrywide and house unions is intended to deal with this problem of linking company loyalty with national purposes. It is not surprising, therefore, that the NTUC is quick to react to the formation of company-sponsored unions—even in the public sector—but equally quick to praise exemplary labor-management cooperation.

Finally, the occupational structures associated with export-oriented industrialization, particularly the increased employment of young, unskilled females in electronics, may contribute to, if not be evidence of, an indifference to government-controlled unionism. In Singapore, a substantial proportion of the work force is not sensitized to the NTUC's socialization efforts, and this remains a problem for an agency whose main function is to generate qualities in the work force consistent with national economic development imperatives. It is a matter of public policy that Singapore's competitive edge will be maintained not by a docile work force but by a high level of worker commitment to work excellence and productivity, and it is for this reason that the continued dependence on unskilled foreign workers is regarded as a major problem and why it remains the government's intention to phase them out and selectively recruit skilled immigrants.

There is evidence to suggest that employees, while accepting the PAP-NTUC symbiosis and the NTUC's proselytizing role, nevertheless identify with their union as part of their cultural domain. This may be more true for the older unions that have survived the restructuring exercise and that have been able to avoid infiltration by young NTUC technocrats.

Such may have been the case with the Singapore Teachers' Union (STU), which, although it was led by a senior PAP member of Parliament and NTUC deputy secretary-general, in 1981 was threatened in Parliament with deregistration by the first deputy prime minister because it had disagreed with aspects of his policy on education (*Straits Times,* 15 April 1981). The effect of the threat was a doubling of STU membership within a month, suggesting some enthusiasm for "sword-of-justice" unionism among NTUC affiliates. Such overt conflict remains exceptional, however.

The imperatives for unions as Singapore achieved industrialization and envisaged a high-tech future were anticipated by the PAP government in the late 1970s. The 1980s saw the transformation of the union movement to meet those imperatives. It is unlikely that in the next decade trade unionism will experience any further substantial transformation. The NTUC is likely to consolidate its current achievements and remain a vigilant agency for ensuring work force compliance with national economic goals, but remain flexible enough to cope with economic recessions such as the one in 1985. Membership strength will continue to be a problem, although the extension of the NTUC's provision of recreational and cultural facilities to its members may prevent the sort of decline experienced from 1979 to 1985. Structurally, the indications are that the number of house unions will grow slowly and that contribution to membership will depend on their success in obtaining company-specific benefits for employees. The growth of house unions could also mean greater flexibility in collective bargaining but with less resort to official dispute-settlement procedures.

Part III.
Advanced Peripheral Countries

9
Australian Trade Unionism and the New Social Structure of Accumulation

Stephen Frenkel

The Australian union movement is in the early stages of a transformation as significant as that experienced in the first decade of the century. The aim of this chapter is to identify these changes and explain their origin as part of a more general restructuring of institutions in response to a crisis in international economic competitiveness. The effectiveness of the unions' response to this challenge will also be explored.

I shall argue that Australian unionism was institutionalized on the basis of a set of political arrangements that assumed that economic development could best be fostered by a strategy that combined the export of primary commodities with import substitution of manufactured goods. This first social contract explicitly included protection of employees' living standards. Although the dominant economic institutions were reorganized and policies altered to fit new circumstances, especially war and severe depression, the institutional framework for economic development remained essentially intact until the 1970s. It was in this period that the idea of developing a more internationally competitive manufacturing and service sector gained ground. It was only after the long

I would like to thank Andrew Brown and Debbie Carey for their research assistance and Ian and Pat Huntley for making data available. My thanks also to Craig Littler, Paul Marginson, David Peetz, and George Strauss for providing useful comments on a draft of this chapter. Responsibility, however, lies solely with the author.

postwar boom had ended, however, that the impact of international competition on the Australian economy had a marked effect. In response, the 1980s witnessed the emergence of what D. M. Gordon, R. Edwards, and M. Reich (1982:23–24) term a new social structure of accumulation, that is, a changed set of institutions that facilitate capital accumulation. As part of this second social contract, a new form of labor organization, known as strategic unionism, is coming to replace the pragmatic economistic unionism of the past.

The chapter begins with a brief examination of early Australian trade unionism in relation to the first social contract. The second section describes the dissolution of Australia's dominant social arrangements in the 1970s and explores the implications of this change for unions. The third section outlines the main features of the new social structure of accumulation, whereas the fourth section focuses specifically on changes in several key aspects of the union movement. These include union goals and methods, union density, external union structure (relations between unions), and internal union organization. In the concluding section, I assess these various changes in relation to contemporary developments and future challenges.

Before proceeding, three caveats need to be made regarding the methodology and accompanying analysis, which is based on information from union records and interviews with federal secretaries (or their equivalent) of the twenty largest Australian unions, statistical data from official sources, and published studies. First, for technical and political reasons, membership data supplied by unions must be treated cautiously. Where appropriate, alternative sources have been used. Second, because of a lack of information, it has not been possible to analyze developments within smaller unions. The majority of members are concentrated in a few large unions, however. Third, and most important, this chapter attempts to generalize about continuity and change; it is not a substitute for exhaustive analysis of the diverse nature of Australian unionism.

Emergence of Unions and the First Social Contract

From the 1850s, prosperity based on natural resources and immigration enabled craft unions in Australia to grow along lines familiar to the largely British immigrant work force: an occupational rather than industrial basis for union organization, decentralized control, and the use of direct action against intransigent employers. Semiskilled-labor organizations followed the path of their craft union predecessors, growing rapidly between the 1860s and the 1890s, when severe economic recession halted their progress. This growth encouraged employers to adopt an aggressive approach to union demands. The issue of management's right to hire, which contravened the principle that prospective employees had to be union members (the closed shop), precipitated the Great Strikes, involving largely semi- and unskilled workers: seamen, transport workers, and shearers. This was a turning point in the history of Australian labor in that the strikes highlighted union vulnerability in the absence of political influence as strikers clashed unsuccessfully with the forces of law and order.

Following the 1890s strike wave, unions began to pay more attention to ensuring political representation through the labor parties, which were founded in each of the states except Tasmania and Western Australia. A federal labor party was created immediately after the establishment of the Federation of Australia in 1901.

Union defeats in the 1890s encouraged labor leaders more readily to accept the involvement of conciliation and arbitration authorities in settling disputes. Laws regulating industrial tribunals were introduced, facilitating such mechanisms in several states.[1] The most important institutional innovation was in the federal sphere, where an arbitration court took on the responsibility of setting wage rates and resolving industrial disputes. This was part of a wider social contract established to ensure prosperity for employers and employees alike.

The first social contract consisted of three elements: a law designed to limit the hiring of immigrant workers; another to prevent and settle industrial disputes through conciliation and arbitration; and another that was declared constitutionally invalid by the High Court but nevertheless became a political norm that extended tariff protection to manufacturers who could show that they were paying "fair and reasonable" wages (Hagan 1989:22; Dyster and Meredith 1990:64). The theory behind the social contract was that employees' wages would be protected from being undermined by restricting the supply of labor, while employers would not be put out of business by unfair competition simply because they were compelled to pay reasonable wages by a state tribunal.

Since resort to industrial tribunals, and hence union recognition and implementation of legally enforceable awards, depended on registration, there was a strong incentive for unions to develop and seek members. The tribunals defined specific occupational areas of coverage for different unions, in effect often providing them with sole jurisdictional rights. Thus, arbitration legislation induced unions to register. After 1907, however, there was little change in their numbers; indeed, official statistics show that there were 323 unions in that year, the same number as in 1985 (Dufty and Fells 1989:146). By contrast, union density varied markedly. Based on official returns (which probably overstate the extent of membership), union density increased from about 12 percent in 1905 to 58 percent in 1927 and declined in 1934 to 42.6 percent. Thereafter, the average density level fluctuated, but it eventually climbed to more than 50 percent, where it remained until the late 1980s (Connell and Irving 1980:281; Dufty and Fells 1989:149).

Australian unionism differed in important respects from its British counterpart. Industrial tribunals enabled weak unions to consolidate and survive by relying on the tribunals to define membership coverage and determine awards. Union leaders developed advocacy skills and looked to legal training rather than relying mainly on strong workplace organization and bargaining skills. The tribunals encouraged the concentration of union power at state and federal levels rather than at the district or workplace level. Further, the tribunals were legally regulated, so it was important to ensure that the laws (at state and federal levels), and hence the tribunals, were not turned against workers. Political activity was therefore an important source of influence. Trades and labor councils—which were associations of unions subsequently organized on a regional basis as state branches of the peak council, the Australian Council of Trade Unions (ACTU)—began to play significant roles in influencing state governments. With the establishment of the ACTU in 1927, the unions had an institutional mechanism for influencing the federal industrial tribunal and successive federal governments.[2]

Except during the 1930s depression, immediately after World War II, and during periodic minor recessions, the Australian economy grew strongly up to the 1970s (Connell and Irving 1980, chap. 5). Full employment and high wages came to be accepted as natural. Unions for the most part focused on a narrow range of issues—chiefly wages and conditions of employment. Significant gains were made: between 1939 and 1974, real wages increased on average by more than 2 percent per year (Gruen 1985:4), while unemployment rates averaged less than 2 percent. The forty-hour workweek was attained in some industries as early as 1921, although it did not become common until the late 1930s. In short, Australia was something of a "workers' paradise," although the country's relative international position vis-à-vis real GDP per capita was slipping by the 1960s (Gruen 1985:8).

Strong unions achieved better pay and conditions by plant bargaining backed by industrial action (as in the metal industry) or, as in construction, by using their bargaining strength at larger work sites to gain arbitration awards for building tradesmen more generally. The majority of weaker unions relied on the tribunals to maintain relative gains and to ensure that wages and employment conditions were increased regularly.

Over time, the federal arbitration tribunal, supported by federal governments, assumed a more dominant role in wage setting than its state counterparts. In some periods, however, its authority was undermined by militant unions that disregarded the tribunal's decisions. This was especially true of the left-wing unions, for example, the Miners and the

Engineers, which had always regarded arbitration as an artifact of the capitalist system. Governments countered by invoking harsh laws that empowered the tribunals to fine and deregister unions. This did nothing, however, to reduce the incidence of industrial disputes.

In short, during the boom that stretched from 1949 to the mid-1970s, Australian unions became accustomed to adversarial industrial relations based on *pragmatic economism*. As we shall see, this reflected the ideological dominance of laborism combined with the combative spirit of radicalism. Various methods were used—bargaining, industrial action, conciliation and arbitration, and political influence (especially in the public sector)—aimed at winning short-term improvements in wages and conditions. Left-wing unions often articulated a more radical agenda, but this was often compromised by their having to work with laborist and sometimes hostile anti-Communist union leaders in a legal context, which, for the most part, protected managerial prerogative. The election of conservative federal governments between 1949 and 1972 also contributed to the development of a reactive, aggressive style of unionism.

Dissolution of the First Social Contract

The unraveling of the main strands of the first social contract were particularly noticeable in the 1970s. Building on earlier changes, a non–racially discriminatory immigration policy was adopted in 1973. The proportion of immigrants arriving from Asia compared with Europe increased substantially. Moreover, from the mid-1980s, immigrants accounted for almost half the annual increase in the national population (Dyster and Meredith 1990:299–306). Immigration policy had become a matter of augmenting the country's resources and demonstrating Australia's commitment to the Asia-Pacific region, rather than protecting workers of Anglo-Celtic heritage from low-paying southern European and Asian labor.

The early 1970s boom, characterized by low unemployment and strong union demands, pushed Australia to near the top of the OECD league in the number of industrial stoppages and the rate of inflation (OECD 1989a:176; Bamber and Lansbury 1987:261). This ranking called into question the appropriateness of existing industrial relations institutions, particularly centralized wage determination by a relatively autonomous arbitration tribunal. The Gough Whitlam Labor government held a referendum in an attempt to gain constitutional power to control prices and incomes, but this failed.

Detailed economic inquiries (Jackson 1975; Crawford 1979) highlighted inefficiencies in the manufacturing and service sectors and argued that these sectors should be opened up to international competition by reducing protection. Such a move, proponents argued, would encourage greater import substitution and the export of secondary goods, a strategy advocated in response to protectionist threats by other industrialized countries and in accordance with changes in world trading arrangements.

In 1973, the government reduced tariffs on manufactured goods by 25 percent, the largest reduction ever in Australian trade protection. This strained relations with the unions, which complained about not being consulted about the decision. Nevertheless, the reduction demonstrated that the government was serious about implementing a new strategy for future development. It did nothing, however, to alter the pragmatic economistic nature of Australian unionism.

In 1975, a conservative administration replaced Labor. This, together with the onset of a deep recession that increased unemployment and reduced inflation and the incidence of strikes, effectively stalled the process of institutional change.

Malcolm Fraser's government had neither the inclination nor any incentive to involve unions in economic decision making. Reliance was placed on the recession and conventional deflationary macroeconomic measures to reduce inflation. In the late 1970s, further reduction of union power was attempted by legislation discouraging the use of industrial action, preventing union amalgamations, and altering the procedures of the federal tribunal. The government also reduced employee and union rights in the federal public sector, sparking retaliatory action by some public-sector unions (Frenkel and Coolican 1984:21–28). At the same time, employers resorted to traditional cost-cutting methods, including redundancies, to improve profits.

This return to confrontation by the government fostered aggressive resistance and inflationary wage demands by stronger unions. A temporary boom in the minerals sector in 1980 and 1981 encouraged unions to seek wage increases and reduced working hours, which effectively undermined the federal tribunal's guidelines. Anticipating a recession, union leaders for the first time pledged not to seek further wage demands for a fixed term. There was also some experimentation with productivity bargaining over reduced hours (Kyloh 1989). Nevertheless, the cost to industry of this return to confrontation at a time of slow economic growth was enormous. Unemployment and company failures began to rise steeply, so that the former reached an annual average postwar record of nearly 10 percent in 1983–84 (Kearney 1989). Governments, employers, and unions were sharply reminded of the need for new economic strategies and a more effective industrial relations system. A nine-month halt to wage increases during 1982 and 1983 permitted strategies to be developed and negotiations to proceed. To understand the subsequent emergence of the joint union-government approach to economic policy, it is necessary first to understand something about the changes in union leaders' thinking as a result of their experiences in the 1970s, and to summarize briefly the state of union organization as unions confronted the challenge of a new social structure of accumulation.

Responding to the Cessation of the Long Boom: Unions in the Late 1970s

When the economy went into recession in 1975, union leaders reacted as if it were a temporary phenomenon requiring caution in the use of industrial action and patience until the economy improved. Accordingly, when economic activity rose temporarily in 1980–81, strikes increased, leading to the breakdown of the wages system noted above. The massive reduction in manufacturing employment, with little prospect of future improvement, prompted a search for a new strategy, especially by leaders of the large left-wing Metalworkers' Union, whose members were most adversely affected by the downturn. The idea of a social contract involving a trade-off between wage restraint and government support for industry regeneration and a progressive social welfare policy was widely canvassed and favored by leaders of the Metalworkers, ACTU leaders, and senior members of the parliamentary Labor Party.

With regard to union organization, union density had held up well. In 1982, union density was estimated at 49 percent, compared with 51 percent in 1976 (Australian Bureau of Statistics, catalogue no. 6325.0). The most notable changes related to the longer-term growth of the tertiary sector, which increased as a proportion of total employment from 64 percent in 1966 to 76 percent ten years later (Gittins 1988:34). White-collar unionism grew very rapidly in this period, particularly under the federal Labor government, which boosted public-sector employment and established the public sector generally as a pacesetter for improved wages and conditions. Consequently, between 1969 and 1976, the number of white-collar unionists grew at an annual average rate of nearly 9 percent, which increased the proportion of white-collar union members to total members from 29.6 percent to 38.3 percent over the same period. This burst of union growth was halted by the decline in job growth in the latter part of the 1970s. Other factors that contributed to the decline included the withdrawal of union dues check-off facilities by the subsequent conservative federal government and some employers (notably in banking) and changes in the law in the state of Queensland prohibiting the closed shop. Thus, by 1981, union density among white-collar workers was only marginally, if at all, higher (39.5 percent) than in 1976 (Crean and Rimmer 1990:9).

White-collar unions had been affiliating with the ACTU in increasing numbers, a process that began to taper off in the mid-1980s.[3] This process involved mergers at the peak council level, which were in part a response to the formation in 1977 of a unified employers' body—the

Confederation of Australian Industry—and to problems negotiating with the conservative government, the ACTU's growing influence over wage policy under centralized wage indexation, and a commitment to the idea of a single peak council by key union leaders (Crean and Rimmer 1990:25). In 1979, the Australian Council of Salaried and Professional Associations decided to disband, and most of its 37 former affiliates and 350,000 members joined the ACTU, which at the time had 140 affiliates comprising 2 million members. Two years later, the Council of Australian Government Employee Organizations, with some 26 affiliates and a membership of about 226,000, merged with the ACTU. These and other changes in the distribution of the unionized work force resulted in an enlarged ACTU Executive (the key decision-making body between biennial congresses) from eighteen members in 1979 to thirty-one in 1985 and additional elected officers. These changes were mainly at the expense of the state-based trades and labor councils (Dufty and Fells 1989:163).

Between 1972 and 1983, there were only three amalgamations of federal unions. In addition to there being little incentive to merge, member commitment to existing structures and problems of job transfer and status maintenance for union leaders inhibited union mergers. Legislation making it virtually impossible for mergers to occur was also a factor.[4] Relations between left- and right-wing unions continued to improve, partly because of the disunity of forces on the extreme left beginning in the 1960s (Martin 1980:17–19) and the growing marginalization of the extreme right. Full-time union officials also acknowledged that working together was necessary to try to resolve common problems, particularly rising unemployment and hostile conservative governments at both state and federal levels.

Toward a Second Social Contract: Labor, the Accords, and Industry Restructuring

Before the election of the federal Labor government under Bob Hawke in early 1983, ACTU and Labor Party officials devised a policy that later came to be known as the main or first Accord. This document, which provided the basis for subsequent variants, reflected a strategy developed by the radically inclined Metalworkers' Union. It was predicated on close, ongoing consultation between the ACTU and the future Labor government and contained several elements that went beyond industrial relations (Frenkel 1988:167–68). Its main aim was to reduce unemployment substantially, but in a way that ensured sustained economic growth through industrial restructuring and an equitable sharing of the adjustment burden. The Accord formed the basis of a return to a centralized wage system in 1983.

On the one hand, the government acknowledged that the economy was overly dependent on export income generated by primary commodities whose prices fluctuated in accordance with changes in international markets. On the other hand, imports were concentrated in the growing, elaborately transformed manufactured goods category. Industry restructuring, particularly in the diverse, protected, and internationally uncompetitive manufacturing sector, was to be accomplished following the stabilization of inflation, job creation, and an improvement in economic growth. In the meantime, the government deregulated the finance industry to increase the supply of investment funds at competitive rates. Foreign banks established offices in Australia, while local banks broadened their services. With increased demand for loans to underpin corporate asset accumulation, an easing of controls over the money supply, and banks eager to increase their market share, the amount of credit increased significantly in the early 1980s. This fostered a large number of corporate takeovers and encouraged short-term portfolio and loan investments, especially by foreigners, rather than longer-term investment in new technology and skill formation (see Dyster and Meredith 1990:280). This key feature of the emerging social structure of accumulation did not last beyond 1989, however, since many firms found it difficult to repay their debts as interest rates climbed to new heights.

With unions cooperating closely with the government, compared with the 1970s, there were fewer working days lost per employee because of industrial disputes (Australian Bureau of Statistics, catalogue no. 6322.0). External trading conditions deteriorated in the early 1980s, however, as Australia's terms of trade declined by 5 percent between 1979–80 and 1984–85. The difference between the inflation rate in Australia and the OECD average was increasing: from less than 1 percent in 1984 to nearly 5 percent in 1985 (OECD 1988:28). Further, overseas corporate borrowing increased substantially following the deregulation of the financial system. This helped to pay for the increasing current account deficit, which reached its peak of more than 6 percent of GDP in 1985–86 and which resulted in a rapidly expanding net foreign debt—from 6.1 percent of GDP in 1980–81 to 31.4 percent in 1985–86 (Australian Bureau of Statistics, catalogue no. 5306.0:6). Lack of international competitiveness dented financial dealers' confidence in the exchange rate, which reduced the demand for Australian dollars. Consequently, in terms of its trade-weighted value, the currency devalued by 40 percent between 1981–82 and 1986–87 (Frenkel 1990).

These critical underlying processes encouraged the development of new institutional relationships. These came to be based on extensive consultation between major industrial interest groups aimed at creating a low-inflation, high-employment economy largely free from protection.

Internationally competitive enterprises characterized by high productivity growth were to be developed in labor markets that enhanced functional flexibility and skill formation.

Several important institutional changes were implemented in the latter part of the 1980s to facilitate this new social contract. These can be grouped under three headings: attempts to improve competitiveness through economic adjustment measures; reforms of industrial relations institutions; and changes in wage-determination principles.

Since 1985, the government has increased its commitment to various measures designed to restructure Australian industry. The effort to reduce manufacturing industry protection is one element that union leaders recognize as necessary but are unwilling to support without adequate adjustment protection. Progress has been slow. In 1981–82, the average effective rate of protection was 21 percent; by 1988–89, it was estimated to be 17 percent (Australia. Industries Assistance Commission 1987, 1989), and there was a government commitment to bring down the protection levels for most protected industries to 10 or 15 percent (depending on the industry) by 1992 (Australia. Industries Assistance Commission 1989:102).

Sectoral plans have also played a role in the restructuring process. These have been introduced selectively—in motor vehicles, heavy engineering, steel, clothes and textiles, and the coal industry—where financial assistance has been provided in exchange for commitments by employers and unions to implement agreed-upon technical and organizational changes aimed at boosting productivity and promoting labor mobility.

The government has also introduced a range of other measures to improve industrial competitiveness. These include tax concessions for research and development, advisory services in marketing and manufacturing, the encouragement of technology transfer, a program to improve the supply of venture capital to entrepreneurs, the fostering of controversial changes in coastal shipping and related services, and the redefinition of government enterprises, giving management more autonomy to pursue commercial objectives (Australia. Economic Planning Advisory Council 1988).

New initiatives have been implemented to reduce unemployment, especially among young people, by increasing the training for occupations in chronic short supply, and to facilitate worker mobility (Australia. Economic Planning Advisory Council 1988:91–92). Active labor market programs, including the development of industry-based skill centers that deliver competency-oriented rather than time-based vocational training, have been established. A training levy on employers was introduced to increase private employers' commitment to training, which in the past was lower than in many other OECD countries (Australian Science and

Technology Council 1987:6; *Australian Financial Review* 1990:1–2). The secondary and tertiary education sectors are also in the process of implementing changes, which are more fundamental than at any time during the postwar period (Australia. Economic Planning Advisory Council 1986:20, 25–26).[5]

With regard to industrial relations reform, the federal tribunal moved to limit managerial prerogative in the 1980s. This was highlighted in 1984, when it began to require employers to notify unions and employees of impending major organizational and technical changes. Provision was also made for redundancy payments (Australian Conciliation and Arbitration Commission 1984). New health and safety laws in several states also prescribed that joint committees examine and resolve work environment problems, while the effect of anti-discrimination laws proscribed certain managerially legitimated practices such as subtle forms of sexual harassment and the last-in, first-off rule when reducing the size of the work force (Dufty and Fells 1989:268–72). A less conservative High Court (which by the mid-1980s included several labor government appointments) made decisions widening the range of issues subject to joint regulation and hence resolution by the federal tribunal. The latter's jurisdiction was extended to include unions previously prevented from applying for federal awards on the grounds they did not cover members of a conventional industry (e.g., teaching and nursing). More generally, the government publicized its support for union-based employee participation (Australia. Department of Employment and Industrial Relations 1986), which prompted an agreement by the ACTU, the Confederation of Australian Industry (CAI), and the Business Council of Australia (BCA) on eliminating restrictive work and management practices (see Australia. National Labour Consultative Council 1988:28–30) and subsequently fostering union-based employee participation over a wider range of issues (CAI/ACTU 1988).

The most significant change occurred in 1988 following an extensive report of a committee of inquiry (Hancock Committee of Review 1985) on reforming industrial relations. In line with the committee's recommendations, which rejected any fundamental shift toward collective bargaining,[6] the Industrial Relations Act of 1988 aimed to simplify, rationalize, standardize, and in some cases establish new procedures for preventing and settling industrial disputes. The major changes introduced were an extension of the federal tribunal's jurisdiction, including giving it the power to resolve union demarcation problems,[7] and a requirement that it take into account the principles of recent anti-discrimination legislation; that explicit cognizance be taken of the interests of the parties and the wider community in the tribunal's deliberations; provision for dual appointments to federal and state tribunals; greater emphasis on grievance procedures and compliance; less onerous provisions for union amalgamation, and the discouragement of small unions.[8]

With regard to wage determination, the government and the unions viewed wage growth as one among several elements of economic policy; others included taxation, social welfare spending, and industry policy. Extensive information on various aspects of the economy were made available through newly established tripartite forums, notably the Economic Planning Advisory Council. Most of the major initiatives in wage policy in the 1980s were made by the ACTU in close consultation with the Labor government. Five Accords, negotiated over the 1983–89 period, were endorsed in large measure by the federal tribunal and hence became law. Employer groups remained disunited and were reluctant to endorse successive wage policies formally (Frenkel 1988). Since 1987, however, the trend toward centrally guided decentralized bargaining, summarized below, has received the qualified support of all the major industrial interest groups. This policy was broadly consistent with the policy advocated by the BCA. Indeed, by the end of the decade, the BCA had established itself as the main vehicle for research and the dissemination of ideas concerning a new form of "employee relations" based on decentralized single-union bargaining (BCA 1989).

It was the dramatic deterioration of the country's current account deficit in the mid-1980s that forced the government and the unions away from centralized wage determination based mainly on rises in the cost of living and national productivity growth. Instead, they were attracted to a system of industry- and workplace-level negotiation based on workplace productivity improvements and skill enhancement, supported by government policies on education and training, labor flexibility, and employee participation (Morris 1989). Arguably, the 1988 and 1989 decisions by the federal tribunal to introduce the structural efficiency principle offer the most far-reaching opportunities in this century for Australian unions and management to recast workplace relations (see Hawke 1988:15). New wage relativities have been established whereby low-paid workers will be protected by enforcement of the centralized guidelines developed by the tribunal.

Most of these changes are consistent with a key strategy document developed by the ACTU and government officials appropriately entitled *Australia Reconstructed* (ACTU/Trade Development Council 1987). This report analyzed the institutional and normative bases of the superior economic performance recorded by several European countries (especially Sweden and West Germany) and drew implications for Australian policy making. Its main message was that industrial restructuring must be embraced as the only panacea for ensuring that there is a growing supply of jobs at satisfactory levels of wages and conditions and that interrelated changes in macroeconomic and micro-level institutions and policies need to be introduced to improve Australia's long-term growth rate. The report also identified the necessary changes required of the union movement if it is to play a key, constructive role in economic and social development. It is to this set of ideas that I now turn.

Reconstructing Australian Unionism: From Pragmatic Economism to Strategic Unionism

In broad terms, two competing ideologies have informed the long-term goals of most Australian union leaders. Laborism, the dominant perspective, sees strong unions and Labor governments as the main means of ameliorating the problems and inequalities generated by economic change (Frenkel and Coolican 1984:1–3; Hagan 1989:22). Labor in government (establishing a favorable social and political framework) and the unions in industry (pressing workers' claims for improved wages and conditions)—each operating in its respective spheres—came to be regarded as the best system of workers' representation under capitalism. The implication for unions was that labor organizations should confine their attention to (fairly narrowly defined) industrial issues and use noncoercive tactics where possible. That unions were structured on occupational lines was seen as natural given Australia's craft union heritage and the institutionalization of the occupational principle of organization as sanctioned by the arbitration tribunals.

By contrast, the adherents of radicalism see capitalism as fundamentally inegalitarian, as requiring transformation based on collective or state property. According to this view, the Labor Party cannot radically reshape society; this can occur only through a revolution involving unity in action by the working class. Although unions must fight for improved wages and conditions, their role is wider: to assist in transforming society by engaging in extra-parliamentary campaigns and organizing more effectively to win power from the ruling class. This view implies that unions must pursue wide objectives, including overtly political issues, through industrial action, which is seen as a symbol of working-class potency. Unions are expected to organize so as to assist in facilitating working-class unity and encourage rank-and-file organization. This position has led to radical union leaders supporting industry rather than occupational unionism and favoring union structures that promote shop steward activity.

Historically, these ideologies were manifested in interunion competition and intraunion factionalism, most clearly visible in the cold war years of the late 1940s and 1950s (Gollan 1975). Thereafter, however, union leaders for the most part cooperated successfully in the pursuit of improved wages and conditions using a variety of methods, including defiance of the law, mainly by left-wing unions (Frenkel and Coolican 1984). I have referred to this style as pragmatic economism.

By the late 1970s, union leaders recognized the need for a new approach to prevent wage increases from exacerbating inflation and thereby inviting deflationary government measures that would reduce employment and leave unions with few gains and less strength. Meanwhile, neo-Stalinism in the Soviet Union and Eastern Europe, together with the failure of Yugoslavia and Maoist China as alternative forms of socialism, discredited the radical ideal. There was an ideological vacuum that came to be filled by the more realistic concept of advanced social democracy epitomized by Sweden, where the union movement played a significant strategic role.

Thus, by the 1980s, both laborist and radical union leaders in Australia were especially receptive to a program of constructive change. In contrast to the anti-union free-market ideology gaining ground among employers and conservative politicians (Plowman 1986), union leaders agreed that significant economic and social progress could best be effected through the aegis of a strong union movement whose strategy and structure were appropriate to the challenges of late-twentieth-century capitalism. The concept of strategic unionism represented a compromise between the laborist tradition of economistic defensive unionism and the radical tradition based on proactive strategies for transforming capitalist social relations. Strategic unionism centered on altering capitalism over an extended period through the participation of a united labor movement in a social democratic political system.

Strategic unionism comprised five main characteristics: first, the proactive pursuit of a broad range of issues, with special emphasis on securing full employment; second, a commitment to income generation in addition to the traditional union concern for income distribution; third, articulation of centrally coordinated long-term goals and integrated strategies at macro and micro levels; fourth, tripartism as the major means of realizing union objectives; and fifth, and finally, the reform of union structure, including extensive informed rank-and-file participation as a crucial precondition for a vibrant union movement (ACTU/Trade Development Council 1987:169).

The need for organizational change was made clear by the union movement's overwhelming endorsement of a document entitled *Future Strategies for the Trade Union Movement* presented at the 1987 ACTU Congress and discussed further at the 1989 Congress (Davis 1988, 1990). Union leaders agreed to implement effective recruiting campaigns, improve communications with their members, broaden their range of services, and, most important, pursue amalgamations and rationalization of union membership (according to agreed-upon principles) to reduce the approximately 350 unions to about 20 mainly industry-based, general organizations. There was now growing concern about the future of Australian unionism (Berry and Kitchener 1989). Lamenting the recent steep decline in union density, the ACTU president told delegates to the 1989 Congress that unions had failed to attract workers in the areas of strongest job growth, that insufficient progress had been made in rationalizing union structures and servicing a more heterogeneous membership, and that self-regulation of interunion conflicts had been less than effective (Crean 1989:14).

Thus, despite barriers to change, by the end of the 1980s, strategic unionism was beginning to emerge. Indeed, some significant developments had already occurred during the previous decade. These are noted below by reference to the main dimensions of union organization: trends in union goals and methods, union density, external union structure, and internal union organization.

Union Goals and Methods

The Accords referred to above imply an extensive range of macro-level goals for most unions in Australia. Support for a wider agenda is also evident in ACTU campaigns for a national health service, superannuation, improvements in health and safety legislation, maternity and adoption leave, and equal pay for women, and against uranium mining and privatization. This activity has necessitated some ceding of negotiating power to ACTU officials and members of key ACTU committees. Changes in wage-determination principles, however, have encouraged consultation between union officials at various organizational levels over changes in awards, while at the micro level improvements in pay have been linked to changes in job design, work organization, skill formation, career development, and productivity growth. Indeed, interviews with leading union officials indicate that the expansion of negotiations to a wider and often unfamiliar range of issues (e.g., superannuation, multi-skilling, vocational training, and career paths) has put pressure on unions to improve their relations with members through new organizational structures and strategies. For example:

> Decisions and problem solving now have to be done at the source. One of the things we are looking at is ways and means of having part-time members become involved in the decision-making process (Secretary, Bank Employees' Union).

> With all the change going on we are trying to consult more with the members via delegate (i.e., steward) meetings across industries and factory by factory. We're also making a bigger effort to keep our full-time officers informed about national issues (Secretary, Miscellaneous Workers' Union).

> Award restructuring is very complex and difficult to communicate with the membership. . . . The whole process is putting a strain on

the branches who have to explain the agreements. . . . This experience has led us to consider ways in which we can bring the membership more closely into the decision-making process (Secretary, Postal and Telecommunications Workers' Union).

With the emphasis on skill formation, we're looking for a direct role for ourselves in the process as there is likely to be privatization of occupational training. We're—jointly with employers—looking at the development of skill centers (Secretary, Electrical Trades Union).

Despite the increase in negotiation, industrial action has declined; indeed, econometric evidence indicates that the Accords reduced the level of industrial conflict significantly (Chapman and Gruen 1990). The period 1983–89 contrasts with the years 1979–82, when conservative government policy reinforced the traditional pattern of employer reluctance to bargain before arbitration, and unions responded by engaging in limited industrial action to encourage a quick settlement either by negotiation, conciliation, or arbitration (Frenkel and Coolican 1984). Employees with little strategic power relied on the tribunals to obtain changes in awards so as to bring wages up to acceptable standards. Figure 9.1 highlights the contrast between the earlier and later periods.

Two caveats need to be made regarding the dramatic decline in days lost because of industrial stoppages since 1983. The first is that there has been a tendency for workers to substitute more covert forms of indus-

Figure 9.1. Working days "lost" per thousand employees in Australia because of industrial disputes, 1979–90

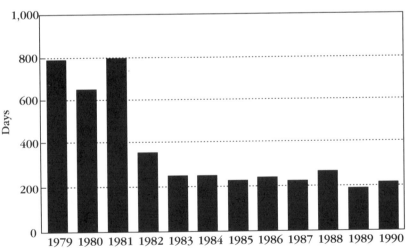

Sources: ABS catalogue no. 6322.0, various; catalogue no. 6321.0, 1990.

trial action for strikes. Thus, between 1977 and 1982, the average annual number of work bans recorded by official sources was 299, compared with more than 455 for the 1983–88 period (Australia. Department of Industrial Relations 1989). Further, Australia experienced a protracted strike by its domestic airline pilots, whose demands went far beyond national wage guidelines and were therefore opposed by virtually all other unions (Davis 1990:106–7). With government support, the union was defeated for the first time. '

Union Density

According to a regular official employee survey that has been conducted since 1976, union density was 51 percent in that year, declined to 49 percent in 1982 and 46 percent in 1986, and fell to a low of 42 percent in 1990 (see table 9.3). This accelerating downward trend reflects structural changes in the economy and a lower propensity by workers to join unions. With regard to the former, there has been a relative expansion in (not mutually exclusive) areas characterized by lower union density: white-collar employment, services, the private sector, and non–full-time employment (Berry and Kitchener 1989; Crean and Rimmer 1990:8–17; Frenkel 1990). D. Peetz (1990) estimates that about half the decline in union density in the 1980s resulted from these changes and that the remainder can be explained by other factors affecting the propensity of employees to join or stay in unions. This is suggested by table 9.1, which contains information showing that union density has been declining in various employment categories (sector, industry, and work status).

Table 9.1 also indicates that density has fallen within demographic categories (birthplace and gender). When sector and broad occupational categories are controlled for, available data show proportionately more unionized men than women.[9] Although a gender effect on union density may be controversial, other work force characteristics may be important, particularly socialization within the family and political attitudes (Deery and De Cieri 1991). This raises the question of whether unions have been sufficiently creative in responding to the changing composition and expectations of the Australian work force. Indeed, as J. Kelly (1990) has argued in relation to the decline in British union density, unions themselves must share some of the responsibility for their lack of attractiveness. This is suggested in Australia by the interunion differences in recruitment policies and the effectiveness of policy implementation. Examples of relatively successful unions include the Building Workers, Miscellaneous Workers, and the Shop, Distributive and Allied Employees' Association (SDA). Although the major sectors in which these unions operate are difficult to organize, each union, using different strategies, has succeeded in maintaining a positive growth rate (see table 9.3), in

Table 9.1. Union density (in percent) in Australia, by selected
characteristics, 1976–90

Characteristics	November 1976	March/May 1982	August 1986	August 1990
Sector				
Public	n.a.	73	71	67
Private[a]	n.a.	39	34	31
Industry				
Agriculture, etc.	20	20	15	13
Mining	63	64	72	63
Manufacturing	57	54	51	46
Electricity, etc.	83	78	82	79
Construction	57	50	48	45
Wholesale and retail trade	27	28	25	23
Transport and storage	73	72	67	58
Communication	88	85	80	76
Finance, property, and services	42	42	34	29
Public administration and defense	72	63	60	60
Community services	56	54	52	49
Recreation and other services	41	36	29	25
Work status				
Permanent	n.a.	n.a.	51	46
Casual	n.a.	n.a.	21	19
Birthplace				
Australia	50	48	45	40
Outside Australia	54	55	48	43
Gender				
Male	56	53	50	45
Female	43	43	39	35
Total	51	49	46	41
No. of union members (in 1,000s)	2,512.7	2,567.6	2,593.9	6,565.6

Source: Australian Bureau of Statistics, catalogue no. 6325.0, various years.
[a]Includes some persons for whom sector could not be determined. Figures rounded to
nearest percent.
n.a. = not applicable.

contrast to counterpart organizations operating in comparable industries.[10]

Other factors explaining the decline in union density are the trend
toward smaller establishments; unfavorable state legislation, especially in
Queensland[11]; changes in management strategies toward nonunion forms

of employment relations; an increase in the volume of industry and workplace concession bargaining in the context of a limited decline in real wages; and, more tentatively, the lagged effect of less favorable employee attitudes toward unions (Peetz 1990).

Changes in Membership Composition

In addition to a decline in union density, the composition of union membership has changed significantly over the past decade, especially among ACTU union affiliates. This is shown in table 9.2. Whereas white-collar workers comprised slightly more than a third (36.5 percent) of all affiliated union members in 1979, by 1989 they constituted close to half (46.3 percent). This change mainly reflects the changing composition of the unionized work force, but it especially reflects the growing affiliation of white-collar unions with the ACTU. Data on membership trends in the twenty largest unions, summarized in table 9.3, provide a similar picture.

Of the five largest unions in 1989, three were nonmanual organizations, and in terms of growth rates, the white-collar/service workers' unions tended to outpace their blue-collar counterparts. The data include membership growth arising from union mergers, of which the most noteworthy boosted the numbers mainly in such blue-collar unions as the Federated Miscellaneous Workers' Union and the National Union of Workers. The Building Workers' Industrial Union absorbed some twenty-three thousand members of the renegade Builders' Labourers Union, which was deregistered in 1986. Table 9.3 is also interesting for the light it sheds on political trends. In 1979, the right-wing tendency would have been clearly dominant; ten years later, however, the balance in the union movement was more or less even.[12]

Table 9.2. Composition of union membership in Australia, 1979–89

	1979	1981	1983	1985	1987	1989
Blue collar as percentage of total	63.4	59.9	56.9	54.6	53.6	53.4
White collar as percentage of total	36.5	39.9	42.9	45.1	47.8	46.3
Number of union members (in 1,000s)	2,281.2	2,283.4	2,444.3	2,624.3	2,719.3	2,743.4

Source: ACTU executive reports, various.
Figures include junior members. Totals do not add up to 100 because a very small proportion of union members belong to unions that cannot be classified as either blue- or white-collar organizations, for example, the Unemployed Workers' Union. The data exclude unions not affiliated with the ACTU. By 1989, these were almost all white-collar organizations accounting for less than 10 percent of total union membership.

*Table 9.3. Membership trends in the twenty largest Australian unions,
1979–89*[a]

Union	Political inclination	Membership (1989)	Average annual membership growth (%)
Shop, Distributive and Allied Employees' Association	right	200,787	3.8
Australian Teachers' Union	left	173,108	3.8
Amalgamated Metal Workers' Union	left	168,455	0.6
State Public Services Federation (state)	left	146,032	0.2[b]
Federated Miscellaneous Workers' Union	left	126,101	5.7
Australian Workers' Union	right	117,536	0
Federated Liquor and Allied Industries Employees' Union	right	111,240	3.5
Transport Workers' Union	right	98,710	5.0
National Union of Storeworkers, Packers, Rubber and Allied Workers	right	87,150	4.1
Federated Clerks' Union	split	84,126	3.6
Australian Public Sector and Broadcasting Union (federal)	left	78,537	5.9
Electrical Trades Union	right	74,934	3.3
Australian Bank Employees' Union	left	73,671	0.8
Building Workers' Industrial Union	left	71,100	7.3
Federated Ironworkers' Association	right	57,619	−2.0
Federated Municipal and Shire Council Employees' Union	right	57,300	1.4
Printing and Kindred Industries Union	left	49,747	0.1
Australian Postal and Telecommunications Workers' Union	right	48,704	0.5
Australian Nursing Federation	left	42,280	1.3
Hospital Employees' Federation	left	39,958	3.3

Source: ACTU executive reports, various.
[a]Twenty largest unions as of September 1989 and union names as of this date. Figures
include junior members.
[b]Annual growth rate is for 1985–89. Federation did not exist before 1985.

External Union Structure

Under this heading there are several key questions. First, with regard
to the notion of strategic unionism, has the union movement become
more concentrated through mergers or does it remain fragmented?

Second, and related, is there evidence of growing cooperation among unions at various organizational levels? Third, to what extent has the institutionalization of the Accords encouraged a centralization of power at the peak council or national union level? Table 9.4 provides relevant data on union concentration.

According to table 9.4, the number of unions declined by less than 7 percent between 1980 and 1990, and the largest unions (fifty thousand or more members) increased their relative share of total union membership by more than 10 percent over the same period. Thus, by 1990, more than half of all union members were in the largest unions. By contrast, close to half of all unions, both in 1980 and ten years later, had one thousand or fewer members. These unions continue to account for less than 2 percent of total membership, however.

The largest relative decline in union membership (slightly less than 10 percent) was in the medium-large unions with ten thousand to fifty thousand members. Mergers between these organizations and larger unions, particularly in the latter part of the 1980s, are mainly responsible for the trend toward concentration of union members shown in table 9.4.

As mentioned earlier, until the latter half of the 1980s, there was little incentive for unions to merge. Improved wages and conditions had been won by traditional means, while immediate restraint under the Accords was expected to bring future benefits. Six factors account for the recent trend toward union amalgamations. First, in the late 1980s, employers increasingly resorted to legal sanctions against unions, leading in some cases to massive financial penalties (Gardner 1987, 1988).[13] Second, as bargaining over workplace issues became more prevalent, reflecting the

Table 9.4. Union membership concentration in Australia, 1980–90

	Percentage of total unions			Percentage of total membership		
Membership	*1980*	*1985*	*1990*	*1980*	*1985*	*1990*
<1,000	46.3	47.7	46.1	1.7	1.7	1.4
1,000–10,000	34.2	32.2	32.5	12.0	10.6	9.8
10,000–50,000	15.1	14.9	15.2	42.2	39.0	33.6
50,000 and more	4.4	5.3	6.1	44.2	48.8	55.3
Total	100	100.1	99.9	100.1	100.1	100.1
Total unions/union members (in 1,000s)	316	323	295	2,943.9	3,154.2	3,422.2

Source: Australian Bureau of Statistics, catalogue no. 6323.0, various.
Totals do not equal 100 because of rounding. Figures for 1980 are as of end of December; figures for 1985 and 1990 are as of end of June.

ongoing process of economic and award restructuring, severe strain was placed on scarce union bargaining skills and union resources more generally. Third, amalgamations were a means of countering the threat of enterprise unionism and fully decentralized bargaining as advocated in various ways by the BCA (1989), the conservative government in New South Wales, and the Liberal-National Party coalition in Parliament. Fourth, in light of the above and information on the decline in union organization in the United Kingdom and the United States under decentralized bargaining systems, senior union leaders urgently counseled unions to embrace organizational change. Fifth, the accelerated decline in union density in Australia over the most recent period brought the issue to center stage. Sixth, and finally, the removal of legislative barriers and support by the federal government for union amalgamations (see n.8) gave union leaders an opportunity to pursue such mergers.

These factors led to a surge in amalgamations in the 1980s, especially toward the latter part of the decade and accelerating markedly in the early 1990s. Thus, between 1986 and 1990, there were twenty-one union mergers under federal legislation, fifteen of which occurred between 1986 and 1990. A further twenty-four took place in 1991 (Australia. Department of Industrial Relations 1992). This contrasts with the 1970s, when, as noted earlier, there were only three such amalgamations. Recent noteworthy mergers have occurred in the public sector to form the Public Sector Union; in manufacturing to form the Federation of Industrial, Manufacturing and Engineering Employees' Union (a counterweight to the left-leaning Metals and Engineering Workers' Union), in the banking and insurance industries to form the Finance Sector Union; and between the building and mining unions to form the Construction and Mining Employees' Union (CMEU).[14]

Interunion cooperation has also been evident at ACTU congresses since 1983 (Burgmann 1984; Davis 1988, 1990), culminating in the 1991 Congress, which was marked by the complete absence of overt factional conflict (Martin 1992:138). Based on their participation in key committees, leading officials provided the same picture of relative harmony. Moreover, although there is no evidence of a rising trend in demarcation disputes occasioned by technical change,[15] in spite of agreements to exchange members with a view to rationalizing union structures, interunion conflicts have sometimes flared, typically because some unions, with employer connivance, have aimed to secure sole bargaining rights in particular industries or workplaces. Examples include the Waterside Workers' Federation and the CMEU, which have sought sole coverage on the docks and in the coal mining industry respectively; the Public Sector Union, which has claimed coverage over customs office workplaces; and the now-defunct Builders' Labourers

Union, which attempted to assert its jurisdiction over all jobs of a semiskilled nature in the construction industry.

Tension has also risen in recent years over union claims to sole coverage of greenfield sites, which the federal tribunal can now legally allocate to a single union.[16] To stem any eruption of interunion conflict arising from attempts by unions and employers to rationalize union membership and bargaining units, the ACTU has established guidelines enabling it to regulate the rationalization of union membership coverage.

Centralizing Tendency in Decision Making

The centralization issue can be approached by examining data on the ACTU's influence and resources and by noting recent trends, mainly in the twenty largest unions. Earlier, reference was made to the growth of the ACTU Executive and elected officials in the 1979–85 period. Expansion has continued: in 1987, the Executive was enlarged to thirty-eight, of which six members are from the ACTU's state branches (the trades and labor councils), eleven from the ACTU, and eighteen from industry groups. Three positions are reserved specifically for women.[17] More growth is planned, which will bring the ACTU Executive to forty-two members and increase the 1989 complement of professional staff, comprising twenty-seven officers and twenty-three administrative employees (ACTU 1989:2; Crean and Rimmer 1990:26).

The growing influence of the ACTU is a product of the close relationship between senior union leaders and key Labor government ministers, including their skills in elaborating the Accords under changing circumstances. But it also reflects five other factors internal to the union movement: first, the centralizing tendency in affiliates, such that state branches are becoming more tightly integrated into national union strategies and structures; second, the more representative nature of the ACTU Executive and its key committees compared with past arrangements (whereby blue-collar union and ACTU branch delegates had greater influence), thereby enabling workable agreements to be made by the most senior and influential union officials; third, the leadership qualities of senior officials of some of the largest unions, who appear to integrate successfully their members' demands with more general concerns regarding aggregate levels of employment, inflation, and international competitiveness; fourth, the vision, commitment, and capacity of leading ACTU officials in formulating strategic compromises, which typically receive the overwhelming support of affiliates; and fifth, and finally, the expertise and professionalism of ACTU staff in assisting affiliates in negotiations and arbitration proceedings. The organization's higher status in the eyes of affiliate leaders has been facilitated by the ACTU's improved financial position: in 1989, ACTU income was more than four times the 1979 level, representing a doubling in the amount of real income per member over the period (ACTU 1979, 1989).[18]

Internal Union Organization

Strategic unionism requires democratic structures that facilitate communication and consultation between cohesive teams of full-time officers and an informed, active membership. Unions are expected to be effective and efficient in delivering services to members. Despite a lack of systematic evidence on these aspects of internal union organization, available data enable some comments to be made concerning variations and trends in internal union structure, the extent of union unity/factionalism, efforts by unions to strengthen workplace union organization, and the provision of specialist services to members.

Union Structure and Factionalism

As noted in the introduction, Australian unions developed from local to national entities. This centralizing process was complicated by the federal structure of the Australian state in which unions tended to register with state tribunals and later extended their influence nationally. Federal rather than national union structures emerged in which considerable power was vested in the state branches of unions, that is, in the middle organizational level between the workplace and the federal union office.

A snapshot of the structure of large Australian unions can be seen in table 9.5, which categorizes selected unions (for which data are readily available) into three groups based on their degree of centralization. Centralization is measured by the ratio of federal office income to income accruing to the largest state branch. This is a plausible proxy for variations in the extent to which decision making is centralized.

Most large Australian unions are in the middle category of centralization, and there is a tendency for those that are highly decentralized to increase their degree of centralization as formerly autonomous state unions combine to form federations (e.g., health employees', teachers', and nurses' unions). This process has been accelerated by ACTU support and recent High Court decisions, which, as noted earlier, permit such associations to register with the federal tribunal. There is also a tendency for unions in the middle category to become more centralized as federal government policies increasingly affect workers' employment and earnings and because decisions by the federal tribunal effectively determine the parameters within which state tribunal decisions are made. State branches of unions have generally been reluctant to cede power to their federal counterparts. Union leaders recognize, however, that state variations in membership composition and demands require that state branches be relatively autonomous and have sufficient resources to cater to their members' needs.

Examining the data in table 9.5 more closely reveals that federal branch income exceeds the income of the largest state branch in only the most centralized unions; in all other cases, federal branches have less income; this is most evident in the highly decentralized category. The contrast between the most and least decentralized unions is stark: in the case of the Metalworkers' Union, all income is collected by the national office and is under its control except an amount that is distributed to the state branches (the largest state substructure received approximately 15 percent of total contributions and entrance fees in 1989). In the Municipal Workers' Union (and most other Australian unions), income is collected by the state branches and is under their control except for the proportion—less than 5 percent in the case of the Municipal Workers' Union—that is ceded to the federal branch.

The arbitration system is sometimes construed as being highly legalistic; in practice, it works routinely with little recourse to legal expertise. This is evident from data collected on legal fees, which, although not shown in table 9.5, indicate that only one of the unions shown in that table spent more than 5 percent of its federal and (largest) state branch expenditures on such fees. This was the Transport Workers' Union, which was engaged in a series of court cases in the latter part of the 1980s involving a secondary boycott.

Data in table 9.5 show the amount of resources unions commit to servicing members' needs through contact with full-time officers at federal and state branch levels. In most unions, state branches tend to spend a greater proportion of funds on full-time officers' salaries than their federal counterparts. This varies, however, seemingly with the dominant level of negotiation and arbitration and with union policy. Thus, bargaining and arbitration in the public-sector unions are split between federal and state levels, involving various federal government departments, while in the case of the Metalworkers', although the federal award is the pacesetter, the emphasis is on changes in workplace relations that require the assistance of state-level full-time officers, so a relatively large proportion of expenditures is channeled into this activity.

In the case of more decentralized unions, such as the Printing Workers', the largest state branch spends only slightly more relatively on full-time officers' salaries than its federal counterpart. By comparison, in the Shop, Distributive and Allied Employees' Association the relative discrepancy is much greater. This is mainly because negotiations and arbitration involving large multiplant printing industry employers have become more centralized in recent years. In the SDA's case, industrial activity tends to be more decentralized, and the dominant awards are under the jurisdiction of the state tribunals.

Table 9.5. Financial indicators of the internal structure of selected
unions in Australia, 1988–89

Union	Income in A. $1,000s	Expenditures in A. $1,000s	Percentage of branch dues to federal branch	Full-time officers' salaries as percentage of total expenditures
Highly decentralized				
Hospital employees				
Federal	283.1	184.0		26.2
Largest state (Victoria)	3,964.7	3,690.5	3.1	4.0
Municipal workers				
Federal	165.3	210.7		6.6
Largest state[a]	3,905.1	3,101.3	5.0	n.a.
Decentralized				
Building workers[a]				
Federal	3,132.7	1,626.7		7.5
Largest state	9,372.2	6,719.7	14.0	24.0
Postal workers				
Federal	1,696.9	1,516.1		10.4
Largest state	2,592.6	2,520.7	25.0	22.7
Printing workers				
Federal	1,015.8	1,009.4		16.2
Largest state	2,171.5	2,032.5	20.0	17.2
Shop assistants				
Federal	1,310.4	827.5		22.0
Largest state (Victoria)	4,323.3	3,054.0	4.1	32.2
Transport workers				
Federal	1,405.3	1,124.6		11.7
Largest state	4,245.8	4,021.0	6.9	23.0
Australian workers[b]				
Federal	2,242.0	2,216.7		3.4
Largest state	6,025.5	6,151.0	14.0	16.3
Centralized				
Metalworkers[b]				
Federal	19,405.8	17,214.9	–	6.7
Largest state	2,619.4	2,607.1		31.9

Table 9.5. (continued)

Union	Income in A. $1,000s	Expenditures in A. $1,000s	Percentage of branch dues to federal branch	Full-time officers' salaries as percentage of total expenditures
Public sector				
Federal	3,767.6	3,764.7		23.6
Largest state	885.6	1,046.2	50.0	28.6

Source: Annual union income and expenditure reports.
ªLargest state is New South Wales unless otherwise specified.
ᵇ1989; remaining data refer to 1988.
ᶜThe New South Wales state council received 14.5 percent of total dues income from the union's federal council.
n.a. = not available.

The presence of six state branches and a federal branch in most large unions, together with legal requirements for union decision makers to be elected by secret ballot at least every four years, has provided the basis for considerable electoral and hence factional competition within branches. In a study of six unions, E. M. Davis (1987:100) notes that of fifty-nine elections (in their respective unions) known to the twenty-one full-time officer interviewees, twenty-four were reported to have been contested.

Union decentralization and electoral requirements also provide opportunities for rivalry between state branches or between state and federal branches of the same union controlled by different factions. This has militated against some unions developing and implementing a national strategy. Examples over the past decade of large unions adversely affected by competition of this nature include those covering electricians (which militated against a merger with the Engineering Trades Union), teachers, transport workers, semiskilled workers (the Australian Workers' Union—to the detriment of a prospective merger with the Ironworkers), insurance employees, municipal government employees, nurses, postal workers, railway workers, and plumbers. The most serious case was the Clerks' Union, in which the competition resulted in a series of court cases between officials of various branches of the union at an estimated cost of A. $1.5 million (*Australian* 1989). Whether factional competition has increased over recent years is difficult to determine, but available evidence suggests that left-wing groups—mainly identified with the left wing of the Labor Party—have been gaining ground.[19]

Workplace Organization and Shop Steward Training

Workplace union organization in the form of shop steward committees has never been a general feature of Australian unionism. This is attributable to several factors: negotiations and arbitration that are conducted primarily above the workplace level; efforts by employers and union officials to retain control over industrial relations outcomes; the relatively few large workplaces;[20] and multiunionism coupled with a multiplicity of awards in any single workplace—a combination that promotes sectionalism. There have been exceptions, however, in the railways, mining, and electricity supply and in the meat, construction, oil refining, aircraft, and metal industries (see Rimmer 1989; Frenkel and Coolican 1984; Frenkel 1978, 1988), where such committees have flourished.

Available evidence suggests continuing weakness of workplace organization but brighter prospects for the future as stewards develop more bargaining skills. Using 1979 data, Frenkel and Coolican (1984:105) found that only 15 percent of the metal industry establishments we visited had a shop committee. Moreover, the extent of consultation and negotiation over issues such as dismissals, distribution of overtime, and work organization was limited. A 1984 survey conducted among metal industry establishments employing fifty or more persons noted that although union density in the great majority of plants was close to 100 percent, only a little more than a quarter (28.2 percent) of these establishments had a shop committee. The same survey also reported that in only 22.7 percent of the plants with more than one steward were stewards able to meet regularly on company time without pay being deducted (Frenkel 1987:44). A subsequent study of productivity bargaining painted a similar picture of union weakness at the point of production. Thus, most stewards were unable to use the federal tribunal's 1987 wage guidelines for workplace bargaining to establish regular consultation and negotiation mechanisms with management (Frenkel and Shaw 1989:103).

Finally, the most authoritative evidence on workplace organization comes from a national workplace survey conducted in 1989–90. This showed that a committee of stewards, all of whom belonged to the same union, existed in 28 percent of workplaces with twenty or more employees, whereas a multiunion steward committee was present in 11 percent of establishments. A full-time steward was present in only 5 percent. Workplace union organization was positively related to workplace size and varied according to industry. Mining sites reported the highest incidence of steward committees (intraunion, 52 percent; interunion, 34 percent). About a third (34 percent) of manufacturing plants claimed to have an intraunion steward committee and 18 percent a multiunion committee. These figures were higher than in most service-sector industries except transport and storage and public administration (Callus et al. 1991:273, 288).

Several recent developments have served to focus official union attention on the need to strengthen workplace organization. These include

Table 9.6. Government-funded trade union training in Australia,
1978–88

Year	Courses	Participants	STDs[a]	Expenditure (in A. $1,000s) in 1984–85 prices
1978–79	367	6,358	23,415	4,299.7
1982–83	474	9,748	31,278	5,612.1
1987–88	1,069	21,660	60,462	7,344.7

Source: TUTA annual reports, various.
[a]STDs (student training days) are the number of participants attending courses in the period multiplied by the length of each course in days.

changes in industrial law facilitating negotiation on such key workplace issues as dismissals, redundancies, organizational and technical change, health and safety, dispute procedures, and most notably, work organization, multiskilling, and training and career paths; the latter of these items are an integral part of the award restructuring process promoted by the federal tribunal (Rimmer 1989). In addition, federal government policy and programs encouraging worker participation (Australia. Department of Employment and Industrial Relations 1986; Morris 1989) are consistent with the ACTU's pursuit of greater "productivity consciousness" through the practice of industrial democracy (ACTU/Trade Development Council 1987, chap. 5; Davis 1990). These policies represent an alternative to the policies of the BCA and the conservative government of New South Wales, which favor the marginalization of industrial tribunals in favor of decentralized bargaining.

The most obvious manifestation of greater union attention to workplace organization is in the amount of resources devoted to steward training. Although, as the data in table 9.6 indicate, this is still relatively small, comments by senior union officials in interviews suggested that this area is becoming more important.

Four percent of our gross budget goes mainly to delegate [steward] training. We want to ensure that the union is able to mobilize support for national campaigns such as anti-privatization. Also, an active rank and file keeps the union responsive and enables us to develop policies in tune with members' needs (Secretary, Public Sector Union).

Industry and award restructuring require us to be effective in getting the message to our members and in developing policy. The role of the delegate as a link in the chain is therefore very important. Our Trade Union Training Authority [TUTA] program for stewards is second to none, and on the migrant side we have been running steward courses in several languages (Secretary, Federation of Industrial Manufacturing and Engineering Employees' Union).

In the last few years union representatives have come into the foreground; they now are resolving some industrial problems and don't just recruit members. We are educating them better, through TUTA. This is a big change (President, New South Wales Nurses' Association).

One reason unions spend so little on steward training is that it is funded by TUTA, a statutory body established in 1975 by a Labor government. Some idea of the growth in training conducted by TUTA—which focuses largely but not exclusively on stewards—is evident from table 9.6.

Table 9.6 indicates that union training has increased appreciably since 1978–79, particularly in the period between 1982–83 and 1987–88, when the number of student training days rose on average by 18.7 percent a year compared with 8.4 percent a year between 1978–79 and 1982–83.[20] This was achieved with slightly lower real increases in funding than in the first period (an annual average increase of 6.2 percent compared with 7.6 percent for the period 1978–79 to 1982–83).

In late 1989, TUTA was reorganized to ensure that its training programs were more flexible and consistent with the trend toward industry and award restructuring. Training has become more tailored to the circumstances and problems of specific industries and enterprises (TUTA 1989:5–7). A major problem seems to be that stewards are not availing themselves of existing training courses. This was revealed in the national workplace survey mentioned earlier, which showed that management in 74 percent of workplaces claimed to allow time off, either paid or unpaid, for union training but only 39 percent of stewards had attended a union training course since becoming a steward at their current workplace (Callus et al. 1991:111). Finally, several resource centers have been established by the government to assist unions and employers with workplace restructuring.

Providing Services to Union Members

Membership dues continue to be comparatively low in Australia: in 1985, an ACTU congress decision criticized union competition on the basis of their low membership fees and suggested that contributions should be no less than 1 percent of the average adult weekly award wage. Very few unions charge fees equivalent to this amount, however. This means that apart from operating mortality funds (which disburse funds on the death of a member to their next of kin) and legal assistance for work-related purposes, only the largest unions are capable of providing a wider range of competitive services. The most prominent examples include the CMEU (whose secretary commented: "Our aim is to make the union relevant to every aspect of a worker's life"), the Metals and Engineering Workers' Union (MEWU), the National Union of Workers (whose secretary favored "twenty-four-hour unionism"), and the SDA.

All four unions have a mortality fund and provide legal advice to members on all matters. Free legal representation is reserved for work-related problems, however. The CMEU and the MEWU employ ethnic affairs officers, and, with the National Union of Workers (in New South Wales), these unions support health centers where members may be diagnosed and treated at low cost. The SDA has a discount dental service and a women's bureau that provides free information and advice to female members. The SDA also distributes textbook scholarships to some sixteen hundred members, enabling them to buy A. $50.00 worth of textbooks for themselves or their children. Some other unique services provided by these unions include the CMEU social club, a counseling service for unemployed members of the MEWU, and a highly successful National Union of Workers' superannuation scheme.[21] The Public Sector Union is noteworthy in that it provides child-care facilities on a regular basis.

In sum, despite relatively decentralized decision-making structures and administrative fragility arising from institutionalized competition for leadership positions, the Accords have been almost unanimously supported by the union movement for several years. In spite of government support for union training and union mergers, however, the combination of weak workplace organization and the multiplicity of small, under-resourced unions—particularly in the context of a more heterogeneous work force and substantial challenges to customary work practices—is probably responsible for the decline in union density referred to earlier.

Conclusion

The structure and behavior of Australian unions owe a great deal to their unique context, characterized by a social contract based on the protection of manufacturers and employees in a federal state and institutionalized by means of statutory tribunals. This first social contract continued until the 1970s, encouraging the persistence of occupational unionism based predominantly on a pragmatic, economistic rationale. The end of the long boom, however, occasioned by international developments and exacerbated by inflationary wage demands and high levels of industrial conflict, led to the highest unemployment rates in the postwar period. Believing this to be a temporary condition and antagonized by a conservative government, the union movement saw no reason to review its traditional strategies and structure. By the early 1980s, however, it was becoming apparent that full employment, low inflation, and rising living standards could not be achieved by traditional means.

Hence, in 1983, the first Accord was developed between the two wings of the labor movement. It was this broad agreement, amended on four occasions during the subsequent six years, that formed the basis of a new form of strategic unionism.

The Accords were only part of a more general process of institutional reordering that I referred to as the second social contract. This emerging social structure of accumulation received a strong impetus during the mid-1980s economic crisis, which was highlighted by rapidly growing foreign debt and substantial currency devaluation. It was in this context that union leaders recognized the need for reform, to preserve their influence at the federal level while fostering participation under a more decentralized, productivity-oriented industrial relations system.

Although it is too early to assess the changes in Australian unions, some preliminary comments can be made. On the positive side, my analysis shows that there has been considerable progress since the first Hawke Labor government came to office in 1983 in creating an effective peak council whose leaders provide strategic vision for the union movement and negotiate acceptable framework agreements with the government. This in turn has led to the reelection of Labor candidates on several occasions and has served to maintain union influence at the macro level. Moreover, as mentioned in the previous section, it is no mean feat to have secured such a high degree of voluntary member consent to the Accords given the fragmented and relatively decentralized structure of Australian unionism and the conditions of total (individual and social) real wage stability for some groups and decline for many others (Bradbury, Doyle, and Whiteford 1990). In exchange, job growth has been among the highest of the OECD countries (Kyloh 1989), and workers have made inroads into managerial prerogative in such matters as technological change, redundancy, health and safety, superannuation, and anti-discrimination. More generally, award restructuring has institutionalized the concept of union participation in a range of workplace issues, including work organization, career development, and productivity enhancement, previously deemed to be outside unions' legitimate purview.

On the negative side, unions have been losing employee support, as reflected by declining union density, which is only partly as a result of structural change. This failure is to some extent related to the persistent dependence on a fragmented external structure, which has only very recently begun to be reconstituted along broad industrial sector lines. Progress in the past few years has been dramatic, however, in spite of the complexities caused by having relatively autonomous state branches, and the tensions created by employer attempts to rationalize union coverage, which have given rise to defensive postures and lack of trust between leaders of different unions. The main union defect has been the reluctance of union leaders to examine critically and change their internal structures and procedures to improve the reach and service of unions to actual and potential members. The changes that have occurred have been limited to variations on such standard themes as the provision of new services and more training for shop stewards. Union officials' thinking about the relationships between the representative and administrative systems and the connection between union strategy and policy implementation remains rudimentary. Unions that do not engage in a fundamental assessment of their goals, strategies, and systems, however, face extinction in the 1990s, for they are unlikely to retain their traditional rights to cover persons employed in particular occupations as they encounter increasingly sophisticated management.

Australian unions face two major challenges in the 1990s: how to augment their power at the workplace level and thereby remain relevant to employees while simultaneously maintaining their influence at federal and state levels; and, second, how to strengthen union solidarity, which is a necessary condition for influencing government policy. Here there are two subsidiary issues: maintaining unity in the face of employer pressure to rationalize union coverage in favor of more compliant unions and ensuring earnings relativities are acceptable not only to manual workers but also to the growing number of professional employees whose comparative reference groups lie beyond the unionized sector. Whether these problems will pose a fundamental threat to the survival of Australian unions sooner rather than later will depend a great deal on changes currently taking place in management policy and practice and the support given to unions by governments and tribunals. It will also depend on the skill, flexibility, and imagination of union leaders in reconstructing organizations that are suited to the demands of the new, less protective social structure of accumulation.

10
Unions in Crisis: Deregulation and Reform of the New Zealand Union Movement

Nigel Haworth

I n 1987, when the New Zealand Council of Trade Unions (CTU) emerged out of an amalgam of the previously separate Federation of Labour (FOL) and the Combined State Unions (CSU), the New Zealand labor movement might well have thought it was in fine shape. Furthermore, after a period of unsympathetic National Party government, the traditional political ally of the union movement, the Labour Party, had come to power in 1984. The union movement anticipated a reinforcement of the accommodations of the 1890s and the 1930s, which had established the legitimacy of union activity in New Zealand. Within union organizations, a new, younger tradition of leadership emerged, often displaying sophisticated strategic thinking, in contrast to the more elemental FOL tradition. The development of a substantial delegate (shop steward) structure began, often coupled with the educational and training inputs of union education officers and the staff of the state-funded Trade Union Education Authority.

The union movement was rapidly disabused of its rosy prospects, however. Before the 1984 electoral victory, the corporatist alternative had been strongly challenged by a free-market, restructuring model promoted within the Labour Party. This was to become the dominant ideological position in the 1984 government and was to pitchfork the union movement into six years of uncertainty and crisis in response to economic and industrial relations restructuring. The commitment shown by some sectors of the union movement and the Labour Party to an Australian-type compact has yet to bear fruit, while record unemployment levels continue to indicate the trauma to the work force induced by what came to be known as Rogernomics.

Historical Background and Characteristics

Although there are many factors that underpin the historical development of the New Zealand union movement—the nature of proletarianization, the characteristics of the settler state and society, and the relationship between immigrant labor and the indigenous population, for example—the most important is the character of the accommodation struck between the state, labor, and capital in the late nineteenth century.

There is an oft-quoted aphorism to the effect that unions in New Zealand are the creation of the legal structure enacted in the 1890s. There is much truth in this saying. Unions were at best in a formative stage before the legislation and were summarily defeated in their first major national confrontation—the maritime dispute of 1890. The government saw the lessons of that dispute in terms of an accommodation with labor. In a highly innovative move, the tradition of enacting English labor legislation was replaced by a formalization of the bargaining process in which unions were faced with a classic dilemma—to register under the 1894 legislation and gain guaranteed bargaining status or refuse to register and face exclusion from the sanctioned bargaining process. Registration implied acceptance of constraints on union action imposed by compulsory arbitration, whereas remaining outside the formal system permitted greater independence of action. The majority of unions chose the formal system and, despite phases of disenchantment, remained with it in principle until its disestablishment in the mid-1980s.

The labor relations accommodation following the 1894 legislation bound unions and employers into a state-patrolled legal framework based on a system of quid pro quos not dissimilar to those enacted in Sweden in the post-1932 period. The accommodation in New Zealand differed, however, in at least one important respect: it was not achieved simultaneously with political accommodation. Despite a second accommodatory phase under the Labour government of 1936, for much of its life labor relations in New Zealand were subject to amendment and interpretation by governments emphasizing the control of labor—politically, organizationally, and in labor market terms—rather than attempting to achieve a social transformation based on a consensus between the two wings of the labor movement on the one hand and capital on the other. Thus, a tension prevailed between the terms of industrial accommodation and the political order that finally precipitated a crisis in the bargaining system, beginning in the late 1960s but coming to a head in the difficult economic environment of the 1980s.

This tension had substantial implications for the labor movement. Once enmeshed in the compulsory arbitration process, the majority of unions came to accept the legitimacy of the system and the bargaining status it conferred. Consequently, they defended a system that was patently an enduring contradiction in that it tied the unions into an economistic bargaining framework that undermined the political sophistication and independence of the union movement, decreed the organizational structures of union activity, determined the internal processes of union life, and determined many membership attitudes toward the union, all in ways likely to undermine union movement autonomy and innovation.

Changing Size of New Zealand Unions

Table 10.1 provides information on the changing number and size distribution of unions in New Zealand. The table indicates a trend toward larger unions as a result of noticeable consolidation in recent years stemming from government efforts aimed at rationalizing external union structure. Thus, according to P. Walsh (1991:14), the number of registered unions declined from 206 in 1987 to 105 in 1990, notwithstanding the inclusion of public-sector unions in the 1990 figure, which were not required to be registered in 1987. Even so, New Zealand continues to be characterized by a large number of small unions.

The average membership in 1989 was estimated at 5,793 persons, a substantial increase over the 1986 figure (2,198). In 1986, only 46 percent of union members were in unions of ten thousand or more; by 1989, the figure had risen to 66 percent. Yet this image of union growth and size has to be seen from a broader perspective: in 1989, there were only twenty-one New Zealand unions with more than ten thousand members (Fuller 1989:appendix 1). This mainly reflects the comparatively small work force (1.3 million persons), but it also reflects union fragmentation.

The proportion of wage and salary earners who are union members has declined from more than 50 percent in the mid-1980s to an estimated 48 percent in 1991. Union density in the private sector is about 40 percent (Boxall 1991:20), versus 85 percent in the public sector. These levels are relatively high given the effects of recession and restructuring on employment indicated by the data in table 10.2

Only limited data are available on the effects of restructuring on the sizes of individual unions, but if we compare the data provided by J. Deeks and P. Boxall for 1989 and by C. Fuller for 1989, some initial conclusions can be drawn. In line with the decrease in manufacturing employment of 18.5 percent between 1986 and 1988, the Engineers

Table 10.1. *Membership in New Zealand unions, 1973, 1983, and 1989*

	1973		1983		1989	
Membership	Number	Percentage of all unions	Number	Percentage of all unions	Number	Percentage of all unions
1–1,000	224	73.4	167	67.3	19	16.9
1,001–2,000	31	10.2	30	12.1	32	28.6
2,001–3,000	17	5.6	13	5.3	–	–
3,001–4,000	6	2.0	5	2.0	29	25.9
4,001–5,000	3	1.0	2	0.8	–	–
>5,000	24	7.9	31	12.5	32	28.6
Total	305	100.1	248	100.0	112	100.0

Sources: Deeks and Boxall 1989:49; Fuller 1989, appendix 1.
Totals do not all add up to 100 because of rounding.

Table 10.2. Absolute and percentage changes in the number of full-time employees in New Zealand unions, by sector, 1985–88

Sector	Employees	Percentage change
Manufacturing	− 48,875	− 18.5
Services	− 31,509	− 5.1
Public sector	− 18,657	− 6.1
Private sector	− 67,455	− 11.5
Total	− 86,112	− 9.6

Source: New Zealand. Labour Department, various.

have lost substantial membership, as have the Meat Processors, Laborers, and Central Clerical Workers. Simultaneously, however, unions such as the Northern Hotel Workers have made great gains, reflecting a dynamic leadership and effective recruitment campaigns, while others have held their own despite restructuring. The biggest union nationally, the Public Service Association, had a membership of more than sixty-nine thousand in 1985 and sixty-six thousand in 1989. There is, of course, a difference between a union maintaining its membership and retaining the power it enjoyed before major restructuring was implemented.

Effects of Restructuring, Real Wages, and Productivity

The effect of unemployment on unions in the 1980s is an important consideration. As table 10.3 suggests, the widespread economic restructuring introduced paradoxically by the fourth Labour government had profound effects on the employment structure. Unemployment in early 1990 ran at an all-time high of 7 percent (109,000 excluding those employed on, or financed by, government schemes), and the "downsizing" has been focused on many of the traditionally important sectors of the economy. With little respite from the unemployment situation likely in the short term, particularly given a very low economic growth rate, unions increasingly recognize that they have little bargaining power.

Data on real after-tax wages indicate very limited, if any, improvement for wage earners in the 1980s. After-tax real wages, calculated on the basis of 1984 equaling 100, fell from 104 in 1981 to 94 in 1985. Thereafter, there was a slow and partial recovery in real after-tax wages. The 1989–90 bargaining round continued this amelioration: annual inflation ran at approximately 4.5 percent and wage settlements at an average of 7.0 percent. This profile is due to the effects of pre-1984 government-imposed wage restraint followed by a limited improvement in wage levels through bargaining under unfettered conditions.

When wage costs are assessed against productivity performance, New Zealand appears to be one of the weakest performers in the OECD

Table 10.3. Working days "lost" in New Zealand (per thousand employees) because of industrial disputes, 1977–90

Year	Days "lost"
1977	418
1978	366
1979	374
1980	366
1981	376
1982	319
1983	362
1984	400
1985	699
1986	1,227
1987	338
1988	254
1989	108
1990	660

Sources: Deeks and Boxall 1989: 248–49; New Zealand. Department of Statistics 1991, mimeo.

(OECD 1989c) although this has begun to change in the 1990s. At times, New Zealand experienced negative productivity growth, in stark contrast with other OECD economies. The causes of this poor productivity performance are complex, but most union strategists argue that responsibility does not lie solely with the unions and their alleged propensity to maintain high wages and anachronistic working practices. Union strategists do, however, recognize the need for improved productivity performance in the context of international market developments. This was a central theme of the government's proposed social compact, which foreshadowed union involvement in macro and microeconomic policy making.

Industrial Conflict

The difficulties of adjusting to the new economic environment have led to a continuation of strike levels similar to those in the 1970s. This is indicated in table 10.3.

The rise in working days "lost" from industrial disputes between 1984 and 1986 reflects the desire of unions to take advantage of bargaining opportunities under the 1984 Labour government. The 1985 figure is higher because of disputes in the traditionally strike-prone meat-processing industry (fostered by seasonal fluctuations in employment, export significance, and particular labor process characteristics, including a strong group consciousness among workers). The substantially higher 1986 figure is accounted for mainly by a major dispute in the wood-processing industry. A. Geare (1988:273) suggests that the five-year average data on stoppages simply indicate the cyclical nature of industrial conflict in New Zealand and that the 1986–90 average may decline substantially from levels reached in 1981–85. This assumes limited structural change, which is untenable for New Zealand in the late 1980s and 1990s. Hence the dramatic rise in days lost in 1990. Further, in response to the introduction by the National Party government of the deregulatory Employment Contracts Act of 1991 (see chap. 11 for further details), the number of longer, more protracted disputes appears to be rising as workers struggle to defend their interests while major changes in bargaining structures work their way through the system.

A final point about industrial conflict relates to the manner in which stoppages are concluded. The majority (75 percent in 1985) are resolved through negotiation between the parties without reference to a third party. Despite the formal conciliation and mediation processes built into the 1894 bargaining model, dispute resolution usually went ahead without reference to these procedures. Perhaps wishing to avoid the formal commitments involved in the mediation and conciliation process, both parties recognized the value of bilateral dispute resolution.

Restructuring, the Labour Government, and the Compact

The union movement was faced with a dramatic crisis in the early 1980s as the Labour Party rejected a corporatist model (Oliver 1989) and important elements of the post-1984 Labour government came to believe that the unions could not deliver an Australian-type social contract (Bertram 1990). This relatively sudden exclusion from influence, particularly over economic policy, was traumatic for the unions that had participated in the 1984 economic summit. For they had done so on the assumption that they would receive a commitment to full employment, growth, economic and social justice, price stability, and industrial democracy. The party's policy was in part underpinned by more pragmatic concerns, in particular the view that unions should receive compensation for Robert Muldoon's wage and price freeze, which had preceded the 1984 election; that compulsory unionism, removed by the Muldoon government in early 1984, should be reintroduced; and that free and direct collective bargaining should be reinstated after the wage freeze.

The supply-side victory in the Labour caucus made the union perspective on economic policy irrelevant, even obstructive. It also disestablished the unions as the key client group of the Labour Party in power. Not only were union economic priorities not relevant but the channels of influence expected to open with a Labour victory were blocked. M.

Wilson (1989) identifies a cabinet faction that rejected the view that the unions and the Labour Party had a special relationship and sought to ensure that the Labour Party was not "captured" by the union movement. Two major consequences followed. First, the union movement was forced into complex, often unproductive faction activity in the Labour Party, both inside and outside Parliament. Second, unions were limited in their influence over the government in response to the effects of restructuring.

The search by the unions for political leverage, made more complex by the creation of the CTU in 1987 after a decade of growing cooperation between the white-collar CSU and the blue-collar FOL, was at its most intense in the policy debates around reform of the bargaining system. Wilson (1989) and Walsh (1989) provide somewhat different interpretations of union input into these debates. As befits the then president of the Labour Party and a contributor to the anti–supply-side policy alternative, Wilson offers the insider's view of the politicking that surrounded the economic summit and the debates on labor relations legislation. She highlights the problem faced by the unions and the party at large in trying to force the government to respond to its constituency's wishes. Wilson describes the process as "constructive engagement," concluding that the legislative changes introduced after 1984 were difficult compromises struck between the party, the unions, government, and the ministries. She sees the period as one that tested the relationship between unions and party yet that saw the relationship survive, even prosper. This conclusion is difficult to accept except in the narrow sense of the compromises struck around labor relations legislation. The broader picture of a Labour Party sponsoring restructuring and large-scale unemployment on a massive scale and facing a breakaway New Labour Party and a defeat in the 1990 elections suggests that the relationship between the unions and the government was at best threatened and at worst terminally damaged. The possibilities of the compact as a means of renewing the relationship are discussed below.

Walsh (1989) sees the legislative outcome as a policy middle ground in which both corporatist and free-market options were rejected in favor of a collectivist legislative consensus derived from the tripartite Long Term Reform Committee (LTRC) proposals produced in 1984. Thus, he views the process of labor relations reform after 1984 not so much as it relates to the ability of the unions to influence the party, but rather as it relates to the willingness of the unions to accept compromises with employers and the government concerning the LTRC proposals, compromises, which, crucially, were defended in policy documents by the Department of Labour and its minister. Walsh's view suggests that union arguments were central to the creation of a coalition that rejected the deregulatory desires of the Treasury, the Business Round Table (BRT), and, to a lesser extent, the New Zealand Employers' Federation as they applied to the private sector. Thus, in the narrow area of labor relations reform, Walsh arrives at a conclusion similar to that of Wilson: in the narrow context, unions were heard and their agendas were partially met.

Whichever view is more accurate—that there was politicking in the party or a powerful "practitioner" consensus—the qualified successes of the union movement in fending off deregulation of the labor relations system and the labor market must be seen against the background of the structural effects of deregulation on the economy as a whole (see Bollard and Buckle 1987; Easton 1989; Walker 1989). The employment effects have been traced above in terms of aggregate and sectoral employment (see table 10.2) and in terms of increasing unemployment. Here, I shall concentrate on the effects of restructuring as experienced through reform of the bargaining process, particularly in the context of the 1986 State-Owned Enterprises Act, the 1987 Labour Relations Act, and the 1988 State Sector Act.

Restructuring the Private Sector

It is possible to draw up a balance sheet of gains and losses by the union movement in relation to the effects of the 1987 act. On the debit side, at least for some unionists, the inclusion in the act of the abolition of compulsory arbitration, first introduced in 1984, stands out. The prohibition on multitier bargaining, the introduction of a mechanism permitting union challenges to existing union coverage, the removal of the government inspectorate from its overseeing role in bargaining, and the requirement that the parties administer their own agreements are further problems created by the act. The pressure toward industry and plant-level bargaining created by the act, and its consequent influence on the traditional occupational award structure, is another problem. As R. Harbridge and Walsh (1989) point out, however, much of the pre-1987 system remained intact, reflecting the impact of the "practitioner" consensus on government policy identified by Walsh (1989). In particular, union membership remained effectively compulsory, compulsory conciliation continued, and union registration was not amended to undermine occupationally based union groups.

The continuity between the pre-1987 and the post-1987 models of labor relations may be judged against the background of the virulent critique of the 1987 legislation by market-model supporters such as the New Zealand Business Round Table (BRT). This organization, which brings together the chief executives of the largest companies in New Zealand, has been the most active group to lobby promoting for continuing and comprehensive deregulation, including proposals for a wider wage settlement range in negotiations to accommodate firms in different market situations. Harbridge (1989) has produced detailed empirical evidence to show that the first round of bargaining, after the 1987 legislation came into effect, produced very little variation around the "going rate." This again suggests continuity between the two models.

Thus, in the private sector, unions faced agendas at two levels. In a narrow sense, deregulation has not inflicted the damage to union practices and expectations as might have been expected, or desired, by the Treasury or the BRT. In a wider sense, there exists the agenda of economic restructuring, which has torn the heart out of the productive sector and, consequently, forced the union movement to consider its role in a new, internationally oriented economic environment. Inevitably, this agenda has led the unions to reappraise their expectations of the bargaining structure.

Public-Sector Restructuring

A further stimulus to this reappraisal has been the experience of the public sector. Under the 1986 State-Owned Enterprises Act, state-owned companies were freed from the requirement to seek wage relativity with the private sector and were empowered to "corporatize" personnel policies, thus breaking down what had been a traditionally centralized personnel strategy. The 1988 State Sector Act introduced similar changes in the core public service, making each government department an employer in its own right and effectively decentralizing personnel policies to these newly autonomous departments. The 1988 legislation also brought the public sector under the aegis of the 1987 Labour Relations Act, which, for the first time, brought the public and private sectors under one bargaining umbrella.

As Walsh (1988) argues, the effects of changes in bargaining in the public sector have been to weaken the power of the public-sector unions. Their consultative rights have been eroded, their members have suffered substantial job losses and changes in job descriptions, and contract labor has been introduced unilaterally. In effect, autocratic management has been the order of the day, the obverse side of which has been a general undermining of union power. Walsh (1989) argues that this managerial success is in part due to the weakness of the "practitioner" consensus in the politicking around reform of the public sector, but it can also be seen as a deliberate government policy to restructure bargaining toward a market model of wage determination, while drawing attention to an alternative model for the private sector. For the unions, the success of this model in the state sector provides a warning regarding the probable future of bargaining reform in the private sector if change is not forthcoming.

Union commentators have tended to couch their analysis of union responses to restructuring in terms of a two-level analysis—micro-level adaptation in the enterprise and macro-level economic planning. Regarding the former, union strategists are contemplating active involvement in moves away from occupational bargaining into a mixture of enterprise and industry bargaining. With regard to the latter, and following frequent consultations with Australian union officials, they have adopted the position of the Australian Council of Trade Unions and initially sought with government a new bipartite accommodation, termed the compact. The compact document, released in late 1989, foreshadows a tripartite consultative arrangement in which appropriate business-sector groups will be involved.

The Compact: Toward Strategic Unionism?

The starting point for union analysts of the compact is realism about the need for change in union bargaining attitudes and practices. Before the release of the compact, A. Kirk (1983) and R. Campbell (Campbell and Kirk 1983), one-time strategists of the FOL, proposed a framework in which unions were key contributors to an alternative strategy covering macro- and microeconomic reform and changes in the wage-fixing structure. Their analyses were prompted primarily by an interpretation of the bargaining and accumulation crises of the 1970s and preceded the strategic victory of supply-side thinking in the Labour Party. The consequences of this victory stimulated further analysis, particularly by what might be described as neocorporatist elements (Sandlant 1988), which are addressed below.

Arguments for change have emerged within the union movement based, in general, on a somber overview of the international victory of deregulation, restructuring, and the internationalization of production and distribution and on a survey of the bleak effects of this model on New Zealand (Harvey 1988). Such arguments have a broadly uniform content. Unions have been excluded from the reform agenda, except to the extent that they bear the brunt of the costs of adjustment. The marginalization of unions from macroeconomic planning, political councils, and enterprise management is seen as a further consequence of this international victory. Even in situations in which unions might have influenced policies to ameliorate the deregulatory surge, unions have been unable to take advantage of the possibilities, primarily because they have little strategic sense of how they should act. In essence, the world has changed irrevocably and the change has been broad in New Zealand, but the union movement has failed either to recognize this sea change or to develop a strategic sense of a new role that it might undertake.

The prevailing union view is that there are two options open in the face of this change. The first is to continue as before and face becoming a weak, ineffective dinosaur, irrelevant to government and to increasingly large numbers of employers and, more important, working people.

The second option, and broadly the model accepted by the Council of Trade Unions in its approach to the compact and change in general, is a strategic approach, drawing heavily on Australian, Austrian, and Swedish union experience. To quote O. Harvey, this option has the following characteristics:

- a tendency for trade unions to go beyond a narrow focus on wages and conditions;
- the generation and implementation of centrally co-ordinated goals and integrated strategies e.g. for full employment, labor market programs, trade and industry policy, productivity, industrial democracy, social welfare and taxation policies which promote equity and social cohesion;
- sophisticated participation in tripartite bodies;
- a commitment to growth and wealth creation as well as its equitable distribution;
- the active pursuit of these goals and strategies in their own right both inside and outside of the arena of industrial relations;
- emphasis upon strong local and workplace organization;
- the extensive delivery of education and research services (Harvey 1988:17).

A key feature of the second option is the creation of a proactive rather than a reactive approach and, consequently, acceptance of a high degree of union responsibility for the performance of the whole economy. Following the Australian ACTU, the dominant view is that unions will always be weak in times of recession and that they should therefore seek to create growth and stability in the economy and thus protect union interests. A final feature of this option is that it emphasizes that unions must win the right to be involved in macroeconomic planning. Such participation is no longer the unions' right but will come to be seen as necessary only because of the advantages it is seen to bring. In these analyses and conclusions, we see the practical working through of the theoretical views developed by, among others, F. Castles (1987), A. Przeworski (1985), and M. Regini (1986).

Strategic unionism has won the day in CTU councils, although there are numerous critics of its main tenets. The left argues that it classically reflects the "let's do capital's work for it" tradition of economistic centralism in the union movement. The treasury, the BRT, and the Employers' Federation are broadly convinced that compact-type models induce rigidity and are anachronistic. Even unionists in the center, battered by restructuring, are concerned about the amount of rhetoric associated with the strategic unionism approach in comparison with the paucity of concrete proposals for its enactment. Some union traditionalists hark back to the days of the 1894 accommodation and believe that its reintroduction would reestablish the old verities. Many observers wonder if the compact concept is sustainable given the defeat of the Labour Party in the 1990 election. Despite these concerns, the leadership of the CTU has committed itself to a version of the Australian/Swedish approach to union policy, and it is unlikely that this line will change even if the compact model fails. The commitment of key younger union leaders, and the lack of an effective alternative, guarantees its future, at least as a guiding idea.

Politics and the New Zealand Union Movement

Two political tendencies have played a particularly important role in union life in the last decade: the Labour Party and the pro-Moscow Socialist Unity Party (SUP). The former's role is in quantitative terms the most significant, though it is declining. Since the formation of the Labour Party in 1916, the union movement has maintained formal affiliation with the party. Since World War II, however, the symmetry between FOL and Labour Party membership has declined sharply. In 1951, for example, more than 86 percent of the FOL membership belonged to the Labour Party. By 1986, this figure had fallen to 40 percent. This decline coincides with the diminished fortunes of the compulsory arbitration system, the extended period in which the Labour Party was in political opposition and in which it perhaps lost much of the ideological commitment on which it had been founded, and, finally, a period of rising living standards. Thus, by the 1980s, it was an error to see the affiliations between the Labour Party and the FOL as necessarily reflecting a basis for concerted political action.

The consequences of Rogernomics have been to distance the party further from the union movement. In addition to their widespread disillusionment with the government caucus, unionists have displayed their opposition in a number of ways. The creation of the breakaway New Labour Party in 1989 involved a number of leading union officials and activists. Constant bickering in local constituencies has also highlighted the gulf created by the imposition of Rogernomics.

The political vacuum arising from the deteriorating relationship between the Labour Party and the unions has not been filled by the left. It is a commonplace to hear statements to the effect that because Ken Douglas, president of the CTU, is a member of the SUP, the Communists have the upper hand in the union movement, but this is unsustainable. There are a number of key SUP personnel in senior positions in the CTU and in regional union structures, but their presence is marked by a pragmatism that generally precludes proselytization. For example, international affiliations of the CTU favor the International Confederation of Free Trade Unions rather than the traditionally pro-Soviet World Federation of Trade Unions. The remaining leftist factions are fragmented, and, although they are active in campaigns against the compact, their effect is greater in terms of the introduction of ideas into debates than in the effective political control of union structures. In sum, the New Zealand movement may be broadly categorized as economistic in its orientation.

Restructuring Bargaining: Whither the Enterprise?

I have noted that a key concern of the 1987 legislation was the promotion of enterprise-level bargaining, thereby making the bargaining process more responsive to the competitive environment in which the enterprise operates. This agenda was promoted assiduously by employers' groups, the treasury, external bodies such as the OECD, and those ministers most closely associated with the "more market" model. It is, of course, a central theme of the international deregulatory approach, but it has struck a special chord in the New Zealand context because of the highly centralized award structure that prevailed between 1894 and the 1980s. Historically, an award was deemed to bind not only those parties negotiating the award but all others carrying out the same task or occupation: the concept of blanket coverage. Thus, employers and employees would find themselves covered by an award in which they had played little part in negotiating. Employers were usually quite sanguine about this system. It avoided substantial transaction costs by centralizing negotiation, and it tended to take wages and conditions out of competition, hence providing a high degree of certainty for wage outcomes. Similar benefits accrued to the unions, particularly with respect to providing minimum wages and conditions.

The 1987 legislation did little to change this system except in relation to the second-tier question. The practice had grown whereby a worker might well be covered by a national award and also be in receipt of a supplementary payment negotiated at the plant level. The 1987 act made this illegal and required that workers be covered by either a national award or an enterprise or workplace agreement but not both. This and other provisions of the act were designed to encourage unions to support decentralized bargaining instead of centralized awards.

In practice, unions have been cautious in their approach to enterprise-based bargaining, preferring to adopt composite awards, which permit local variations, rather than withdraw from the award structure altogether. Employers have pursued enterprise bargaining but have often obtained acceptable settlements within the traditional framework. Table 10.4 indicates a trend toward agreements, but this is more gradual than some observers had anticipated.

According to table 10.4, there was a shift of about 5 percent away from awards and agreements over the four-year period. Harbridge and S.

Table 10.4. Registered settlements (in percent) in New Zealand, by document type, 1984–85 and 1988–89

Settlement	1984–85	1988–89
Awards	42.4	33.5
Composite awards	–	3.9
Agreements[a]	57.6	62.6
Total	800.0	818.0

Source: Harbridge and McCaw 1991:378.
[a]Includes voluntary collective agreements made with nonunion worker collectivities and composite agreements.

McCaw (1991:376) suggest that even this magnitude of change is exaggerated because of the inclusion of public-sector settlements in the 1988–1989 figures. In line with microeconomic reform, a more decentralized bargaining structure is, however, contemplated by the union movement. Strategic thinkers (e.g., Harvey 1988) see industrial revitalization as a vital concern for the union movement, arguing that technological change, work organization, skill formation, and the issue of flexibility are all determinants of New Zealand's economic performance. Moreover, microeconomic reform will proceed regardless of whether the unions are or are not involved. It is therefore better that responsible unions make their involvement in change invaluable rather than be left outside the process. Such involvement requires enterprise-level bargaining with the employer, and unions should accept and appropriate this reality. They should become key managers of the bargaining structure (Harvey 1988:11).

Angela Foulkes, the vice-president of the CTU, echoes much of Harvey's analysis (Foulkes 1989). Her argument recognizes that the occupationally based wage system became obsolete because it no longer suited either employers or employees and was affected by intense technological change. She envisages an amalgam of industry- and enterprise-based bargaining in which workers in smaller units are covered by the former and those in larger units by the latter. This arrangement, she argues, is the realistic way to achieve more flexible bargaining patterns without disadvantaging the weaker work forces in the small-plant sector. Two sources of difficulty in achieving these changes are noted. The first is union opposition, which is crumbling in line with growing support for the concept of strategic unionism; the second is employer opposition to the industry/enterprise mix. This is a bigger problem in which Foulkes sees short-sighted management attempting to subvert a collaborative reform process.

The trend-setting Engineers' Union supports Foulkes's argument in many respects but identifies three principles underlying union moves toward decentralized bargaining (Eichbaum 1989). First, from both the unions' and the employers' perspectives, occupationally based bargaining is less than rational because of its compliance costs. Second, industry agreements may be, and should be, responsive to the bargaining requirements of enterprises and their subunits. Third, bargaining agendas need to encompass the wider issues of micro-level reform outlined by Harvey. If the parties are willing to accept these principles, the tradition of enterprise bargaining at an informal level, which has always existed apart from the formal award structure, will be developed and improved.

Several unions, led by the Engineers, have been active in promoting a combination of industry/enterprise bargaining and new models of training, skill formation, career path development, and payment systems, similar to recent Australian initiatives (see chap. 9). It is fair to say that in these areas the unions have been at least as innovative as management. The result has been an unusual situation in which the Engineers have implored management to restructure their work organization and bargaining structures in line with the demands of a high-technology, high value-added economy. Clouding employers' responses to these initiatives have been a combination of factors: skepticism about the motives of the unions, uncertainty about the ability of the unions to deliver on productivity, and an unwillingness to recognize unions as partners in the restructuring process. At the same time, there are several cases in which the model is working very effectively; New Zealand Steel and Fisher and Paykel—leading metal industry employers—are often cited as the most successful.

Union Reform: Rationalization, Membership, and the CTU

I have already touched on the impact of the 1987 legislation on union size. The intention of the legislation was to reduce the number of unions from 250-plus in 1986 to more manageable numbers. To this end, the act required that amalgamations of unions take place within a given period so that no union would have fewer than one thousand members. Tied in with this rationalization process were a number of objectives, including the need for unions to be viable without subsidies or the legislative props of compulsory unionism and perpetual coverage; that they be viable only if they have membership support; that their rules be reasonable, democratic, fair, and nonprejudicial; and that coverage be clear-cut and not overlapping (Fuller 1989). As we shall see, these goals conformed broadly to the CTU's model of union development in an industry/enterprise bargaining framework.

Union amalgamations have been the central feature of the rationalization process. Table 10.1 above outlines the relevant data. C. Fuller identifies three patterns of amalgamation. The first pattern—the craft occupation type—brought together occupational groups nationally, such as the watersiders or the footwear workers. The second pattern is consistent with an industry union structure, for example, distribution workers and local government employees. The third pattern is of a more general type, for example, the Rubber Workers with the New Zealand Workers. Given the impetus to amalgamate, this pattern is not surprising in that it reflects the contingent nature of union alliances, subject as they are to historical rivalries, interpersonal frictions, and regional diversity. With respect to the objectives implicit in the act, it is not yet clear whether these amalgamations provide more resources and better services to members. Fuller (1989:5–6), however, quotes Department of Labour research that supports the view that the larger unions in New Zealand are developing more sophisticated services and that this is likely to become more widespread as unions consolidate.

Exclusive Coverage

The issue of exclusive coverage is more complex. A number of sanctions are available that are designed to prevent overlapping coverage—chiefly refusal by the Arbitration Commission to register an award and supervision of the registration process by the union registrar. The process of achieving rule changes by negotiation or ballot to eliminate overlapping membership is difficult and time-consuming, however. Similarly, when ownership patterns are changed, traditional coverage by a union may be lost, as in the case of the privatization of state-owned enterprises, whereby the Public Service Association stands to lose coverage and therefore power. Not surprisingly, where exclusive coverage prevails, union rationalization is slow, although the union registrar has commented favorably on the CTU's positive orientation to union rationalization.

Fuller argues that, in the main, unions have been happy to accommodate their rules to the standards and guidelines laid down by the registrar's office. These provisions have been designed to ensure that union rules are "unambiguous, easy to read and transparent." They cover the organization and running of unions, the rights and responsibilities of elected officers, disciplinary processes, and mechanisms for balloting the membership. There are some areas of contention, such as the right to an appointed secretary, the appropriateness of disciplinary procedures, the election of officers other than by postal vote, the voting rights of members, the right of paid officers to stand for office, and the provision of audited accounts. Generally, however, the requirement that unions act in a democratic and responsible manner is being fulfilled.

Contestability

The final aspect of union structure affected by the 1987 act relates to compulsory union membership and the thorny issue of contestability. Ballots have been carried out under the "principled supervision" of the registrar's office in cases in which employers refused to negotiate a union membership provision appropriate to the existent award structure. All such ballots (forty-four by late 1989) have been successful, and the relevant workers have won the coverage of the union and, where denied, the award. Presumably this evidence contradicts the traditional employer assertion that compulsory union membership offends the democratic rights of workers. It also suggests that, despite low levels of participation in both these ballots and in other areas of union life, those who participate are firmly committed to independent union membership.

The issue of contestability was a central theme in the debates around the 1987 act. The right of a union to challenge for the coverage of a group of workers is permitted under the act under two conditions: first, when a new union claims coverage of workers who are members of an existing union that arguably offers "no service" to those workers and, second, when a registered union challenges for coverage of a group of workers already covered by another registered union. There have been relatively few of these claims—perhaps four of the first and seven of the second during recent years. The existence of such procedures, however, may stimulate a greater concern about the services offered to members by their unions. In a context in which rationalization of union structures is an inevitable, long-term development, the question of contestability may come to play a more frequent and disruptive part in labor relations. The key to whether this will occur will be the response to restructuring by the unions and the CTU.

Union Rationalization

The CTU, in line with its acceptance of the need for change in the bargaining environment, is promoting dramatic and controversial rationalization of the union movement. Complementing its commitment to industry-level bargaining and drawing on the experience of other economies in which large union bodies have enjoyed organizational, political, and financial stability, the CTU introduced a discussion document in 1989 in which an amalgamation of the union movement into fourteen large bodies was aired. Behind the proposal was a belief that the existing unions were too small, too underresourced, too narrowly focused on wages and conditions, and too small to integrate into the international union context. The CTU strategists believe that the services that must be delivered by unions if they are to be effective cannot be provided under the current fragmented structure and that there is only one solution: massive rationalization.

It is still early in the discussion of the CTU proposals. Unions facing amalgamations required by the 1987 act are still enmeshed in discussions with potential partners. Nevertheless, as mentioned earlier, the number of registered unions has declined substantially in recent years. The added imposition of even greater levels of unity is a daunting prospect. More important, a number of unions are unhappy about the structure proposed by the CTU. It is common knowledge, for example, that the country's biggest union, the Public Service Association, fears the loss of its independence under the CTU proposals. A question mark hangs over some of the interpersonal relationships within the union movement. As elsewhere, individual antipathies play an important role in union policy making; their effects on the CTU proposals should not be underestimated.

Building the Cadre: The Internal Development of Unions

So far, we have looked primarily at the wider issues facing the New Zealand union movement. Now we turn to several micro-level organizational issues that are also subject to change. These include participation in the union, union services, union education, the role of the organizer, and, most important, the development of delegates (shop stewards).

Some comments have already been made concerning the cultural and structural reasons for the relatively low levels of participation in union activities. Centralized bargaining made an active rank and file less necessary than in, say, the voluntarist U.K. system. A narrow wages and conditions orientation, coupled with the relatively limited services offered by the union, were compounding factors. It is arguably the case that compulsory unionism exaggerated this low participation rate, creating a tension between the individual and the institution. Union leaders and activists, it is often asserted, simply paid little attention to membership involvement in the wider life of the union. Decentralized bargaining and the effects of the 1987 act on union procedures may encourage greater participation rates. Employers have thought otherwise; some believed that the dinosaur quality of the union movement would be revealed if a National Party government reintroduced voluntary unionism after the 1990 elections (Marshall 1989). This was in part borne out after the passage of the Employment Contracts Act of 1991, when many unions reported very substantial decreases in membership—some of the order of 50 percent—as a result of the legislation, which promoted a workplace-based, contractual model.

Much will depend on the level and quality of the services unions offer their members. There are two aspects to their response. First, according to the CTU (CTU, n.d.), the existing functions of unions are becoming more onerous as change affects technology, management practices, and the wider economic environment. Issues such as redundancies, personal grievances, and breaches of awards are increasingly common, complex, and time-consuming and demand increasingly more sophisticated responses.

Second, new services are emerging directed at such matters as health-hazard training, industrial democracy, and skill formation. Services outside the workplace—for example, medical centers, investment societies, and union-run superannuation schemes—are also expanding. As elsewhere in the OECD, insurance, banking, and credit services may well appear in time. The CTU recognizes that in both new and traditional areas, services must be delivered at an acceptable quality and cost if unions are to be effective. Clearly, there is a long road ahead for many unions.

Union Funding

Two elements crucial to the provision of better services are long-term financial stability and high-caliber staff. Financial issues have been central to the amalgamation process since 1987. C. Fuller (1989) notes that a major feature of union mergers has been an increase in the level of union dues, which for the twenty largest unions are currently (1990) equivalent to 1.2 percent of the average adult minimum wage. Union leaders emphasize the difficulties of operating with such meager funding. It adversely affects union officials' salaries and hence filling of positions. It also limits travel, education, and the ability to purchase technical equipment and get the message across to the rank and file. In contrast, the resources available to management are often superior even to those of the best-equipped unions, such as the Engineers and the Northern Hotel Workers. Clearly, funding is a fundamental problem not only for the CTU's constituent unions but also for the CTU, which is frequently the object of rumors alleging that it is having serious financial problems.

Union Personnel

Leaving the role of leadership aside, there has been a marked change in the profile of union personnel in the last decade. In line with international experience, there are more younger, better-qualified paid officials and women, and more officials are of Maori or Islander ethnic background. In the larger and more dynamic unions and in the CTU, previous experience in a relevant occupation or industry is less important as a selection criterion for a union position than possession of the requisite skills.

Given the resource problems noted above, a common feature of union work experience is the burnout syndrome, caused by large workloads characterized by numerous workplace visits involving increasingly complex negotiating issues and responsibility for improving delegate organization, leading to fatigue. The only effective answer is a larger staff. Job rotation can also help. When union officials share front-end work with research and other staff, they suffer less stress and become more familiar with all aspects of union activity. Providing appropriate equipment— portable phones, for example—is another way to increase union effectiveness. Unions could take a leaf out of management's book in the area of improving their human resource policies.

Creating a Delegate Structure

Developing an effective delegate structure is perhaps the greatest priority for the New Zealand union movement. The same process of decentralization of bargaining and service that has moved the CTU and the union movement in general toward industry/enterprise bargaining has highlighted the limited quality of the lay representatives at the workplace level. The reasons for this deficiency derive from the formalized, centralized, and fragmented nature of the New Zealand bargaining tradition. Historically, there has never been a combination of plant-level bargaining and political mobilization of the work force. Thus, the idea of shop committees made up of lay union members within an industry or of a combined committee uniting stewards across the branches of a multiplant employer is novel.

Only in the 1980s did the issue of creating and supporting delegate structures become urgent, and in recent years much effort has been expended in trying to equip a new layer of delegates with the range of skills they need to negotiate at the workplace level. Once again, there has been a correlation between active delegate development and recognition of the changing pattern of bargaining, especially since the 1987 act. Some unions, working in sectors with a high degree of membership dispersion—the clerical workers, for example—face major problems in delegate development. The success of union efforts at developing delegate structures more generally is not yet evident: indeed, this is an uphill task given the job insecurity posed by economic restructuring, a management offensive against oppositional elements in the work force, and the many other issues that unions have had to address with inadequate resources. Nevertheless, the trend toward decentralized bargaining encouraged by the 1987 legislation will tend to focus union activity at the workplace level and, if only or mainly by practice, will assist in developing stronger union organization at the workplace.

There has been growing recognition, particularly in the Auckland region, of the importance of ethnicity in creating effective union organization. The Trade Union Education Authority and the larger unions have sought to respond to Maori and Pacific Islander issues by means of specially appointed personnel and targeted educational sessions. These responses, though seeking to achieve the appropriate cultural sensitivity and focus, have had limited success, in part because of ethnically related separatist political traditions within the union movement. Separatism focuses attention on the rights of the indigenous Maori, many of whom claim a preeminent right as a colonized people to determine the future of New Zealand and consequently enter union activities with a complex agenda of both union and ethnic politics. While it would be wrong to overemphasize the effects of this debate on the union movement, it is a powerful and permanent influence on the membership.

On a positive note, the Trade Union Education Authority, established in 1986 with a national and a regional structure, has provided a national infrastructure of delegate education and training that has been a lifeline for unions unable to develop an internal education structure and a great aid to unions in more fortunate circumstances.[1]

Changing Leadership

The quality of union leadership is currently receiving considerable attention by New Zealand unions. The 1980s saw a substantial change in the role of union leaders and their incumbents, as exemplified by Ken Douglas. Douglas, for many years the "coming man" in the FOL, took over as the preeminent national union leader from the traditionalist Jim Knox when the CTU was formed. Although a leading member of the pro-Moscow SUP, with a long history of union politicking, Douglas was a major catalyst in the shift of union policy away from the 1894 model to a recognition of the need for union rationalization and for a clear strategy in the new production and market circumstances of the late 1980s. Douglas also has the political influence within the union movement to facilitate change.

Douglas's characteristics are found elsewhere in the union movement. I have already commented on the changing profile of the full-time official. The rise to prominence of younger leaders brings to the union movement bright, well-informed, competent strategists whose knowledge extends far beyond the wage and conditions issues of the old-style bargaining structure. For want of a better description, they combine strategic vision with practical organizational and bargaining skills and, consequently, have been able to influence the CTU and wider union thinking about the need for comprehensive change. There is still an "old guard" who are less committed to change and who display a traditionalism grounded in the compulsory arbitration model. In many cases, this traditionalism is related to membership needs not yet greatly challenged by change or to the existence of members in traditional, even decaying sectors, but in others it is simply a conservatism on the individual leaders' parts that permeates their union activities. Delicate negotiations at the CTU level have helped reconcile the promoters of change and the traditionalists.

Conclusion

There is a consensus in New Zealand that unions are in crisis. They are assailed on a number of fronts: their relevance to their members, their role in the bargaining process, their role in restructured and competitive production, their involvement with the Labour Party, and their ability to change. On all fronts, the unions are on the defensive and must rely on the quality of the leadership to produce effective responses. There are some signs that appropriate responses are forthcoming, thereby reducing the appeal of decentralized bargaining to employers and the government. But matters are still fragile.

The National Party's victory in the 1990 elections may bring about dramatic changes for New Zealand's union movement. The party's intention is to sweep away the traditional bargaining framework and introduce a system based essentially on the individual employment contract. The Employment Contracts Bill, introduced into Parliament in December 1990 and enacted in 1991, proposes voluntary unionism, the removal of the union's sole right of representation of a particular group of workers, bargaining based on the individual employment contract rather than collective agreements, the end of the award system established in 1894, markedly more limited personal grievance procedures, greater limitations on the right to strike, and a range of other changes.

In the short term, it is the effects of voluntary unionism on the private sector that will have the greatest effect as many unions, particularly in service industries, anticipate losses of membership of up to 50 percent. These losses will have an inevitable effect on the resources available to unions in the period of major bargaining reform. In that unionism has always been voluntary in the state sector, state-sector unions are likely to feel the effects of this measure to a lesser extent.

The proposed changes in bargaining on paper are draconian, but it is not clear to what extent they will lead to a decay of the collective bargaining system. Many employers, particularly major companies, are likely to continue to have collective bargaining agreements for reasons of efficiency, industrial order, and tradition. Some smaller employers may well take the opportunity to move to a more fragmented, contract-based model, but it is difficult to say how widespread this option is likely to be. It may not be the actual demise of collective bargaining as much as the threat of such a demise that will have the most significant effect on the unions. Unions will be operating in a framework in which management may at any time seek to move from collective agreements to either an individual-contract model or collective bargaining with other nonunion bargaining agents. Weak unions, or unions operating in sectors that are difficult to organize, may find their effectiveness compromised by this situation. Strong unions in well-organized sectors will be less likely to face problems on this front.

It is clear that the New Zealand union movement faces a further period of radical change in its bargaining system that promises to be far more difficult than that experienced after 1984. The need to respond strategically to the changes of the 1980s is even more urgent in the 1990s. It is difficult to be sanguine about the future of unions in the coming decade.

Part IV.
Overview

11
Variations in Patterns of Trade Unionism: A Synthesis

Stephen Frenkel

Previous chapters in this volume examined the nature of trade unionism in each of nine Asia-Pacific countries. They present a diverse picture in which each union movement appears to be unique in its structural and causal features. In this chapter I abstract from the detail in a search for cross-national commonalities. These are expressed in the form of a typology of union patterns. Care will be taken, however, not to overemphasize the similarities in unions, which would lead to an oversimplified view of union behavior. In addition, I shall adopt a perspective that acknowledges change, especially since some union movements are in a process of transition and others are likely to be affected imminently by political developments.

I begin by elaborating on some of the concepts referred to in the first chapter. These ideas, particularly those on the nature of state-union relations, are then used to identify three principal union patterns—state corporatist, state exclusionary, and state collaborative—as well as several variations on these themes, including Japanese enterprise-based unionism. In the second section, I examine this interpretation of unions in light of the twelve hypotheses summarized in chapter 1. I find relatively

I would like to thank the contributors for supplying additional information for this chapter. My thanks also to Bowhoa Song and Karen Shire for data on Korea and Japan respectively. Christian Berggren, Fred Deyo, Chris Leggett, David Levin, Paul Marginson, and George Strauss provided useful comments on a previous draft of this chapter.

strong evidence for conjectures relating political elements such as party systems, state development strategies, and labor policies to trade unionism, although the role of various elites, including MNCs, in determining government policy lay beyond the scope of the current inquiry. The third section looks at the 1990s, noting recent developments and attempting to predict future union patterns. In the final section I offer some suggestions for further research on unions in the Asia-Pacific region.

Trade Union Patterns

Comparative analysis requires a broad consensus on the variables to be selected for comparing cases and adequate measures of these factors. As indicated in chapter 1, the variables and analytical distinctions considered critical to our research are grounded in a well-established literature. As for the measures, there is room for disagreement where measurement is based essentially on a reading of qualitative data derived from national case studies. Disagreement cannot be avoided in exploratory research whose primary aim is to discover, categorize, and interpret limited data, unlike tests of well-defined theories based on accumulated information and knowledge. I did, however, take the precaution of checking my interpretation of variables against other research findings, leading in some cases to a revision of the initial assessment of a variable. Confidence in the interpretation of certain variables is thereby strengthened, despite the subjective nature of the measures. Table 11.1 provides a summary of the findings for 1989–90 for Japan and each of the nine countries examined in this book (Hong Kong is not a country but is referred to as such). Subsequent change is reserved for later discussion.

The first three columns on the left side of table 11.1 summarize state-union relations. State control over unions is ordered along a continuum from high to low. As with other subjective measures, the terms *high* and *low* are used relative to other union movements included in the study. As noted in chapter 1, involvement in state decision making can vary independently of state control; for example, given high state control over unions, governments may wish to include unions in economic decision making and/or prescribe significant union involvement at the workplace level, or state managers may choose to exclude unions from both macro and micro arenas. Trends in government policy provide a guide to current and future tendencies. Governments may seek various goals ranging from preservation of the status quo to changing extant arrangements in the direction of weakening or maintaining the union movement's role.

The next five columns in table 11.1 summarize various aspects of union structure. The inclusive/exclusive dimension is denoted chiefly by

Table 11.1. Union configurations in ten Asia-Pacific countries, 1989–90

Country	State control of unions	Involvement in state decision making	Government policy	Union density (%)	Principle of membership aggregation	Enterprise unions[a] (%)	No. of unions	Unity and no. of peak orgs.	Central-ization	Joint regulation
DCs										
China	high	high	preserve/worker support	90	mainly industry	0	15	high; 1	high	low
Thailand	medium	low	weaken	6	enterprise/industry	65	713	low; 5	med./low	low
Malaysia	medium	low	weaken	14	enterprise/industry	55	411	low; 2	low	low
NICs										
Korea	high	low	weaken	24	enterprise	>90	7,883	low; 2	low	low
Taiwan	high	low	ambivalent	33	occupational/enterprise	42	3,462	low; 2	low	low
Hong Kong	low	low	preserve	19	occupational/other	<20	452	low; 3	low	low
Singapore	high	high	preserve/worker support	17	enterprise/other	45	83	high; 1	high	medium
APs										
Australia	low	high	rationalize	41	occupational/general	<10	295	high; 1	high	high
New Zealand	low	medium	rationalize	48	occupational/general	<10	112	high; 1	medium	med./high
Advanced Core										
Japan	low	low	preserve	26	enterprise	>90	72,605	low; 3	low	medium

Sources: Matsuzaki 1992; Nagamine 1991; New Zealand union density based on estimate by Peter Boxall (personal communication); other New Zealand data from Hince and Vranken 1991:491.

[a] Denotes the percentage of enterprise unions in relation to the total number of unions. Union density refers to the percentage of the nonagricultural work force that is unionized. For Australia, Hong Kong, Singapore, and Japan the density figure includes agricultural employees. Apart from Japan, where about 7 percent of employees work in agriculture, the size of this sector is very small and so does not affect international comparisons.

union density (union members as a proportion of nonagricultural employees) and the principle of membership aggregation (the main contours along which employees are organized in unions). Industry-based unions are inclusive, whereas occupational and especially enterprise-based unions are said to be exclusive. Thus, the number of enterprise unions as a proportion of the total and the total number of unions provide further empirical indicators. The extent of union unity gives some idea of the factionalism and rivalry within the movement, especially when the number of peak councils is taken into account. The centralization of decision making conveys a picture of the concentration or dispersion of power, although, as noted in chapter 1, a union movement need not be centralized to be powerful. The joint regulation variable is included to take account of this point and as an indicator of union methods. High levels of joint regulation imply consensus over a relatively wide range of issues at any one or more organizational levels and hence reliance on bargaining, while low levels of joint regulation imply the unilateral imposition of wages and conditions, usually by employers. This may evoke industrial action when circumstances permit. To facilitate identification and discussion of union patterns, figure 11.1 applies these ideas to unions in the ten countries.

Figure 11.1 shows three main configurations or ideal types with several variants. The main ordering principle is the nature of state-union relations, while structural features represent secondary means of distinguishing different union patterns. State-union relations vary according to the relative power of the state. Strong states may incorporate or exclude unions from decision making (Valenzuela 1989), but where the distribution of power between the state and unions is less unequal, the state is more likely to enter into collaborative arrangements with unions and other interest groups. State corporatism reflects the presence of a strong state in which unions are strictly controlled by the government yet included in decision-making bodies at the macro and/or micro level. China represents a socialist version, whereas Singaporean unionism differs in ways that are explored below.

Figure 11.1. Union patterns in ten Asia-Pacific countries, 1990

Union pattern	Variant	Country
State corporatist	socialist	China
	capitalist	Singapore
State exclusionary	repressive	Thailand, Malaysia
	autonomous, market	Hong Kong
	autonomous, enterprise	Japan
	transitional	Korea, Taiwan
State collaborative	autonomous, market	New Zealand
	bargained corporatism	Australia

The second pattern is characterized by state exclusion or union marginalization that relies mainly but not exclusively on repression in addition to the law, which is intended to prevent unions from becoming politically involved by confining unionism largely to the labor market. These characteristics are evident in Thailand and Malaysia, although repression is more evident in the former country.

Where the law is the primary instrument guaranteeing autonomy in the industrial sphere, unions will tend to differ in strategy and methods according to their principles of membership aggregation. Thus, we distinguish Hong Kong from Japanese unionism; the former is based mainly on the occupational aggregating principle, which encourages coordination of demands across firms in the local labor market, and contrasts with the enterprise union principle, which favors intraorganizational wage comparisons and coordination. A transitional variant is represented by the notion that a mixture of more than one union type can arise from organizational change in which past forms are not completely superseded by emerging structures.[1] Thus, Korea and Taiwan combine state corporatist and exclusionary repressive union patterns in which the autonomous variant was on the ascendant in the late 1980s.

The third type, state collaborative, more commonly approximates the institutional arrangements in advanced societies. It implies a formal class compromise involving employers' and workers' representatives and the state. This may occur following a particularly momentous bout of industrial conflict—as, for example, in the late 1930s in Sweden, or as part of a process of major social and economic reconstruction, as in Germany, Japan, and the United States immediately following World War II. It tends to take the form of an agreement on fundamentals enshrined in a raft of new labor legislation. This may institutionalize bargaining by autonomous unions, or it may assume a variety of bargained corporatist forms, some involving closer relationships between capital and the state, others fostering union involvement in national-level decisions (Katzenstein 1985; Frenkel 1991).

State Corporatist Pattern

Beginning with the state corporatist pattern, the Chinese socialist and Singaporean capitalist variants are quite similar vis-à-vis the three union-state relations variables and two of the three other union structure variables shown in table 11.1. Some differences are evident in terms of state control and the extent of joint regulation. There are much larger differences with respect to union inclusiveness, insofar as China has a high union density and membership aggregation based mainly on industrial lines. In Singapore, union density is low and declining, and although 45 percent of its unions are organized along enterprise lines, a proportion that is increasing over time, this gives a false impression, for nearly two-thirds of its unionists are members of 20 percent of the unions. These are relatively large occupational, industrial, and to a lesser extent general unions (see tables 8.1, 8.3, and 8.4).

The similarities and differences between unions in China and Singapore reflect different forms of state corporatism. In both cases, the state supports and involves unions in decision making through a single encompassing peak council, but this is achieved in quite different ways (see chaps. 2 and 8). In China, the party and the government compel employees to join the appropriate union. Although the Chinese Federation of Labor is included in consultations with the government over labor and welfare legislation, there is no evidence that it exerts any independent influence (see chap. 2). Indeed, party control over key union positions appears to ensure official union compliance.

In Singapore, the state does not require employees to be union members. In fact, the incentive to join unions has been limited by labor shortages, rising real wages, and statutory requirements for the provision of benefits, which amounted to nearly 40 percent of wages in 1990 (ADB 1991:73–74). Employers and unions are, however, allowed to support the union-shop principle in particular enterprises. As in China, senior union officials are members of the ruling party, which is the People's Action Party.[2] Unions are permitted more influence in decision making at the national level through the National Wages Council and in the public sector through joint consultation machinery. In addition, at the workplace level, almost all union members (15 percent of the work force) were covered by collective bargaining agreements in 1990. Moreover, in recent years the government has devolved greater responsibilities for social insurance, education, and welfare to the enterprise (Deyo 1992:303), thereby encouraging unions to focus their efforts at the workplace level. With or without unions, the aim is to foster employee integration into the enterprise. This contrasts with China, where less than 10 percent of employees are covered by collective bargaining agreements, whose capacity to protect and advance employees' interests, especially in foreign joint venture firms, is doubtful (see chap. 2). In addition, there are few legal requirements in China inducing management to pursue employee-involvement strategies. In both countries the state effectively prohibits industrial action. The incorporation of union and worker surveillance by state and party officials has hitherto ensured that strikes are rare and unofficial in China (chap. 2) and virtually unheard of in Singapore (chap. 8).

In sum, Chinese unionism reflects Communist Party ideology, which views unions as transmission-belts for the achievement of largely productionist goals. Singapore's government policy toward unions is pragmatic, shaped by a concern to advance workers' material interests within the scope of the state's development strategy and to elicit workers' continuing commitment to economic growth and PAP support, at least to the extent of not favoring an opposition party.

State Exclusionary Pattern

Unions in Thailand and Malaysia are not controlled by the state to the same extent as in China and Singapore. For example, unions are able to organize according to various aggregating principles (in contrast to China), and, unlike China and Singapore, most unions are not party ancillaries. Government policies in both countries have, however, been oriented toward marginalizing and splitting the union movement. This is seen in Thailand in the lack of labor law enforcement, which is tantamount to condoning labor exploitation and repression by employers, privatization, and, more recently, the disbanding of state enterprise unions (chap. 3).

In Malaysia, similar intentions are illustrated by the imprisonment without trial of the secretary-general of the MTUC, the main peak union council (Standing 1992a:328), the prohibition of unions in "pioneer" industries for three years and the restrictions on issues subject to bargaining in these sectors, the establishment of PUSPANITA as an alternative to unionism for women employed in the public sector, and strong indications of government support for a new peak council (Malaysian Labour Organization) in opposition to the MTUC (chap. 4).

In other respects, unions in these countries are similar. They have relatively few members, especially in Thailand, where enterprise unionism is increasing in importance. Both union movements lack unity, in part because of fragmentation stemming from the size of the organizations (membership in Thailand averages 550 members per union and 1,412 in Malaysia) but also because there are competing peak councils. Around 1990, Thai unions were slightly more centralized than in Malaysia. This reflects the concentration of power in the State Enterprise Labor Relations Group (chap. 3). In both countries union power is very limited, as demonstrated by the low levels of joint regulation, the limited capacity to mobilize employees for industrial action in support of workers' claims, and indebtedness. Thus, in 1990, less than 5 percent of employees were covered by collective bargaining agreements in Malaysia and Thailand, and, as noted in chapter 3, strikes in Thailand were often the result of spontaneous action rather than orchestration by unions, whereas industrial disputes in Malaysia declined substantially in the 1980s (chap. 4). Finally, by the end of the decade, Thai unions appeared to be influenced by foreign organizations (chap. 4), while their Malaysian counterparts were in a difficult financial position (chap. 5).

Hong Kong and Japanese unionism are autonomous variants of the state exclusionary pattern. The former will be touched on briefly, whereas more attention will be paid to Japanese unionism since this is not covered elsewhere. Hong Kong and Japanese unionism share the important characteristic of being subject to limited state control; state strategies are aimed at maintaining close ties between governments and business elites, to the virtual exclusion of the trade unions. In both societies, however, unions are acknowledged by senior government officials as performing a useful function in the labor market as long as they are not a challenge to the status quo.

Unionism in Hong Kong and Japan is dominated by exclusivity: low union density—bearing in mind the developed nature of these economies—and fragmented structures. In the former society, unionism in the private sector is particularly weak, density is about 10 percent, compared with approximately 33 percent in government employment (chap. 7). Although the density is increasing slightly, it reflects the impact of patriarchal and paternalistic forms of management and the efficacy of personal and community networks in resolving work-related problems (Whitley 1992:76–81; Deyo 1989, chap. 5). Union density in Japan is slowly declining from an estimated 30.8 percent in 1980 to 25.2 percent in 1990 (Japan Institute of Labor [JIL] 1991a:48). Density is highest in the largest enterprises, but firms employing five hundred or more regular employees comprise less than 1 percent of Japan's enterprises and are declining over time relative to smaller firms (Nagamine 1991, table 1).[3] In this context it is important to note the decline in the relatively highly unionized public sector, where density, according to the JIL (1991a:49), is about 75 percent, which is more than twice the rate in the largely privately owned manufacturing sector (30.1 percent). Privatization has adversely affected some of the strongest left-wing unions.[4] The fragmentation of Japanese unions reflects the enterprise-based structure of unionism whereby most unions restrict their membership to permanent employees, who comprised nearly 75 percent of the approximately 47 million total employees in 1990 (JIL 1991a:25).[5] Union members are spread over a vast number of relatively small enterprises, so that unions in Japan are probably on average smaller than in Hong Kong (1,032 persons).[6] In the latter society, unions are organized on various bases, the most common being according to occupation (chap. 7). It is this difference that distinguishes these two variants of state exclusionary autonomous unionism. Its significance lies in the labor market and political consequences of these different bases of union organization, a subject I shall return to shortly.

With regard to other organizational features, the differences are less striking and consequential than the similarities. Thus, Hong Kong's peak councils have been divided along political lines, but, as noted in chapter 7, the pro-Taiwan TUC is declining and the China-oriented FTU is increasingly challenged by the recently formed, politically independent Confederation of Trade Unions of Hong Kong. In Japan, the major private-

and public-sector union confederations merged in 1989 to form Rengo (Japanese Trade Union Confederation), which covers an estimated 62 percent of union members (JIL 1991b). The other two peak councils are Zenroren (aligned to the Japan Communist Party), with nearly 7 percent of total union members, and Zenrokyo (aligned with the left wing of the Japan Socialist Party and other left-wing groups), with 2.4 percent (JIL 1991b). The remaining 29 percent of unionists are members of non-affiliated unions.

In addition to the limited authority of peak councils and federations vis-à-vis enterprise unions, conflicting political policies between Rengo and the other two peak councils, Zenroren and Zenrokyo, are complicated by major policy differences within Rengo (JIL 1991c). These are mainly between public-sector unions previously affiliated with Sohyo, representing the staunchly socialist Social Democratic Party of Japan (previously called the Japan Socialist Party), and those previously affiliated with Domei, dominating the more right-wing, Western-oriented, social democratic Democratic Socialist Party. The political views of unions associated with these two parties and those of nonaligned unions within Rengo have as yet been impossible to reconcile in support of Rengo's espoused position (JIL 1991c; Nitta 1991). This is to facilitate a merger of the main opposition parties (excluding the Japan Communist Party) to create a viable alternative to the Liberal Democratic Party, which has dominated Japanese postwar politics (JIL 1992a:3). The absence of any clear moves toward unity thus far justifies Japanese unionism being designated low on the unity dimension in table 11.1.

Although Japanese unions may be more dependent on management than in most other advanced societies, they have certainly been more effective in promoting their members' interests than their Hong Kong counterparts. As we shall see, this is less evident at the macro level. In Hong Kong, unions are represented on the Labour Advisory Board and are gradually expanding their representation on advisory committees, but they have very limited influence in the Legislative Council and no presence in the colony's Executive Council. At the national level, Japanese unions are arguably not much better off. They are generally excluded from the corridors of power (Pempel and Tsunekawa 1979; Wade 1990:327) but are involved in tripartite consultations over industry restructuring, budget expenditures, and labor legislation (Matsuzaki 1992; Nitta 1988:8; Taylor 1989:114). At enterprise and workplace levels, however, Japanese employees benefit from relatively well-financed unions whose average dues are set at 1.8 percent of wages, which is well above the rate in Hong Kong and in the other countries discussed in this volume.[7] Moreover, in Hong Kong, only about 4 percent of employees are covered by collective bargaining agreements (chap. 7); the corresponding figure for Japan is 25 percent. Industrial action is low in both societies. According to T. Inagami (1988), in 1986, nearly 71 percent of collective bargaining agreements in Japan contained a clause requiring eligible employees to join their relevant union, thereby guaranteeing unions a sound financial base.

The incidence of joint consultation in Japan is also extensive: about 70 percent of firms report the use of this mechanism. Joint consultation is found most commonly in large, highly unionized establishments (Inagami 1988; Kuwahara 1990:161). It is widely used to disseminate and discuss sensitive information, and is more likely where establishments are large, labor-intensive, and operate with continuous-process technology (Morishima 1992). Joint consultation is viewed positively by both management and employees, which partly explains the trend toward expanding the scope and use of this mechanism to deal with wages and bonuses, working hours, welfare benefits, rationalization of production through new technology, and organizational change. This trend may be interpreted as reflecting a decline in union power as the bargaining agenda is narrowed to make way for an expansion of joint consultation (Eccleston 1989:83). Alternatively, one might argue that the expanded process of consultation is a consequence of management vulnerability to more competitive and unstable markets, which in turn leads to greater dependence on employees and unions, as illustrated by the more frequent use of joint consultation over wage rises prior to the formal Shunto negotiations (Morishima 1992). Since consultation and bargaining are not as sharply differentiated in Japan as in other Western countries, the result is decisions that more often take account of union views (see Inagami 1988:25). Recent research showing the adverse impact of unionization or productivity and profitability in 979 Japanese manufacturing plants suggests that Japanese unions do indeed exert substantial influence on management (Brunello 1992). The controversial issue of trends in union influence cannot, however, be resolved without further research, but three factors—one favoring more union influence and two limiting union power—need to be borne in mind. On the one hand, persistent labor shortages in the context of fierce product market competition give the unions leverage; on the other hand, rapid firm and industry restructuring on the basis of advanced technology, and the increasing use of multitrack employment systems and payment procedures emphasizing ability rather than seniority (Inagami 1988; Whittaker 1990) can be expected to weaken the unions' hand.

More generally, despite the achievements of Japanese unionism in terms of job security, wage increases, and the reduction of inequalities between regular blue- and white-collar employees (Koike 1988:249–60; Shimada 1988), the aggregation of members on an enterprise basis has restricted union power and hence the extent of joint regulation. The main effects include reinforcement of an enterprise rather than social or class consciousness among employees and segmentation of the work force so that labor aristocrats co-exist with disadvantaged workers. These tendencies have resulted in weak organization at the industrial and national level and a consequent failure to prosecute effectively issues that compromise the interests of individual firms. The most notable examples involve labor effort (Shimada 1992:8), working time (Deutschmann 1991), and social welfare (Eccleston 1989:96–99).[8]

The state exclusionary transitional variant is exemplified by Korea and Taiwan. Unionism in these societies bears the imprint of both a repressive past and a more liberal present associated with the emergence of democratic politics. Until recently, state control over unions was strong in both countries. This involved infiltration by government officials (Korea) and party members (Taiwan) and the election of senior union leaders to the party-controlled legislative assembly (Taiwan) (Sharma and Sephton 1991:430). At the micro level, consultative councils were expected to integrate workers into the enterprise (Deyo 1989). In both countries, repressive and corporatist elements co-existed, although the former were more dominant in Korea and the latter more prominent in Taiwan. The state's goals in Korea and Taiwan were the same: to exclude and marginalize autonomous unions. In response to popular demonstrations in Korea, however, the government eased its repressive policies and introduced some reforms, which were noted in chapter 1. But, as suggested in chapter 5, there has been little change in the overall thrust of government policy toward autonomous unionism. Continued state repression is evident from the rise in the number of workers sentenced for industrial action or associated activities.[9] The new unions have therefore had no legal basis from which to strengthen their position (chap. 5; Ogle 1990:160–61).

Union behavior is less predictable than in the past, however, as the old-style unions begin to reflect the expectations of a younger generation of employees. In Taiwan, the lifting of martial law in 1987 signaled an end to repression and the growth of opposition political parties, but by the end of the decade enthusiasm for autonomous unionism and the struggle for higher wages and better conditions had dissipated. The KMT was regrouping in the face of a divided political opposition, while a less buoyant economy gave employers an opportunity to dismiss new-style union leaders (chap. 6 and personal communication, Nai-teh Wu). Meanwhile, the state remained ambivalent, "caught between the government's traditional role of suppressing labor's demands to advance economic growth, and its role as the champion of workers' rights" (Kleingartner and Peng 1991:431).

Union density is relatively low in Korea and especially in Taiwan, given that home workers and self-employed persons have joined occupational unions for insurance purposes (chap. 6). Nevertheless, union membership increased rapidly in the second half of the 1980s (chaps. 5 and 6), reflecting the surge in collective assertiveness following two decades of rapid economic growth and limited progress toward democracy.

With regard to the aggregation of union members, in 1980, the Korean government restructured the union movement on an enterprise basis (chap. 5), whereas in Taiwan, unions were not compelled to organize along enterprise lines. Indeed, occupational unionism has proved more popular, reflecting the preferences of small-enterprise employees and eligible independent contractors. Nevertheless, 42 percent of unions are of the enterprise type.

By the end of the decade, the union movements in both societies were divided between new, more radical unions and those sanctioned and nurtured by the state. With the emphasis on industrial action and organization at the point of production, the rise of the new unions tended to decentralize the movement further. In Korea, the FKTU attempted to stabilize labor relations by establishing a tripartite consultative council, but this was superseded by a body without government representation (see chap. 1). Not surprisingly, joint regulation remained limited in both countries, with employers preferring to assert their rights and eliminate so-called agitators from the work force. But whether workers, particularly in Korea, will accept the limited role assigned to them by employers and the state is a moot point.

State Collaborative Pattern

State collaborative unionism is the third type of pattern. It is distinguished by legislation guaranteeing a major role for unions in the labor market. In Australia and New Zealand, historically significant class compromises were struck following the defeat of unions in large-scale industrial unrest in the 1890s (Deery and Plowman 1991, chap. 10; Deeks and Boxall 1989, chap. 2). These social contracts involved jurisdictional guarantees regarding union membership and access to statutory conciliation and arbitration systems. Membership has been fostered by awards permitting employment preference clauses to be included for unionists and through the practice of the closed shop. Unions have also been able to prosecute their claims, sometimes in contravention of decisions by arbitration tribunals. State controls over union structure have regulated union competition and ensured a minimum level of democracy in these organizations.

With regard to involvement in state decision making, Australian unions, together with federal and state governments and employers, have for many years been represented in national wage cases in which the nation's industrial relations guidelines were periodically reviewed and decided upon. Until recently in New Zealand, similar jurisdictional guarantees and advantages accrued to unions, although award making has tended to be at the industry level, usually with assistance from a statutory tribunal. Australian unions have also been more highly involved in national-level decision making on account of the macro-level Accords negotiated between the ACTU and the Labor government during the 1980s (chap. 9). Despite differences in union involvement in state decision making, the governments and peak union councils in both countries have been keen to rationalize the number and structure of unions and to reorganize bargaining units, thereby facilitating "strategic unionism.".

The structure of unions in Australia and New Zealand reflects a common ancestry in British occupational unionism, which took root in the early nineteenth century. Thus, many unions in these countries had their origins before the burst of industrialization following World War I. This contrasts with small countries such as Norway and Sweden, where occupational unions were virtually swept away by rapid industrialization based on high levels of industrial concentration, relatively advanced technology, and a more specialized product range, all of which facilitated membership aggregation along industry lines (Ingham 1974).

Unions in Australia on average are nearly twice the size of similar organizations in New Zealand, although the civilian work force is more than six times the size. Australian unions are thus smaller than might be anticipated given the size of the labor force. This reflects the distribution of the urban work force among several cities separated by large distances, and the federal constitution, which permits industrial relations legislation and associated union registration to operate on both state and federal levels. Unions originally registered in one of six states and only later, with the help of federal legislation, spread nationwide. Many organizations never expanded or did so haphazardly. Also relevant is the impact of recent legislation encouraging union mergers, especially among smaller unions. This has already had time to have an effect in New Zealand (chap. 10), whereas it is only beginning to have an impact in Australia (chap. 9).

Both union movements are relatively unified, although the creation of single peak councils has occurred only recently—in 1981 in Australia and in 1987 in New Zealand. Factionalism exists, but it is muted compared with the past. On account of the Accord and the Australian Labor government's commitment to inclusion of the ACTU in economic decision making, Australian unions are more centralized than in New Zealand. In the latter case, the Labour government, which held office from 1984 to 1991, was not prepared to enter into the so-called compact that leading officials in the CTU were advocating (chap. 10). Moreover, despite continuing government support for union involvement in wage determination, the policy of economic deregulation and decentralization of industrial relations limited the extent of joint regulation. Hence, New Zealand is rated lower (medium/high) on this dimension in table 11.1.

This analysis has shown that although union patterns vary cross-nationally, they can be grouped into three theoretically coherent categories (state corporatist, state exclusionary, and state collaborative) and several subcategories based on state power and strategy, and particular structural attributes. In the following section I return to the theme of state-union relations and politics more generally after discussing national union patterns in relation to the hypotheses based on modernization and international labor market theories outlined in chapter 1.

Union Patterns and Relevant Theorizing

Modernization theory

I begin with the conjecture of C. Kerr and his colleagues on the role of elites in shaping industrialization and unionism. Our study was too limited to explore the complex issue of the characteristics and dynamics of elites; nevertheless, a picture of elites can be constructed from information provided in chapter 1 and secondary sources. Using Kerr et al.'s (1975) concepts, this picture suggests that the following elites are key agents in the industrialization process of their respective countries: China—revolutionary intellectuals; Thailand—military/nationalist leaders; Malaysia—dynastic/nationalist leaders; Korea, Taiwan, and Singapore—nationalist leaders; Hong Kong—colonial administrators; Australia and New Zealand—middle-class/nationalist leaders; and Japan—dynastic leaders.[10]

Reference to figure 11.1 suggests some correspondence between elites and union patterns even at similar levels of industrialization. Consistent with their different elites, China's, Hong Kong's, and Japan's union patterns have no parallels. This is not so in relation to Korea's and Taiwan's elites, on the one hand, and Australia's and New Zealand's, on the other. There is a close correspondence between union patterns within the two pairs of countries but marked differences between unions across these two sets of societies. The hypothesis does not explain, however, why Thailand and Malaysia have similar union patterns; nor does it account for Singapore's state corporatist form of unionism. It is nevertheless possible that a more detailed analysis and conceptualization of elites could explain Singapore's distinctive form of unionism. Commonalities and differences in some but not all elements of Thai and Malaysian unions might also be explained by a finer examination of the characteristics of their elites. For example, the Thai union pattern is distinguished from its Malaysian counterpart by a greater use of coercion in repressing autonomous unionism. Consequently, industrial conflict assumes more violent forms. There is a parallel here with Korea, where, as noted in chapter 5, workers have been especially militant compared with Taiwan, where the KMT has been more successful in channeling dissent by incorporation and limited democratization. In both Thailand and Korea, as distinct from Malaysia and to a lesser extent Taiwan, the military has been a pivotal influence within the ruling elite.

The proposition linking greater use of coercion against unions with a strong military presence in a society's industrializing elite appears to be supported by a consideration of the remaining six societies. Only in China did the military occupy a key position. It is thus not coincidental that autonomous unionism has been brutally suppressed and union leaders severely punished, as highlighted in the aftermath of the 1989 Tiananmen Square massacre (chap. 2). Thus, if this line of approach is to succeed, the primary bases of power need to feature in the definition of each of the types of elites. More generally, shortcomings of the elite theory highlight the need for its integration into a wider state-centered approach. This would involve linking the types of elites to the generation of specific labor strategies and tracing the extent to which labor policies are implemented effectively. In sum, the evidence tends to support the elite hypothesis, but this perspective would be more useful if it were included in a broader reformulation that accounted for weaknesses noted above.

There is very limited support for the well-known convergence on the pluralistic industrialism hypothesis. At the most general level, the hypothesis accounts for our findings, that is, that unions in the developing countries of China, Thailand, and Malaysia have the least influence in shaping labor relations in the workplace, while their counterparts in the advanced peripheral countries of Australia and New Zealand have the most influence. Unions in Korea and Taiwan fit the argument since they appear to be on the road to achieving more influence. But what of Japan, whose influence (outside the largest companies) is probably no greater than in the latter two countries? From the standpoint of this hypothesis, Hong Kong and to a lesser extent Singapore are also problematic in that the impact of unions in the workplace is limited yet the economic structures of these societies—as shown in table 11.1—more closely resemble those in the advanced countries than in the developing countries.

An untenable assumption of the conventional convergence thesis is that industrialization will lead to a more powerful working class. The experiences of Hong Kong and Singapore show that without mass production in heavy industries, workers' power is limited, especially where the state shapes union patterns before or at an early stage of the industrialization process (Singapore) and where employers adopt paternalistic employment practices (Japan).

The next hypothesis focuses on those conditions in developing countries that are expected to encourage political unionism. Transposed to advanced societies, this hypothesis suggests that political strategies will be paramount where unemployment is high and persistent by recent historical standards. In that only two advanced countries in our sample experienced continuous high unemployment, this conjecture cannot be adequately assessed. A comparison between Australia—which supports the hypothesis—and New Zealand—which does not—is nevertheless instructive insofar as it suggests three conditions that distinguish these cases. First, the union movement in Australia retained substantial influence in the Labor Party through the maintenance of strong ties between senior union leaders and government ministers. Second, the Australian union movement was led by a group of particularly impressive, strategically minded officials. And third, being more centralized than its New Zealand counterpart, the Australian industrial relations system was more amenable to a national-level bipartite approach to policy making. These conditions need to be taken into account in a revised hypothesis. A final, more speculative point is that although the existence of a left-oriented government tends to increase the probability that a union movement will adopt a political strategy when the labor market is chronically weak, the New Zealand experience suggests that governments may perceive bargained corporatist arrangements as barriers to effecting rapid structural adjustment. With limited pressure from the unions, governments may prefer to avoid such arrangements.

S. Lash and J. Urry (1987) are pessimistic about the future of political bargains negotiated by trade unions in advanced countries. According to their alternative convergence hypothesis, structural changes (summarized in chap. 1) are "disorganizing" unionism and undermining corporatist arrangements. Again, there are too few cases to gauge the efficacy of this hypothesis; however, evidence on union density for Australia, New Zealand, and Japan are consistent with the thesis. At the same time, depending on one's interpretation, the Australian case poses a problem for the argument regarding the decline of bargained corporatism, for, as noted in chapter 9, the Accords emerged for the first time in 1983 and have been sustained for ten years in spite of declining union power in the labor market. A contrary argument favoring the hypothesis is that since 1987, national-level bargaining has devolved an increasing number of labor relations decisions to the enterprise, signifying a decline in the content, though not as yet the institutional form of bargained corporatism.

Proponents of the next hypothesis argue that later developers will emulate Japan and hence adopt enterprise unionism. Two mechanisms identified in chapter 1 were government policy and Japanese corporations engaged in foreign direct investment. Considering the latter aspect first, the relevant data are as follows. Over the period 1951–88, the largest five recipients of Japanese direct investment in Asia were Indonesia (30.6 percent), Hong Kong (19.2 percent), Singapore (11.9 percent), Korea (10.1 percent), China (6.3 percent), and Thailand (6.2 percent) (ADB 1991:46). In addition, data presented in chapter 1 covering the second half of the 1980s show that Thailand received especially large injections of Japanese capital.

Evaluation of the hypothesis needs to take two points into account. First, levels of foreign investment relative to domestic sources vary between countries, and, second, with the exception of Thailand, Malaysia, and Singapore (see chap. 1), the absence of data on foreign direct investment from countries other than Japan should make us cautious about assuming a strong Japanese influence, at least from this source. Nevertheless, with the exception of China, where foreign investment comprises a very small proportion of total investment, it is reasonable to suppose that these societies will show evidence of Japanese labor practices, including enterprise unionism.

There is support for a hypothesis linking Japanese investment *and* commodity chains (based on supplier-producer networks) to union patterns.[11] Consider the evidence. Korea is almost entirely based on enterprise unionism, and this form of unionism is relatively strong in Thailand. It is less significant in Singapore and even more limited in Hong Kong. Thus, in Thailand but also Malaysia, where Japanese investment is less significant but nevertheless important, enterprise-based organization is one of the main aggregating principles. This is also true of Singapore, although to a more limited extent, partly because of the dominance of U.S. capital but also because restructuring industry-based and general unions is a protracted and difficult process. In line with the hypothesis, it is worth noting that state-controlled Indonesian unions are structured according to enterprise and sector (ILO 1991a:67).

Korea and Taiwan are more problematic cases in terms of the hypothesis. Neither is a large recipient of Japanese investment relative to other sources, yet Korean unionism is very largely enterprise-based whereas, as shown in table 11.1, only a substantial minority of Taiwanese unions are similarly organized. By contrast, Hong Kong receives considerable Japanese foreign direct investment but has very few enterprise-based unions. Can these three anomalies be explained?

Employers have played a significant role in shaping enterprise-based unionism in Korea (chap. 5). The strong supplier-producer relations between Japanese and Korean firms—which encourage conformity to Japanese manufacturing requirements, including enterprise-based unionism—are additional sources of support. The same argument applies to Taiwan, though with less force since the United States appears to have had more influence on that country's labor policies and U.S. firms have been more prominent investors in Taiwan. With regard to Hong Kong,

compared with local enterprises, Japanese companies have limited influence in labor relations. Moreover, the weak union presence in the private
sector (where union density is about 10 percent) permits Japanese
companies to operate substantially without unions, which they prefer.
Hence, the incidence of company-based unionism is low in Hong Kong.

The second major mechanism, emphasized by R. Dore (1974), is the
role of the state. More specifically, I refer here to government policy that
seeks to adapt the Japanese model to take account of domestic priorities
and endowments. This is most explicit in Malaysia's Look East policy,
although E. F. Vogel (1991:90–91) claims that the Japanese development
model was closely studied by the governments of Korea and Singapore
and was also influential in Taiwan and Hong Kong. Given a connection
between development strategy and labor policies—which later I demonstrate exists—there is strong prima facie support for this argument.
Indeed, further research would probably show that the state effect is
more important than the foreign investment effect since nonunionism is
a viable option for Japanese companies in many industrializing countries.
Nevertheless, in the absence of detailed information on the origins of
government labor policies, a partial exception being Korea (see Choi
1989), my assessment must remain somewhat tentative.

To conclude, the evidence supports the convergence on Japan thesis
but only to the extent that Japanese foreign direct investment is significant and/or governments favor and are capable of implementing Japan-
oriented policies. This is subject to the qualification that differences in
institutional and cultural contexts are likely to result in structures that
bear only a limited likeness to their Japanese counterparts.

The final hypothesis in the tradition of modernization theory is restricted to industrializing and recently industrialized countries. This
states that the level of industrialization strongly influences the nature of
unionism. Thus, unions in the developing countries of China, Thailand,
and Malaysia should be similar, focusing primarily on economic matters
and hence leading to conflict with the state. At a higher economic level,
unions in the four Asian NICs should resemble one another as they
become incorporated by the superior power of the state. This hypothesis
is too simplistic. According to the summary in Table 11.1, developing
countries fall into one of two categories—state corporatist (socialist) or
state exclusionary, repressive variant.

The Chinese case suggests that a state corporatist strategy can predate
any substantial conflict with the modern union movement but that it is
probably more likely to arise after a showdown with the unions, as
occurred in Singapore and to a lesser extent in Taiwan. The alternative
emphasis on repression has prevailed in Thailand and Malaysia. So, as
Deyo (1989) has convincingly argued, challenges to the power of the

state and employers can be preempted to varying extents by government policy at early stages of the industrialization process.

The hypothesis is also unconvincing in relation to the NICs. Although Singapore confirms the hypothesis, Hong Kong does not, for there is little state control of, or involvement in, Hong Kong unions. The cases of Korea and Taiwan are interesting, for they suggest that under particular conditions—highly competitive markets coupled with unilateral management relying on low-cost, disciplined, semiskilled workers (see Amsden 1990:17–18) and authoritarian governments—the frustration of an expanded and more powerful working class will eventually explode, leading to increasing support for unions and other groups demanding industrial and political participation, and to higher levels of conflict. The consequences of this activity in terms of inflation, reduced investment, and slower growth may create opposition from other (middle-class) groups, at least in the short term. A reintegration of unions into the state is not likely, but neither is a historic class compromise favorable to labor inevitable. Various forms of settlement are possible, including the institutionalization of autonomous enterprise unionism, highlighted by postwar Japan.

International Labor Market Theory

Turning now to international labor market theory, what evidence is there that the location of low-cost manufacturing in industrializing countries has led to union repression and marginalization by the governments of these societies and those of advanced countries? One answer to this question is that MNCs have been a leading factor in countering unions, inasmuch as their behavior in doing so is condoned by governments in host countries. A stronger interpretation is that MNCs have pursued such strategies *and* have directly influenced government labor policy. These claims are difficult to assess with existing data. Available evidence suggests that, in general, American and European MNCs are no more likely to oppose unions than are local firms (Banaji and Hensman 1990; Enderwick 1985). This may not be true of particular sectors, however, and may be less applicable to Japanese and ethnic Chinese firms.

Regarding government policy, it appears that foreign corporations in the special economic zones of China and in Malaysian manufacturing industry have influenced the labor policies of the respective governments. Indeed, governments in the region generally are likely to take this factor into account, but we do not know to what extent this is a result of consultation with, and influence by, foreign corporations.[12] Moreover, there are other reasons for attempting to incorporate or marginalize unions, not least of which is to suppress political opposition. There are also good reasons governments choose not to pursue this

strategy. For instance, such action must be weighed against the consequences of reduced government legitimacy both at home among a
growing working class and overseas, for, as we have observed in relation
to China, Thailand, Malaysia, and Taiwan, foreign states and international
organizations do apply pressure on governments to moderate repressive
labor policies.

Efficacy is another consideration, for the Japanese model shows that
repression is not the only means of domesticating workers' organizations.
Indeed, state control has not proved to be a viable long-term solution, as
evidenced by the growth of alternative union movements in Korea and
Taiwan.

Finally, as regards the advanced peripheral countries, both Australia
and New Zealand have experienced deindustrialization and growing
unemployment, arguably arising from too little local and foreign investment. There is no evidence that foreign MNCs have been more active
than similar-sized local firms in marginalizing unions (Huybregts 1988).
The Australian federal government and the tribunals have protected the
institutional interests of the union movement, albeit within limited
parameters (chap. 9). In New Zealand, the government was more forth-
right about economic restructuring, although unions were spared fundamental changes in labor market policy (chap. 10). Large corporations
played a role in the shift toward labor market deregulation in 1990
following the conservative National Party's victory in the election, but
foreign MNCs did not appear to be especially influential in shaping this
policy.

In sum, available evidence does not confirm the connection between
the changing division of labor and union marginalization through the
direct role of MNCs. Although some governments have been pursuing
labor market policies that seek to minimize union involvement, the
sources of such policies remain unclear. The hypothesis thus awaits
further research.

Political/Sociological Theory

I now consider the impact of political factors, first by examining the
hypothesis that trade unionism at the peak council level broadly reflects
the existing party system. I take union purpose—productionist versus
consumptionist[13]—together with the extent of unity, number of peak
organizations, and degree of union centralization in each of the countries
as indicators of unionism at a general level.

According to the unions' purpose and the indicators in table 11.1
(which are assigned equal weighting), the following sets of union
movements closely resemble one another: China and Singapore; Korea
and Taiwan; and to a slightly less extent, Australia and New Zealand.[14]

At the peak council level, unionism is most different when China and

Singapore are grouped together and compared with the other NICs and DCs. References to figures 11.1 and 1.7 and accompanying discussion indicate that these conjectures are consistent with the party system hypothesis. Thus, China and Singapore are variants of a state corporatist pattern associated with a one-party state whereas Korea and Taiwan represent transitional forms of unionism reflecting—according to this theory—the emergence of a competitive party system from single-party (Taiwan) and multiparty/military dominance (Korea). Australia and New Zealand reflect different variants of state collaborative–type unionism, both based on competitive and mainly two-party systems.

Finally, a distinguishing feature of the most different unions are the party systems with which they are associated. China and Singapore are single-party systems whereas the other NICs and DCs have systems characterized by party competition. In sum, the evidence supports the two hypotheses set out in chapter 1, that is, that unionism at a general level is causally related to the type of party system that exists and that changes in the latter lead to changes in the former.

This conclusion raises questions about the origin and status of party systems as an explanatory variable. Are not party systems a consequence of the political process? And if they are, does this not imply that the party system should be regarded as a mediating rather than an independent variable?[15] These assumptions are embodied in an argument from political sociology. Essentially, this is that except for Australia and New Zealand—where party systems are the product of electoral systems decided by referenda, contending pressure groups, *and* the influence of state institutions (especially the judiciary)—these and other institutional arrangements that shape trade unionism are determined largely by the politics of the elites that occupy key positions within the state. This view is supported by evidence on the *general* role of governments in the various societies, summarized in such notions as the strong state (which applies to all eight states) and the developmental state (which applies most readily to the NICs, China, and to a more limited extent contemporary Japan) (see chap. 1; Wade 1990; Castells 1992:56–66).[16] This invites the question whether the evidence specifically on trade unionism supports the state-centered thesis embodied in the three related hypotheses noted in chapter 1.

If the typology established earlier in this chapter is valid, then the power and policies of the state can be regarded as the major factor shaping trade unionism. To paraphrase the argument underlying this typology, states with the greatest power over society are those that tend most severely to limit the emergence of independent collectivities, including autonomous unions. China and Singapore are examples of what I termed state corporatist unions. In the case of China, this approach to trade unionism is consistent with suppressing political opposition and the maintenance of a compliant labor force under conditions of relatively low labor costs. In Singapore, the government has fostered a form of politically loyal unionism that seeks to secure employee commitment to advanced technology firms and that simultaneously supports employees' needs both at work and increasingly beyond the workplace. This position is in line with the government's high-technology, export orientation.

The levels and trends in union density are not, however, encouraging. Where the state's power is circumscribed to some extent by social forces, there is a tendency to repress unionism to forestall further challenges to state power (Thailand and Malaysia) or to settle on a modus operandi that effectively restricts the role of unions to the labor market (Hong Kong and Japan). The former strategy is consistent with competing in low-wage global product markets, while the latter facilitates the political continuity of existing elites and assists in stabilizing the political system. It also gives employers considerable discretion in dealing with employees and their representatives. Hence, the variations in the forms of workplace relations and unionism in Hong Kong and Japan cannot be explained solely by the role of the state. In Korea and Taiwan, the state has responded to the growth of opposition movements by tentatively initiating democratic reforms, some of which include the lifting of controls over autonomous unions. In both countries, however, the government has not extended the law to allow these organizations to challenge the jurisdiction of the official unions. At the same time, the official unions appear to be more responsive to workers' demands.

An important point that parallels that made in relation to Hong Kong and Japan is that the nature of workplace relations and trade unionism in Korea and Taiwan is also a reflection of employer strategy, which is influenced by a variety of structural factors (see chap. 1). In Korea, employers have tended to favor repression, although important interfirm differences exist among the Chaebol (Ogle 1990, chap. 6). Paternalism is more common in Taiwan (Deyo 1989; Whitley 1992), although this probably masks considerable diversity in management style that has yet to receive the attention it deserves.

The state-centered argument also applies to Australia and New Zealand, where state collaborative unionism prevails. In these cases the existing labor relations systems, including trade union patterns, reflect a class compromise institutionalized around the turn of the century. Strong economic pressures arising from the success of the NICs and now the DCs are leading to demands for a change in the terms of this compromise. In Australia, we see this unraveling in the form of a second social contract (see chap. 9), which includes a major restructuring of unions in which industry (broadly defined) is replacing occupation as the main principle of membership aggregation. This is giving rise to general unions that are more strategic and mindful of the need to compete internationally. This is less evident in New Zealand, as the state has presided over the trend toward decentralizing labor relations consistent with efforts to deregulate the economy. The marginalization of unions has since accelerated as employers and the conservative government seek to reduce unit labor costs.

The second state-related hypothesis asserts the presence of a variety of mechanisms through which the state implements its labor relations and union policies, resulting in patterns of unionism that reflect development policies. Thus, similarities in the former should be associated with commonalities in the latter and vice versa. There is substantial evidence concerning the various ways in which the state influences trade unionism. Examples of such mechanisms taken from our ten countries are as follows: party control of union influence in Chinese factories; government/NTUC restructuring of particular unions in Singapore; violence against senior union officials in Thailand;[17] legislation restricting union coverage and the scope of bargaining in Malaysia; union representation in Hong Kong's Legislative Council; restriction of national-level negotiations in Japan; confinement of unions to enterprise-based organizations for bargaining purposes in Korea; legal provision for employee rather than union-based consultative councils in Taiwan; until very recently, statutory provisions stipulating union coverage and worker representation through unions in New Zealand; and in Australia, decentralized bargaining within a macro-level framework designed by a state tribunal, mainly in response to an agreed-upon strategy formulated by the government and union movement.

More contentious is the connection between development policy and patterns of unionism. Indeed, five difficulties stand in the way of evaluating this hypothesis with any confidence. First, development strategies vary in comprehensiveness, as highlighted by the contrast between Singapore and Hong Kong (Castells 1992:35–37, 45–49). Second, it is often unclear to what extent government plans are implemented effectively. A case in point is the Malaysian government's Bumiputra policy (Lubeck 1992:181–82). Third, priorities and even plans may change over time—for example, Korea and Taiwan during the 1980s (Cheng 1990)—making it difficult to interpret state strategy. Fourth, what appears subsequently as a coherent development strategy is in fact a post facto rationalization of less coordinated behavior (Cheng 1990:141). Fifth, and finally, since development policies comprise a wide range of economic goals and means (see Wade 1990; Bradford 1990), it is difficult to establish which aspects are most likely to tie in with the state's policy toward labor.

Bearing these problems in mind, it is possible to proceed by crudely categorizing development strategies according to three criteria: whether they are based on high- or low-wage competition and high- or low-technology products and whether government policy is export- or import-oriented. On this reckoning, state labor strategies should be most similar within the following sets: Thailand and Malaysia (low on all three criteria); Singapore and Japan (high on all three criteria); Korea and Taiwan (medium on the three criteria); and Australia and New Zealand (high on the first criterion and medium on the second and third criteria). Nevertheless, very different state labor strategies and union patterns should be evident from comparisons between these three sets of countries.

Figure 11.1 suggests that the evidence supports the hypothesis. Union exclusion and repression are characteristic of state labor strategies and accompanying patterns in Thailand and Malaysia, whereas corporatism is a feature of the Singaporean state, made possible by a combination of corporate welfarism at the enterprise level and state inclusion of unions at the national level. Similarities between the Australian and New Zealand state strategies are indicated by a basic agreement on the labor relations framework. The current terms of this relationship differ, however, and are in the process of changing. This raises the question of whether any collaborative framework acceptable to the unions is compatible with the trend toward greater international exposure to foreign competition. In summary, broad similarities and differences in state labor policies and union patterns do appear to reflect wider development strategies, although this does not preclude detailed differences in such policies consistent with the overall thrust of state strategy.

Finally, from political sociology we have the contention that an emphasis on high technology will promote the growth of company paternalism and enterprise unionism in order to foster employee commitment to the organization. In the absence of firm- or industry-level data, it is difficult to say anything about trends in company policies except that paternalism has been common in Hong Kong, Taiwan, and to a lesser extent Singapore, independent of the use of advanced technology. This reflects the dominance of small-scale organization, characteristics of major industrial sectors, responses to chronic labor shortages, the role of the state in the latter two societies, and cultural values (Deyo 1989:152–208). The evidence from industry structure and government development policies as noted in chapter 1, together with information from the chapters that follow, suggests that Hong Kong and Singapore are the most technologically advanced of the Asian countries and are probably at an overall technological level similar to Australia and New Zealand. By contrast, China, Thailand, and Malaysia are the least technologically advanced. This raises two questions: first, does the distribution of enterprise unionism follow this pattern, and, second, how can the spread of enterprise-based unionism be explained, acknowledging that the latter is by no means synonymous with Japanese unionism?

Table 11.1 suggests that there is no technology–enterprise unionism relationship, at least not at a relatively high level of data aggregation. Thus, Singapore has a minority of unions structured on enterprise lines, which, as noted earlier, overstates their importance relative to membership numbers. That house unions are becoming more important has a great deal to do with the fact that government policy on this form of unionism is seen as more pertinent in technologically advanced, competitive economies. On the one hand, Hong Kong, like Australia and New Zealand, has very few enterprise unions. On the other hand, some of the least technologically advanced societies—Thailand and Malaysia—have a greater proportion of enterprise unions than Hong Kong and more technologically advanced NICs. In Thailand, this probably reflects the concentration of house unions in the state enterprise sector and to a lesser extent the impact of Japanese organizational ideology through foreign investment and supplier-producer links. In Malaysia, government policy has explicitly favored enterprise unionism as an integral part of the New Economic Policy. This is reflected in the practice of restricting registration of previously deregistered industrial unions to enterprise unions and confining registration of new unions to enterprise-based organizations (Wad 1988:222). To halt the growth of industrial unionism, the government has also denied requests by unions to amalgamate. By comparison, Japanese companies—which are in any case less influential than in Thailand (see chap. 1)—have not played a major role in diffusing enterprise unionism in Malaysia (Wad 1988:223–24).

In short, enterprise unionism is more a creature of government policy—undoubtedly influenced by Japanese industrial success—than an organizational imperative associated with advanced technology. It is noteworthy that although this view supports the state-centered explanation of unionism, evidence indicates that enterprise-based unionism has been introduced relatively slowly in countries where the state is favorably disposed to it. This observation testifies to the political sensitivity and practical difficulties of restructuring trade unionism when it is not in the interests of incumbent leaders and their supporters.

Summary

Having examined the twelve hypotheses in light of the empirical evidence, it is clear that the most convincing arguments tend to be those that focus on the role of the state and political processes. These include the hypotheses relating to party systems, state power, development strategy, labor policies, and implementation mechanisms. In addition, I argued for a revised typology of elites that could be incorporated into a theory of state strategy formulation and implementation. I also noted that the tendency toward enterprise-based unionism in several countries was largely a consequence of government policy. The importance of the

state in shaping patterns of unionism raises questions about key influences on state politics and policy.[18]

Notwithstanding the significance of particular historical periods, of
note here are the far-reaching contemporary changes taking place in the
world's geopolitical and economic structure. There was no hypothesis
regarding the former—which clearly needs to be developed—whereas
the impact of structural change on unions in advanced societies was
difficult to assess given the size of our sample. Changes in the world
division of labor did not support any direct connection between MNCs
and labor repression; however, this did not rule out the possibility that
foreign direct investment and trade considerations figure prominently in
government development and labor policy considerations. In short, any
conceptualization of the state vis-à-vis unions will require detailed
consideration of the impact of factors both external and internal to
national societies.

Unions in the Future

Based on our comparative union analysis covering the decade ending
in 1990 and subsequent developments, what will be the character of the
unions in the ten Asia-Pacific countries examined here as we approach
the end of the century? This question cannot be answered with any
certainty partly because the world economy—which affects states' development strategies and their economic and labor policies—is at a
turning point. One possibility is that there will be a significant multilat-
eral reduction in trade barriers, as foreshadowed by the Uruguay round
on the General Agreement on Tariffs and Trade. Another option is that
multinational trading blocs will dominate, with the European Community and the North American Free Trade Association playing a leading
role. Perhaps the most likely outcome is a combination of the two, which
will lead to intensified international competition not only in secondary
goods and services but also in primary commodities. This will benefit
many industrializing countries and such advanced peripheral exporters
as Australia and New Zealand.

Caution is also necessary in making predictions about unionism insofar
as most of the countries discussed in this volume are facing or have
recently experienced major political events, the outcomes of which are
likely to influence not only government policy and economic growth
but also in some cases political institutions. Leadership changes are
inevitable among the Chinese gerontocracy, while in Taiwan, Taiwanese-
born members of the KMT reformist faction are in positions of ascendancy. By 1993, Korea's president, Roh Tae-woo, will have served the
maximum term permitted under the law.[19] In Thailand, the resignation
of Prime Minister Suchinda Kraprayoon in May 1992 following bloody

protests in Bangkok was part of a constitutional crisis in which the king played an unusually important role in the formation of an interim government under former Prime Minister Panyarachun Anand pending a national election.[20] In September 1992, the election was narrowly won by an informal coalition of four pro-democracy, anti-military parties. Prime Minister Chuan Leckpai and the Democratic Party are keen to reduce the power of the military in politics (*Economist* 1992g:25–26). A protracted crisis of a different kind is the lead-up to China's accession of Hong Kong in 1997. In Singapore, new leader Goh Chok Tong has yet to establish his credentials. In December 1992, important elections were held in Korea and Taiwan.[21] Australia held a federal election in March 1993, and elections in New Zealand were scheduled for later in the year. In the latter country, these are likely to follow a referendum on whether a new mixed-member proportional electoral system (giving more opportunities to smaller parties) will replace the current first-past-the-post system (*Economist* 1992h:28). Japanese voters went to the polls in late July 1992 to elect half the membership of the upper house of the Diet. The result favored continuity as the embattled Liberal Democratic Party won with a slim majority in an election that attracted only half the eligible voters. Union strategy will certainly be reconsidered in the wake of the failure of all twenty-two of Rengo's candidates to win seats (*Economist* 1992f:29).

Given a more open and competitive world economy and particular assumptions regarding the consequences of the political events noted above, to what extent are the patterns of unionism identified earlier likely to change in the foreseeable future? Based on the three categories used in figure 11.1, change can be thought of as *minimal*, in which case the pattern remains stable; *moderate*, involving a shift from one variant to another within the same union pattern; or *major*, implying a shift from one pattern to another. Where the future is particularly problematic, I offer two alternative scenarios—a probable and a possible future pattern respectively. In figure 11.2, which serves as a guide to the discussion, the ten societies are grouped according to the extent of probable change in unionism during the 1990s and the direction and nature of those changes. I begin by considering countries in the minimal change category.

Minimal Change: China, Singapore, Hong Kong, and Japan

The current tendency toward economic reform in China, involving the substitution of markets for planning, is likely to continue, particularly with the discrediting of the planned economies of the former Soviet bloc and the poor performance of Chinese state-owned enterprises. This situation will contrast with that in the people's sector and the capitalist economies of neighboring countries. Decentralization of decision mak-

Figure 11.2. Probable changes in union patterns in ten Asia-Pacific countries during the 1990s

	Future union pattern and main sources of probable change
	Minimal change
China	State corporatist, socialist; ascendant autonomous management
Singapore	State corporatist, capitalist; member-responsive services
Hong Kong	State exclusionary, autonomous market; more political involvement
Japan	State exclusionary, autonomous enterprise; declining influence
	Moderate change
Thailand	State exclusionary, autonomous enterprise; political democratization
Malaysia	State exclusionary, autonomous mixed form; political democratization
Korea	State exclusionary/qualified, autonomous enterprise; middle and working class ascendancy
Taiwan	State exclusionary, autonomous mixed form; labor law reform, democratization
Australia	State collaborative, autonomous market; weak economy
	Major change
New Zealand	State exclusionary, autonomous, market; right-wing government; weak economy; changes in labor law

ing will increase the power of factory managers. On the one hand, the reduced power of the party within the enterprise is likely to be filled by unions, but these will be shaped by management and so take on an enterprise-based form. On the other hand, for mainly political reasons, unions external to the enterprise are likely to continue under party control so that state corporatist unionism will persist, resulting in a form of unionism in some ways similar to that which existed in Taiwan before liberalization in the late 1980s. A less likely scenario is that the political system will be reformed from within, allowing limited pluralism along Taiwanese lines. This would encourage autonomous organizations and a transitional form of unionism.

Like their Chinese counterparts, Singapore's political leaders show no signs of wanting to democratize the political system, particularly since the economy has been growing rapidly and the People's Action Party still commands a large majority of support despite recent election setbacks (see chap. 1, n. 25). The peak union council, the NTUC, is intensifying its search for ways to increase union support (Leggett, n.d.). In the future we are likely to see a limited increase in the unionization of executive, managerial, and technical employees, whose coverage by unions has recently been permitted. The growth of union-supplied consumer services—consumer cooperatives, clubs, holiday facilities, a labor college, and so on—together with associate membership provisions for retired members and full members' kin is another area likely to yield results in increased membership and income. The government is likely to continue to encourage enterprise-based unionism through the restructuring of relatively large general and industry-based unions. This strategy will be legitimated in terms of economic efficiency and will serve to restrict the potential organizational base for political opposition.

Unions in Hong Kong will certainly become more politicized as 1997 draws closer and political parties become more active. This can be seen today among the public-sector unions, whose members are concerned about their future under Chinese rule.[22] This trend will ensure that the unions remain divided, especially now that there is a pro-Chinese political party (formed in May 1992), which will be supported by affiliates of the pro-China peak council, the FTU. On the basis of developments in the special economic zones in China and commitments given by the Chinese government, Hong Kong industrialists will probably see little change. Unions may even be weakened by the easing of government restrictions on the entry of mainland workers into Hong Kong. In sum, except for heightened politicization and further competition, unions in Hong Kong are unlikely to change very much. After 1997, the pro-Chinese unions will probably be favored by the government, thereby weakening autonomous unionism especially in the public sector and bringing Hong Kong unions into line with the emerging Chinese model referred to above.

As long as the Japanese economy continues to deliver better-paying jobs, affordable consumer items, and a limited respite from work pressure (none of which are as assured as in previous decades), Japanese enterprise-based unionism will continue its slow decline. There is no evidence that unions are succeeding in organizing temporary workers and no sign that industrywide federations are capable of securing collective agreements containing minimum wages and conditions that might attract the vast number of nonunion employees working in small firms (JIL 1991a:21; Nakamura 1991). Although many Japanese workers, particularly those of the younger generation, are dissatisfied with the extent of commitment and work effort traditionally expected of them and hence may be more supportive of greater union independence from management (Salmon 1992), legislation and corporate strategies are likely to preempt the channeling of discontent into union militancy. In the political sphere, the Liberal Democratic Party's grip on power does not appear to be waning despite endemic corruption and possible changes in the rules relating to the financing of political campaigns.

Rengo's capacity to unite most of the unions under an opposition political umbrella party seems a long way off in spite of the collapse of communism and the decline of the public sector, factors that are likely to bring the Social Democratic Party and the Democratic Socialist Party closer together. In short, Japanese unionism will continue to provide other countries with a conservative model in the 1990s.

Moderate Change: Thailand, Malaysia, Korea, Taiwan, and Australia

By the end of the decade, the elected Thai government under Chati-chai was especially unpopular among state enterprise union leaders who, anticipating a reversal of the government's privatization policies and related corruption, welcomed the coup. What followed was a policy of more intense public-sector union repression underpinned by new legis-lation (see postscript to chap. 3), which included changes in the Labor Relations Act of 1975 aimed at further marginalizing the weak private-sector unions.[23] These changes weakened the union movement, whose popularity among the urban public was limited by perceptions of state enterprise unions as narrow, self-interested organizations. By dissolving the state enterprise unions, the government deprived the peak councils and federations of their most experienced and knowledgeable leaders and strongest union affiliates.

Political events and trends are likely to have more positive conse-quences. The successful protests against Prime Minister Suchinda in May 1992 and consequential constitutional and political changes signify the rising power of middle- and working-class opinion based on the country's rapid economic growth during the 1980s. These changes, together with more peaceful prospects in neighboring countries, seem to be leading to a decline in the power of the military, offering more scope to civilian-based parties. With encouragement from foreign governments and inter-national agencies, successive governments will attempt to institutional-ize a form of liberal democracy. Ensuing labor policies will substitute a strategy of fostering state exclusionary, autonomous, enterprise-based unionism—the seeds of which were already evident in the 1980s—for the repression and marginalization of unions. Should the military succeed in restoring its political hegemony, however, as has been the pattern in the past, the most likely outcome will be the repression of unions.

In Malaysia, a similar trend toward state exclusionary, autonomous unionism is apparent in the wake of current efforts to marginalize unions. These include the removal of all joint consultative and bargaining machinery from the public sector and the probable privatization of the telecommunications and electricity industries. This will continue to weaken CUEPACS, the state-sector union federation. In addition, the government has not permitted union amalgamations, which are contrary to its preferred enterprise-based union model.[24] Continuing rapid economic growth has increased the size and power of the middle and working classes, however, resulting in chronic shortages of skilled labor. Over the longer term, it is difficult to see how the government will be able to eliminate unionism from the public sector. In addition, the MTUC, the most prominent peak union council, has altered its policy of political neutrality and several senior union leaders are playing a prominent role in opposition political parties. The ruling party, the UMNO, is less powerful; indeed, Malaysia is experiencing a slow process of major political change reflected in the fragmentation of political parties. Ultimately, there will be a realignment that will benefit the union movement. In the meantime, union repression is less easily tolerated, at least in public, by foreign governments. This is true of the United States, although U.S. companies, which dominate Malaysia's large electronics sector, tend to oppose unions (Kuruvilla 1992).

The most likely scenario for the late 1990s is one characterized by labor exclusion rather than repression, with enterprise-based unions coexisting with industrial and general unions. A less probable prognosis is that if the UMNO continues to dominate Malaysian politics, the government will rely on immigrant workers to limit union power in the labor market and embark on a strategy of splitting existing industry and general unions into enterprise-based organizations. This would maintain the current pattern of state exclusionary, repressive unionism.

In Korea, the early 1990s witnessed a decline in support for autonomous unions and a reduction in industrial disputes and strikes associated with economic slowdown.[25] Growth has resumed at a lower rate since the economy is now suffering from inflation and balance of payments problems. Other factors contributing to the reduction in disputes include government retaliation against militant unionists, a swing of public opinion against industrial instability, and the emergence of modern personnel and labor relations systems in some companies. Continuing labor shortages and political change, however, are likely to encourage the reemergence of the spirit of autonomous unionism, leading eventually to state exclusionary, autonomous enterprise unionism.

Five reasons can be advanced for this prediction. First, younger, educated workers, particularly those who have been active as student protesters and supporters of the alternative labor movement, will continue to oppose authoritarianism in the workplace and in the wider community.[26] Second, the old politics of Korea have been discredited. People are seeking new paths that eventually will be followed. So, although the Democratic Liberal Party retained power in the 1992 parliamentary elections, it was by a much reduced margin. It will be more difficult to continue with repressive labor policies, especially if incoming president (Kim Young-sam gradually democratizes Korean institutions. In the longer term, a coalition of progressive managerial, white-collar, and skilled urban workers and intellectuals can be expected to influence Korean politics. Notwithstanding the variable and sometimes inconsistent political projects favored by elements of the new middle class (Koo 1991), a more democratic society is a common objective among these and working-class groups. Third, continuing economic growth based on a more highly educated and skilled work force will bolster the power of skilled labor in the economy, making repression a less feasible option for the government and employers. Fourth, U.S. sensitivity to alleged human rights violations against Korean workers and union leaders in the context of domestic pressure to reduce foreign competition, together with the admittance of Korea to membership in the ILO in 1991, can be expected to restrain government repression of trade unions. Fifth, and finally, the image of an alternative order is already visible: the Chaebol, whose senior management will be increasingly drawn from professionals rather than family members, are introducing welfare schemes, performance-related pay, and improvements in working conditions. Changes of this kind, coupled with participatory, enterprise-based unionism, foreshadow the shape of unionism in large enterprises. Elsewhere, unionism will be weaker, reflecting a trend toward labor market segmentation, but the government will discourage the reemergence of radical unionism by confining unionism mainly, but not exclusively, to the enterprise. Unions in designated industries will be permitted to combine at periodic intervals for the purpose of negotiating minimum wages and conditions at industry or national levels. Government concern with wage-push inflation will be reflected in regular consultation with employers' representatives and a reformed FKTU, the peak union council. Maximum wage increases and minimum wages and conditions are likely to be legislated on a regular basis.

A less likely scenario is one characterized by a consolidation of Democratic Liberal Party power under a new president committed to a major assault on all oppositional elements, especially trade unions and students. A climate of continuing repression might be legitimated by the need for order while South and North Korea agree on unification terms. Following unification, the integration of authoritarian parties across the previous borders may serve to further contain democratic aspirations, leaving unions divided and weak.

With limited information on current trends, the future of Taiwanese unionism is particularly difficult to predict. There is some evidence that occupational unions are splitting into smaller units and that where elements of new-style autonomous unions remain, management in large firms is encouraging enterprise-based unions to divide into workplace-based organizations.[27] New unions have lost influence, although traditional unions are not as compliant as they were in the years before liberalization. The labor market remains tight as economic growth continues at about 6 percent per year, based on large foreign trade surpluses (ADB 1991).

Industry restructuring, leading to the use of more highly educated, skilled labor with stronger participatory aspirations, is encouraging management and the government to adopt formalized, consensual labor relations policies in lieu of the informal paternalist and repressive policies characteristic of the past. Especially noteworthy are draft amendments to the union and labor standards laws currently under review in the Legislative Yuan. These include provisions aimed at ensuring workers' rights to organize, including protection of union organizers and representatives against unfair employer practices, greater union autonomy, and more negotiating functions for unions.

The new Labor Standards Law includes stronger fines against employers who dismiss workers illegally. Notwithstanding a history of procrastination in legislating change in labor relations and a failure to enforce the law, the new legislation will eventually take effect and is likely to be bolstered by changes in the political arena. Both the KMT and the opposition Democratic Progressive Party are vying for union support, making union involvement in politics inevitable.[28]

With continuing democratization, particularly in light of the opposition's showing in the 1992 legislative yuan elections, Taiwan seems to be moving toward a competitive party system. As R. M. Martin's (1989) theory suggests, this will foster autonomous unionism. The KMT's advantage derived from its continuous control over the government and its enhanced legitimacy arising from presiding over a successful economy and a democratized polity will virtually guarantee the party political hegemony. The new leadership will be more receptive, however, to demands by the expanding white-collar and progressive managerial strata.

In the labor sphere, the state will nevertheless attempt to ensure order by limiting union competition based on political affiliation. The absence of any strong preference for enterprise unionism is likely to lead to a continuation of the current mixture of occupational and enterprise-based unions, and negotiations are likely to be confined largely to the enterprise or workplace level. National-level union involvement is less probable against a background of relatively weak unionism.

In sum, the trend in Taiwan is toward state exclusionary, autonomous unionism with organization based on occupational and enterprise principles. An alternative, less probable scenario might result from an emerging KMT policy commitment to integrating enterprise-based unionism into a rejuvenated Chinese Federation of Labor (the sole union peak council) that has consultative rights over government labor and welfare policy; in other words, the KMT could endorse a weak yet comprehensive form of corporatism.

The future of unionism in Australia depends on the state of the economy and the outcome of the 1993 federal election; the former has considerable bearing on the latter. The first two years of the 1990s saw the Australian economy plunge into deep recession: in 1992 unemployment exceeded 10 percent. This was largely a product of excessive company borrowing, which was used to finance nonproductive ventures. On the positive side, inflation declined to zero and the proportion of working days "lost" from industrial disputes remained low. In addition, union amalgamation and rationalization continued at a rapid pace in the context of further decentralization of the industrial relations system (Jamieson 1992:166–67).[29] The large deficit on the balance of payments current account remained, putting increasing pressure on the government to speed up microeconomic reform and labor market deregulation (OECD 1992b).

In a surprise March 1993 election that reflected the electorate's support for continued government intervention in the economy, Australians reelected a federal Labor government for the fifth successive time. Industrial relations featured as one of the key policy differences among the major parties. The electorate apparently preferred Labor's managed decentralization, based on union representation, to the Liberal–National coalition parties' labor market deregulation policy, which aimed to severely limit the application of awards in favor of workplace agreements. Union rights to automatically represent employees in negotiations would also have been undermined (*Australian Financial Review* 1992a:10–11).

The trend toward workplace bargaining is set to continue within the framework established by further accords between the government and the unions. Pressure to improve economic growth and reduce unemployment will put a premium on low wage increases achieved through centralized arbitration, with the bulk of wage increases and other improvements initially coming from productivity-related, registered workplace agreements, which might later be supported by industry-level framework agreements. Currently, the scope of issues addressed by workplace agreements is limited and cover only about 10 percent of the work force. Progress has been slow, partly because previous legislation led to delays and restrictions by the Australian Industrial Relations Commission (AIRC).[30] Negotiation of more comprehensive agreements appears to be accelerating following the change in legislation limiting the power of the AIRC (see n. 29) and following the introduction of an enterprise bargaining principle by the AIRC in October 1991. This promotes decentralized bargaining subject to certain limitations (AIRC 1992:15–16), including negotiation with unions via a single bargaining unit. The principle aims to encourage orderly wage increases based on productivity improvements supported by union co-operation and rationalization of workplace structures. Emerging agreements indicate that there are fewer unions in organized workplaces because of work reorganization and the elimination of jobs, and union mergers. Meanwhile, unions are facing growing pressure to adequately service their shop stewards at a time when new structures are being developed to govern and administer larger unions with more heterogeneous memberships.

These trends seem set to continue for the foreseeable future. The anticipated growth and importance of workplace bargaining represents a tendency toward a state-collaborative, autonomous market form of unionism, although elements of corporatism will remain. These include centralized negotiations over the social wage, a safety net for lower-paid workers, and procedural rules that extend the scope of the federal system, including support for union recognition. This may, however, involve a mechanism for encouraging limited competition between unions in order to promote further union rationalization and better membership representation, which might also help to stem declining union density. Some union influence on a more interventionist industry policy may emerge, although this will be limited to individual unions. Over the longer term, and depending on the outcome of industrial relations change in New Zealand, the accession to power of a Liberal–National coalition will probably lead to the state-exclusionary union variant discussed below.

Major Change: New Zealand

In New Zealand, major change is already under way, the foundations having been laid by the previous Labour government (as described in chap. 10). This change has shifted New Zealand unions from a pattern of state collaborative, bargained corporatism to the autonomous market variant. Since the National Party came to power in 1990, massive cuts in government expenditure, further deregulation of the economy, and economic decline have followed. This is reflected in an average annual decrease in real GDP of 0.3 percent between 1987 and 1992 and an unemployment rate of more than 10 percent, which is unlikely to decline in the next three years.[31] The main instrument of change in industrial relations is the Employment Contracts Act of 1991, which affects private-sector employees and unions. This legislation involves the substitution of individual, fragmented "negotiation" for union-based collective bargaining.[32] Employers and employees can now negotiate contracts on an individual basis or through representation by an "incorporated society," which need not be a union. Union preference in agreements or awards is prohibited, as is any requirement that employees be members of unions. Unions cannot legally enforce collective agreements on employers other than those with whom they have made agreements. Finally, union (and employer) access to compulsory arbitration is severely restricted. In short, the legislation invites employers to disregard unions and to "negotiate" individual contracts. Alternatively, collective contracts can be negotiated with an "incorporated society."

It is difficult to distinguish the impact of the Act from other factors. Moreover, there is no systematic evidence on the consequences of the legislation. A widespread view is that union-negotiated collective agreements have declined substantially, especially in relation to small firms. Union density is conservatively estimated to have diminished by 20 percent over the past two years. Clearly, the combination of recent government policies and economic recession have sent the union movement into disarray.[33] This is highlighted by the disaffiliation of the large Amalgamated Workers' Union from the CTU (the peak council), and the massive decline in membership of the strategically oriented Engineers' Union from sixty thousand in the early 1980s to thirty-six thousand a decade later (Stutchbury 1992:14). The only possible alternative to further decline is that the Labour Party could be returned to power in the 1993 election. But even this is unlikely to reverse completely what has already occurred, namely, a major shift from autonomous market unionism, based on state collaboration, to a similar variant, based on state exclusion.

The Research Challenge

This volume has outlined recent features and probable directions for trade unionism in nine Asia-Pacific countries. We have also attempted to synthesize the research results by using an inductively developed framework that identifies patterns of unionism without underplaying differences in structure, goals, and methods of union operation. Inevitably, the analysis revealed gaps in both our knowledge of important elements of trade unionism and in explanatory details. Here, I want to highlight some of the more important areas and issues that might be addressed in further research.

Because our study aimed at providing a general picture of unions, it was not possible to examine union strategy, goals, or policy implementation systematically. Such a project is in any case difficult since unions frequently react to, rather than shape, events and there can be substantial differences across organizational levels and between regions. Research on these issues therefore raises complex conceptual and methodological questions. Nevertheless, such an examination, together with a comparative study of internal union structures (i.e., governance and administrative systems), is essential for a more complete understanding of trade unionism.

Our study also points to the need for further research on the political role of trade unions. Of primary importance are the relations between unions and various branches of government, particularly the legislature, labor departments, industrial tribunals and courts, the military, and the police. Relations with the ruling political party and networks of influential officials may mediate the relationship between unions and government. Party-union relations, particularly in terms of financing and the flow of information and advice, including the extent of dual position holding (union officials holding political party positions and vice versa), merit research in their own right. In some countries, relations with church groups (Taiwan), student organizations (Korea), and international organizations (Thailand) also have a strong bearing on union behavior. In this context it would be useful to know more about the role and limitations of international unions in the Asia-Pacific region (see Berdiner 1987:178–80).

Our study was designed to account for variations in the stability of union patterns by covering the 1980s. To understand the basic features of labor organization, however, it is necessary to undertake comparative research spanning a much longer period. The notions of critical historical junctures that exert especially powerful effects on subsequent developments (Collier and Collier 1991) and the preemptive state subordination of labor in the NICs (Deyo 1987, 1989) are particularly noteworthy in this regard. These issues raise the question of how a state-centered approach to unionism might be elaborated on in studies of contemporary unionism. To begin with, it is necessary to theorize more adequately the essential features of the state. We have used the term *state* mainly to refer to one of its faces—its authoritative, decision-making role—but as acknowledged in our discussion of elites and the role of MNCs, the state is also the product of group interests and the site of distributional struggles (Jessop 1990:338–69). While so-called hard, developmental states are less likely to be influenced by pressure groups, in part because of the social cohesion associated with the meritocratic selection of their leaders from elite institutions (Evans 1989), we know very little about conflicts between departments and between senior state officials that affect state labor policies and the effectiveness with which these policies are implemented. Moreover, the impact of foreign states has also been noted in relation to the connection between access to foreign markets and the pressure on certain countries to raise their labor standards. International financial agencies such as the World Bank also exert influence on governments to adopt particular policies.

Also worth exploring are the social networks and directions of influence that connect representatives of the ruling elites: senior state managers (including military officers), party officials, employer representatives, and, in some cases, union officers. Such work would assist in developing a typology of elites whose effects on development strategy and labor policy could then be studied cross-nationally. There is also what S. Lukes (1974) refers to as the second and third faces of power respectively. Thus, decisions regarding state development and labor policies might be institutionalized in a way that precludes union involvement. Our research shows that this is commonplace, but less obvious is the way decision makers' ideologies contain assumptions that favor capital in general, and possibly MNCs in particular, while being prejudicial to the autonomous development of unions. Thus, the role of ideology requires examination, including the state's legitimating function, which might encourage particular types of trade unions and discredit others.

The state's role in setting labor policies and shaping union patterns should be appropriately located and qualified. Changes in the world economic system influence state development strategies. With the increasing openness of national economies and mobility of capital, governments may have less power to influence firms' investment and employment decisions than in the past. This issue warrants further analysis. The factors and mechanisms that account for this selectivity, which in many countries is likely to be biased against unions, deserve careful examination. So do the strategies used by different employers to avoid unions or to shape them according to their own interests. In particular, more work could usefully be directed toward comparisons of the labor practices of domestic and foreign-owned firms of various nationalities in selected industries and the extent to which labor issues are taken into account when making key investment decisions.

Thus far we have suggested further research on the nature and determinants of unionism. Such work would benefit from an examination of unions in a wider array of countries within and beyond the Asia-Pacific region, and it would provide a more reliable basis for developing and testing theory.

Finally, we also favor research on the effects of various union patterns. Economic rationalists claim that unionism of any kind that interferes with market forces has deleterious consequences and should therefore be eliminated. A contrary view is that unionism has positive welfare and efficiency consequences and should therefore receive state support. More nuanced arguments relate to union power and structure, with some commentators (Standing 1992a, 1992b) claiming that variations in structural forms have different consequences for industrial efficiency and equity. The effects of unionism should not, however, be restricted to the economy; political consequences deserve at least as much attention, especially since political change is likely to be a feature of the Asia-Pacific region for the foreseeable future.

Notes

1. Theoretical Frameworks and Empirical Contexts of Trade Unionism

1. In addition, there were the intellectuals and the military, the so-called floating forces that "guide the march to industrialization mostly when the march is faltering or changing course" (Kerr et al. 1975:74).

2. The effects of MNCs are often assumed rather than demonstrated, reflecting adherents' failure to theorize and test conjectures concerning variations in the characteristics and power of these organizations. In addition, little attention is paid to the influence of foreign governments and international agencies on trade unionism. There is also insufficient recognition of domestic capital, whose cohesion and influence vary considerably between countries and sectors. Most important, the role of the state is given limited attention, yet governments and other official agencies are often responsible for implementing development initiatives and hence structuring the terms under which foreign and domestic companies conduct their employment relations. R. Cohen (1991:133–46), an influential scholar in this tradition, has noted, however, that the growth of the international division of labor is complex, advancing historically in a series of stages. He warns against confining analysis to the manufacturing sector and overestimating the significance of multinational capital.

3. Relevant factors include the attenuation of the strength of the local middle class; local political elites that have a resource base so they can insulate themselves against domestic pressure; the creation of a labor aristocracy uninterested in wider working-class issues; growing inequality, leading to potential disorder and hence increased authoritarianism to forestall such a possibility; and the discipline of world market competition, which requires competitive labor costs (Deyo 1981:17).

4. Deyo argues that variations in the effectiveness of such systems in part reflect international variations in industrial structure. Thus, Korean labor, which

is based on a large heavy-industry sector, is stronger than in the other three NICs.

5. A historical approach might have focused on critical junctures in the development of unionism in the nine countries, tracing their legacy in a manner suggested by R. B. Collier and D. Collier (1991). Such a project would have been well beyond our capacity, however, especially in the absence of detailed histories of the union movements in the various countries.

6. Care must be taken in analyzing the role of variations in key variables. For a discussion of the assumptions underlying comparisons of this kind in some small N studies, see Lieberson (1991).

7. It proved impossible to find a local researcher willing to do a critical examination of unionism in Indonesia, probably at least in part because of a fear of government reprisals. The Philippine study became part of a bureaucratic wrangle from which it never recovered. The Japanese study fell by the wayside mainly because of illness in the researcher's family.

8. Structure is defined here as relations between unions. External structure should be distinguished from internal structure, which refers to the representative and administrative arrangements of unions (Donaldson and Warner 1974), an aspect requiring examination in a separate study.

9. See Bello and Rosenfeld (1990) for details concerning the electronics and auto industries, which shows that Korean and Taiwanese manufacturers are especially dependent on Japanese high-technology components and marketing organizations. This strategy is not confined to Japanese firms. The United States encourages such activity: items 806.30 and 807.00 of the U.S. tariff code allow duty-free entry of U.S. components sent abroad for assembly or reprocessing. If the items are reexported back to the United States, only the value added by foreign labor is subject to tariffs (Bello and Rosenfeld 1990:245). In this context it is noteworthy that Malaysia is "the world's largest exporter of [electronics] components that are assembled and tested by mostly American firms in export processing zones" (Lubeck 1992:179).

10. In some cases this ratio exceeds 100 percent, indicating that foreign trade generates more value than domestic economic activity. The relevant 1990 figures unless otherwise specified are as follows: Singapore, 360 percent; Hong Kong, 232 percent; Malaysia (1989), 125 percent; China, 34 percent; Australia, 27 percent; and New Zealand, 44 percent. Corresponding data for the remaining countries are Thailand, 70 percent; Korea, 56 percent; and Taiwan, 77 percent (*FEER* 1991; ADB 1990: 235, 240).

11. For example, U.S. investment in Taiwan over the period 1951–85 accounted for 43 percent of total foreign investment, compared with 28 percent by Japan. This excludes investments by overseas Chinese in Taiwan, which was slightly greater than the Japanese contribution (Bello and Rosenfeld 1990:245). U.S. investment in Malaysia in 1990 was relatively modest. Of total foreign investment approved in Malaysia for that year, U.S. companies invested an amount similar to Singapore (8.2 percent of total), which was much less than Taiwan (35.7 percent) and Japan (31.2 percent).

12. While almost all of Taiwan's population is Chinese, E. G. Redding (1990:28–32) notes that Chinese immigrants comprise 72 percent of Singapore's population and 37 percent of Malaysia's. Slightly less than 10 percent of Thailand's population are Chinese, but they are estimated to control more than 50 percent of industry. It is noteworthy that in contrast to most other societies, the Chinese are highly integrated into Thai society through intermarriage. Although Chinese immigrants constitute less than 2 percent of the population in Australia

and New Zealand, they are important in certain branches of industry. Only in Korea are Chinese entrepreneurs conspicuous by their absence.

13. Between 1987 and 1990, Japanese investment in Thailand increased by 41 percent, reaching U.S. $1.6 billion. The corresponding increase for NIC investment was nearly 31 percent, totaling U.S. $1.2 billion in 1990. Korea contributed the smallest proportion (less than 3 percent) of NIC investment (Wu 1991:105).

14. In the period 1985–88, New Zealand nationals accounted for 8.4 percent of Australian foreign direct investment, while the corresponding figure for Australians investing directly in New Zealand was 23.1 percent.

15. Alternative estimates for Australia suggest that in 1989–90, 23.3 percent of immigrants arrived from Southeast Asia and 13.5 percent from Northeast Asia. Corresponding data for 1990–91 are 24.2 and 18.2 percent respectively (N = 121,688 persons) (Business Council of Australia 1992:20). In 1990–91, the six most common sources of immigrant labor were the United Kingdom and Ireland (about 22 percent); Hong Kong and Vietnam (nearly 13 percent each), New Zealand (7 percent), and China (6 percent). The number of immigrants from Hong Kong, who tend to be highly skilled, has increased mainly in response to the return of Hong Kong to China in 1997.

16. Across the Hong Kong border in China's Guandong province, for example, more than 2 million workers are reported to be employed, directly and indirectly, by Hong Kong businesses on a fifth of the wages paid to equivalent Hong Kong workers (*Economist* 1990e:30). In Singapore, there is a growth triangle with Singapore as its apex that includes the Malaysian state of Johore, northern Sumatra, and various Indonesian islands. The aim is to encourage labor-intensive production to move away from Singapore and into these lower-cost areas (*Economist* 1991a:27).

17. The real exchange rate for Hong Kong increased over the period 1980–89. This was true of Taiwan in the late 1980s, while Korea had still not attained its real level by the end of the decade. This is in contrast to the three DCs, whose real exchange rates declined substantially over the same period (see ADB 1990, table A26). Regarding comparative labor costs, a diagram showing relative wage costs in manufacturing (expressed in U.S. dollars) for twenty-five countries was summarized as follows: "In 1990 manufacturing wages in the four [NIC] economies (at between $3.20 and $4.16 an hour) were still only a quarter of those in America and less than a fifth of western German wages. Labour is even cheaper, however, in the newly emerging economies of Indonesia, Malaysia and Thailand, where hourly wages are less than $1" (*Economist* 1992d:117).

18. This is highlighted by the failure of the Asia Pacific Economic Co-operation Group to achieve anything substantial in its four years of existence. At a January 1992 meeting of ASEAN, however, member countries agreed to reduce tariffs on fifteen groups of manufactured products to no more than 5 percent within the next fifteen years, a move that is likely to promote a regional market and therefore help ASEAN "to compete for investment with countries like Mexico and Portugal, in rival free trade areas (*Economist* 1992a:25).

19. GDP growth per capita at constant prices, as shown in table 1.1, tends to be lower than GDP growth because it takes into account population growth. Over the period 1981–90, the annual average percentage changes for the DCs were estimated as follows: China's GDP per capita, 7.7; GDP, 9.0; Thailand's GDP per capita, 5.4; GDP, 7.4; and Malaysia's GDP per capita, 3.0; GDP, 5.8 (World Bank 1989; ADB 1991).

20. Tariffs have been cut substantially, the aim being to reduce them to an

average of about 17 percent by 1992. According to *FEER* (1992:171), tariffs were levied on only 7 percent of imports by value and other types of assistance were used very little.

21. This did not, however, mean the eclipse of import substitution, for the government continued to emphasize the growth of specific heavy industries, whose inefficiencies led to the replacement of Malay managers by Japanese and private-sector managers and a privatization drive beginning in 1989 (Kuruvilla 1992).

22. In elections to the expanded central committee of the KMT, Taiwanese-born members increased their share from 20 to 45 percent, and in the policy-making standing committee they claimed to have won a majority of the seats. The average age of central committee members fell from seventy to sixty-three years, while the age of standing committee members dropped from seventy to fifty-nine years (*FEER* 1989:233).

23. Before the National Assembly elections, held in December 1991, 470 of the older deputies retired. The assembly includes 325 new members, who joined 80 others elected in 1986 to form the new 405-seat National Assembly. The KMT won 179 of 225 seats and was awarded another 75 on the basis of votes won nationwide. The main opposition party, the Democratic Progressive Party, won 41 seats directly and 25 indirectly (*Sydney Morning Herald* 1991:8). The opposition's poor showing probably had much to do with its campaign for an independent Taiwan.

24. The British government has been more receptive to speeding up the democratization of Hong Kong because it sees this process as a way to reinforce public confidence in the future. The Chinese government has opposed such moves, preferring to build an administrative structure that can more easily be controlled (*FEER* 1990:123–24). In September 1991, for the first time in the British colony's 150-year history, 3.6 million Hong Kong residents became eligible to elect eighteen of the sixty members of the Legislative Council (*Economist* 1990d:29).

25. In the August 1991 election, four members of the opposition parties were elected, and the ruling party received only 59.7 percent of the votes cast. The PAP continues to limit freedom of speech and restrict political activity (*FEER* 1992:186).

26. In 1980–81, the average effective rate of assistance for manufactured items was estimated at 24 percent; the corresponding figure for 1988–89 was 17 percent (Australia. Industries Assistance Commission, various).

3. Union Unevenness and Insecurity in Thailand

1. This figure, which is the only one available, understates the rate of unionization since it includes employers, the self-employed, and children eleven years old and older.

2. The newsletter from which this information is taken also reports (p. 4) a case in which the house of a union leader at Omnoi was searched by the police because they were ostensibly looking for illegal firearms. The police were actually looking for union documents and records. It was suggested that the reason for the incident was that the factory committee had come into conflict with the wife of the local police chief, who had monopolized the sale of food at the factory and was charging exorbitant prices.

3. During the 1980s some important state enterprises or parts thereof were privatized. These included the pulp and paper factory at Bang Pa-in, the Glass

Organization, the Alum Organization, the Naraipin Shop, the Erawan and Bang-
saen hotels, the Instant Food Organization, three routes formerly run by the State
Rail Authority, three ports previously controlled by the Port Authority, and the
installation of new telephones, which was previously the responsibility of the
Telephone Organization of Thailand.

4. According to Limqueco, McFarlane, and Odhnoff (1989), more than 50
percent of Thai employers pay less than the legal minimum rate, while those
employees who do receive the minimum rate claim that it is insufficient to meet
rising costs. These figures serve to highlight the substantial inequalities of wealth
and income in Thailand, where an estimated 25 percent of the population live
below the poverty line (U.S. Department of Labor 1990:1) while political and
economic power are in the hands of a relatively small elite (Mackie 1988:303–
5).

5. The earnings of state-enterprise employees contrast with those of unorganized public servants. Although strictly comparable data are unavailable, it is
noteworthy that before 1989 the lowest-paid public servants earned less than
the minimum wage. In January 1989, these employees received their first pay
rise in more than six years. This brought their salary to a level equivalent to the
minimum rate (U.S. Department of Labor 1990:4).

4. State Regulation and Union Fragmentation in Malaysia

1. In the year of independence (1957), only 20 percent of union members
were Malay; 24 percent were Chinese, 58 percent were Indian, and 4 percent
were classified as other. By 1986, 57 percent were Malay, 17 percent were
Chinese, 25 percent were Indian, and 1 percent were in the other category
(Malaysia. Ministry of Labour annual reports).

2. Such developments in connection with union autonomy were clearly
foreseen by one expatriate adviser to the MTUC, who cautioned against unions
having too much involvement in the running of business enterprises. Although
the organization he represented, the Friedrich-Ebert-Stiftung (FES), had been the
major contributor to the MTUC Education and Development Program, he was
immediately informed by the Ministry of Home Affairs that he was permanently
banned from Malaysia for commenting on the Malaysian union situation. This
arbitrary action was condoned even by the president of the MTUC, who argued
that the FES representative had been "in the country too long" (*New Straits
Times*, 14 Jan. 1987).

3. The MTUC boycotted the National Labor Advisory Council over the tabling
of a bill to amend the Trade Union Act of 1959 that would have allowed the
registration of in-house unions in industries in which there were already national
unions. The CUEPACS supported the MTUC on this matter. The protests were to
no avail, however. (*New Straits Times*, 11 March 1989).

4. In 1986, the MTUC suggested an accord with CUEPACS under an umbrella
organization to be called the United Malaysian Labor Movement. Its constitution
was submitted to the registrar but was not accepted (*Suara Buruh*, Jan. 1987).

5. The Korean Union Movement in Transition

1. For a detailed description of the Korean labor movement before the late
1970s, see Federation of Korean Trade Unions (1979) and Kim (1982).

2. The Korean Labor Mutual Aid Association was broken up in 1922 because
of ideological conflicts among its leaders. The Federation of Korean Labor

changed its name to the Confederation of Korean Labor and Farmers in 1924. After 1927, when the confederation divided into the Confederation of Korean Labor and the Confederation of Korean Farmers, these two organizations became inactive because of suppression by the Japanese government. All the local unions and other labor organizations were directly affiliated with the national centers.

3. Firms in the following sectors are exempted from the act's requirements: agriculture; hunting, forestry, and fishing; construction, in cases where enterprises operate for less than one year; newspapers; and finance, insurance, and real estate services.

4. In November 1987, clerical and financial workers who were not working for banks established a federation separate from the Korean Federation of Bank and Financial Workers. The Federation of Taxi Transport Workers' Union did the same in 1988, separate from the Federation of Auto and Transport Workers. The major reasons for these splits were conflicts about group interests and ideological differences.

5. The participating councils were the Council of Democratic Publication and Press Unions and the National Council of Unions of Facility Maintenance Employees. The observers were the National Teachers' Union; the Council of Researchers', Professionals', and Technicians' Unions; and the freight transportation unions.

6. In 1987, Korean workers averaged 51.9 hours a week; manufacturing workers averaged 54.0 hours a week. The fatal occupational injury rate was also high by international standards (see ILO 1991b:982–96). In the second quarter of 1990, working hours were reduced to 48.8 in all industries and to 50.4 in manufacturing (Bai 1990:13). Recent incidence rates of fatal occupational injuries per thousand workers also indicate a declining trend: the average annual rate between 1980 and 1984 was 0.36 compared with 0.33 for the period 1985–89 (Korea. Ministry of Labor 1990:988).

7. The objectives included: (1) expansion of the scope of activities through the reform of the labor laws; (2) participation of the working masses as active agents in struggles for better economic and political systems and the awakening of elementary class consciousness and political consciousness; (3) organization of the working class and the development of a national solidaristic union movement through the spread of nationwide joint struggle; and (4) the encouragement of solidarity among all democratic power groups and the realization of social democratization through the reform of antidemocratic laws (National Council of Labor Movements Organisation 1989:118).

8. The two parties mentioned thus far were major oppositional organizations until January 1990, when they merged with the ruling party, thus creating the Democratic Liberal Party, which now dominates the Korean legislature.

9. According to the National Alliance of Trade Unions, as of 2 June 1990, 364 workers had been arrested, 134 workers booked, and 224 sued in violation of labor-related laws (*Korean Economic Daily,* 23 June 1990, 19).

10. For 1987 and 1989, Bai (1990:3) reports the unemployment rate as 3.1 and 2.6 percent respectively, which is lower than for 1985 (4.0 percent) and earlier years. According to Bai, severe labor shortages in textiles, electronics, and toys led to a severe bottleneck in economic growth. It is noteworthy that the Korean economy grew by an annual average of 11.8 percent over the years 1986–88. In 1989, it declined to 6.1 percent, but based on data for the first six months of 1990, it then increased to 9.5 percent (Zerby 1990). The annual average inflation figure for the 1986–88 period was 4.3 percent (7.1 percent in 1988), 5.7 percent in 1989, and 8.0 percent in 1990 (based on the first six months) (Zerby 1990).

6. *The Resurgence and Fragility of Trade Unions in Taiwan*

1. A self-employed person is eligible for social insurance if she or he joins an occupational union that subscribes on her or his behalf (Lee 1988:190).

2. A contrary official view is that the Trade Union Law, which has regulated union activity since the KMT established its rule over Taiwan, provides for regular elections of union officials and that the unions' quiescence had much more to do with the existence of martial law. When this was lifted and political parties were permitted, the formal union procedures facilitated the emergence of union leaders more willing to oppose the KMT line.

3. A similar law—the Factory Law of 1929—applied specifically to factories using power-driven machinery, but since 1984 this law has been subsumed by the Labor Standards Law. Some laws were enacted while the KMT was in control of the mainland before the Communists established the PRC.

4. Taiwanese employees in manufacturing work considerably longer hours than workers in industrialized countries (CLA 1988; Ying 1990:23–24). Compared with their counterparts in other NICs, the data for 1987 show that they worked an average of 48.2 hours per week, which is very slightly in excess of the legal limit (CLA 1989b:27), less than their Korean (54.0 hours) and Singaporean counterparts (49.2 hours), and more than Hong Kong workers in the same sector (44.5 hours).

5. As late as 1975, 30.5 percent of the work force was engaged in agriculture, hunting, forestry, and fishing. By 1989, the proportion had declined to 12.9 percent (China. DGBAS, n.d.:8).

6. Similar to other Asian NICs, Taiwan has been characterized by a relatively egalitarian distribution of income compared with most other developing countries (see Haggard 1990:227–29).

7. There are five central government branches that control ministries and departments. These branches are the Legislative Yuan, the Executive Yuan, the Judicial Yuan, the Examining (staff recruitment) Yuan, and the Control (administrative coordination) Yuan.

8. According to a 1986 survey covering 8,344 workers in the manufacturing industry, 25.3 percent claimed to be union members. In the establishment size category ten to forty-nine employees (N = 2,165), slightly less than 3.5 percent of respondents stated they were union members, compared with 72 percent in the size category five hundred or more employees (N = 1,560) (Social Department of Taiwan Provincial Government 1986:154–55). In the same survey, 59 percent of employees with primary school education (N = 1,975) stated that they needed a union, while 60.5 percent of employees with tertiary education (N = 358) expressed this view.

9. Almost 60 percent of private manufacturing-sector employees were working in establishments employing fewer than thirty employees, and a further 17 percent worked in establishments employing thirty to forty-nine employees. In the service sector, small establishments were even more predominant (China. DGBAS, n.d.: 28).

10. Between 1986 and 1989, government-approved direct overseas investment increased by more than 1,600 percent in nominal terms, rising most strongly between 1988 and 1989 but continuing strongly into 1990. Countries attracting the most Taiwanese investment were the United States, Malaysia, Thailand, and the Philippines (Taiwan. Ministry of Economic Affairs. Investment Commission 1990:49–56). Both approved investment through subsidiaries and unapproved investment in the PRC is rising steeply.

11. Some member unions of the TBU joined the NFIU, so the two organizations have overlapping memberships; the latter is the major federation in northern Taiwan. The NFIU receives administrative support from the Taiwan Association for Labor Movement, which was the first civil organization formed on May Day 1984 with the intention of promoting workers' rights (see Ying 1990:73–74).

12. In a 1988 survey that was not confined to manufacturing, union members were asked whether they preferred the welfare function to be unilaterally or jointly administered. More than two-thirds (67.5 percent) of the respondents preferred it to be run solely by the union, 22.9 percent preferred joint administration with management, and 12.5 percent wanted it to be run solely by management. Members of enterprise unions, which predominate in manufacturing, were far less inclined to want schemes run solely by the union (32.2 percent), preferring joint control (55.8 percent), in contrast to occupational union members, who overwhelmingly preferred (91.4 percent) union-run schemes. This difference possibly reflects the greater independence of occupational unions from management.

13. Official statistics use the term *compensation benefits* rather than *bonuses*, but as far as we can ascertain, the great majority of disputes under this heading concern bonuses. Chao, Wu, and Wu (1988) also adopt this position. A small minority of disputes in the broader category focus on the alleged failure of employers to pay the requisite retirement benefits required by law.

14. The Labor Standards Law states that work done on holidays, on workers' vacations, or in emergency situations must be paid at double the normal rate. G. San (1988:359) observes that there have been many disputes over whether the total pay for such overtime work should be paid at triple (2 plus 1) or double (1 plus 1) workers' usual wage rates.

15. Chao (1988:262) argues that Taiwan's progress in the area of health and safety has been slow because of the shortage of inspection personnel: 232 inspectors for some 150,000 enterprises; the reluctance of employers to upgrade health and safety standards; and the lack of worker consciousness of proper health and safety procedures. Ying (1990:24–25) notes that a large proportion of Taiwan's employees are beyond the reach of the inspectorate because they work in small enterprises. He believes that official records considerably understate the incidence of health and safety problems. According to the official statistics, the rate of industrial injuries in the 1980–89 period declined very slightly, but this may reflect the changing distribution of employment away from the hazardous mining and construction sectors toward the less accident-prone service sector. In manufacturing, the average industrial injury rate over the 1980–84 period was 8.04 and 8.53 percent for the 1985–89 period (China. DGBAS, n.d.: 34–35). This is relatively high by international standards (CLA 1989b:428–29).

16. A question in the survey of manufacturing employees asked what the government should do to improve unions. "Providing more conciliation services to resolve disputes" was the second most popular response (given by 19.8 percent of respondents) after "clarification of workers' rights and obligations under the Labor Standards Law" (28.4 percent). Third was "explaining to employers the advantages of unions" (15.2 percent) (Social Department of Taiwan Provincial Government 1986:214).

17. For example, 35.3 percent of firms with fewer than thirty employees claimed to have some kind of employee-participation scheme, while 81.3 percent of firms employing five hundred or more employees made this claim (CLA 1989b:366–67).

18. This assumes that trends in industrial disputes in manufacturing and for all industries are highly correlated. This is likely since it is the manufacturing sector that accounts for about 80 percent of industrial disputes in Taiwan (Lin 1988:393).

7. Dependent Capitalism, a Colonial State, and Marginal Unions: The Case of Hong Kong

1. Under the existing Trade Unions Ordinance, a trade union is defined as "any combination the principal objects of which are under its constitution the regulating of relations between employees and employers or between employees and employees, or between employers and employers." This definition encompasses three types of trade unions according to the employment status of members: employees' unions, employer associations, and mixed organizations of employers and employees. "Trade union" is used in this chapter to refer only to unions of employees. There are other organizations in Hong Kong concerned with workers' welfare, however, that are not registered under the Trade Unions Ordinance. The most important of these are the trade union federations, which are registered under the Societies Ordinance because of provisions in the Trade Unions Ordinance that limit the formation of federations to unions in the same trade, industry, or occupation. Every registered trade union is required to provide the Registrar of Trade Unions with an annual form showing the membership of the union as of 31 December. These figures are reported by the registrar as declared membership and are the figures used in this chapter. Declared membership figures do not necessarily provide an accurate picture of paid-up membership, however, and the registrar also reports estimated paid-up membership based on trade union accounts. In 1988, the ratio of estimated paid-up membership to declared membership for all employee unions was 86.3 percent.

2. The Trade Unions and Trade Disputes Ordinance of 1948 generally followed the U.K. model with several variations, including the following three requirements: (1) all trade unions had to be registered; (2) officers of a trade union had to be employed or engaged in the industry or occupation with which the trade union was connected; and (3) there had to be prior consent of the governor of Hong Kong for a trade union to be affiliated with trade unions or other organizations outside Hong Kong. In 1961, this ordinance was replaced by the Trade Unions Registration Ordinance and the Trade Disputes Ordinance. The former retained provisions relating to trade union registration but added new provisions regarding the definition of, and procedures for, forming trade union federations and union amalgamations. Restrictions were also added pertaining to the use of trade union funds, including a requirement that welfare funds be kept separate from general funds. Relatively minor amendments were introduced in 1971 and 1977, and the ordinance was retitled in 1977 the Trade Unions Ordinance. See Chan (1988:35–39) for a review of these changes.

3. In 1966, 121 of the 240 unions had between 50 and 250 members, 71 had between 251 and 1,000, and 30 had more than 1,000. Of this 30, only 7 had more than 5,000 members, 5 of them affiliates of the FTU.

4. The FTU's strength lay mainly in its industrial union affiliates in transport, parts of manufacturing, utilities, and the service sector, while the TUC's base was in smaller trades, construction, and the restaurant industry.

5. For discussions of these disturbances, the role of the FTU unions in the events of 1967, and the effects of these disturbances on government social policy, see Scott (1989:81–126) and England and Rear (1981:17–23).

6. One stimulus for the growth of white-collar unions in the civil service was

the restructuring of the internal labor market in line with recommendations of the 1971 Salaries Commission. This gave rise to grievances over occupational pay structure and promotion opportunities. A number of occupational groups apparently became convinced that they could press their claims more effectively as registered trade unions rather than by working through one of the three servicewide unions entitled to sit on the Senior Civil Service Council, a consultative forum established in 1968.

7. The sharp drop in union membership between 1980 and 1981 was due to the reclassification in 1981 of the Hong Kong Graziers Union, whose membership (22,655 in 1981) consists of persons working in jobs related to agriculture. The reclassification was from an employees' union to a mixed organization of employees and employers. The sharp rise in union membership between 1987 and 1988 was due largely to a more than doubling of the membership of the Hong Kong Chinese Civil Servants' Association from 22,526 to 49,425.

8. A Hong Kong Census and Statistics Department (1983:50) special sample survey (conducted as part of the general household survey) on labor mobility found that in the first quarter of 1982 15.6 percent of the estimated employed population had changed jobs during the previous twelve months. This compares with a wastage rate (resignations, retirements, completions of agreements, dismissals, terminations of service, and death) of 4.2 percent for the civil service in 1983–84 (Burns 1988:94).

9. The Labour Relations Service of the Labour Department and the Labour Tribunal, established in the early 1970s, have become important means by which employees seek help when they face employment problems. In 1978, the number of claims (mostly by employees for a sum of money arising from a breach of a contract of employment or from failure to comply with the provisions of the Employment Ordinance and thus an indicator of individual grievances) recorded by the Labour Department was 10,060, of which about 50 percent were settled through the Labour Department and 29 percent were referred to the Labour Tribunal. In 1987, the number of claims rose to 16,232, of which about 76 percent were settled through the Labour Department and 23 percent were referred to the Labour Tribunal. Claims typically involve arrears of wages, payment in lieu of notice, severance pay, end-of-year bonuses, holiday pay, annual leave pay, maternity leave, sickness allowances, and long-service payments (England 1989:225).

10. The only details Turner (1988:178) provided about the 1985 survey are that it was composed of a sample of 500 employees and a further sample of 250 workers in certain industries.

11. The origins of the CSGU go back to the Pre-Amalgamation Coordinating Team, formed in 1974. To register as a trade union under the provisions of the Trade Unions Ordinance, the CSGU had to recruit individual civil servants as ordinary members while affiliating with other civil service unions. Only union federations are registered under the law. A number of the unions affiliated with the CSGU are also affiliated with the Public Services International Trade Secretariat.

12. The CCSA has a special status as one of only three staff associations that sit on the Senior Civil Service Council. Of the three, it is the only one open to all Chinese civil servants regardless of their rank. Affiliation with the CCSA enabled unions without direct access to the Senior Civil Service Council to send representatives to general and Executive Council meetings of the CCSA. It should be noted that the boundaries among federations and quasi-federations in the public sector are not very clear-cut since the same trade union may belong to two or more of these federations.

13. One reported case occurred in 1983 at the Hong Kong International Terminal Ltd. Some employees belonged to the Union of Godown and Wharf Workers (UGWW), affiliated with the FTU, while others belonged to an independent union, the Storehouses and Transportation Staff Association (STSA). When the STSA called a strike in support of twelve workers who were dismissed for opposing a management retrenchment plan, the UGWW did not support the strike. In 1986, the UGWW sponsored the formation of the Container and Transportation Employees' General Union, and the STSA sponsored the HIT Limited Company Employees' General Union. Both were therefore competing for members and company recognition. In the Hong Kong post office, an FTU-affiliated Postal Workers' Union was formed in 1948, and the Union of Post Office Employees (UPO), originally affiliated with the TUC but which became an independent union in 1977, clashed in 1978 and again at the end of 1987 over the UPO's call for industrial action against management for improved working conditions. A representative from the independent Association of Government Nursing Staff has reported numerous conflicts with an FTU-affiliated union over a ten-year period (Leung and Leung 1988:28–30).

14. S. Yeung (1989:21), for example, has commented as follows: "In terms of the value orientation of the left- and right-wing unions, I think they emphasize collectivism more and neglect individualism and social justice. There are two levels of meaning for this collectivism. The first is the object of loyalty, or the symbol of the 'collectivity' for these two groups. On the one side is the Chinese government; on the other is the Taiwanese government; but in neither case is it the members of the unions. Second, the approaches of the two groups of unions tend to be tailored to the political lines of the two governments. It seems that the opinions of union members do not have much influence on the unions' centrally determined orientations and stands. In the formulation of the unions' directions, it is likely that both left- and right-wing unions will adopt a top-down approach. I doubt whether there has been sufficient discussion with the members in the process of formulation" (our translation).

15. The annual income was calculated using the average daily basic wage for the two occupations in September 1988 times the number of standard working days per month times twelve months. Data are from the Hong Kong Census and Statistics Department (1989a:1, 5).

16. The closest response, given by only 8.7 percent of the respondents, was "ask for pay rise from employer." This leads to the question of how the mass of unorganized workers deal with employment problems and grievances. Seeking help through the Labour Department and the Labour Tribunal is a common response when the employment relationship is terminated. Approaching the CIC is another strategy. The most common informal approaches are probably labor mobility and ad hoc group bargaining at the place of work when, for example, a group of workers goes on a brief strike. Such bargaining does not necessarily involve trade unions, although unions are sometimes in the background giving advice and support, and bargaining is typically focused on a specific issue such as piece rates or the sacking of employees. The ad hoc nature of the dispute and of the bargaining process in these cases means that these temporary and spontaneous arrangements typically dissolve after the dispute.

17. Another form of dispute is the "trade" or labor dispute, which usually involves a conflict between an employer and a group of workers (though not necessarily a trade union) who have resorted to some form of industrial action. The causes of labor disputes are classified officially under such categories as employer insolvency or cessation of business for other reasons, prolonged layoff,

removal of factory, redundancy or retrenchment, dispute between principal contractor and subcontractor, changes of terms of employment, and dismissal. England and Rear (1981:313) note that the overall number of such disputes is small, though the number rose from 29 to 182 between the mid-1960s and 1978. At the end of 1987, the number was 140, of which about half the cases involved insolvency and cessation of business. Only 8 involved changes in terms of employment.

18. The three are the Hong Kong Chinese Civil Servants' Association, the Association of Expatriate Civil Servants, and the Senior Non-Expatriate Officers' Association. The SCSC includes representatives from the official side as well as the staff side. The secretary for the civil service branch serves as the chairperson of the official side, and other members of the official side include senior representatives from the civil service and finance branches. The staff side is composed of nine representatives, three from each of the staff unions.

19. While the structure is generally similar to that of the SCSC, six instead of three staff unions make up the staff side—the six with a large membership among manual staff. Police associations are represented on a separate Police Force Council. At the departmental level, consultation is practiced through departmental consultative committees, now mandatory for departments with one hundred or more staff. Finally, the Standing Commission on Civil Service Salaries and Conditions of Service has become part of the consultative machinery in that it serves as an independent body. Both staff and management can approach or consult its members, who are appointed by the governor, on matters of pay, structure, and conditions of service (Tso 1988:61–66; Cheek-Milby 1984:187–226).

20. This does not exhaust all forms of political participation by trade unions. Trade unions also make representations to government organizations, notably the Labour Department, but also to the Executive Council and Legislative Council, on matters of interest to labor. In the 1980s, individual trade unionists were also appointed by the governor to other advisory committees.

21. K.Y.P. Chiu (1986:41) claims there are tacit understandings about sharing seats. If the FTU wished to dominate the elections, it could do so by splitting up its larger unions into smaller ones. Chiu argues that the policy of the FTU is instead to "produce a positive image as an organization to unite different forces in the Hong Kong society."

22. Independent trade unionists outside the civil service had the option of running for representative of one of the other functional constituencies. Thus, the president of the Hong Kong Professional Teachers' Union chose to run (successfully) for representative of the education constituency.

23. The government of the PRC, in an early elaboration of its basic policies regarding Hong Kong, stated that Hong Kong's capitalist system and lifestyle will remain unchanged for fifty years after 1997 and that existing rights and freedoms, including those of speech, assembly, association, occupation, and to strike, are to be ensured by the Basic Law. Strong doubts about China's commitment to maintain existing rights and freedoms and to allow Hong Kong autonomy in domestic affairs—exacerbated by the crackdown on students and the democracy movement at Tiananmen Square in June 1989—have contributed to Hong Kong's middle-class "brain-drain" problem.

24. In sharp contrast to the FTU's active participation in the drafting of the Basic Law, the TUC abstained from the process on political grounds. The TUC recognizes the nationalists in Taiwan as the sole legitimate government of China. Participating in the drafting of the Basic Law would be tantamount to accepting

the sovereignty of the Communists over Hong Kong. Thus, the TUC had little choice but to boycott the Basic Law Consultative Committee and the Joint Conference.

25. The FTU's new proposal was for the legislature to be divided into two chambers, a functional chamber and a regional chamber. Each chamber would have thirty seats, and those in the functional chamber would be elected from functional groups while those in the regional chamber would be elected by direct elections. Each of the chambers would have equal power, and a bill would have to pass through both chambers before it became law (FTU Press 1989b).

26. The case of the Mass Transit Railway illustrates the precariousness of unions when faced with a resourceful and recalcitrant management. In 1984, after finally extending recognition to the Mass Transit Railway Operating Department Staff Union, management implemented a flexible rostering system against the opposition of the union. When the union called a strike, the management retaliated immediately by dismissing the strikers for breach of contract (for failing to give proper notice). All the strikers were subsequently offered reemployment, however, except for thirteen union activists. For details, see Kong (1988:144–45).

27. The major exception is the government, where civil servants have become relatively well organized and formal consultative machinery has been in existence since 1968. Some larger companies in the private sector have set up joint consultative committees that provide alternative forms of employee representation and participation, but few are found in manufacturing. C. K. Yeung (1988:54–66) reports that there were seventy-seven joint consultative committees in 1984, covering 61,550 employees. Only eleven were in manufacturing, covering an estimated 6,100 workers.

28. W.K.S. Chiu's (1986) study of a metal industry union found that union organizers were able to recruit and hold on to members living in the squatter areas using a variety of means, including providing relief to workers suffering from fire (which was quite frequent in these areas). A veteran union organizer interviewed in the same study acknowledged that the geographical dispersal of members in the 1960s prevented the union from holding on to existing members.

29. For instance, the impact of the political strikes by the left-wing workers in 1967 was minimized by the right-wingers who served as strikebreakers.

30. Growing labor unrest in the late 1980s included, within the civil service, the disciplined services (staff of the immigration department, correctional services, and the police force), doctors, nurses, and other health personnel. There were also several labor disputes in the private sector, involving workers of Swire Air Caterers, flight attendants at Cathay Pacific, and drivers at the two major bus companies. One view is that this industrial militancy reflects a new mood among employees, specifically a declining willingness to compromise in light of the heightened political and economic uncertainties since June 1989. It should be noted, however, that the aims of these industrial actions were specific improvements in terms of employment, which are negotiable; they were not aimed at securing the institutionalization of collective bargaining or the advancement of the procedural status of organized labor.

31. Directly elected members are in a minority, however, since there are twenty-one appointed members (including three civil servants) and twenty-one indirectly elected members from functional constituencies. Unions favor having more seats allocated to the labor functional constituency; they were therefore disappointed that the government kept their number at two seats while increasing the number of seats allotted to business and professional interests.

32. The legal path has already been opened for trade unions to use their financial resources to support candidates: in June 1988, the Trade Unions Ordinance was amended to permit the use of union funds to support candidates standing for elections to the Legislative Council and other public bodies. Although only two unions had amended their rules as of the end of 1988 to enable them to use their funds for this purpose, others are expected to follow.

33. In August 1988, a conference was organized to discuss the future development of the independent labor movement in Hong Kong (Leung and Leung 1988). In January 1989, a preparatory committee was formed to discuss the possibility of establishing an alliance of independent unions in which the CIC would play an instrumental role.

8. Corporatist Trade Unionism in Singapore

1. In 1965, when Singapore became an independent sovereign republic, statutes previously entitled ordinances were retitled acts, and subsequent legislation is so titled. Legislation cited in the text is variously referred to as ordinance or act according to historical context.

2. A legal strike in Singapore "is virtually impossible without the tacit consent of the government" (Wilkinson and Leggett 1985:12), but in this case the NTUC did not veto its affiliate's decision and the minister of labor did not choose to refer the dispute to the Industrial Arbitration Court.

3. Unless otherwise cited, details of events from 1945 to 1965 are from, or corroborated by, material supplied by the NTUC library (NTUC 1985b). Statistics in this chapter on industrial stoppages and working days "lost" from 1955 to 1977 are from a mimeographed document supplied by the NTUC.

4. Membership statistics for 1946 to 1965, unless otherwise cited, are from or calculated from the Singapore Ministry of Labor (annual) and the NTUC (1985b).

5. Except for the brief stoppage in 1985, the last strike in Singapore was in 1977 at the Metal Box Company, where the non-NTUC house union was provoked into making an illegal demand and forfeited the help of the Ministry of Labor. Subsequently, the union was dissolved and the workers organized by an NTUC affiliate (Deyo 1981:50).

6. Data on industrial structure and union density are from the Singapore Ministry of Labor (1984).

7. The nine unions were the Building Construction and Timber Industries Employees' Union, the Chemical Industries Employees' Union, the Food and Beverage Industrial Workers' Union, the Metal Industries Workers' Union, the National Transport Workers' Union, the Shipbuilding and Marine Engineering Employees' Union, the Singapore Industrial and Services Employees' Union, the Textile Industries Workers' Union, and the United Workers of Electronics and Electrical Industries.

8. Calculated from figures supplied to me by the Ministry of Labor.

9. *Japan as No. 1* (Vogel 1979), *Theory Z* (Ouchi 1981), and *In Search of Excellence* (Peters and Waterman 1982) were virtually compulsory reading for Singapore's technocrats in the early 1980s when human resource management became a buzz term for training and development courses sponsored by the National Productivity Board and financed through a Skills Development Fund (Wilkinson and Leggett 1985).

10. In 1989, when the Singapore government announced an amnesty before applying corporal punishment to workers found guilty of staying beyond the expiration of their permits, ninety-eight hundred Thai workers offered themselves for repatriation (*Straits Times Weekly*, overseas edition, 22 April 1989).

In addition to foreign workers on construction sites, there are increasing numbers of foreign domestic servants, most from the Philippines, employed in Singaporean households, who are not covered by the Employment Act and who are effectively excluded from trade union protection.

11. The state-managed Central Provident Fund, established in 1955, requires monthly contributions from employers and employees toward employees' superannuation, medical benefits, and purchase of public housing.

12. An example of the government's placement of technocrats in key organizational roles in the NTUC is offered by Ng Pok Too. Ng, an able administrator whom the prime minister had wanted in the counsels of government, was humiliatingly defeated as a PAP candidate in the 1984 general election. He was subsequently appointed deputy director of the NTUC. Another technocrat and PAP member of Parliament, Goh Chee Wee, as an assistant secretary-general became the NTUC's "hatchet man" during the house union-creation exercise and, after the 1988 general election, was responsible for purging the NTUC of supporters of opposition parties (*Straits Times Weekly,* overseas edition, 15 Oct. 1988). Ng and another technocrat and PAP member of Parliament, Lim Boon Heng, eventually became deputy secretaries-general of the NTUC, leaving among the chief officers only the NTUC's presidency to a "grass-roots" nominee.

13. Dispute statistics are from Singapore Ministry of Labor (annual).

14. That the Ministry of Labor intends to take "preventive mediation" further was evidenced by its 1988 "corporate mission statement," which read, "We will foster, together with workers and employers, a conducive work environment to help in the creation of more and better jobs for a productive and disciplined workforce," and the accompanying "corporate goals" of (1) "a harmonious industrial relations climate," (2) "a safe and healthy work environment," (3) "adequate employment standards and welfare for our workers including savings for old age," (4) "an efficient labor market," (5) "a productive and disciplined work force," and (6) "more and better jobs for Singaporeans" (Singapore. Ministry of Labor 1988:5–6).

15. Deyo (1981:98–101) attributes the demoralization of the Singapore work force to rapid industrialization that has atomized the work force. He views the activities of the NTUC as seeking to create a sense of industrial community through symbolic inclusion.

16. In 1985, after a colleague at the National University of Singapore and I had published by invitation an analysis of human and industrial relations in Singapore in a Paris-based business journal (Wilkinson and Leggett 1985), we were publicly vilified by a senior NTUC official (who was also a PAP member of Parliament), condemned in the local press as distorters of the truth, and, in one case, advised not to seek a renewal of his employment contract if he wished to receive references.

17. In his 1990 May Day speech (May Days in Singapore are occasions for affirmation of the PAP-NTUC "symbiosis" and celebration of the contributions of the NTUC to nation building), NTUC Secretary-General Ong Teng Cheong emphasized the importance of continued education and training in increasing productivity and tried to convince skeptical employers of the value of cooperative relations with trade unions. He also emphasized the welfare provisions of the NTUC unions for their members and set as a target that Singaporean workers would enjoy recreational and cultural facilities comparable to those enjoyed by managers and executives (*Straits Times Weekly,* overseas edition, 5 May 1990). Among the May Day pledges by the NTUC were the maintenance of tripartism and industrial harmony, a commitment to political stability, and an enhanced standard of living for workers.

9. Australian Trade Unionism and the New Social Structure of Accumulation

1. Tribunals were established in Western Australia in 1900, New South Wales in 1901, and the Commonwealth of Australia in 1904. They were introduced in 1912 in Queensland and South Australia, while Victoria and Tasmania operate with wage board systems to this day.

2. Other interunion bodies of note were the ACTU's predecessor, the Commonwealth Council of Federated Unions, established in 1923, and the Council of Australian Government Employee Organisations, which was created in 1915 (Dufty and Fells 1989:161–62).

3. Evidence for this comes from ACTU Executive reports, which show that between 1979 and 1983 there were forty-one new ACTU affiliates, thirty-seven of which were white-collar unions. This compares with eighteen new affiliates over the period 1985–89, of which fifteen were white-collar unions.

4. In 1972, a conservative government changed the law. A successful amalgamation required at least 50 percent of the respective memberships of the merging unions to vote in a secret ballot and a majority of votes to be cast in favor of the merger (Dabscheck and Niland 1981:117). The subsequent Labor government tried unsuccessfully to amend the legislation. Legislation was probably not the main impediment to amalgamation, however, in that before 1972 there were also few union mergers.

5. According to a report in the *Economist* (1990a:37), Australia spends a relatively small amount on primary and secondary education compared with other advanced societies. The participation rate in education for persons aged sixteen to twenty-four years has also been low relative to comparable societies. Like Britain, Australia has one of the lowest ratios of persons qualified for undergraduate degrees among major OECD countries (Australia. Economic Planning Advisory Council 1986:32). These deficiencies are currently being addressed.

6. The act enables the tribunal to certify collective agreements that may not comply with extant general wage guidelines. Such agreements must be for a fixed term and contain grievance procedures and must not be varied for the length of time they are in force. For further details, see sections 115–17 of the act.

7. The tribunal may grant coverage or extend the coverage of a particular union, and in making an award it may favor one union over another.

8. There now must be a simple majority in favor of amalgamation; there is no minimum turnout requirement if the tribunal has deemed there to be "a community of interest" among the merging organizations; if this is lacking but the tribunal permits the merger to proceed, the turnout must be at least one-quarter of the members in each organization who are eligible to vote, and a simple majority must vote in favor. The perpetuation of small unions was discouraged by section 193 of the Industrial Relations Act of 1988, although it allowed for a review of unions with a membership of fewer than one thousand members. Such unions were required to convince the arbitration commission that special circumstances warranted continued registration. The ACTU subsequently lobbied the government to increase the minimum threshold to ten thousand members. This amendment was enacted in December 1990. Unions in this category that are registered in the federal jurisdiction have a three-year grace period before commencement of their review (Griffin 1991:13). Finally, mention should be made of financial assistance that the federal government

provides to amalgamating unions. This totaled nearly A. $2 million in 1990–91, and an additional A. $2 million was committed for 1991–92.

9. For example, male paraprofessionals in the public sector are more highly unionized (70.5 percent) than their female counterparts (58.3 percent), though this is not so for the private sector. A similar picture emerges, however, when comparing tradespersons in the private sector (male density, 44.7 percent; female, 21.7 percent) and low-skilled workers (laborers and related workers), whose respective densities are as follows: males in the public sector, 81.1 percent; females in the public sector, 56.8 percent; males in the private sector, 43.5 percent; females in the same sector, 36.9 percent (Australian Bureau of Statistics, catalogue no. 6325.1:19). Such comparisons are still inexact since the status of the employee (full time or part time) is not controlled for and the comparisons are not based on matched samples with respect to detailed industry and occupational categories. Women are underrepresented at various organizational levels (Winters 1987; Doran 1989:200), although some unions, such as the major public-sector unions, including the Australian Nursing Federation, have successfully fostered dramatic increases in female participation. Also worth noting is the finding that although more than 25 percent of the members of many unions have non–English speaking backgrounds, full-time officers are overwhelmingly Australian or British born (Quinlan 1989:218). The strong underrepresentation of Asians among full-time officers may be one of the reasons for the decline in union density.

10. This discussion takes into account growth arising from amalgamations. The construction section of the CMEU has an estimated density of about 60 percent, which is probably among the highest in the world for the occupations it covers. Until March 1992, when it merged with the main union covering the hospitality industry, the Federated Miscellaneous Workers' Union organized broadly similar employees as the Australian Workers' Union, yet the record of growth for the former union is far superior. In contrast to these unions, the SDA emphasizes cooperation with employers and hence closed-shop arrangements to secure a high density.

11. S. Crean and M. Rimmer (1990:21) observe that in the period 1976–88 union density declined most strongly in the Australian Capital Territory (21 percent), the Northern Territory (16 percent), and Queensland (14 percent), where conservative governments adopted such anti-union policies as the withdrawal of check-off facilities, union preference employment clauses, and closed-shop provisions in awards and agreements.

12. It is important to note, however, that according to union officials, several of whom sit on the ACTU Executive, it was officials associated with the left who tended to initiate strategy. Right-wing officials were seen by others and themselves as less influential. The growing ideological sophistication of union leaders, derived from their advanced educations and the exhaustion of various forms of communism, has begun to blur the distinctions between right and left positions in union debates, making it more difficult to distinguish union officials on ideological grounds.

13. The most conspicuous case involved the Meatworkers' Union, which was ordered to pay damages of A. $1.7 million in a secondary boycott action in 1986. In the following year, the Plumbers' Union was ordered to pay damages of A. $280,000 a day for disobeying a court order and A. $140,000 for each day work bans were implemented against employers.

14. Most amalgamations in the federal jurisdiction in the period 1980–90 involved large unions merging with smaller organizations. Twelve of the twenty-

one mergers involved blue-collar unions based mainly in the private sector, while a further six were between white-collar unions whose coverage spanned both the private and public sectors. The remaining three mergers were more complex in terms of union composition. There have also been some unsuccessful attempts at amalgamation, notably in the building industry in 1989 and between the Electricians' and the Ironworkers' unions in 1986. In 1990, the Electricians' Union and a small engineering union failed to obtain the necessary votes. A dispute ensued within the Electricians' Union leading to a court case that resulted in a decision whereby unions are prevented from using funds to support or oppose amalgamation campaigns (*Sydney Morning Herald* 1990:2). Partly in response to this case, the ACTU has urged the government to ease legal limitations on the pace of amalgamation.

15. Prominent examples over the decade include members of the Railway Union and its craft counterpart (the locomotive drivers) with respect to new jobs involving elements of work previously executed separately by members of these unions; storepersons—typically members of the National Union of Workers—undertaking additional clerical duties associated with computerized systems, traditionally the province of members of the Clerks' Union; and fitters being trained to undertake electrical work on sophisticated machinery, previously executed solely by members of the Electricians' Union.

16. As mentioned earlier, this power is provided for in the Industrial Relations Act of 1988 and was used in 1990 to award single-union coverage at an aluminum plant to the Ironworkers' Union, which since May 1991 has been the largest union comprising the Federation of Industrial, Manufacturing and Engineering Employees' Union. The Ironworkers were criticized by the MEWU for seeking to extend its coverage to a tourist site via a sole union agreement with the employer and for marketing itself as the appropriate union with whom employers should cooperate on a single-union basis.

17. It was only in 1983, after fifty-six years, that the first woman was elected to the ACTU Executive (Burgmann 1984:98). This remained unchanged until 1987, when five women were elected (Davis 1988:127), and an additional woman was elected before the 1989 congress. Female representation was reduced to five following the 1989 ACTU Congress. In 1992, only six of the thirty-five members of the Executive were women, although women comprised more than 40 percent of the ACTU's senior staff.

18. The ACTU's greater influence both within and outside the union movement has not gone unnoticed. In 1979, the editorial of a leading financial newspaper commented, perhaps with only a little exaggeration: "Of all the trade-union central organizations of the developed world, it [the ACTU] is one of the weakest, the most uninfluential, and the most devoid of the kind of basic staff structure which the responsibilities of a trade-union organization require in the complicated modern world." By 1987, the editorial described the ACTU as "one the smoothest machines in the country" (see Davis 1988:128).

19. Over the past decade left-wing factions have won control or made significant inroads in banking, clerical, insurance, public-sector (federal and some states), hospital employees', nurses', theatrical and amusement workers', and some teachers' organizations. In addition, from mid-1988, for the first time in many years, the left gained the upper hand in the Victorian Trades Hall Council, the state affiliate of the ACTU.

20. A comparison with Sweden is instructive. Available data suggest that whereas close to 9 percent of union members associated with the ACTU attended TUTA training courses in 1987–88 (see tables 9.4 and 9.6), the corresponding

figure for Swedish unionists associated with LO (the Swedish peak union body) was 14.3 percent in 1986 (ACTU/Trade Development Council 1987:183).

21. The Building Workers' and the Metal Workers' unions were in the forefront of the push for superannuation schemes in the mid-1980s. The former union, together with the construction employers, runs the successful building industry superannuation scheme. Superannuation schemes spread rapidly through industry following the 1985 Accord Mark 2 agreement, which included government support for increases in payments to these schemes. This agreement was endorsed in a qualified way by the federal tribunal. For further details, see Plowman and Weaven (1989:264).

10. Unions in Crisis: Deregulation and Reform of the New Zealand Union Movement

1. In 1992, after a major review by the National Party government, the Trade Union Education Authority and its act were abolished. This was despite the review's strongly positive statement about the efficiency and usefulness of the Trade Union Education Authority and in spite of widespread protest from many quarters. The government's intention is to make funds available for employee training and education that would be subject to competitive bidding by employers' organizations, unions, educational institutions, and others.

11. Variations in Patterns of Trade Unionism: A Synthesis

1. Ideal types cannot easily accommodate changing forms. This problem can be handled in two ways: by stating that particular empirical cases do not fit any type because they are transitional or by creating hybrid types. I have opted for the latter option since it enabled me more clearly to summarize the cases being analyzed. The question of changing union types might be more usefully considered, however, by pursuing the first option and developing ideas about the key mechanisms that shift unions from one type to another.

2. According to C. Leggett (n.d.), the NTUC's secretariat comprises the second deputy prime minister as secretary-general and three PAP members of Parliament as deputy secretaries-general. Until mid-1990, a fifth member was from the prime minister's political office. Only one member was originally a trade unionist.

3. Based on 1989 survey data, average union density in large Japanese firms—defined as employing 1,000 or more regular workers—was 58.7 percent, compared with 23.3 percent in firms with 100 to 999 regular employees. Density was only 1.8 percent in firms with fewer than 100 regular workers. Workers in these firms comprised more than 54 percent of the total employees in 1990 (Japan Institute of Labor 1992b:2–3).

4. Privatization has effectively destroyed the Japan National Railways Union, the Japan Telephone and Telecommunications' Union, and the Tobacco Corporation Union. The Teachers' Union has been racked by internal political differences.

5. While enterprise unionism usually takes the form of one union per enterprise, in 1988, 14.5 percent of surveyed establishments reported the presence of two or more unions, these being most common in mining and several areas of the service sector, such as electricity, gas, water, and heat supply (31 percent) and transport and communication (22.0 percent) (JIL 1991a:54). H. Kawanishi's (1992) research suggests that multiunionism typically arises where a right-wing union has been formed as a splinter group to the dominant left-wing union. He also points to the emergence of smaller fringe unions that organize nonperma-

nent employees. It is unclear whether these alternative unions have been expanding or declining in recent years.

6. If the number of union members is divided by the number of unions based on "workers in a factory, site, etc. or an enterprise" (JIL 1991a:48), the average union size in Japan is 170 members. This is an understatement, however, because members of workplace unions in multiworkplace organizations are also members of larger enterprise unions.

7. A useful case study illustrating the resources, issues, and dynamics of enterprise unionism in a large Japanese auto firm is provided by M. Nomura (1991b).

8. Working hours in Japan have declined only slightly from an average of 2,110 per year in 1980 to 2,052 in 1990 (calculated from JIL 1991a:41). According to P. Pons (1992:16), Japanese employees spent 2,016 hours at work in 1991, whereas the figures were 1,957 hours for U.S. workers, 1,646 for French, and 1,638 for Germans. Pressure from foreign governments, the views of a few outspoken corporate leaders, union claims based on younger workers' demands, and the rising incidence of *karoshi* (death from overwork) have encouraged the government to legislate on this issue.

9. Seventy-nine workers were sentenced for such activities in 1988. The figure rose more than sevenfold, to 601, in 1989 and declined, to 482, in 1990. In the first seven months of 1991, 377 workers received sentences for work-related "crimes" (Korea. National Alliance of Trade Unions 1991).

10. The use of hybrid or mixed categories is necessary to align the ideal types more closely with the reality of elites in the countries being analyzed. There may be disagreement with this initial classification. For example, Australia and New Zealand could be regarded as comprising middle-class elites, but this would seriously underestimate the role of political and administrative leaders in the industrialization process.

11. An implication of a wider reading of this hypothesis is that in countries where there is considerable non-Japanese foreign direct investment and/or supplier-producer networks involving non-Japanese foreign companies, management preferences for particular forms of unionism, including nonunionism, would mirror this diversity, especially if it is also reflected in public policy. This argument applies to Thailand and Malaysia, where investment from Taiwan and Hong Kong has been significant (see chap. 1). In these countries, nonunionism either has tacit government support or has been officially endorsed with respect to particular sectors.

12. Two examples—one illustrating corporate power, the other indicating its limitations—are worth noting. Apparently in response to AFL-CIO pressure to restrain the Malaysian government from denying workers' rights, the U.S. government threatened to review Malaysia's eligibility for trade preferences. This may have led the Malaysian government in 1988 to announce that it was lifting the ban preventing workers in the electronics industry from joining unions and that henceforth employees could join organizations of their choice. This position was strongly opposed by employers, with U.S. MNCs embarking on union-avoidance programs and threatening to dismiss workers who participated in union activities. A compromise was worked out whereby unionism is restricted to company-based organizations even if there is an industrial union in the industry (Standing 1992a:329). In the second example, MNCs were unable to prevent the Singapore government from introducing its high-tech, high-wage strategy in the early 1980s.

13. From previous chapters we would argue that on a productionist-consump-

tionist continuum, the union movements can be arrayed as follows: China and Singapore (relatively strongly productionist); Japan (moderately productionist); and Korea and Taiwan (dual productionist/consumptionist). Malaysian, Thai, and Hong Kong unions appear to be relatively strongly consumptionist, as are unions in Australia and New Zealand.

14. Note that although unions in China and Singapore resemble their Australian counterparts in structure at the confederal level, the purpose of Australian unions is essentially to facilitate the satisfaction of affiliates' largely consumptionist interests. Differences in the purposes of unions are also striking when the peak union councils of Hong Kong and Japan are compared.

15. A parallel problem arises with H. Clegg's (1976) theory of unionism, which is most applicable to state collaborative unionism, typically found in advanced societies. He assigns explanatory status to bargaining structure but acknowledges that bargaining structures are shaped by employers and/or the state.

16. I am grateful to Fred Deyo for pointing out that, although the Thai state is politically autonomous, it does not possess other important attributes associated with developmentalism. These include an overriding developmental mission, a unified development planning and implementation structure, and extensive policy networks. The Malaysian state lacks integration with the economic elite and consequently is unable to enforce implementation of its economic plans (see Lubeck 1992).

17. In June 1991, Thanong Po-arn, who had been president of the Labor Congress of Thailand, disappeared after threats to kill him. Thanong had led protests against the policies of the military junta, which had toppled the elected Chatichai government in February 1991.

18. The state's visibility as a factor in shaping labor relations varies; it is less apparent under state exclusionary autonomous and state collaborative autonomous regimes. When these conditions co-exist with weak labor markets and competitive product markets, employers appear as the main source of change. The state's role nevertheless remains significant (see Turner 1991).

19. The presidential election followed national assembly elections in 1992, which represented a setback for Roh's Democratic Liberal Party. Its two-thirds majority was reduced to about 50 percent of the 299 seats (*Economist* 1992c:21).

20. General Suchinda was at the center of the February 1991 army coup that appointed Anand as prime minister. Suchinda repeatedly claimed to have no political ambitions but, following elections in March 1992, permitted himself to be chosen as a nonelected prime minister by a coalition of pro-military parties. This was opposed by pro-democracy protesters, led by opposition leader, Chamlong Srimuang, the ascetic former governor of Bangkok. A conservative estimate of the death toll put it at fifty-one, and more than six hundred were injured. Many more people were beaten and imprisoned by the military (*Economist* 1992e:25, 1992g:25–36).

21. Kim Young-sam, the candidate of the ruling DLP, won 42 percent of the twenty-four million votes cast in Korea's December 1992 presidential election, ahead of rivals Kim Dae-jung (33.6 percent) and Hyundai president Chung Ju-yung (16 percent). Kim is Korea's first civilian president in thirty-two years (*Sydney Morning Herald* 1992a:7). In Taiwan, bipartisan democracy appeared to be closer following the outcome of the legislative yuan elections, which saw the ruling KMT party win only 53 percent of the vote compared to 31 percent for the opposition DPP. Remaining votes went to minor parties and KMT members who did not have the party's support (*Sydney Morning Herald* 1992b:7).

22. In the September 1991 Legislative Council elections, members of various liberal pro-democracy parties succeeded in winning a large majority of the eighteen elected seats. Most successful was the United Democrats of Hong Kong, a new party that includes some of the leaders of the so-called independent unions under the umbrella of the Confederation of Trade Unions of Hong Kong. This has enlarged union affiliates' opportunities to influence government policy.

23. These changes included restrictions on outside advisers to two persons who must be qualified and registered with the Department of Labor. This measure is intended to control the amount of advice unions receive. The right to strike was limited further by requiring that a secret ballot be held before taking action and that more than 50 percent of all workers vote affirmatively.

24. An example was the denial of the intended merger between the Malaysian Airways' Union and the Transport Workers' Union.

25. Industrial disputes (number of strikes in parentheses) declined from 1,616 (899) in 1989 to 322 (183) in 1990 to 234 (93) in 1991 (Korea Employers' Federation 1992:31). According to the ADB (1991:278), in 1989, Korea's GDP growth rate dropped to 6.5 percent from 11.5 percent the previous year. In 1990, the growth rate increased to 8.7 percent, and further growth of about 7 percent was predicted for the immediate future. Inflation in 1991 was running at around 9 percent, considerably higher than that of Korea's competitors. The balance of payments trade deficit reached nearly U.S. $9.6 billion in 1991 (Korea Employers' Federation 1992:14).

26. There is no detailed information on the relationship between the student movement and the new unions in Korea, but it appears that many union leaders of the new unions were student activists. Radical students also established what came to be known as "night school," where they passed on their knowledge to union leaders and workers. Students have also been active in workers' protests and have sought employment as a means of joining the industrial struggle. Many of these so-called disguised employees have been discharged in recent years (personal communication, Hwang-Joe Kim).

27. An example of the former is the Taiwan railroad workers forming a separate union in the north of the country, while demands by the fifth transportation section of the Taiwan Bus Company Union to form a separate union highlight the latter tendency.

28. The growing political importance accorded to unions by political parties is illustrated by the recent election of the chairman of the National General Union to the thirteenth KMT Central Standing Committee.

29. There were seven federal union amalgamations in the first six months of 1992 and an additional five pending as of 24 June 1992 (Australia. Department of Industrial Relations 1992). A significant recent development is the January 1993 merger of the Metalworkers' Union (MEWU) with the Vehicle Builders' Union; the Printers' Union and the National Union of Workers may be incorporated into this new union before 1995. The new general union, based on the manufacturing sector, would probably be Australia's largest trade union. In July 1992, the Industrial Relations Act of 1988 was amended to stipulate criteria to facilitate workplace bargaining. The criteria, which supported union involvement and the protection of workers' current standards of employment, have to be met for agreements to be certified by the AIRC. The commission could no longer delay or prevent certification of single-employer agreements because it was against the public interest.

30. Certified enterprise or workplace agreements have been permitted since 1988 under section 115 of the Industrial Relations Act of 1988 and more recently

under Division 3A. A recent analysis of the use of Section 115 concluded that very few agreements were comprehensive in scope, aiming to substitute for award provisions. Most such agreements supplemented existing award provisions or regulated employment covering unusual and short-term circumstances (Plowman 1992).

31. With substantially reduced real wages and rising unemployment, it is not surprising that changes in unit labor costs have been low in recent years relative to other OECD countries (see Boxall 1991:18).

32. For further details, see Hince and Vranken (1991) and Boxall (1991).

33. As we were going to press, Peetz et al. (1993, chap. 4) published a thorough analysis of recent developments in New Zealand. Referring to recent research, the authors suggest that the Act has had a differential impact on unions. The survival of unions in the private-service sector, which traditionally relied on compulsory unionism, has been threatened. By contrast, unions in manufacturing, construction, and the public sector suffered large membership losses from redundancies during the 1980s recession, but have remained relatively stable since (1993:265). This implies that if the tendency toward dualism alluded to above continues, unionism in New Zealand is converging on the contemporary U.S. pattern, a prime example of the state-exclusionary, autonomous market variant.

References

Abella, M. I. 1991. "Manpower Movements in the Asian Region." Mimeo.

Aldrich, H., and D. A. Whetton. 1981. "Organization-Sets, Action-Sets, and Networks: Making the Most of Simplicity." In *Handbook of Organizational Design*, ed. P. C. Nystrom and W. H. Starbuck, 385–408. New York: Oxford University Press.

All-China Federation of Trade Unions. 1988. *The Eleventh National Congress of Chinese Trade Unions*. Beijing.

Amsden, A. 1989. *Asia's Next Giant: South Korea and Late Industrialization*. New York: Oxford University Press.

———. 1990. "Third World Industrialization: 'Global Fordism' or a New Model?" *New Left Review* 182: 5–31.

Arn, J. 1984. "Public Sector Unions." In *The Hong Kong Civil Service: Personnel Policies and Practices*, ed. I. Scott and J. P. Burns. 227–57. Hong Kong: Oxford University Press.

Asian Business. 1988. *Thailand Economic Report.* June.

Asian Cultural Forum on Development. 1984. *Newsletter,* July–Aug.

Asian Development Bank (ADB). 1990. *Asian Development Outlook.* Manila.

———. 1991. *Asian Development Outlook.* Manila.

Australia. Department of Employment and Industrial Relations. 1986. *Industrial Democracy and Employee Participation.* Canberra: Australian Government Publishing Service.

Australia. Department of Industrial Relations. 1989. "Work Stoppages and Bans, 1977–88." Mimeo.

———. 1992. "Union Amalgamations under Federal Legislation since 1975." Mimeo.

Australia. Economic Planning Advisory Council. 1986. *Human Capital and Productivity Growth.* Canberra: Australian Government Publishing Service.

———. 1988. *An Overview of Microeconomic Constraints on Economic Growth.* Canberra: Australian Government Publishing Service.

Australia, Government of. 1990. *Economic Round-up.* Canberra: Australian Government Publishing Service.

Australia. Industries Assistance Commission. 1987. *Assistance to Agricultural and Manufacturing Industries.* Canberra: Australian Government Publishing Service.

———. Various. *Annual Report.* Canberra: Australian Government Publishing Service.

Australia. National Labour Consultative Council. 1988. *Wages Policy and Productivity Improvements: Achieving a Better Balance between Macro and Micro Objectives.* Canberra: Australian Government Publishing Service.

Australian. 1989. "Clerks' Civil War Costs Union $1.5 Million." Nov. 10, 4.

Australian Bureau of Statistics. 1982–90. *Australian Demographic Statistics Quarterly.* Catalogue no. 3101.0. Canberra: Australian Government Publishing Service.

———. 1990. *The Labour Force: Australia.* Catalogue no. 6203.0. Canberra: Australian Government Publishing Service.

———. Various. Catalogues nos. 5306.0., 6322.0., 6323.0, and 6325.0. Canberra: Australian Government Publishing Service.

Australian Conciliation and Arbitration Commission. 1984. *Termination Change and Redundancy Case.* Mis 250/84. MD Print F6230. Melbourne.

———. 1988. *National Wage Case.* Print H4000. Canberra: Australian Government Publishing Service.

Australian Council of Trade Unions. 1987. "Future Strategies for the Trade Union Movement." Mimeo.

———. 1979. *Finance Report to ACTU Congress.* Melbourne.

———. 1989. *Finance Report to ACTU Congress.* Melbourne.

———. Various. *Executive Report.* Melbourne.

Australian Council of Trade Unions/Trade Development Council. 1987. *Australia Reconstructed.* Canberra: Australian Government Publishing Service.

Australian Financial Review. 1990. "Government to Trigger Training Levy Time Bomb." 11 April, 1–2.

———. 1992a. "The Hewson-Howard Blueprint for a Revolution in Industrial Relations." 21 Oct., 10–11.

———. 1992b. "Strike Crisis Looms but Kennett Stands Firm." 11 Nov., 3.

Australian Industrial Relations Commission. 1992. *National Wage Case* (Oct. 1991). Decision 1150/91. M Print K0300. Canberra: Commonwealth Government Printer.

Australian Science and Technology Council. 1987. *Wealth from Skills: Measures to Raise the Skills of the Workforce.* Canberra: Australian Government Publishing Service.

Bai, M. K. 1990. "Recent Developments in Korean Labour Conditions." Mimeo.

Bamber, G., and R. Lansbury, eds. 1987. *International and Comparative Industrial Relations.* London: Allen & Unwin.

Banaji, J., and R. Hensman. 1990. *Beyond Multinationalism: Management Policy and Bargaining Relations in International Companies.* New Delhi: Sage.

Banks, J. 1974. *Trade Unionism.* London: Collier/Macmillan.

Barraclough, S. 1984. "Political Participation and Its Regulation in Malaysia: Opposition to the Societies (Amendment) Act, 1981." *Pacific Affairs* 57 (3): 450–61.

BBC. 1988. *Summary of World Broadcasts.*

———. 1989. *Summary of World Broadcasts.*

Bello, W., and S. Rosenfeld. 1990. *Dragons in Distress: Asia's Miracle Economies in Crisis.* San Francisco: Institute for Food and Development Policy.

Berdiner, B. 1987. *International Labour Affairs: The World Trade Unions and the Multinational Companies.* Oxford: Clarendon Press.

Berry, P., and G. Kitchener. 1989. *Can Unions Survive?* Melbourne: Industrial Printing and Publicity, Building Workers' Industrial Union.

Bertram, G. 1990. "Review of Easton and Walker, eds." *Listener,* 26 Feb., 110.

Biggart, Nicole Wollsey. 1990. "Institutionalized Patrimonialism in Korean Business." In *Comparative Social Research: A Research Annual: Business Institutions,* ed. C. Calhoun, 113–33. Greenwich, Conn.: JAI Press.

Bjorkman, M., S. Lauridsen, and H. S. Marcussen. 1988. "Types of Industrialization and Capital-Labour Relation in the Third World." In *Trade Unions and the New Industrialisation of the Third World,* ed. R. Southall, 59–80. London: Zed Books.

Blum, A. A., and S. Patarapanich. 1987. "Productivity and the Path to House Unionism: Structural Change in the Singapore Labour Movement." *British Journal of Industrial Relations* 25 (3): 389–400.

Bognanno, M. F. 1988a. "Labour Disputes in Korea: Recent Developments." In *Proceedings of the Conference on Labor and Economic Development,* 435–70. Taipei: Institution for Economic Research, China Productivity Center.

———. 1988b. "Korea's Industrial Relations at the Turning Point: A Report to the Korea Development Institute." Mimeo.

Bollard, A., and R. Buckle. 1987. *Economic Liberalisation in New Zealand.* Wellington: Allen & Unwin.

Boxall, P. 1991. "The New Zealand Employment Contracts Act 1991: An Analysis of Background Provisions and Implications." *Australian Bulletin of Labour* 17 (4): 284–309.

Bradbury, B., J. Doyle, and P. Whiteford. 1990. "Trends in the Disposable Incomes of Australian Families, 1982–83 to 1989–90." Discussion Paper no. 16. Sydney: Social Policy Research Centre, University of New South Wales.

Bradford, C. I., Jr. 1990. "Policy Interventions and Markets: Development Strategy Typologies and Policy Options." In *Manufacturing Miracles: Paths of Industrialization in Latin America and East Asia,* ed. G. Gereffi and D. L. Wyman, 32–54. Princeton, N.J.: Princeton University Press.

Brosnan, P. 1978. "Attitudes towards the Union in a Changing Economic Environment." *New Zealand Journal of Industrial Relations* 3 (3): 118–20.

Brosnan, P., J. Burgess, and D. Rea. 1991. "Two Ways to Skin a Cat: Government Policy and Labour Market Reform in Australia and New Zealand." Mimeo.

Brown, E. C. 1966. *Soviet Trade Unions and Labor Relations.* Cambridge: Harvard University Press.

Brunello, G. 1992. "The Effect of Unions on Firm Performance in Japanese Manufacturing." *Industrial and Labor Relations Review* 45 (3): 471–87.

Burgmann, M. 1984. "Australian Trade Unionism in 1983." *Journal of Industrial Relations* 26 (1): 91–98.

Burns, J. P. 1988. "Succession Planning and Localization." In *The Hong Kong Civil Service and Its Future*, ed. I. Scott and J. P. Burns, 87–106. Hong Kong: Oxford University Press.

Business Council of Australia. 1989. *Enterprise-Based Bargaining Units: A Better Way of Working.* Melbourne.

———. 1992. "Australian Trade Policy Priorities and the Asia Pacific Region." *Business Council Bulletin* 86 (May): 6–12.

Callister, P. 1991. *Expanding Our Horizons: New Zealand in the Global Economy,* Wellington: New Zealand Planning Council.

Callus, R., A. Morehead, M. Cully, and J. Buchanan. 1991. *Industrial Relations at Work: The Australian Workplace Survey.* Canberra: Australian Government Publishing Service.

Campbell, R., and A. Kirk. 1983. *After the Freeze: New Zealand Unions in the Economy.* Wellington: Port Nicholson Press.

Castells, M. 1992. "Four Asian Tigers with a Dragon Head: A Comparative Analysis of the State, Economy, and Society in the Asian Pacific Rim." In *States and Development in the Asian Pacific Rim,* ed. R. P. Applebaum and J. Henderson, 33–70. London: Sage.

Castles, F. 1985. *Working Class and Welfare: Reflections on the Political Development of the Welfare State in Australia and New Zealand.* Sydney: Allen & Unwin.

———. 1987. "Neocorporatism and the Happiness Index." *European Journal of Political Research* 15 (4): 381–93.

Chan, A.W.K. 1988. "The Trade Unions Ordinance: Its Enactment and Subsequent Development." In *Labour Movement in a Changing Society,* ed. Y. C. Jao et al., 35–39. Hong Kong: Centre of Asian Studies, University of Hong Kong.

Chan, M. K. 1975. *Labor and Empire: The Chinese Labor Movement in the Canton Delta, 1895–1927.* Ann Arbor: University Microfilms International.

———. 1981. *A Historiography of the Chinese Labor Movement.* Palo Alto, Calif.: Stanford University Press.

Chao, S. P. 1987. "Labor Policies and Implementation in Taiwan," (in Chinese). *Labor Research Quarterly* 89: 10–22.

———. 1988. "Labor Policy and Legislation in the Republic of China on Taiwan." In *Proceedings of the Conference on Labor and Economic Development,* 245–76. Taipei: Institution for Economic Research, China Productivity Center.

Chao, T. C., C. S. Wu, and H. L. Wu. 1988. "The Year-End Bonus System and Taiwan's Economic Development." In *Proceedings of the Conference on Labor and Economic Development,* 567–94. Taipei: Institution for Economic Research, China Productivity Center.

Chapman, B. J., and F. Gruen. 1990. "An Analysis of the Australian Consensual Incomes Policy: The Prices and Incomes Accord." Discussion Paper no. 221. Canberra: Centre for Economic Policy Research, Australian National University.

Cheah, H. B. 1988. "Labour in Transition: The Case of Singapore." *Labour and Industry* 1 (2): 258–86.

Cheek-Milby, K. 1984. "Staff Relations." In *The Hong Kong Civil Service and Its Future*, ed. I. Scott and J. P. Burns, 187–226. Hong Kong: Oxford University Press.

Cheetham, J. 1988. "The Perspective of Employers on Trade Unions." In *Labour Movement in a Changing Society*, ed. Y. C. Jao et al., 77–80. Hong Kong: Centre of Asian Studies, University of Hong Kong.

Chen, C. L. 1988. "The Development of the Union Movement in Taiwan" (in Chinese). *Labour Research Quarterly* 92: 102–12.

Chen, K. C. 1986. "The New Topic of Labor in Taiwan" (in Chinese). *Association of Industrial Relations, ROC*, 180–84.

Chen, P. K. 1985. *The Labour Movement in China*. Hong Kong: Swindon Books.

Cheng, T.-J. 1990. "Political Regimes and Development Strategies: South Korea and Taiwan." In *Manufacturing Miracles: Paths of Industrialization in Latin America and East Asia*, ed. G. Gereffi and D. L. Wyman, 139–78. Princeton, N.J.: Princeton University Press.

Cheng, Y. T. 1988. "The Role of a Trade Union Centre in a Changing Society: The Case of the Hong Kong Federation of Trade Unions." In *Labour Movement in a Changing Society*, ed. Y. C. Jao et al., 113–16. Hong Kong: Centre of Asian Studies, University of Hong Kong.

Chesneaux, J. 1968. *The Chinese Labor Movement, 1919–1927*. Stanford, Calif.: Stanford University Press.

Child, J., R. Loveridge, and M. Warner. 1973. "Towards an Organizational Study of Trade Unions." *Sociology* 7 (2): 71–91.

Child, J., and X. Xinzhong. 1989. "The Communist Party's Role in the Enterprise Leadership at the High-Water of China's Economic Reform." Working paper. Economic Management Institute, Beijing.

China, Republic of. Executive Yuan. Directorate-General of Budget, Accounting, and Statistics (DGBAS). n.d. *Abstract of Employment and Earnings Statistics in Taiwan Area, Republic of China, 1989*. Taipei: DGBAS and Coordination Council for North American Affairs Office in USA.

Chiu, C. H. 1989. "The Adjustment of Trade Union Organizations under Social Change" (in Chinese). *Symposium on Social Development and Labor's Needs*, 57–63.

Chiu, K.Y.P. 1986. "Labour Organizations and Political Change in Hong Kong." M.Soc.Sc. diss., University of Hong Kong.

Chiu, W.K.S. 1986. "A Brief History of the Metal Industry Workers' Union" (in Chinese). In *Dimensions of the Chinese and Hong Kong Labor Movement*, ed. M. K. Chan et al., 138–44. Hong Kong: Christian Industrial Committee.

———. 1987. "Strikes in Hong Kong: A Sociological Study." M.Phil. thesis, University of Hong Kong.

Cho, Changhwa. 1978. "Labour Movement in Korea." *Journal of Labour Economics* 2 (1): 73–86.

Choi, J. J. 1989. *Labor and the Authoritarian State: Labor Unions in South Korean Manufacturing Industries, 1961–1980*. Seoul: Korea University Press.

Christian Institute of Industrial Development. 1990. *Recent Labor Movement and the Issues of Industrial Relations*. Seoul: Chung-arm Mun-whasa.

Chua, B. H. 1982. "Singapore in 1981: Problems in New Beginnings." In *Southeast*

Asian Affairs 1982, ed. Institute of Southeast Asian Studies, 315–55. Singapore: Heinemann Asia.

———. 1985. "Pragmatism of the People's Action Party Government in Singapore: A Critical Assessment." *South East Asia Journal of Social Science* 13 (2): 29–46.

Church and Society Study Group. 1985. *Focus on Labour.* Singapore.

Clegg, H. 1976. *Trade Unionism under Collective Bargaining: A Theory based on Comparisons of Six Countries.* London: Basil Blackwell.

Cohen, R. 1991. *Contested Domains: Debates in International Labour Studies.* London: Zed Press.

Collier, D., ed. 1979. *The New Authoritarianism in Latin America.* Princeton, N.J.: Princeton University Press.

———. 1991. "The Comparative Method: Two Decades of Change." In *Comparative Political Dynamics: Global Research Perspectives,* ed. D. A. Rustow and K. P. Erickson, 7–31. New York: HarperCollins.

Collier, R. B., and D. Collier. 1991. *Shaping the Political Arena.* Princeton, N.J.: Princeton University Press.

Confederation of Australian Industry and Australian Council of Trade Unions. 1988. "Joint Statement on Participative Practices." Canberra: Australian Government Publishing Service.

Connell, R. W., and T. H. Irving. 1980. *Class Structure in Australian History.* Melbourne: Longman Cheshire.

Council of Seoul Trade Unions. 1989. *Seonohyup Shin Min* (newspaper), 7 Jan.

Crawford, J. 1979. *Report of Study Group on Structural Adjustment.* Vol. 1. Canberra: Australian Government Publishing Service.

Crean, S. 1989. *Presidential Address to ACTU Congress.* Melbourne: ACTU.

Crean, S., and M. Rimmer. 1990. *ILO Study on the Adjustment Problems of Trade Unions in Industrialised Market Economies.* International Labour Organisation. Mimeo.

Crouch, C. 1977. *Class Conflict and the Industrial Relations Crisis.* London: Macmillan.

Dabscheck, B., and J. Niland. 1981. *Industrial Relations in Australia.* Sydney: Allen & Unwin.

Damri Phophangpum. 1990. "Thailand Country Paper." In *Report of the ILO/ Japan Asia and Pacific Regional Tripartite Evaluation Meeting on Labor Management Cooperation and Productivity,* 179–80. Manila.

Davies, S.N.G. 1977. "One Brand of Politics Rekindled." *Hong Kong Law Journal* 7 (1): 44–84.

Davis, E. M. 1987. *Democracy in Australian Unions.* Sydney: Allen & Unwin.

———. 1988. "The 1987 ACTU Congress: Reconstructing Australia?" *Journal of Industrial Relations* 30 (1): 118–29.

———. 1990. "The 1989 ACTU Congress: Seeking Change Within." *Journal of Industrial Relations* 32 (1): 100–110.

Deeks, J., and P. Boxall. 1989. *Labour Relations in New Zealand.* Auckland: Longmans.

Deery, S., and H. De Cieri. 1991. "Determinants of Trade Union Membership in Australia." *British Journal of Industrial Relations* 29 (1): 59–73.

Deery, S., and D. H. Plowman. 1991. *Australian Industrial Relations.* Sydney: McGraw-Hill.

Deery, S. and R. Mitchell, eds. 1993. *Labour Law and Industrial Relations in Asia.* Melbourne: Longman Cheshire.

Deutschmann, C. 1991. "The Worker-Bee Syndrome in Japan: An Analysis of Working-Time Practices." In *Working Time in Transition: The Political Economy of Working Hours in Industrial Nations,* ed. K. Hinrichs, W. Roche, and C. Sirianni, 189–202. Philadelphia: Temple University Press.

Deyo, F. C. 1981. *Dependent Development and Industrial Order: An Asian Case Study.* New York: Praeger.

———. 1984. "Export Manufacturing and Labor: The Asian Case." In *Labor in the Capitalist World-Economy,* ed. C. Bergquist, 267–88. Beverly Hills, Calif.: Sage.

———. 1987. *The Political Economy of the New Asian Industrialism.* Ithaca, N.Y.: Cornell University Press.

———. 1989. *Beneath the Miracle: Labor Subordination in the New Asian Industrialism.* Berkeley: University of California Press.

———. 1992. "Newly Industrialized Countries." In *States and Development in the Asian Pacific Rim,* ed. R. P. Applebaum and J. Henderson, 289–306. London: Sage.

Deyo, F. C., S. Haggard, and H. Koo. 1987. "Labor in the Political Economy of East Asian Industrialization." *Bulletin of Concerned Asian Scholars* 19 (2): 42–53.

Djao, W. 1975. "Dependent Development and Social Control: Labor Intensive Industrialization in Hong Kong." *Social Praxis* 5 (3–4): 275–93.

———. 1981. " 'Traditional Chinese Culture' in the Small Factory of Hong Kong." *Journal of Contemporary Asia* 11: 413–25.

Donaldson, L., and M. Warner. 1974. "Elections and Bureaucratic Control in Occupational Interest Associations." *Sociology* 8 (1): 47–58.

Dong, X. 1989. "Labour Contract System." *Chinese Trade Unions* 2: 27–29.

Doran, J. 1989. "Unions and Women." In *Australian Unions: An Industrial Relations Perspective,* ed. B. Ford and D. Plowman, 190–202. Melbourne: Macmillan.

Dore, R. 1974. *British Factory–Japanese Factory: The Origins of National Diversity in Industrial Relations.* Oxford: Allen & Unwin.

———. 1979. "Industrial Relations in Japan and Elsewhere." In *Japan: A Comparative View,* ed. A. M. Craig, 324–70. Princeton, N.J.: Princeton University Press.

———. 1986. *Flexible Rigidities, Industrial Policy and Structural Adjustment in the Japanese Economy, 1970–1980.* London: Athlone.

———. 1989. "Where Are We Now: Musings of an Evolutionist." *Work, Employment and Society* 3 (4): 425–46.

Dufty, N. F., and R. E. Fells. 1989. *Dynamics of Industrial Relations in Australia.* Sydney: Prentice Hall.

Dyster, B., and D. Meredith. 1990. *Australia in the International Economy in the Twentieth Century.* Melbourne: Cambridge University Press.

Easton, B., ed. 1989. *The Making of Rogernomics.* Auckland: Auckland University Press.

Eccleston, B. 1989. *State and Society in Post-War Japan.* Cambridge, U.K.: Polity Press.

Economic Intelligence Unit. 1991. "Profile of Singapore, 1990–91." *London Economist* paper.

Economist. 1987. 1 Aug., special ed.

————. 1988. *South East Asia on Business.* London: Collins.

————. 1990a. "Spending on Schools: Pick Your Number." 17 Feb., 37.

————. 1990b. "Thailand Waits for Its Second Wind." 14 April, 28.

————. 1990c. "China's Economy Still Dead-Ended." 18 Aug., 18.

————. 1990d. "Hong Kong: A Whisper of Democracy." 3 Nov., 29.

————. 1990e. "China America's Fair-Haired Boy Again." 8 Dec., 30.

————. 1991a. "South Korea's Economy Stumbles." 23 Feb., 26–27.

————. 1991b. "ASEAN Debates a Trade Block." 9 March, 30.

————. 1991c. "Malaysia, Slicing the Cake." 4 May, 31–32.

————. 1991d. "China's Economy: They Couldn't Keep It Down." 1 June, 17–20.

————. 1992a. "ASEAN: The Eye of Japan." 1 Feb., 24–25.

————. 1992b. "Asian Economies: Freedom Pays." 14 March, 26.

————. 1992c. "A Blow to Roh." 28 March, 21–22.

————. 1992d. "Economic and Financial Indicators." 4 April, 117.

————. 1992e. "Thailand, the Generals and the King." 23 May, 25–26.

————. 1992f. "Miyazawa's Moment." 1 Aug., 29–30.

————. 1992g. "Thailand's Day of Angels." 19 Sept., 25–26.

————. 1992h. "New Zealand: Vote, Vote, Vote." 26 Sept., 28.

Edelstein, J. D., and M. Warner. 1979. *Comparative Union Democracy.* New Brunswick, N.J.: Transaction Books.

Edwards, R., P. Garonna, and F. Tödtling. 1986. *Unions in Crisis and Beyond.* Dover, Mass.: Auburn House.

Eichbaum, C. 1989. "Workplace Bargaining: Implications for Trade Union Organisation and Strategy." In *Restructuring Industrial Relations: The Challenge of Industry and Enterprise Bargaining.* Auckland: Longmans.

Ellison, C., and G. Gereffi. 1990. "Explaining Strategies and Patterns of Industrial Development." In *Manufacturing Miracles: Paths of Industrialization in Latin America and East Asia,* ed. G. Gereffi and D. L. Wyman, 368–404. Princeton, N.J.: Princeton University Press.

Enderwick, P. 1985. *Multinational Business and Labour.* London: Croom Helm.

England, J., and J. Rear. 1975. *Chinese Labour under British Rule.* Hong Kong: Oxford University Press.

————. 1981. *Industrial Relations and Law in Hong Kong.* Hong Kong: Oxford University Press.

————. 1989. *Industrial Relations and Law in Hong Kong,* 2d ed. Hong Kong: Oxford University Press.

Essenberg, B. 1981. "The Interaction of Industrial Relations and the Labour Process in Developing Countries." *Labour and Society* 6 (1): 91–102.

Evans, P. B. 1985. "Transnational Linkages and the Economic Role of the State: An Analysis of Developing and Industralized Nations in the Post–World War II Period." In *Bringing the State Back In,* ed. P. B. Evans, D. Rueschemeyer, and T. Skocpol, 192–226. Cambridge: Cambridge University Press.

————. 1989. "Predatory, Developmental and Other Apparatuses: A Comparative Political Economy Perspective on the Third World State." *Sociological Forum* 4: 561–87.

Fairbank, J. K. 1989. "Why China's Rulers Fear Democracy." *New York Review of Books,* 28 Sept., 32–33.

Far Eastern Economic Review (FEER). 1986. "Asia's Unions: An Organised Disunity." 3 April, 43–67.

———. 1989. *Asia 1989 Yearbook.* Hong Kong: Review Publishing.

———. 1990. *Asia 1990 Yearbook.* Hong Kong: Review Publishing.

———. 1991. *Asia 1991 Yearbook.* Hong Kong: Review Publishing.

———. 1992. *Asia 1992 Yearbook.* Hong Kong: Review Publishing.

Fathers, M., and A. Higgins. 1989. *Tiananmen: The Rape of Peking.* London: Independent and Doubleday.

Federation of Korean Trade Unions. 1979. *History of Labor Union Movement.* Seoul.

———. 1984a. *Analysis of Collective Agreements.* Seoul.

———. 1984b. *Annual Report 1983.* Seoul.

Flanders, A. 1975. *Management and Unions: The Theory and Reform of Industrial Relations.* London: Faber & Faber.

Foulkes, A. 1989. "Industry Bargaining in Restructuring Industrial Relations." In *Restructuring Industrial Relations: The Challenge of Industry and Enterprise Bargaining.* Auckland: Longmans.

Frenkel, S. J. 1978. "Industrial Conflict, Workplace Characteristics and Accommodation Structure in the Pilbara Iron Ore Industry." *Journal of Industrial Relations* 20 (4): 386–406.

———. 1987. "Managing through the Recession." *Labour and Industry* 1 (1): 39–60.

———. 1988. "Australian Employers in the Shadow of the Labour Accords." *Industrial Relations* 27 (2): 166–79.

———. 1990. "Containing Dualism through Corporatism: Changes in Contemporary Industrial Relations in Australia." *Bulletin of Comparative Labour Relations* 20: 115–45.

———. 1991. "State Policies and Workplace Relations: A Comparison between Thatcherism and Accordism." In *The Future of Industrial Relations: Proceedings of the Second Bargaining Group Conference,* ed. H. C. Katz, 47–71. Ithaca, N.Y.: ILR Press.

Frenkel, S. J., and A. Coolican. 1984. *Unions against Capitalism?: A Sociological Comparison of the Australian Building and Metal Workers' Unions.* Sydney: Allen & Unwin.

Frenkel, S. J., and M. Shaw. 1989. "No Tears for the Second Tier: Productivity Bargaining in Australia." *Australian Bulletin of Labour* 15 (2): 90–114.

FTU Press. 1988. "Comments of the FTU on the Draft Basic Law Consultative Document" (in Chinese). Oct.

———. 1989a. "Mourning Our Compatriots Killed on June 4th in Beijing" (in Chinese). July.

———. 1989b. "Comments of the FTU on the Political System Section of the Draft Basic Law" (in Chinese). Dec.

Fuller, C. 1989. "The Functioning of the Labour Relations Act 1987—Unions." In *Evaluating the Labour Relations Act 1987,* ed. R. Harbridge. Wellington: Industrial Relations Centre, Victoria University of Wellington.

Galenson, W., ed. 1962. *Labour and Economic Development.* New York: Wiley.

Gamba, C. 1962. *The Origins of Trade Unionism in Malaya.* Singapore: Donald Moore.

Gardner, M. 1987. "Australian Trade Unionism in 1986." *Journal of Industrial Relations* 29 (1): 102–10.

———. 1988. "Australian Trade Unionism in 1987." *Journal of Industrial Relations* 30 (1): 147–54.

Garnaut, R. 1989. *Australia and the North East Asian Ascendancy.* Canberra: Australian Government Publishing Service.

Geare, A. 1988. *The System of Industrial Relations in New Zealand.* Wellington: Butterworths.

Gereffi, G. 1990. "Big Business and the State." In *Manufacturing Miracles: Paths of Industrialization in Latin America and East Asia,* ed. G. Gereffi and D. L. Wyman, 90–109. Princeton, N.J.: Princeton University Press.

Gittings, J. 1989. *China Changes Face: The Road from Revolution, 1949–1989.* Oxford: Oxford University Press.

Gittins, R. 1988. "It's Time to Start Taking the Services Sector More Seriously." *Sydney Morning Herald,* 30 Jan., 34.

Goldman, M. 1989. "Vengeance in China." *New York Review of Books,* 9 Nov., 5–9.

Gollan, R. 1975. *Revolutionaries and Reformists: Communism and the Australian Labour Movement, 1920–1955.* Canberra: ANU Press.

Gong, Y. 1989. "Chinese Trade Unions' Function of Democratic Participation and Social Supervision." *Chinese Trade Unions* 2: 2–5.

Gordon, D. M., R. Edwards, and M. Reich. 1982. *Segmented Work, Divided Workers: The Historical Transformation of Labor in the United States.* New York: Cambridge University Press.

Gourevitch, P., et al. 1984. *Unions and the Economic Crisis: Britain, West Germany and Sweden.* London: Allen & Unwin.

Griffin, G. 1991. "Changing Trade Union Structure." Working Paper no. 61. Centre for Industrial Relations and Labour Studies, University of Melbourne.

Gruen, F. H. 1985. "How Bad Is Australia's Economic Performance and Why?" Discussion Paper no. 127. Centre for Economic Policy Research, Australian National University, Canberra.

Guillermaz, J. 1972. *A History of the Chinese Communist Party.* New York: Random House.

Hagan, J. 1989. "The Australian Union Movement: Context and Perspective, 1850–1987." In *Australian Unions: An Industrial Relations Perspective,* ed. B. Ford and D. Plowman, 18–48. Melbourne: Macmillan.

Haggard, S. 1988. "The Politics of Industrialization in the Republic of Korea and Taiwan." In *Achieving Industrialization in East Asia,* ed. H. Hughes, 260–82. Cambridge: Cambridge University Press.

———. 1990. *Pathways from the Periphery: The Politics of Growth in the Newly Industrializing Countries.* Ithaca, N.Y.: Cornell University Press.

Hancock Committee of Review. 1985. *Australian Industrial Relations Law and System.* Vol. 2. Canberra: Australian Government Publishing Service.

Harbridge, R. 1989. "Evaluating the Bargaining Provisions of the Labour Relations Act, 1987." In *Evaluating the Labour Relations Act 1987,* ed. R. Harbridge. Wellington: Industrial Relations Centre, Victoria University of Wellington.

Harbridge, R., and P. Walsh. 1989. "Restructuring Wage Bargaining in New Zealand, 1984–1989." In *Issues and Trends in Australasian Industrial Relations,* ed. M. Bray and D. Kelly, 60–84. Sydney: Industrial Relations Academics Association of Australia and New Zealand.

Harbridge, R., and S. McCaw. 1991. "Trends in Wage Bargaining in New Zealand: The 1988–89 Wage Round." *Labour and Industry* 3 (2–3): 372–88.

Harris, N. 1987. *The End of the Third World: Newly Industrialising Countries and the Decline of an Ideology.* Harmondsworth, U.K.: Penguin Books.

———. 1992. "States, Economic Development and the Asian Pacific Rim." In *States and Development in the Asian Pacific Rim,* ed. R. P. Applebaum and J. Henderson, 71–84. London: Sage.

Harvey, O. 1988. "Towards a Union Strategy for the 1990s." Auckland. Mimeo.

Hawke, R. J. 1988. "The Government's Reform Agenda." *Business Council Bulletin* 48 (Oct.): 15.

Hawke, R. J., P. Keating, and J. Button. 1991. *Building a Competitive Australia.* Canberra: Australian Government Publishing Service.

Haworth, N. 1990. "Industrial Restructuring and Industrial Relations in New Zealand: Towards a New Consensus." *Bulletin of Comparative Labour* 2: 167–90.

He, B., C. Hao, and J. Guo. 1989. "Conditions of Workers' Material and Mental Lives." *Chinese Economic Studies,* Summer, 32–37.

Henley, J. S., and M. K. Nyaw. 1986. "Introducing Market Forces into Managerial Decision Making in Chinese Industrial Enterprises." *Journal of Management Studies* 23 (6): 635–56.

———. 1989. "The System of Management and Performance of Joint Ventures in China." In *Reform Policy and the Chinese Enterprise,* ed. J. Child and M. Lockett, vol. 1, pt. A, 277–94. London: JAI Press.

Hewison, K. J. 1989a. *Power and Politics in Thailand: Essays in Political Economy.* Manila: Journal of Contemporary Asia Publishers.

———. 1989b. *Bankers and Bureaucrats: Capital and the Role of the State in Thailand.* Monograph Series no. 34. New Haven, Conn.: Yale University Southeast Asia Studies, Yale Center for International and Area Studies.

Hill, H. 1990. "Foreign Investment and East Asian Economic Development." *Asia-Pacific Economic Literature* 4 (2): 21–57.

Hince, K., and Vranken, M. 1991. "A Controversial Reform of New Zealand Labour Law: The Employment Contracts Act 1991." *International Labour Review* 130 (4): 475–92.

Hing Ai Yun. 1990. "Capital Transformation and Labour Relations in Malaysia." *Labour and Industry* 3 (1): 76–92.

Hong Kong. Census and Statistics Department. 1979. *Hong Kong by Census 1976: Main Report.* Vol. 2. Hong Kong: Government Printer.

———. 1982. *Hong Kong 1981 Census: Main Report.* Vols. 1 and 2. Hong Kong: Government Printer.

———. 1983. *Social Data Collected by the General Household Survey: Special Topics Report 1.* Hong Kong: Government Printer.

———. 1988. *Hong Kong 1986 by Census: Main Report.* Vols. 1 and 2. Hong Kong: Government Printer.

————. 1989a. *Quarterly Report of Wages, Salaries and Employee Benefits Statistics, September 1988.* Vol. 2. Hong Kong: Government Printer.

————. 1989b. *Estimates of Gross Domestic Product: 1966 to 1988.* Hong Kong: Government Printer.

Hong Kong. Labour Department. 1989. *Annual Departmental Report 1988.* Hong Kong: Government Printer.

Hong Kong. Registrar of Trade Unions. 1989. *Annual Departmental Report 1988.* Hong Kong: Government Printer.

————. Various. *Annual Report.* Hong Kong: Government Printer.

Hong Kong Economic Journal. 1988. "The Long-Run Cause of the Internal Dissent within the TUC." 28 Nov.

Hong Kong Federation of Trade Unions. 1988. *Carry Forward the Fine Traditions, Open up a New Prospect.* Hong Kong.

Hong Kong Hansard. 1987–88. *Reports of the Sittings of the Legislative Council of Hong Kong* 1. Hong Kong: Government Printer.

Hongladarom, C., et al. 1985. *Research Report of Labour Relations at the Level of the Enterprises.* Bangkok: Human Resources Institute, Thammasat University.

Huang, J. 1988. "The Development of Newly Emerged Labor Movement in Taiwan and Its Implications for Human Resource Management." In *Proceedings of the Conference on Labor and Economic Development,* 281–308. Taipei: Institution for Economic Research, China Productivity Center.

Huang, P. T. 1988. "The Problem of Taiwan" (in Chinese). *Labour Research Quarterly* 93: 70–85.

Huybregts, G. 1988. "The Labor Relations Practices of Foreign-Owned Firms in Australia." Ph.D. diss., University of California, Los Angeles.

Inagami, T. 1988. *Japanese Workplace Industrial Relations* (in Japanese). Japanese Industrial Relations Series no. 14. Tokyo: Japan Institute of Labor.

Ingham, G. K. 1974. *Strikes and Industrial Conflict: Britain and Scandinavia.* London: Macmillan.

Inkson, K. 1980. "Factors Influencing Workers' Involvement in Their Unions." *Journal of Industrial Relations* 22 (4): 442–52.

International Labour Organisation. 1962. *The Trade Union Situation in the Federation of Malaya.* Geneva: International Labour Office.

————. 1989. *International Financial Statistics, Yearbook 1989.* New York.

————. 1990. *1989–90 Year Book of Labour Statistics.* Geneva: International Labour Office.

————. 1991a. *ILO in Asia and the Pacific: A Review of Activities in 1990.* Bangkok: International Labour Organisation.

————. 1991b. *Report of the ILO/Japan ASEAN Subregional Tripartite Seminar on the Development of Sound Labour Relations.* Bangkok: International Labour Organisation.

International Monetary Fund. 1989a. *International Financial Statistics, December.* New York.

Ismail, A. 1989. *Hong Kong 1989: A Review of 1988.* Hong Kong: Government Information Services.

Jackson, G. 1975. *Policies for Development of Manufacturing Industry.* Vol. 1. Canberra: Australian Government Publishing Service.

Jain, H. 1990. "Human Resource Management in Selected Japanese Firms, Their Foreign Subsidiaries and Locally Owned Counterparts." *International Labour Review* 129 (1): 73–89.

Jamieson, S. 1992. "Trade Unions in 1991." *Journal of Industrial Relations* 34 (1): 162–69.

Japan Institute of Labor (JIL). 1990. "Major Moves Prior to Revision of Immigration Control Law." *Japan Labor Bulletin* 29 (7): 4.

———. 1991a. *Japanese Working Life Profile: Labor Statistics 1991–1992.* Tokyo.

———. 1991b. "Labor-Management Relations: Basic Survey on Trade Unions." *Japan Labor Bulletin* 30 (2): 2–3.

———. 1991c. "Labor-Management Relations: Labor Unions' Political Activities: Rengo Searching for Its Political Policy." *Japan Labor Bulletin* 30 (9): 3–4.

———. 1992a. "Labor-Management Relations: Rengo Decides on Action Policy for 1992–93." *Japan Labor Bulletin* 31 (3): 3.

———. 1992b. "Labor-Management Relations: Unionization Hits Record Low." *Japan Labor Bulletin* 31 (3): 2–3.

Jessop, B. 1978. "Capitalism and Democracy: The Best Possible Shell?" In *Power and the State,* ed. G. Littlejohn, B. Smart, J. Wakeford, and N. Yuval-Davis, 10–51. London: Croom Helm.

———. 1990. *State Theory: Putting Capitalists in Their Place.* State College: Pennsylvania State University Press.

Jomo, K. S. 1983. *The Sun Also Sets: Lessons in Looking East.* Petaling Jaya, Malaysia: Institute for Social Analysis.

Kassalow, E., ed. 1978. *The Role of Trade Unions in Developing Societies.* Geneva: International Institute for Labour Studies.

Katzenstein, P. J. 1985. *Small States in World Markets: Industrial Policy in Europe.* Ithaca, N.Y.: Cornell University Press.

Kawanishi, H. 1992. *Enterprise Unionism in Japan.* London: Kegan Paul.

Kearney, C. 1989. "The Australian Macroeconomy, 1971–89." Mimeo.

Kelly, J. 1990. "British Trade Unionism, 1979–89: Change, Continuity and Contradictions." *Work, Employment and Society,* May (special issue), 29–65.

Kerr, C. 1983. *The Future of Industrial Societies: Convergence or Continuing Diversity?* Cambridge: Harvard University Press.

Kerr, C., J. T. Dunlop, F. H. Harbison, and C. A. Myers. 1975. *Industrialism and Industrial Man.* Harmondsworth, U.K.: Penguin Books.

Khoo Kay Kim. 1972. "Chinese Labour Unrest in Malaya in the Late 1930s." *Pentadbir* 2.

Kidd, J. B. 1992. "Globalism through Localism: Reflections on the Japanese Production Subsidiaries in the UK." Mimeo.

Kim, H.-J. 1984. *New Directions for the Development of Appropriate Industrial Relations in Korea* (in Korean). Seoul: Korean Chamber of Commerce and Industry.

———. 1988. "Industrial Relations in Korea: Issues and Perspectives." *Journal of East and West Studies* 17 (2): 1–16.

Kim, H.-J. and B. N. Sung. 1990. "Union Activities and Economic Effects." *Yonsei Business Review* 27 (2): 55–93.

Kim, T. 1990. "Industrial Relations and Collective Bargaining in Korea: Recent Developments" (in Korean). Mimeo.

Kim, Y. 1982. *History of Korean Labor Movement* (in Korean). Seoul: Chungsa.

Kirk, A. 1983. "The Trade Union Response to Structural Change." *New Zealand Journal of Industrial Relations* 8 (3): 211–21.

Kleingartner, A., and H.-S. Peng. 1991. "Taiwan: An Exploration of Labour Relations in Transition." *British Journal of Industrial Relations* 29 (3): 427–45.

Koike, K. 1988. *Understanding Industrial Relations in Modern Japan.* London: Macmillan.

Kong, T. C. 1988. "The Strikes at the Mass Transit Railway: Causes and Implications." In *Labour Movement in a Changing Society,* ed. Y. C. Jao et al., 143–46. Hong Kong: Centre of Asian Studies, University of Hong Kong.

Koo, H. 1991. "Middle Classes, Democratization and Class Formation." *Theory and Society* 21 (4): 485–509.

Korea. Ministry of Labor. 1987. *Annual Report.* Seoul.

———. 1990. *Yearbook of Labor Statistics.* Seoul.

Korea. National Alliance of Trade Unions. 1991. *National Labor Newspaper* (unofficial newspaper of the National Alliance of Trade Unions), 15 Aug.

Korea Employers' Federation. 1992. *Quarterly Review* 46 (March).

Korea Labor Institute. 1989a. *Quarterly Labor Review* 2 (May): 31–37.

———. 1989b. *Quarterly Labor Review* 2 (Aug.): 30–34.

Korean Productivity Center. 1987. *The Environment of Labor Relations and Labor Disputes* (in Korean). Seoul.

———. 1989. *Industrial Society and Labor Culture of Korea* (in Korean). Seoul.

Kromraenggnan (Thai Labor Department). 1984. *Ruam Kotmai Raenggnan* (Collected Labour Laws). Bangkok.

Kumon, K. 1991. "Japanese Affiliated Automobile Plants in the U.S. and Taiwan." Mimeo.

Kuruvilla, S. 1992. "Industrialization Strategy and Industrial Relations Policy in Malaysia." Paper presented to the Labour, Management and Industrialization Conference, Sydney, 4–5 Sept.

Kuwahara, Y. 1990. "Changing Industrial Relations in the Context of Industrial Restructuring: The Case of Japan." *Bulletin of Comparative Labour Relations* 20: 147–65.

Kwanmo, S. 1989. "Distribution of White Collar in Korea." In *Labor Movement of Clerical Workers in Korea,* ed. S. Kwanmo and S. Sungmo, 7–32. Seoul: Tae-am.

Kwok, Y. H. 1988. "Staff Representation on the Senior Civil Service Council: Consultation, Collective Bargaining or Participation." In *Labour Movement in a Changing Society,* ed. Y. C. Jao et al., 147–49. Hong Kong: Centre of Asian Studies, University of Hong Kong.

Kyloh, R. 1984. "Productivity Bargaining within a Centralised Wage System." Wages and Incomes Policy Research Paper no. 1. Australian Government Publishing Service, Canberra.

———. 1989. "Flexibility and Structural Adjustment through Consensus: Some Lessons from Australia." *International Labour Review* 128 (1): 103–23.

Lambert, R. 1990. "Social Movement Unionism in the Philippines." *Labour and Industry* 3 (2–3): 258–80.

Lange, P., G. Ross, and M. Vannicelli. 1982. *Unions, Change and Crisis: French and Italian Union Strategy and the Political Economy, 1945–1980.* London: Allen & Unwin.

Lansbury, R. D., S. K. Ng, and R. B. McKern. 1984. "Management at Enterprise Level in China." *Industrial Relations Journal* 15 (1): 56–64.

Lash S., and J. Urry. 1987. *The End of Organized Capitalism.* Cambridge, U.K.: Polity Press.

Lau, S. K. 1982. *Society and Politics in Hong Kong.* Hong Kong: Chinese University Press.

Law, P. 1988. "White-Collar Unionism: The Case of Teachers." In *Labour Movement in a Changing Society,* ed. Y. C. Jao et al., 163–66. Hong Kong: Centre of Asian Studies, University of Hong Kong.

Lee, B. H. 1979. "Public Sector Labour Relations in the Singapore Context." Occasional Paper no. 37. Department of Political Science, National University of Singapore.

Lee, J. S. 1988. "Labor Relations and the Stages of Economic Development: The Case of the Republic of China." In *Proceedings of the Conference on Labor and Economic Development,* 177–204. Taipei: Institution for Economic Research, China Productivity Center.

Lee, L. T. 1984. *Structure of the Trade Union System in China, 1949–66.* Hong Kong: Centre of Asian Studies.

———. 1986. *Trade Unions in China: 1949 to the Present.* Singapore: Singapore University Press.

Leggett, C. 1984. "Airline Pilots and Public Industrial Relations: The Case of Singapore Airlines." *Indian Journal of Industrial Relations* 20 (1): 27–43.

———. 1988. "Industrial Relations and Enterprise Unionism in Singapore." *Labour and Industry* 1 (2): 242–57.

———. n.d. "Singapore's Industrial Relations in the 1990s." In *Singapore Changes Guard: Social, Political and Economic Directions in the 1990s,* ed. G. Rodan. Melbourne: Longmans Cheshire. Forthcoming.

———. n.d. "Singapore." In *Labor Organisations in Asia and the Pacific,* ed. J. Scoville. Westport, Conn.: Greenwood Press. Forthcoming.

Leung, P. L. 1988. "Promoting Workers' Interests outside the Trade Union System: The Experience of the Christian Industrial Committee." In *Labour Movement in a Changing Society,* edited by Y. C. Jao et al., 117–19. Hong Kong: Centre of Asian Studies, University of Hong Kong.

Leung, S. H. 1983. "Industrial Relations in Cable and Wireless: A Unionist's View." In *Contemporary Issues in Hong Kong Labour Relations,* ed. S. H. Ng and D. Levin, 123–33. Hong Kong: Centre of Asian Studies, University of Hong Kong.

Leung, T., and A. Leung. 1988. *At the Crossroads: Hong Kong's Independent Trade Union Movement and the International Trade Secretariats.* Hong Kong: Hong Kong Trade Union Education Centre and Asia Monitor Resource Center Ltd.

Leung, W. 1988. *Smashing the Iron Rice-Pot: Workers and Unions in China's Market Socialism.* Hong Kong: Asia Monitor Resource Center.

Leung, Y. H. 1989. "Corporatist Trends in Public Policy Making in Hong Kong." M.Soc.Sc. diss., University of Hong Kong.

Levin, D. A., and Y. C. Jao. 1988. "Introduction." In *Labour Movement in a*

Changing Society, edited by Y. C. Jao et al., 1–23. Hong Kong: Centre of Asian Studies, University of Hong Kong.

Levine, S. B. 1980. "Changing Strategies of Unions and Management: Evaluation of Four Industrialised Countries." *British Journal of Industrial Relations* 18 (1): 70–81.

Li, H. 1989. "The Democratic Management of Enterprises and Workers' Awareness of Democracy." *Chinese Economic Studies,* Summer, 69–80.

Li, W. W. 1990. "The Tensions in Labour Relations Are about to Explode," (in Chinese). *Pai Shing,* 16 Jan., 9–17.

Liang, S. X. 1986. "Whither the Hong Kong Labor Movement? On the Lau Chin-sek Incident" (in Chinese). *Undergrad* (University of Hong Kong) 5: 28.

Lieberson, S. 1991. "Small N's and Big Conclusions: An Examination of the Reasoning in Comparative Studies Based on a Small Number of Cases." *Social Forces* 70.(2): 307–20.

Lim, L., and E. F. Pang. 1984. "Labour Strategies and the High-Tech Challenge: The Case of Singapore." *Euro-Asia Business Review* 3 (2): 27–31.

Limqueco, P., B. McFarlane, and J. Odhnoff. 1989. *Labour and Industry in ASEAN.* Manila: Journal of Contemporary Asia Publishers.

Lin, C. 1988. "The Development of the Labor Movement and Labor Disputes in Taiwan." In *Proceedings of the Conference on Labor and Economic Development,* 383–96. Taipei: Institution for Economic Research, China Productivity Center.

Littler, C. R., and M. Lockett. 1983. "The Significance of Trade Unions in China." *Industrial Relations Journal* 14 (4): 31–42.

Littler, C. R., and G. Palmer. 1987. "Communist and Capitalist Trade Unionism: Comparisons and Contrasts." In *Trade Unions in Communist States,* ed. A. Pravda and B. A. Ruble, 253–72. London: Allen & Unwin.

Liu, T. 1989. "Chinese Workers and Employees Participate in Democratic Management of Enterprises." *Chinese Trade Unions* 2: 5–10.

Lo, S. H. 1989. "Colonial Policy-Makers, Capitalist Class and China: Determinants of Electoral Reform in Hong Kong's and Macau's Legislatures." *Pacific Affairs* 62: 204–18.

Lubeck, P. M. 1992. "Malaysian Industrialization, Ethnic Divisions and the NIC Model: The Limits to Replication." In *States and Development in the Asian Pacific Rim,* ed. R. P. Applebaum and J. Henderson, 176–98. London: Sage.

Lui, T. L. 1989. "Social Structural Change and the Development of White-Collar Unionism" (in Chinese). In *The Directions of the Hong Kong Trade Union Movement,* ed. the Hong Kong Federation of Trade Unions, 45–58. Hong Kong: New City Cultural Service Ltd.

Lukes, S. 1974. *Power: A Radical View.* London: Macmillan.

Ma, C. 1955. *History of the Labour Movement in China.* Taipei: China Cultural Service.

Mabry, B. D. 1977. "The Thai Labour Movement." *Asian Survey* 17 (10): 931–51.

———. 1979. "The Development of Labor Institutions in Thailand." Data Paper no. 112. Southeast Asian Program, Department of Asian Studies, Cornell University, Ithaca, N.Y.

————. 1987. "The Labour Movement and the Practice of Professional Management in Thailand." *Journal of Southeast Asian Studies* 17 (2): 303–26.

Mabry, B. D., and K. Srisermbhok. 1985. "Labor Relations under Martial Law: The Thailand Experience." *Asian Survey* 25 (6): 613–37.

Mackie, J. A. C. 1988. "Economic Growth in the ASEAN Region: The Political Underpinnings." In *Achieving Industrialization in East Asia,* ed. H. Hughes, 283–326. Cambridge: Cambridge University Press.

Malaysia. Ministry of Labour. 1985. *Annual Report, 1984–1985.* Kuala Lumpur.

————. 1988. *Labour and Manpower Report, 1985–86.* Kuala Lumpur.

————. 1989. *Labour Indicators, 1987–88* (in Malaysian). Kuala Lumpur.

————. n.d. "Labour and Manpower Report, 1987–1988." Draft.

————. Various. *Annual Report.* Kuala Lumpur.

Malaysia. Prime Minister's Department. 1981–85. *Fourth Malaysian Plan (1981–1985).* Kuala Lumpur: Government Printer.

————. 1986–90. *Fifth Malaysian Plan (1986–1990).* Kuala Lumpur: Government Printer.

Malaysian Trade Union Congress. 1985. "Conference on Unemployment and Retrenchment in Malaysia: Proceedings." Mimeo.

Manning C., and P. E. Fong. 1990. "Labour Market Trends and Structures in ASEAN and the East Asian NICs." *Asian-Pacific Literature* 4 (2): 59–81.

Marshall, R. 1989. "Time's Up for Relics." *NBR* 11 (Aug.).

Martin, R. M. 1980. *Trade Unions in Australia.* Melbourne: Pelican Books.

————. 1989. *Trade Unionism: Purposes and Forms.* Oxford: Clarendon Press.

————. 1992. "The ACTU Congress of 1991." *Labour History* 62 (May): 138–50.

Matsuzaki, H. 1992. *Japanese Business Unionism: The Historical Development of a Unique Labour Movement.* Monograph 1. University of New South Wales Studies in Human Resource Management and Industrial Relations in Asia. Sydney: Industrial Relations Research Centre, University of New South Wales.

Miners, N. 1988. "The Representation and Participation of Trade Unions in the Hong Kong Government." In *Labour Movement in a Changing Society,* ed. Y. C. Jao et al., 40–47. Hong Kong: Centre of Asian Studies, University of Hong Kong.

Ming Pao. 1985. "Labor Organizations Protest in Front of the Legislative Council against the Long-Service Payment Bill" (in Chinese). 19 Dec.

————. 1989a. "Labor Representatives Walk Out from LAB Meeting" (in Chinese). 13 May.

————. 1989b. Letter to the Editor from a Group of FTU Members (in Chinese). 30 Nov.

Mirsky, J. 1989. "China's Democratic Crisis." *Britain-China Newsletter,* 1–5.

Morell, D., and S. Chaianan. 1981. *Political Conflict in Thailand: Reform, Reaction, Revolution.* Cambridge, Mass.: Oegeschlager, Gunn and Hain.

Morishima, M. 1992. "Use of Joint Consultation Committees by Large Japanese Firms." *British Journal of Industrial Relations* 30 (3): 405–23.

Morris, P. 1989. *Award Restructuring: The Task Ahead.* Canberra: Australian Government Publishing Service.

Munck, R. 1988. *The New International Labour Studies: An Introduction.* London: Zed Books.

Nagamine, H. 1991. "Is the Japanese Employment System Changing?" Mimeo.

Nair, C. V. Devan. 1976. "Trade Unions in Singapore: Model of an Alternative to Futility in a Developing Country." *In Socialism That Works: The Singapore Way*, ed. C. V. Devan Nair, 97–103. Singapore: Federal Publications.

Nakamura, K. 1991. "Types and Functions of Industry-wide Labor Organizations in Japan." *Japan Labor Bulletin* 30 (3): 5–8.

Narong Petprasirt. 1982. *The Political Economy of Thai Labour Movement.* The Hague: Institute of Social Studies.

National Council of Labor Movements Organisation (NCLMO). 1989. *Policy Document of NCLMO 2*, March. Seoul.

National Trades Union Congress (NTUC). 1970. *Why Labour Must Go Modern.* Singapore.

————. 1979. *Plan of Action for the '80s: Secretary-General's Report to the Adjourned Third Triennial Delegates' Conference of the NTUC.* Singapore.

————. 1980. "Work and Excel for an Even Better Quality of Life: NTUC's Position Paper." Singapore.

————. 1984. *Secretary-General's Report to the NTUC Ordinary Delegates' Conference, 27–29 April '84.* Singapore.

————. 1985a. *Standing Up as One for Singapore: Secretary-General's Report to the NTUC Triennial Delegates' Conference, 1–3 April 1985.* Singapore.

————. 1985b. "Chronology of Trade Union Development in Singapore, 1940–1984." Mimeo.

New Zealand. Council of Trade Unions. 1988. "Towards a Compact." Mimeo.

————. n.d. "The Need for Change." Mimeo.

New Zealand. Department of Statistics. 1988. *Monthly Abstract of Statistics* (March). Wellington.

New Zealand. Labour Department. Various. *Quarterly Survey*. Auckland: New Zealand Government Printer.

Ng, S. H. 1982. "Labour Administration and Voluntarism: The Hong Kong Case." *Journal of Industrial Relations* 24 (2): 266–81.

Nitta, M. 1988. "Birth of Rengo and Reformation of Union Organisations." *Japan Labor Bulletin* 27 (2): 5–8.

————. 1991. "Probing Rengo's Political Policy." *Japan Labor Bulletin* 30 (3): 5–8.

Nolan, P. 1989. "History, Democracy and Economic Change." *China Now* 131 (Aug.): 12–14.

Nomura, M. 1991a. "Japanese Personnel Management Transferred: Transplants of the Electronic Industry in Asia and Europe." Paper presented to international symposium, "The Production Strategies and Industrial Relations in the Process of Internationalization," 14–18 Oct., Tohoku University, Sendai, Japan.

————. 1991b. "Organization and Activities of the Japanese Enterprise Union: A Case of the Automobile Industry." *Okayama Economic Review* 22 (Feb.): 153–76.

Nongyao Reecharoen. 1988. "Thailand." In *The Problem of Union Recognition: A Survey of the Current Situation in ASEAN*, ed. International Labour Organisation, 89–101. Geneva.

Odhnoff, J., et al. 1983. *Industrialization and the Labour Process in Thailand (Bangkok Area)*. Stockholm: Swedish Center for Working Life.

O'Donnell, G. A. 1977. "Corporatism and the Question of the State." In *Authoritarianism and Corporatism in Latin America*, ed. J. M. Malloy, 47–87. Pittsburgh: University of Pittsburgh Press.

Ogle, G. 1990. *South Korea: Dissent within the Economic Miracle.* London: Zed Books.

O'Leary, G. 1989. "The Impact of Economic Reforms on Chinese Trade Unions." Paper presented at the Labour-Management in the Asia and Pacific Region Conference, 28–30 Aug., University of Hong Kong.

Oliver, W. H. 1989. "The Labour Caucus and Economic Policy Formation, 1981–84." In *The Making of Rogernomics*, ed. B. Easton, 11–52. Auckland: Auckland University Press.

Organization for Economic Cooperation and Development (OECD). 1984. *OECD Economic Outlook* 36. Paris.

———. 1986. *OECD Economic Outlook* 40. Paris.

———. 1987. *OECD Economic Outlook* 42. Paris.

———. 1988. *OECD Economic Outlook* 44. Paris.

———. 1989a. *OECD National Accounts: Main Aggregates, 1960–1988.* Paris.

———. 1989b. *OECD Economic Outlook* 46. Paris.

———. 1989c. *New Zealand.* Paris.

———. 1990. *OECD Economic Outlook* 47. Paris.

———. 1992a. *OECD Economic Outlook* 51. Paris.

———. 1992b. *OECD Economic Surveys: Australia, 1991/1992.* Paris.

Ouchi, W. G. 1981. *Theory Z: How American Business Can Meet the Japanese Challenge.* New York: Avon Books.

Pang, E. F. 1981. "Singapore." In *International Handbook of Industrial Relations: Contemporary Developments and Research*, ed. A. Blum, 481–97. Westport, Conn.: Greenwood Press.

———. 1982. *Education, Manpower and Development in Singapore.* Singapore: Singapore University Press.

Pang, E. F., and L. Cheng. 1978. "Changing Patterns of Industrial Relations in Singapore." In *The Role of Trade Unions in Developing Societies*, ed. E. M. Kassalow and U. G. Damachi, 31–50. Geneva: International Institute for Labour Studies.

Pappas, Carter, Evans, and Koop/Telesis. 1990. Final Report. *The Global Challenge: Australian Manufacturing in the 1990s.* Melbourne: Australian Manufacturing Council.

Parmer, N. J. 1964. "Chinese Estate Workers' Strikes in Malaya in March, 1937." In *Economic Development of Southeast Asia*, ed. C. D. Cowan, 154–73. London: Allen & Unwin.

Patarapanich, S., B. Wilkinson, and C. Leggett. 1987. "Labour Management in Singapore: The Management of Thai Workers in the Construction Industry." Paper presented at the Second European Regional Congress of Industrial Relations of the International Industrial Relations Association, 13–17 Dec. 1987, Herzlia, Israel.

Peetz, D. 1990. "Declining Union Density." *Journal of Industrial Relations* 32 (2): 197–223.

Peetz, D., et al. 1993. "Workplace Bargaining in New Zealand: Radical Change at Work." In *Workplace Bargaining in the International Context*, ed. D. Peetz,

A. Preston, and J. Docherty, 195–328. Canberra: Department of Industrial Relations/Paragon Printers.

Pempel, T. J., and K. Tsunekawa. 1979 "Corporatism without Labor: The Japanese Anomaly." In *Trends Towards Corporatist Intermediation*, ed. J. Schmitter and G. Lehmbruch, 246–68. London: Sage.

Peters, T., and R. H. Waterman. 1982. *In Search of Excellence: Lessons from America's Best-Run Companies*. New York: Harper and Row.

Plowman, D. 1986. "Economic Forces and the New Right: Employer Matters in 1986." *Journal of Industrial Relations* 29 (1): 84–91.

———. 1992. "Opting Out: The Operation of Section 115 of the Industrial Relations Act, 1988." University of New South Wales. Mimeo.

Plowman, D. and G. Weaven. 1989. "Unions and Superannuation." In *Australian Unions: An Industrial Relations Perspective*, ed. B. Ford and D. Plowman, 251–68. Melbourne: Macmillan.

Podmore, D. 1971. "The Population of Hong Kong." In *Hong Kong: The Industrial Colony,"* ed. K. Hopkins, 21–54. Hong Kong: Oxford University Press.

Pons, P. 1992. "Japanese Ponder How to Stop Working." *Guardian Weekly,* 12 April, 16.

Poole, M. 1986. *Industrial Relations: Origins and Patterns of National Identity*. London: Routledge & Kegan Paul.

Poulantzas, N. 1973. *Political Power and Social Classes*. London: New Left Books.

Pravda, A., and B. A. Ruble, eds. 1987. *Trade Unions in Communist States*. London: Allen & Unwin.

Productivity Digest. 1984. Singapore: National Productivity Association.

Przeworski, A. 1985. *Capitalism and Social Democracy*. Cambridge, Mass.: Cambridge University Press.

Quinlan, M. 1989. "Unions and Immigrants: The Post Second World War Experience." In *Australian Unions: An Industrial Relations Perspective*, ed. B. Ford and D. Plowman, 203–24. Melbourne: Macmillan.

Ramos, E. T. 1990. *Dualistic Unionism and Industrial Relations*. Quezon City, Philippines: New Day.

Rear, J. 1971. "One Brand of Politics." In *Hong Kong: The Industrial Colony*, ed. K. Hopkins, 55–139. Hong Kong: Oxford University Press.

Redding, E. G. 1990. *The Spirit of Chinese Capitalism*. New York: de Gruyter.

Regini, M. 1986. "Political Bargaining in Western Europe during the Economic Crisis of the 1980s." In *Economic Crisis, Trade Unions and the State*, ed. O. Jacobi, B. Jessop, H. Kastendiek, and M. Regini, 61–78. London: Croom Helm.

Rimmer, M. 1989. "Work Place Unionism." In *Australian Unions: An Industrial Relations Perspective*, ed. B. Ford and D. Plowman, 120–44. Melbourne: Macmillan.

Rodan, G. 1989. *The Political Economy of Singapore's Industrialization: National State and International Capital*. London: Macmillan.

Rosen, S., ed. 1989. "The All-China Federation of Trade Unions' Survey of China's Workers and Staff." *Chinese Economic Studies,* Summer.

Ross, R.J.S. and Trachte, K. C. 1990. *Global Capitalism: The New Leviathan*. Albany: State University of New York Press.

Roth, H. 1978. "The Historical Framework." In *Industrial Relations in New*

Zealand, ed. J. Deeks, H. Roth, J. Farmer, and G. Scott, 19–57. Wellington: Methuen.

———. 1983. "The State of the Unions." *New Zealand Journal of Industrial Relations* 8 (1): 47–56.

Rueschemeyer, D., E. Huber Stephens, and J. D. Stephens. 1992. *Capitalist Development and Democracy.* Cambridge, U.K.: Polity Press.

Salaff, J. 1981. *Working Daughters of Hong Kong.* New York: Cambridge University Press.

Salmon, J. 1992. "The Impact of Developments in Welfare Corporatism upon Japanese Workplace Trade Unionism." *International Journal of Human Resource Management* 3 (2): 247–66.

Samrej Zeeponsekul. 1987. "Organised Labour in Thai Society: A Critical Analysis of Its Action, 1973–1985." Master's thesis, School of Social Sciences, La Trobe University.

San, G. 1988. "A Critical Review of the Labor Standards Law in Taiwan, ROC." In *Proceedings of the Conference on Labor and Economic Development,* 343–66. Taipei: Institution for Economic Resources, China Productivity Center.

Sandlant, R. 1988. "Strategic Unionism: The Australian and New Zealand Trade Union Movements and Economic Liberalisation." Paper presented at the conference of the Australasian Political Studies Association, Armidale, Australia, University of New England.

Scott, I. 1989. *Political Change and the Crisis of Legitimacy in Hong Kong.* Hong Kong: Oxford University Press.

Scoville, J. G. 1973. "Some Determinants of the Structure of Labor Movements." In *The International Labor Movement in Transition: Essays on Africa, Asia, Europe and South America,* ed. A. Sturmthal and J. G. Scoville, 58–78. Urbana: University of Illinois Press.

Sharma, B. 1985. *Aspects of Industrial Relations in ASEAN.* Singapore: Institute of Southeast Asian Studies.

———. 1991. "Industrialisation and Strategy Shifts in Industrial Relations." In *International Comparisons in Human Resource Management,* ed. C. Brewster and S. Tyson, 92–109. London: Pitman.

Sharma, B., and P. Sephton. 1991. "The Determinants of Union Membership Growth in Taiwan." *Journal of Labor Research* 12 (4): 429–37.

Shimada, H. 1988. "Japanese Trade Unionism: Postwar Evolution and Future Prospects." *Labour and Society* 13 (2): 203–23.

———. 1992. "The Globalization of Business and the New World of Work." *Japan Labor Bulletin* 31 (4): 4–8.

Shirai, T. 1983. *Contemporary Industrial Relations in Japan.* Madison: University of Wisconsin Press.

Siengthai, S. 1988. "Three Case Studies in Thai Labour-Management Co-operation." In *Case Studies in Labour-Management Co-operation: Successful Experiences from Eight Asia-Pacific Countries,* ed. International Labour Organisation, 265–308. Bangkok: International Labour Organisation.

Singapore. Department of Statistics. 1983. *Economic and Social Statistics Singapore, 1960–1982.* Singapore: Singapore National Printers.

Singapore. Economic Committee. 1986. *The Singapore Economy: New Directions.* Singapore: Ministry of Trade and Industry.

Singapore. Ministry of Labor. 1984. *1984 Singapore Yearbook of Labor Statistics.* Singapore: Ministry of Labor, Research and Statistics Department.

————. Various. *Annual Report.* Singapore.

Singapore. Ministry of Trade and Industry. 1991. *Economic Survey of Singapore, 2nd Quarter 1991.* Singapore: Singapore National Printers.

————. Various. *Economic Survey of Singapore.* Singapore: Singapore National Printers.

Singapore. National Productivity Board. 1981. *Report of the Committee on Productivity.* Singapore.

Singapore. National Wages Council Secretariat. 1986. *Report of the National Wages Council Subcommittee on Wage Reform.* Singapore: Ministry of Labor.

Sing Tao Evening News. 1989. "The Inevitable Trend of Union Participation in Politics." 10 Feb.

Sit, V.F.S., and S. L. Wong. 1989. *Small and Medium Industries in an Export-Oriented Economy: The Case of Hong Kong.* Hong Kong: Centre of Asian Studies, University of Hong Kong.

So, A. Y. 1986. "The Economic Success of Hong Kong: Insights from a World-System Perspective." *Sociological Perspectives* 29: 241–58.

Social Department of Taiwan Provincial Government. 1986. *An Investigation into the Current Status of Employees' Working Life.* Taipei.

Song, H. K. 1992. "The State and Organized Labor in Transition to Democracy in South Korea." Working Paper no. 2. Institute for Social Research, Hallym University, Kangwon-do, Korea.

Sopon Wichitrakon. 1991. "Good Labour Relations a Key to Industrial Peace and Economic Prosperity." Paper presented at ASEAN Subregional Tripartite Seminar on the Development of Sound Labour Relations, 5–8 March, Kuala Lumpur.

Southall, R. 1988. "Introduction." In *Trade Unions and the New Industrialisation of the Third World,* ed. R. Southall, 1–34. London: Zed Books.

South China Morning Post. 1990a. "FTU Plans to Contest 1991 Direct Polls." 23 April, 2.

————. 1990b. "Union Group Looks for More Members." 24 April, 6.

————. 1990c. 28 June,

Standing, G. 1992a. "Do Unions Impede or Accelerate Structural Adjustment? Industrial Versus Company Unions in an Industrializing Labour Market." *Cambridge Journal of Economics* 16 (3): 327–54.

————. 1992b. "Identifying the 'Human Resource Enterprise': A Southeast Asian Example." *International Labour Review* 131 (3): 281–95.

Statistical Outline of China (in Chinese). 1989. Beijing: Zhongguo tongji chubanshe.

Stephens, J. D. 1976. *The Transition from Capitalism to Socialism.* London: Macmillan.

Sturmthal, A., and J. G. Scoville, eds. 1973. *The International Labor Movement in Transition.* Urbana: University of Illinois Press.

Stutchbury, M. 1992. "Shake-up on NZ Shop Floor." *Australian Financial Review,* 3 July, 14.

Sumalee Pitayanon. 1984. "Labour Market Changes in Thailand." ASEAN-Australia Working Paper no. 11. Canberra.

Suphachai Manatphaibun, et al. 1984. *Human Rights and Waged Employees in Thailand* (in Thai). Bangkok: Thai Studies Centre, Thammasat University.

Swidler, A. 1986. "Culture in Action: Symbols and Strategies." *American Sociological Review* 51: 273–86.

Sydney Morning Herald. 1990. "Court Gets Blamed for Failed Union Merger." 16 June, 2.

———. 1991. "Taiwan: China Unchanging." 30 Dec., 8.

———. 1992a. "South Korea Opts for Safer Choice of Two Freedom Campaigners." 21 Dec., 7.

———. 1992b. "Poll Marks New Era for Taiwan." 21 Dec., 7.

Tai, H. C. 1989. "The Oriental Alternative: An Hypothesis on Culture and Economy." In *Confucianism and Economic Development,* ed. H. C. Tai, 6–37. Washington, D.C.: Washington Institute Press.

Taiwan. Council of Labor Affairs. 1988. *Yearbook of Labor Statistics, Taiwan Area, Republic of China, 1987.* Taipei: Council of Labor Affairs, Executive Yuan.

———. 1989a. *Labor Laws and Regulations of the Republic of China.* Taipei.

———. 1989b. *Yearbook of Labor Statistics, Taiwan Area, Republic of China, 1988.* Taipei: Council of Labor Affairs, Executive Yuan.

———. 1990a. *Major Labor Statistics Indicators* (July) (in Chinese). Taipei.

———. 1990b. *The Current Status of Unions: A Survey (March)* (in Chinese). Taipei: Council of Labor Affairs, Executive Yuan.

Taiwan. Ministry of Economic Affairs. Investment Commission. 1990. *Statistics on Overseas Chinese and Foreign Investment, Technical Cooperation, Outward Investment and Outward Technical Cooperation, Republic of China.* Taipei.

Taylor, A. 1989. *Trade Unions and Politics: A Comparative Introduction.* London: Macmillan.

Thailand. Ministry of Interior. Department of Labor. 1981. *Yearbook of Labor Statistics (1979–1980).* Bangkok.

———. 1989. *Yearbook of Labor Statistics 1989.* Bangkok.

———. 1990. "Unions and Industrial Relations in Thailand." Mimeo.

Thailand. Ministry of Interior. Department of Labor. Labor Relations Division. n.d. *Major Labor Councils in Thailand* (in Thai). Bangkok.

Ting, K. Y. 1988. "The Impact of Containerization on Seamen's Employment: The Hong Kong Experience." In *Labour Movement in a Changing Society,* ed. Y. C. Jao et al., 120–23. Hong Kong: Centre of Asian Studies, University of Hong Kong.

Todd, P., and K. S. Jomo. 1988. "The Trade Union Movement in Peninsula Malaysia 1957–1969." *Journal of South Asian and African Studies* 23 (1–2): 102–24.

Trade Union Training Authority. 1989. *Annual Report.* Melbourne.

Translation Services for Social Development. 1991. *Public Enterprise Trade Unions.* Bangkok.

Tso, M.T.T. 1983. "Civil Service Unions as a Social Force in Hong Kong." M.Soc.Sc. diss., University of Hong Kong.

———. 1988. "The Industrial Relations System in the Hong Kong Civil Service." In *Labour Movement in a Changing Society,* ed. Y. C. Jao et al., 61–66. Hong Kong: Centre of Asian Studies, University of Hong Kong.

Tsuen Wan District Board. 1987. *A Report on the Survey on the Conditions of Work for Female Workers in Tsuen Wan, 1986.* Hong Kong.

Tsui, T. F. 1979. "The Bargaining Process in Hong Kong: The Development of Labour and the Government's Role in Labour Relations in Hong Kong." In *Contemporary Labour Relations in the Asian-Pacific Region,* ed. T. W. Casey, 20–28. Hong Kong: Libra Press.

Turner, H. A. 1988. "The Prospects for Trade Unions in Hong Kong." In *Labour Movement in a Changing Society,* ed. Y. C. Jao et al., 177–90. Hong Kong: Centre of Asian Studies, University of Hong Kong.

Turner, H. A., et al. 1980. *The Last Colony: But Whose?* Cambridge, U.K.: Oxford University Press.

Turner, L. 1991. *Democracy at Work: Changing World Markets and the Future of Labor Unions.* Ithaca, N.Y.: Cornell University Press.

Turton, A. 1984. "Limits of Ideological Domination and the Formation of Social Consciousness." In *History and Peasant Consciousness in South East Asia,* ed. A. Turton and S. Tanabe, 19–74. Osaka: National Museum of Ethnology.

United Nations. 1961. *A Proposed Industrialisation Programme for the State of Singapore.* Report of the U.N. Commission for Technical Assistance. Geneva: U.N. Department of Economic and Social Affairs.

———. 1988. *Statistical Yearbook for Asia and the Pacific.* New York.

U.S. Department of Labor. Bureau of International Labor Affairs. 1990. *Foreign Labor Trends, Thailand.* FLT 90-20. Washington, D.C.: U.S. Government Printing Office.

Valenzuela, J. S. 1989. "Labor Movements in Transition to Democracy: A Framework for Analysis." *Contemporary Politics* 21 (July): 445–72.

Visser, J. 1989. "In Search of Inclusive Unionism." *Bulletin of Comparative Labour Relations* (special issue) 18.

Vogel, E. F. 1979. *Japan as Number One: Lessons for America.* Cambridge: Harvard University Press.

———. 1991. *The Four Little Dragons: The Spread of Industrialization in East Asia.* Cambridge: Harvard University Press.

Wad, P. 1988. "The Japanization of the Malaysian Trade Union Movement." In *Trade Unions and the New Industrialisation of the Third World,* ed. R. Southall, 210–29. London: Zed Books.

Wade, R. 1988. "The Role of Government in Overcoming Market Failure: Taiwan, Republic of Korea and Japan." In *Achieving Industrialization in East Asia,* ed. H. Hughes, 129–63. Sydney: Cambridge University Press.

———. 1990. *Governing the Market: Economic Theory and the Role of Government in East Asian Industrialization.* Princeton, N.J.: Princeton University Press.

Walder, A. G. 1986. *Communist Neo-Traditionalism: Work and Authority in Chinese Industry.* Berkeley: University of California Press.

———. 1989. "Factory and Manager in an Era of Reform." *China Quarterly* 118 (June): 242–64.

Walker, S., ed. 1989. *Rogernomics: Reshaping New Zealand's Economy.* Wellington: Centre for Independent Studies and Government Printing Office.

Walsh, P. 1988. "The Struggle for Power and Control in the New Corporations." *New Zealand Journal of Industrial Relations* 13 (2): 178–89.

————. 1989. "A Family Fight: Industrial Relations Reform under the Fourth Labour Government." In *The Making of Rogernomics*, ed. B. Easton, 149–70. Auckland: Auckland University Press.

————. 1991. "Trade Unions in New Zealand and Economic Restructuring." Working Paper no. 17. Australian Centre for Industrial Relations Research and Teaching, University of Sydney.

Warner, M. 1986. "Managing Human Resources in China." *Organisation Studies* 7 (4): 353–66.

————. 1987a. "Industrial Relations in the Chinese Factory." *Journal of Industrial Relations* 23 (2): 217–32.

————., ed. 1987b. *Management Reforms in China.* London: Pinter.

————. 1989. "Microelectronics and Manpower in China." *New Technology, Work and Employment* 4 (1): 18–26.

Webster, E. 1988. "The Rise of Social-Movement Unionism: The Two Faces of the Black Trade Union Movement in South Africa." In *State Resistance and Change in South Africa*, ed. P. Frankel, N. Pines, and M. Swilling, 174–96. London: Croom Helm.

Wehmhorner, A. 1983. "Trade Unionism in Thailand: A New Dimension in a Modernising Society." *Journal of Contemporary Asia* 13 (4): 481–97.

Whitley, R. 1992. *Business Systems in East Africa: Firms, Markets, and Societies.* London: Sage.

Whittaker, D. H. 1990. "The End of Japanese-Style Employment?" *Work, Employment and Society* 4 (3): 321–47.

Wilkinson, B., and C. Leggett. 1985. "Human and Industrial Relations in Singapore: The Management of Compliance." *Euro-Asia Business Review* 4 (3): 9–15.

Wilson, J. L. 1987. "The People's Republic of China." In *Trade Unions in Communist States*, ed. A. Pravda and B. A. Ruble, 219–52. London: Allen & Unwin.

Wilson, M. 1989. *Labour in Government, 1984–1987.* Auckland: Auckland University Press.

Winters, S. 1987. "Women and the Future of Unions." In *Union Strategy and Industrial Change*, ed. S. Frenkel, 155–60. Sydney: New South Wales University Press.

Wong, E. S. 1983. "Industrial Relations in Singapore: Challenges for the 1980s." In *Southeast Asian Affairs 1983*, ed. Institute of Southeast Asian Studies, 263–74. Singapore: Gower.

Wong, R. 1990. *The Other Hong Kong: Report 1990.* Hong Kong: Hong Kong University Press.

Wong, S. L. 1988a. *Emigrant Entrepreneurs: Shanghai Industrialists in Hong Kong.* Hong Kong: Oxford University Press.

————. 1988b. "The Applicability of Asian Family Values to Other Sociocultural Settings." In *In Search of an East Asian Development Model*, ed. P. I. Berger and H.H.M. Hsiao, 134–52. New Brunswick, N.J.: Transaction Books.

World Bank. 1989. *World Bank Atlas 1989.* Washington, D.C.

————. 1990. *World Development Report, 1990.* Oxford: Oxford University Press.

————. 1991. *World Development Report, 1991: The Challenge of Development.* Oxford: Oxford University Press.

Wu, F. 1991. "The ASEAN Economies in the 1990s and Singapore's Regional Role." *California Management Review* 34 (1): 103–14.

Wu Min Aun. 1982. *The Industrial Relations Law of Malaysia.* Kuala Lumpur: Heinemann.

Yeung, C. K. 1988. "Joint Consultation, Collective Bargaining and Trade Union Recognition: Status and Prospects." In *Labour Movement in a Changing Society,* ed. Y. C. Jao et al., 54–60. Hong Kong: Centre of Asian Studies, University of Hong Kong.

Yeung, S. 1989. "Looking at the Trade Union Movement as a Social Movement" (in Chinese). In *The Directions of the Hong Kong Trade Union Movement,* ed. Hong Kong Federation of Trade Unions, 17–24. Hong Kong: New City Cultural Service Ltd.

Ying, H. S. 1990. *Taiwan—After the Long Silence: The Emerging New Unions of Taiwan.* Hong Kong: Asia Monitor Research Center.

Zerby, J. 1990. "The Korean Economy: Overview of Recent Developments." Mimeo.

Zhang, G. X. 1988. "Changes in the Chinese Trade Union Movement in the Light of the Current Reforms." M.A. thesis, Institute of Social Studies, The Hague.

Contributors

Andrew Brown is a doctoral student in the Department of Politics, Sociology and Philosophy at Murdoch University in Western Australia. His thesis topic is industrial relations and labor politics in Thailand. Brown has a master's degree in Asian studies from the Australian National University, Canberra.

Ponniah Arudsothy is a senior lecturer in the Division of Asian and International Studies at Griffith University in Australia. He has a Ph.D. from the University of Glasgow. His dissertation focused on Malaysian labor markets and industrial relations. He is currently completing work on a comparative study of industrial relations systems in the ASEAN countries.

Stephen Chiu is a lecturer in sociology at the Chinese University of Hong Kong and has recently been awarded a Ph.D. in sociology from Princeton University. His dissertation focused on development strategies in the newly industrialized countries of East Asia.

Stephen Frenkel is a professor at the Centre for Corporate Change in the Australian Graduate School of Management at the University of New South Wales. He has a Ph.D. in economics and politics from Cambridge University. His major publications include *Shop Stewards in Action* (1975) (co-authored with E. Batstone and I. Boraston), *Unions against Capitalism?* (1984) (co-authored with A. Coolican), and *Economic*

Restructuring and Industrial Relations in Industrialised Countries (1990) (co-edited with O. Clarke).

Nigel Haworth is a professor of international studies in the Faculty of Commerce at the University of Auckland. He holds a Ph.D. in sociology from the University of Liverpool. He has published widely on industrial development and labor relations in South America.

Jon-Chao Hong is a professor of industrial education at the National Taiwan Normal University. He holds a Ph.D. from the University of Illinois.

Hwang-Joe Kim is director of the Industrial Management Research Centre at Yonsei University in Seoul. He has a Ph.D. in economics from the University of Massachusetts and has published widely in the areas of wage structure and economic development. His major publications include *New Directions in Industrial Relations Systems in Korea* (1984) and *Modern Society and Marxism* (1984) (co-authored with others), both in Korean.

Bih-Ling Lee has been a research assistant at the National Taiwan Normal University and is currently a researcher at the Taiwan Industrial Development Bureau in the Ministry of Economic Affairs.

Chris Leggett is a senior lecturer in the School of Industrial Relations and Organizational Behaviour at the University of New South Wales. He holds an M.Sc. in management studies from the University of Bradford in the United Kingdom. His publications include *Industrial Relations and the Political Process in the Sudan* (1980). He has also written extensively on labor relations and trade unionism in Singapore.

David A. Levin is a senior lecturer in the Department of Sociology at the University of Hong Kong. He has a master's degree in labor and industrial relations from the University of Illinois and has written widely on labor relations in Hong Kong. His publications include *Contemporary Issues in Hong Kong Labour Relations* (1982) (co-edited with Ng Sek Hong).

Craig Littler is a professor of management at the University of Southern Queensland. He has a Ph.D. in sociology and economics from the London School of Economics. His major publications include *The Development of the Labour Process in Capitalist Societies* (1982) and *Class at Work: The Division, Allocation and Control of Jobs* (1984) (co-authored with G. Salaman). Littler is also the founding editor of the journal *Labour and Industry.*

Malcolm Warner is a fellow of Wolfson College and the Judge Institute of Management Studies at Cambridge University. He has a Ph.D. in politics and economics from Cambridge University and has written extensively in the fields of industrial sociology and industrial relations. His major publications include *Comparative Union Democracy: Organisation and Opposition in British and American Unions* (1975) (co-authored with J. D. Edelstein), *Management Reforms in China* (1987) (editor), and *How Chinese Managers Learn* (1992).

Index

Abella, M. I., 25
Accidents, industrial, 206–7, 210. *See also* Workers' compensation
ACFTU. *See* All-China Federation of Trade Unions (ACFTU)
ACTU. *See* Australian Council of Trade Unions (ACTU)
Advanced core countries, 5. *See also* Japan
Advanced peripheral countries (APs): economic development of, 27, 40–45; immigration of workers to, 26; service sectors in, 18; unemployment in, 42. *See also* Australia; New Zealand
Ahmad Kamthetthong, 93, 94
All-China Federation of Trade Unions (ACFTU): constitution of, 65, 71–72; development of, 60, 75, 164; organizational structure of, 62, 66, 67–68, 69–70, 81; purpose of, 61, 68–69, 70–74, 79, 80
Alliance government, Malaysia, 112
Amalgamated National Union of Local Authorities, Malaysia, 120–21
Amalgamated Union of Public Employees (AUPE), Singapore, 225, 227, 228
Amalgamated Workers' Union, New Zealand, 344
American Federation of Labor-Congress of Industrial Organizations (AFL-CIO), 18, 104; Asian-American Free Labor Institute (AAFLI), 92
APs. *See* Advanced peripheral countries (APs)

Arbitration. *See* Collective bargaining
Arom Phongphagnan Foundation, Thailand, 92
ASEAN. *See* Association of Southeast Asian Nations (ASEAN)
Asia Labor Monitor Group, 63
Asian Cultural Forum of Development, Thailand, 92
Asian tigers, 4. *See also* China, People's Republic of; Malaysia; Thailand
Association of Female Employees in the Government Sector (PUSPANITA), Malaysia, 108, 123, 129, 315
Association of Southeast Asian Nations (ASEAN), 26
AUPE. *See* Amalgamated Union of Public Employees (AUPE), Singapore
Australia: anti-unionism in, 262; debt service ratio of, 40–41; direct foreign investment in, 25; economic development of, 18, 40–43, 249, 252, 342; economic reforms in, 41–43, 53–54, 254, 256–61, 280; and foreign trade, 22, 23, 250; immigration of workers to, 26, 250, 251, 253; inflation rates in, 41–42, 253, 254, 257, 262, 279, 342; interunion relations in, 261, 270–71; and intraregional trade, 22; labor disputes in, 251, 252–53, 254, 255, 257, 261, 264–65, 342; labor productivity in, 277; as model for New Zealand, 293, 294, 297; organizational structure of unions in, 268–71, 272–79,